THE CRAIC

Born in Cambridge in 1958, Mark McCrum is the author of two previous travel books, *Happy Sad Land* about South Africa and *No Worries* about Australia. In a varied career he has worked as an advertising executive, street artist, cinema manager, copywriter, video-games salesman and Father Christmas. As a journalist he has written for the *Evening Standard*, the *Independent*, the *Daily Mail*, the *Sunday Times*, *Vogue* and *Punch*, and for two years had a regular column in *Screen International*. In 1986 his comedy *The Swap* was produced at the Boulevard Theatre in London's West End.

THE CRAIC

A Journey Through Ireland

MARK McCRUM

VICTOR GOLLANCZ

LONDON

First published in Great Britain 1998
by Victor Gollancz
An imprint of the Cassell Group
Wellington House, 125 Strand, London WC2R 0BB

A Gollancz Paperback Original

A catalogue record for this book is
available from the British Library.

ISBN 0 575 06573 7

Typeset by SetSystems Ltd, Saffron Walden, Essex
Printed and bound in Great Britain by
Guernsey Press Co. Ltd, Guernsey, Channel Isles

98 99   5 4 3 2 1

for Leonie

Contents

Author's Note

I have changed the names of many of the private figures who appear in this book. The hardest part of a travel writer's job is having to record honest reactions to people who have been kind to you. I hope, as always, that I have not caused offence. If I have, I can only apologize. Wherever I went, I made it clear that I was writing a book; and it would be a pointless and tedious exercise if I was untruthful about what I heard, saw and felt.

Preface

Now I'm back in England. Even as everyone talks optimistically of peace, there's another of those terrorist trials going on, for the two men who allegedly planted the Canary Wharf bomb that ended the first ceasefire in February 1996, killing an Asian newsagent and his colleague. Another pair of evil IRA terrorists, mad bastards with no respect for human life who will undoubtedly go to jail for a very long time.

But J—— M—— comes from Crossmaglen. I look at that chunky, oblong, moustachioed face in the courtroom-drawing and remember Sean, the not dissimilar-looking man who showed me round that bizarre little village, its pretty central square squatted on by the giant dalek-like pyramid of the British Army observation post. (Opposite was a bar called Chums, where we lunched on Bisto-drenched shepherd's pie.)

Up the lane, past the bakery, the Gaelic football pitch had been invaded – by the massively fortified monster that is the local 'police station'. No, there are no friendly village bobbies for the folks of Crossmaglen, although if the border line had been drawn just a few miles further up ('in accordance', as the original treaty stipulated, 'with the wishes of the inhabitants'), it would have been a shambling member of the Garda Siochana keeping order, rather than this barbed wire festooned citadel.

I study that face, and I know where that guy is coming from. You think I'm some sort of woolly-headed apologist for violence, don't you? That police station, I hear you say, is only a fortress because of men like J—— M——. What about our brave lads who have to make the terrifying journey from citadel to observation post, never quite knowing where the death bullet may come from? Crossmaglen men are famous snipers. Sean, indeed, proudly showed me the places where the individual British soldiers had fallen, and at the turning to the village, there's the famously ghoulish roadsign, which has a black silhouette of a gunman inside the usual crimson triangle. SNIPER AT WORK it says underneath. These guys know what they're doing.

Of course they do. I just said I knew where he was coming from; I have some understanding now of why he planted that bomb.

My own family, as it happens, comes from not far from Crossmaglen. Just across the county, in fact. Turn left at the third bristling look-out mast and you'll be there.

They were Protestants. My great-great-grandfather did so well out of his linen factory that he built a village of neat, red brick cottages for his employees (with streets named after his two children, William and Anne). He paid them in vouchers, which they could exchange for goods at the store he owned. He didn't want them to drink, you see.

But it was drink that ruined William, my great-grandfather, who gambled away the family money at Monte Carlo and ended up dying alone in one room in Armagh. The big house was sold, the factory went to the Bank of Ulster, and the days when people would cycle from Belfast to gawp at the famous drive way, with the novel electric lanterns every thirty yards, were over. The ornamental lake was drained and the jacuzzi-fitted bathrooms were overrun by the gymslipped pupils of the Manor School for Girls.

William's son, my grandfather Cecil, had moved to England by then. My uncle remembers, as a child, being rich, then suddenly not so rich. Having to move out of a big house into something smaller is what made him a socialist, he jokes.

Despite those Irish roots, I'd visited the island only twice. Once for a wedding in Wicklow; once for a short September holiday by the exquisite mountains of the Dingle peninsula. On both occasions we were treated to suitably 'Irish' behaviour. The staff were all very jolly at the nuptial hotel, and Guinness flowed from the bar until well into the small hours. In Kerry we drank illegal poteen, I rode a horse for the first time in my life along a wild and empty curve of beach, and we laughed at pot-bellied priests cheerfully betting and swilling back the booze at the Tralee races.

But like most English people I had only a superficial understanding of the country. If you followed popular myth, you'd imagine that the South was peopled by loquacious, stout-sipping amateur poets who, like the Murphy's, were 'not bitter'. They spoke in cod accents and had buxom, raven-haired daughters with flashing dark eyes who were either riding black horses across fields of the deepest green or practising their jigs for the Friday night *ceilidh*, while mother was gossiping over the washing or at Confession.

The North, of course, was an entirely different country. Against a bleak backdrop of concrete, graffiti and razor wire, the hatchet-faced residents pursued incomprehensible vendettas that stretched back hundreds of years. The 'Prods' were Orangemen and had (did they?) an enduring loyalty for William of that name, 1690 and all that, Battle of the Boyne, can't remember what or exactly where it was, but crucial. The Catholics were basically in the right, suppressed and down-trodden, with a much nicer accent, of course, wasn't Stephen Rea great in *The Crying Game*, have you seen *Michael Collins*, explains a lot, but isn't it time, in this day and age, to grow up and leave history behind? I mean, what have their problems got to do with *us*?

It was (I think now) truly incredible that I was so ignorant of the affairs and grievances of these people who were just an hour's flight away, who spoke the same language, and from whose stock I largely come.

But I was hardly alone. On my return from my journey, I amused myself by asking friends and acquaintances the most elementary questions about Irish history. Well-informed graduates, who would be shocked at newspaper reports that there are children around who don't know what happened in 1066, admitted that 1798 meant nothing to them. They'd never heard of Wolfe Tone. Who or what was it? (A kind of Irish tweed, I explained to one friend. 'Oh, *right*,' she said.) Parnell, generally, yes. O'Connell, generally, no. 1916, yes, 'but only through Yeats'. Henry Grattan, Robert Emmet, Thomas Davis, Patrick Pearse – forget it. Mitchel, Stephens, Allen, Larkin, O'Brien, Redmond – don't even think about it.

But why should they have known? For us English, as
children, the Irish were no more than comic butts, just as
Poles and Tasmanians are elsewhere. 'How d'you hurt an
Irishman? Ring him up while he's ironing.' 'Have you heard
the one about the Irish stuntman? He jumped over twenty
motorbikes in a double-decker bus.' 'An Irishman went for a
walk in the woods and met a girl. "I'm game," she said. So he
shot her.' And so on.

When I was an adolescent, the Irish 'question' or 'problem'
was a tedious sub-section of A-level history. Poor old Glad-
stone. Things were always just starting to go well for him when
the Irish Question (with a host of dull new names and dates
to learn) would come along and screw it all up again. One
friend remembers a recurring sentence in her school history
book – at the end of every chapter 'the Irish entered the next
century full of bitterness'. Why, it seemed, was never
explained.

In the background of my growing-up consciousness the
Northern 'Troubles' lurked consistently, however. I was eleven
when they got going in earnest; fifteen at the time of the
Sunningdale agreement; just starting work when Bobby Sands
died; going freelance at the time of the Anglo-Irish agreement.
At times, when there was even a vague promise of peace, I'd
take an interest, hoping that by some miracle *this* time the
bloody thing would be solved and that, finally, it would be safe
to walk down Oxford Street at Christmastime.

At other times page two, Home News, was something I
generally skipped over. Another bomb in Belfast, another
'sectarian killing'. I didn't understand it, didn't particularly
want to understand it, didn't think it had anything to do with
me – I was, frankly, bored by the repetitive nature of the
subject. Then a bomb would go off on the mainland and once
again, for a few days, you'd think, 'Oh for Christ's sake, will
this never end?'

It was the wrecking of the Grand National in 1997 that got me
going. Ever since I'd journeyed around South Africa and
discovered how just travelling through a place opens its problems to you, giving you an understanding that no books can
give (always a very different, arguably better, understanding

than the parish-bound locals have), I'd had this idea of a journey through Ireland, ending up in the North, at the old family home.

Before the first ceasefire I remember having a conversation with a friend from Belfast about it. Should this be my next trip? He shook his head. He wasn't sure it would be wise. An Englishman in the North – they might think I was an undercover agent. Did I know what they did to suspected undercover agents who got caught? He told me. I decided to leave the idea alone and go to Australia, where the worst that could happen was being eaten alive by a shark.

But three years later it was still nagging away when the world's most famous horse-race was stopped. 'IRA halts London by phone,' read the headline on the front page of the *Evening Standard* a week or so later. Then the technique had spread to the motorways. Before I knew it, I was having one of those over-excited lunchtime conversations that lead to a contract.

Rapidly garnering contacts, I discovered that I was not alone in having an Irish connection. Almost everyone I knew seemed to have a relative 'over there'. They were almost all 'mad'; more specifically, 'barking'. Talking to these friends and acquaintances of mine, you could have been forgiven for thinking that the entire island was an institution for expatriate English who'd gone off the rails.

Having signed my contract, I had my usual reservations, which were duly encouraged by those closest to me. 'Nobody's interested in Ireland,' said one friend. 'Not *another* book about Ireland,' said another. A search through the British Library computer threw up 49,045 books with Ireland in the title, 16,026 of which had been published since 1975.

I read five of them and left.

1

An Irish Dimension

A friend had told me that the first thing he'd seen in Ireland, disembarking from the ferry at Dun Laoghaire, was a priest being thrown out of a pub. Nothing, sadly, so symbolic for me. Just an airport arrivals lounge crowded with the usual kaleidoscope of fluorescent-clad tourists and backpackers. Outside in the summer sunshine a cheery man in a cap was on hand to direct me to a numbered taxi.

There was not a hint that I'd just landed on an island one part of which was in a state of serious civil disorder, even though, since the Orange march through Drumcree, Co. Tyrone, the previous Saturday and the ensuing riot at Garvaghy Road, Portadown, the following day, there had been 550 attacks on the security forces, 700 separate bombings, 57 civilians and 46 police injured, 150 ambulance and 500 fire service call-outs and 41 arrests in the six-county statelet that lay just sixty miles away from where I stood.

The taxi sped down the half-empty motorway towards Dublin. My middle-aged driver sat silent, entirely failing to regale me with long quotes from *Ulysses* or powerful tales of Cuchulainn and Finn McCool. Did he hate me for being English? Fresh from my first reading of Irish history, I was still feeling a bit insecure. It was to take me several days before I realized that most of the Irish had really had plenty of time to get used to the injustice of it all. But for now there was definitely a part of me that expected the driver to turn round in his seat and say: 'Wolfe Tone slit his own throat with a penknife because Cornwallis wouldn't allow him to die by firing squad. O'Connell spent his entire life negotiating with your lot – and failed even to get Home Rule. Pearse said that slavery was worse than bloodshed – and look what you did to him. Get out of my cab. Now!'

I sat back and let impressions of the fabled country seep into me. Green fields had rapidly given way to suburbs dotted with swankily pristine developments. 'Pembroke Square, new apartments of outstanding quality,' said a placard. Dublin was booming, I'd been told often enough in London. Ireland's *per capita* GNP had just overtaken ours, for the first time in history. *The Economist* had described her as the Celtic Tiger (conjuring up an image of a splendid tricoloured beast prowling through the Celtic twilight). They'd done 'incredibly well' out of Europe. It was great in one way, an Anglo-Irish friend had said, 'because it was doing away with some dreadful poverty'; but in another way it was 'sad', because there were lots of wonderful things about the old Ireland that were going as well.

The man from Bord Failte (the Board of Welcome, otherwise known as the Irish Tourist Board) had offered me, in return for journalistic commissions, three nights in a bed and breakfast that he'd described as 'central as you'll get, albeit you'll get more central than it'. (Trained in childhood, we English still keep a chuckle for the quaintness of Irish ways.) This semi-peripheral hostelry was in the charmingly named district of Ballsbridge and not at all the grubby dive I'd feared. An ivy-covered mansion with a flight of fifteen steps up to the front door, a phone by the bed, and would I like tea and biscuits in the lounge, asked soft-voiced, bob-haired Deirdre, who was surely the daughter of the house.

'If I visit Dublin, will I become a poet?' asked the glossy *Ireland – live a different life* brochure. I headed off to find out. Until now it had been entirely a city of fantasy, based on teenage immersions in Donleavy and, more substantially, Huston's film of Joyce's *The Dead*, in which horses and carts trotted along snowy boulevards by Parisian-looking river bridges. For years, too, my imagination had been locked on an image of narrow streets with dark pubs and Guinness flowing in grimy, mahogany-panelled interiors. A seat at the bar by a row of garrulous locals. A couple of grubby kids, perhaps, with a pet horse in a snug at the side.

Instead, I found the Dart, a sunny overground tube full of

pallid white faces. Direct from London, the absence of colour was startling. It was one stop into town, rattling above the backs of houses and factories and church spires to a station where the guard really did say 'dat's grand' as he took each ticket. (It was the lack of a 'th' sound in Gaelic, it was explained to me later, which produces the 'dat's and 'tink's and 'tird's so beloved, back home, of ham actors, Victorian cartoonists and pub bores.)

Round the corner was *a secondhand book shop, which doubled as a post office and stationers*. And upstairs, on a wooden stepladder half-way up a wall of ancient tomes in a dust-speckled shaft of sunlight was *a spluttering, crimson-faced man in a tweed jacket with leather patches at the elbows*. This was all as it should be.

Round another corner I came to St Stephen's Green, which for some reason I'd seen as a scrubby triangle of grass, with, perhaps, a few plane trees and a fret of traffic. Instead, through a gate and past a modernistic statue of the great Wolfe Tone (known to the irreverent locals, on account of the oblong granite blocks of stone that surround him, as 'Tone Henge') was a secret little park with a lake, complete with island, at its centre. Swans glided past on the deep green mirror, on to which brightly backlit seedfluff coasted down. Over a twinky little bridge was a rose garden, where, on a bench, sat a white-haired gent very deliberately *doing embroidery*. There was a *park keeper*. Now when had I last seen one of those? 1966, for sure.

Strolling back down the street and into Foley's I immediately distinguished myself as a tourist by ordering a pint of Guinness. The other men at the bar were drinking spritzers. The pint glass was half-filled, then put aside to settle. Later, when I understood this sacred process, I learned to sit down and wait for the drink to be brought over. Now, I hung around uselessly, smiling inanely, holding out my money in a friendly fashion, longing to do the right thing, to be accepted as a local in this bar that, ten minutes later, surrounded by Japanese with big sunglasses eating chicken nuggets, I realized was hardly the heart of the Dirty Old Town.

In my private oak-panelled booth in the corner I flicked through the Irish papers, the serious *Times* and the more gossipy *Independent*. Their perspective on the recent days of

violence was subtly different from the English versions I'd
read on the plane. 'The Government', obviously, was 'the
British Government'; the 'police' was the 'RUC'; Londonderry
was Derry; and in the *Independent* there was a photo-feature
on Gary Lawlor, a fourteen-year-old Catholic boy shot in the
back of the head by an RUC plastic bullet and now critical in
hospital. I hadn't seen anything about that in the *Daily Mail*,
whose page two headline had been 'Policeman shot as Ulster
riots turn to burning hatred'.

Absolut Ronnie Wood

Back in my B & B room at ten to nine it was altogether too
sad to go to bed and watch *Coronation Street* on TV. I played
lucky dip with my contacts, and after a couple of answerphones
and a wrong number reached Sinead, who'd been intending to
stay in and watch the news but sure, she'd be tempted out
after all. She had a mane of frizzy red hair, chunky black
leggings and an almost self-consciously gossipy manner, as if,
having been repeatedly told she was a bit of a gossip, she had
decided to major on this aspect of her personality in public.

'Let's see,' she said, grabbing my list of contacts. 'I probably
know most of them.' She did.

But then our conversation veered inevitably to the subject
of the moment. When I'd phoned she'd been watching the
riots and burning cars on the TV news and thinking, 'This is
like the seventies when I was a child. Have we really got to
return to that?' She could get ITV and Channel 4, as well as
both BBC channels and the Irish station RTE. It was interesting switching between the different perspectives of what was
going on in the North. Yes, I agreed, I'd been having an eye-
opening time with the newspapers. But truly, she said, the
Northern Irish were 'a shower of gobshites', they really were.
And Belfast was a 'kip'.

'A kip?'

'A dump.' I should go to Donegal, which was picturesque,
but the rest was a kip. 'You can have it. And d'you know what
the nice thing is,' she grinned. 'It belongs to you.'

No, the people there were horrible. On both sides. Most of

the Catholics were 'knackers' too. 'Don't go anywhere near them because you'll lose your knees.' The Catholics were dirty, the Protestants were mean. The Catholics didn't wash their front doorsteps, and the Protestants were so tight they'd only buy meat once a week. They were *all* bitter. 'There used to be advantages living up there, because of the Welfare State, and the National Health, because things were cheaper than in the South, but not any more . . .'

'D'you know what you really want to do to make your book great,' she enthused. 'Skip the North. It's a fecken kip. Do the twenty-six counties and that's it. That would be so great, because they always expect to get written about up there. Leave them out! It's a kip, kip, kip!'

So we returned with relief to glamorous, happening, peaceful Dublin. Who else should I try and see? Well, Marianne Faithful lived in a cottage on an estate not far from town; and Mia Farrow had just bought a house in Wicklow; and Ronnie Wood – did I know he was also a painter? – was having a show at this restaurant called the Baton Rouge, which he'd managed to get sponsored by Absolut Vodka. It was called Absolut Ronnie Wood. 'There's many a bitter artist in Dublin,' said Sinead, her gossipy grin returning.

Coming down for breakfast in the morning I found that I'd been joined by Sean, my host from the Board of Welcome, who was clearly taking a hands-on approach to his job. Deirdre (who was not the daughter, but the mother of the house) served us a breakfast big enough for several Celtic tigers. We munched manfully through cereals, stewed fruit, bacon, sausage, tomato, mushrooms, fried bread, black pudding and, something entirely new to me, white pudding.

Sean had brought a piece of headed Bord Failte notepaper with him.

TO WHOM IT MAY CONCERN

IT IS MY PLEASURE TO INTRODUCE MARK MCCRUM, FREELANCE JOURNALIST, WHO IS ON ASSIGNMENTS IN IRELAND.
MARK IS WRITING A BOOK WITH AN IRISH DIMENSION.

I carried it with me like a talisman; and in my darkest moments was always consoled by that 'Irish dimension'.

Sean also had some leaflets on the sights of Dublin, about which his advice was refreshingly frank. The famous eighth-century Book of Kells, for example, in Trinity Library: 'People ask and ask about it, but it's just another book.' The National Wax Museum: 'I wouldn't get too excited about that, it's mainly local figures.' As for the Joyce Tower: 'Well, if you're that way inclined it's probably worth a look.'

In contrast to this mellow Southern approach, the North was still, in what the papers were excitedly calling 'the countdown to 12 July', dominating the headlines. Last night, indeed, the Dublin to Belfast train had been petrol-bombed by masked men claiming to be from the IRA. It was the second train to have been set alight in three days. The whole thing was such a shame, Sean said. Last year, during the ceasefire, there'd been such optimism on both sides of the border. Bord Failte had even started to have joint trips with the Northern Irish Tourist Board. Not any more. Sean was as worried now as he'd ever been.

His twelve-year-old son was at this moment on holiday in Donegal, and he didn't know how he was going to get him home. He'd probably have to fly him back. That or take the long way round, via Sligo. He certainly wasn't going to drive the direct route across the North, with all the hijackings and all. (In addition to the train attacks, there'd been 221 'car-hijackings' since last Saturday, the *Irish Times* had reported, another detail not mentioned in the papers at home.)

It was an instructive irony that the British papers, although technically covering the conflict as a home matter – 'the Government', 'the Army' – on the home pages, treated Ulster in practical terms as if it were abroad. The Irish papers, on the other hand, while describing it – correctly, of course – as the affairs of a foreign country, helpfully reported that the AA had 'advised people not to travel North if the trip can be postponed' and other such useful domestic advice.

But the people in the North *were* different, Sean said. When his daughter had got married to a Northerner last year he'd made a speech in which he'd praised her patience, politeness, perspicacity – everything beginning with 'p', in fact, except her principles. This was a kind of dig at her new father-in-law, 'because they all have principles up North'. The marches were all 'on principle' – and look at the havoc they caused. 'And what are principles, except for yourself.' Sean tapped the pale blue shirt under his beige jacket. 'They're just for yourself. Poor Jesus,' he concluded, 'with these people following him.'

It was a beautiful summer's day, so I folded the Northern troubles away on the bed and headed off lightheartedly into town. 'Dat's grand, dat's grand, dat's grand,' went the ever-friendly ticket-taker at Pearse Street Dart station, where for some reason the five automatic gates were all set for incoming passengers, so he had to deal with the morning rush outwards entirely by hand.

In Merrion Square I turned into the National Gallery, which Sean had told me was supported by the estate of George Bernard Shaw. 'Every time there's a production of *My Fair Lady* they get another picture.'

Here was yet more ignorance on my part. Did you know that Yeats had had a brother who painted? I'd never even heard of the celebrated Jack B. Yeats; nor yet of W. B.'s artist father, John Butler Yeats. Nor indeed of the Irish School, and James Barry, whose *Temptation in Paradise* features a very Irish-looking Adam holding an apple whose leaves conveniently cover his parts, while a plump, shy-smiling Eve whispers, 'Jaysus, take the fockin' ting.'

Irish subjects, Irish preoccupations. From Daniel Maclise's *The Marriage of Strongbow and Aoife*, through Edwin Hayes's *An Emigrant Ship, Dublin Bay, Sunset*, to Howard Hemlick's *News of the Land League* – all the big moments were there. None of it would have meant much to me a month before.

I walked on. Donleavy's 'last shy elegant young man', Baltha-zar B, had come this way, *removed in a hansom cab from the Shelbourne Hotel to go prancing down Kildare Street towards the wall and fence and trees of Trinity College. To smile suddenly at this city. The red faces of the men and white faces of the women.* A dream of my teenage years. Particularly I had fallen in love with Beefy, Balthazar's boisterous friend. And, of course, Miss Fitzdare.

'Miss Fitzdare. Will you dance with me?'
'I'd love to.'
To take her hand. And put mine on the soft satin of her back. The blazing log fire throws red shadows. So far away from all the rain.

By the wall and fence and trees of Trinity College was a large sign advertising a Multimedia Show, the Dublin Experience, which I decided to eschew, not wanting to disappoint myself with all the loud tourists who jostled down Nassau Street buying Celtic pots and Aran jerseys and horrid little pottery leprechauns. One, most super-kitsch of all, lurked in a 'snowstorm' of fluorescent green shamrocks.

Instead, I wandered on into the wide cobbled courtyard of my imagination. *Odd lights here and there in College. To stare out the window. And wait for commons. Put on one's gown for warmth. The bell rings. Down the dark stairs. Gas lamps glowing along the dark squares.* Sadly not. But either I was having a mind-blowing *déjà vu* or I'd been on these sunny green lawns before. Just as I was starting to think I might have been Oscar Wilde in a previous life, it dawned on me – it was the location of *Educating Rita*. The college, I later discovered, was picked on account of its resemblance to 'a typical English university'.

Outside the fine stone portico stand Edmund Burke and Oliver Goldsmith, two non-fictional alumni of this fine Protestant foundation of Elizabeth I's, which accepted Catholics only if they were prepared to 'take the soup' and change their religion. Right up till 1970, long after this rule had been dropped by Trinity, Catholics still had to gain special dispensation to study here, or risk excommunication.

Beyond them, on tiny College Green, gesturing towards his purpose-built parliament, stands another graduate, Henry Grattan. 'Ireland is now a nation,' he declared, somewhat prematurely, in 1782. Nineteen years later, Pitt's Act of Union robbed the Anglo-Irish leaders of the island of their short-lived independence. The Irish parliament created an unusual precedent by voting themselves out of existence; and the first building in the world designed to house a parliament was turned into a bank, the Bank of Ireland, which it remains today.

History is indeed everywhere in these dirty streets, where

honking, fuming traffic, driven, Beefy tells me, by 'pasty-faced bogmen', rattles on into the ever-booming Euro-future. Were you to stop and remark on everything of interest, he adds, you'd be here all week.

With Beefy pacing beside me in his black *chapeau*, I walk on, down Anglesea Street and Crown Alley to Temple Bar, the very epicentre of modern Ireland, on whose narrow, oblong-cobbled streets are swish nineties bistros and galleries and secondhand shops, and the Project Arts Centre, and the Irish Film Centre and, up steps under three maroon sunshades, the oak-panelled Octagon Bar of the Clarence Hotel, which is, as everyone will tell you, owned by U2, conferring on its architecture and ambience an unimpeachable certificate of trendiness. Beefy and I, hoping we are hip enough to get served, pause for a few minutes for a double *espresso*.

Refreshed, we stride on, past Central Perks and the Back Lounge and down a narrow alley to Ha'penny Bridge, Dublin's only pedestrian river crossing, a quaint cast-iron affair that predates Queen Victoria. Below, the Liffey is a grey-brown low-tide murk, where gulls swoop above beds of vivid green seaweed. On the dirty wall on the far side a quote from Joyce is picked out on a long metal plaque: 'the sea the sea crimson sometimes like fire.' I recognize it as a quote from Joyce, even though, to my shame, I've never read more than seventeen pages of *Ulysses*. How often have I tried, though. I must have been through that shaving sequence ten times on various occasions. Buck Mulligan, Stephen Dedalus – figures of shame. I must be thick not to understand. What the feck is going on in the tower? Though why, I wonder now, should any mere Englishman understand *What Arthur Griffith said about the headpiece over the* Freeman *leader: a homerule sun rising up in the northwest from the laneway behind the bank of Ireland.*

These tatty side streets in the less fashionable area north of the river are much more like the Dublin of imagination. Here are old ladies gossiping in an open doorway; there a Venetian perspective of washing lines. Round a corner two rolled carpets poke from a skip overflowing with pallets. The alley is strewn with rotting potatoes, and there's no sign of the Old

Chapter House of the great Cistercian Abbey of St Mary, founded by the Benedictines in 1139, only a doorway and a sign saying 'Open Wed 10–5.00'. A stroke of luck! It's Wednesday and 12.30, in the height of the summer season. But no, the door is firmly locked. I head back to the river. The walls read PUSHERS OUT. SCUM OUT. DRUG FREE ZONE.

Just up the Quay are the Four Courts, famously occupied by anti-Treaty forces in 1922, at the start of the Civil War. ('What were they fighting about?' I hear you ask. Land, potatoes, the allocation of green beer on St Patrick's Day? No. The murderous squabble was about a *difference in policy*, over that perennial common objective – getting rid of the British from all parts of the island.) After two months Michael Collins's patience with his ex-comrades ran out and forces of the new Free State Government opened fire on the rebels with field guns, destroying the dome and the nearby Public Records Office.

Creak. I push through the tall oak front doors and into an echoing corridor. Sunlight fans in neat beams from square windows high in the restored dome down to a marble floor where groups of black-gowned, grey-wigged barristers gossip. To one side the defendants and their families wear shell suits and trainers.

In Court One a softly spoken teenage girl in a white top is being quizzed about an accident. She slipped down a muddy slope by a waterfall on a school trip and crippled herself.

'What kind of countryside were you walking over?'

'Through fields and forests.'

'And how were they all getting on now?'

'Everyone was falling.'

'Was it good fun?'

'Not at this stage, we were scared.'

'And how were you for pain?'

'I was numb.'

So? says Beefy, as I emerge a few minutes later into the traffic. 'It's interesting,' I reply. 'I'm trying to put my finger on something. A lilt of language that is the basis for your story, and Joyce, and Doyle and McCourt, and all the rest of them. It was unselfconsciously there, in that exchange. It's poetic, and it's genuine.'

Beefy raises his *chapeau*, makes a deeply ironic *moue* and strides off without a word.

There were still horses drawing the box-piled carts that queued on the cobbles outside the arched red and yellow brickwork of the Dublin fruit and vegetable market. Further along Capel Street, beyond the massed bargains of a £1 shop, I stopped for lunch in a pub straight out of *The Commitments*. 'All children must be off the premises by 7 pm' read a sign behind a large mum, jogging a chubby-faced toddler on each knee.

Round the corner was a fine exhibit for anyone who wanted to muse on the deeper resonances of the religious divide. St Mary's Church, where Sheridan, Wolfe Tone and Sean O'Casey were baptized, Arthur Guinness was married, and John Wesley preached his first sermon in Ireland. Being a Protestant foundation there's not much use for it these days, the 3 per cent or so of Southern Irish who are of that persuasion being more than well catered for by two huge cathedrals, Christ Church and St Patrick's, in the centre of the city. So, waste not, want not, they've turned the place into Ryan's DIY Centre. Look up, and see the lovely ceiling, in blue turquoise and crimson, the light filtering through stained-glass windows beyond the chandelier; look down and see Ireland's Best Exterior Stone Paint £15.95, wallpaper rolls, curtain samples, tiles, wood dyes . . .

I wandered on, through all the streets named for Irish heroes with a common aim: Wolfe Tone Street, Parnell Square, O'Connell Street, Lord Edward Street. Finally, back over the river, in the vast interior of Christ Church, I found the man who had started all the trouble. Richard Fitzgilbert de Clare (known as Strongbow) lies with his palms flat together on his chest in prayer, his eyes closed. This is what you get, 827 years later, for daring to be the first completely successful non-Celtic invader of Ireland – a pink-cardiganed matron from Akron, Ohio, leaning over you and cooing, 'Liddle Bo Pee-ep.'

The Ego of the Irish

'Welcome to Dublin!' says Liam McShane, as he raises his first pint to his lips. As we stand sipping, this dapper, gleaming, ever-so-slightly convex young lawyer, in his neat grey suit and crimson tie, seems rather anxious that I'm enjoying myself and that I'm impressed with his choice, the Long Bar of the Shelbourne Hotel. He keeps looking around the noisy crowd of suits and skirts pressed up against the pink 'n' black granite counter for someone to recognize him, hail him, verify his claim that this is the place to be in Dublin on a Friday night.

'You see that fellow there,' he says, as we enjoy our second.

'Yes.'

'He's a complete *eejit*.'

'Right.'

On our third, Liam relaxes a little and tells me how fed up he is with his job. Because he went to Trinity, his colleagues in the firm regard him as a 'West Brit', even though he's a Catholic.

Now, as the thick white foam slides slowly down the sides of our fourth, and the two wooden eagles above the porphyry fireplace assume ever-friendlier expressions, he's decided to tell me the truth about Ireland and the Irish. 'We have this idea,' he shouts against the din, 'that we invented the entire universe. Everything developed from us. We actually discovered the States before Christopher Columbus – St Brendan did it, long time before. Europe, forget it!'

He laughs, takes a deep swig, licks the creamy foam from his lips. 'We had the monasteries, we dispersed all the monasteries to the Outer Hebrides. We were the best, we're the dog's bollocks in that regard. Europe was conquered. Africa – we have runners from Ethiopia and Kenya, keep doing it, who have they been taught by? Christian brothers!'

He beams at me. 'South America,' he yells. 'We have Chile and Argentina. We have guys like, what's his name, Bernardo O'Higgins, became dictator of the place. Our convicts went out to Australia. We built all the railroads with the Japanese and the Chinese. The only place we haven't done is Southeast Asia, because we couldn't handle the climate, I'm sure. Like, we are the greatest country in the world. We are the dog's bollocks. The ego of the Irish is just frightening – we must be the biggest egotists in the world. Even though it's just three and a half million people here, there would have been much more except for the Famine, we'd have had fifteen and a half million people here by now, and we'd never have got into this bar at this time of the evening, not a fuckin' chance . . .'

We decide to move on, round the corner to Café en Seine, which punningly titled venue is, Liam explains, nothing like as stuffy as the Shelbourne. It's much friendlier, and you'll find 'the most gorgeous looking girls'. And indeed, as we push in to the dazzling modern Irish crowd under the row of globed chandeliers, he's greeted by two young women, a skinny mouse-haired Maire, and a bulky Sheena, whose large nose is well set off by her flashing brown eyes and mass of dark curls. Friday night is sacred in Dublin, Maire tells me, as Liam pushes off through the throng to get the requisites. You go out straight from work and get boxed. Or, to put it another way, you try to move on, to go with the flow, but then you end up going with the sludge, and the sludge ends up being really good fun, so you stick with the sludge.

'Welcome to Dublin!' says Liam, rejoining us. 'Another thing you need to do, Mark,' he continues, 'is be fed by an Irish mother. You need to be taken into the womb and fed – Jesus!' he says, interrupting himself, head swivelling, 'the most amazing pairs of breasts keep coming through here . . .'

But oh no, all of a sudden we've been joined by Liam's girlfriend Katrina, who shouldn't be here because they'd agreed this would be a boys' night out, but what was she supposed to do? Stay in? She wasn't to know he'd be coming to Café, and anyway if it was a boys' night out, what's he doing with a huge grin on his face surrounded by a bevy of gorgeous looking girls?

'Welcome to Dublin!' says Liam, with a rapid half-wink.

Katrina was, she explains to me now she's been introduced, actually going on a girls' night out with her sister Therese, who has bobbed blonde hair and a fetching laugh, and I'll have no problem in Ireland because Ireland is the kind of place where people *take care of you*. It is. It is, Katrina agrees. They were once, the pair of them, stuck in Rosslare with no money, and the people on the bus had a whip-round for them, you know, 'to bring the girls home'. That's the kind of country it is. People have respect, Katrina says, 'for the sorts of things your mother told you'.

The North, though, is different. Katrina's voice rises to sudden fury as she shouts in my ear about how she'd been to visit some relatives who'd become Protestants and how they were ashamed to be seen with her family, Catholics, and how they'd been made to park their car round the back of the house so it wouldn't be recognized as a Catholic car. 'And this was three years ago!' she yells.

'Welcome to Dublin!' says Liam, lurching towards me. Café's closing, so we're moving on, to Lily's Bordello, which is where, Liam tells me, as we float through the bright crowds and late-night buskers of pedestrianized Grafton Street, all the most pretentious human beings in Ireland come, and it's all naff but it's great fun and you meet the nicest people in the world. But somehow this doesn't happen this evening, even though Therese, who has got us in, seems extremely happy with her arms around a mean-looking guy in a black shirt buttoned up to the neck. Katrina apologizes for her. She's been rocky in the three months since she split up from her husband.

'Welcome to Dublin!' says Liam, as, still grinning, he passes out on the arm of our black leatherette alcove seat.

Emerging sometime in the small hours I find the city packed with young people gorging on take-aways. Half of Dublin's population is under twenty-five, and three-quarters of them are out tonight. The bright lights of McDonald's dazzle out on to the orange-brown brick floor of Grafton Street. In murky corners there's snogging and rowing and vomiting going on.

I look for taxis but find only a rickshaw, pedalled by a bearded scarecrow with hair half way down his Nirvana T-shirt. He has dark, Charles II ringlets and a ferocious scowl. Jake is English, filling in for a friend. Last week he was in Glastonbury; now, he moans, as he pedals me very slowly along in the lowest gear, he's got stuck with this.

Lamplit faces passing on the pavement turn as we crawl down Baggot Street, back past the splendid façade of the Shelbourne and on by the clean-bricked Georgian houses.

This guy is useless, repeatedly veering in towards the curb, grumbling on about how he'd rather be in London.

It's only a glorified tricycle, for Christ's sake! With a surge of inebriated impatience, I've suggested I take over. And yes, Jake's more than happy to lounge in the back, as I mount the high, narrow saddle and – Jesus, he's heavy – take us much more speedily over the little canal bridge, down past the crowds outside Abrakebabra and the Late-Nite Supermarket, controlling that repeating leftwards swerve with all the skill of my Gaelic ancestors.

After the Fall

In the North the Orangemen had decided not to march through key sectarian flash points. Hardline Unionists had condemned the gesture as a sell-out to the IRA, while in other quarters the compromise was greeted with 'praise and relief'. But down here in the South some fresh news had pushed this story into second position in the headlines. Charles Haughey, celebrated former Taoiseach, whose super-extravagant life-style – a mansion in north Dublin, a private island off Kerry, a yacht called *Celtic Mist*, a string of racehorses – had long led to allegations of corruption, had finally, it seemed, been caught out. He'd admitted that he'd accepted £1.3 million from Ben Dunne, the owner of the Ireland-wide Dunnes Stores. It was Ireland's 'biggest political scandal for years', and the weekend papers were full of gloating headlines: 'The charade is finally over', 'After the fall', 'The descent of man' and the like.

By 10.30 in the morning, when I arrived at Dublin Castle, the tribunal room was full. A gaggle of journos hung around by the arch in the corner of the cobbled courtyard for a glimpse of the (once) great man.

Down a couple of flights of stairs, in a spacious basement across the way, the Videolink was also packed. A buzzing crowd of two or three hundred sat in front of the huge screen at the far end, at present relaying a view of an empty witness box, a shuffling room full of lawyers and press.

Suddenly there was movement. 'Mr Charles J. Haughey, please,' called the judge. There was a mighty hush, in both courtroom and Videolink, as the star of the show shuffled in and took his seat. On screen his features were giant, in a face six feet tall.

It was one of the most extraordinary performances I'd ever seen. The ex-Taoiseach was so clearly trapped in a corner, yet he refused to come clean and admit that, yes, while in office he'd known about the acceptance of £1.3 million from Mr Dunne. Sitting there in a shaft of sunlight, his hooded eyes shifting, lizard-like, from side to side, he somehow successfully managed to adopt the ridiculous line that the manager of his financial affairs, Mr Des Traynor, (now conveniently deceased) had kept him in the dark to such an extent that he didn't know how he'd received this money, even when three bank drafts worth £210,000 were put in his hand by Mr Dunne in person.

'I have absolutely no recollection of the meeting,' he told the tribunal (to howls of laughter in the Videolink) 'but it is clear from the evidence that the late Mr Des Traynor received the money and that I got the benefit of it ... In hindsight it is clear I should have involved myself to a greater degree in this regard.'

'As an accountant you *must* have known,' tried his interrogator, a little later. (Was he deliberately trying to catch him out with his conciliatory tone, or just cowed by the legend before him, I wondered.)

'I was a very quiescent accountant, I hadn't known the accountancy world for many decades.'

'You may not have been an accountant for some time, but you'd been Minister of Finance.' Roars in the Videolink.

And so it went on. 'My private finances were perhaps peripheral to my life', 'I didn't have a lavish lifestyle', and 'Des Traynor was a man of few words', particularly bringing the house down.

'I have no knowledge of any Cayman accounts. I never had any knowledge. I still have no knowledge.'

After the bizarre charade was over, as the audience got to their feet and pushed for the doors, the man on my right leant over. 'I don't like to say it,' he said with a chuckle, 'but he was always a rogue.' He shook his head. 'They say they forget. If someone gave you a million pounds would you forget? You wouldn't.'

Outside, the entire crowd, it seemed, was waiting to see the ex-Taoiseach emerge.

'The number of times he had to stop to recollect his thoughts . . .'

'Why didn't he specifically ask . . .?'

'He concluded that he was of such a benefit to the State that the State owed him a living . . .'

'In Ireland we love a rogue, we love a character . . .'

Then, suddenly, there he was, a little man running for a big car. There was a ragged cheer. Then a lone boo. Then everyone was booing. It was a casebook example of a mob changing mood.

'Yer ratbag! Yer chancer!' screamed a dark, pig-faced little woman. 'He's a *chancer*!'

'He got the dinner for nothing, didn't have to pay for it!'

'Charles J. Haughey.'

That evening I met up with Sinead again. We sat over a bottle of wine in a downstairs 'club' full of check-clothed, candlelit tables. Despite everything, she was still cheering the fallen leader. 'Don't be cruel, Mark,' she said, when I'd finished giving her my description of the morning's proceedings. When she was a child, she said, her grandmother had had three pictures over her bed. 'One was Pope Pius, one was John F. Kennedy, and one was Charles J. Haughey.' Her grandmother had been a good practising Catholic, always talking about the Holy Trinity. 'And the Holy Trinity is three blokes.' It was a long while before Sinead had realized it wasn't these three blokes.

But her grandparents had been huge supporters of Fianna Fail, 'the Soldiers of Ireland', the party that had emerged from the uncompromising anti-Treaty side of the Civil War. 'She was in love with Charlie, definitely. She used to send him money for his party, because she supported him, and, you know, she didn't want to see him *short*.'

Haughey had always had the reputation of being a bit of a rogue. 'And now it turns out that he accepted a bit of money.'

'A *bit*?'

'Well a lot. But it's only money, Mark. Because, I mean, it could have been a lot worse. It could have been child abuse, which I think is appalling.' Sinead was bright-eyed, swigging the red wine. 'Sure he blamed everything on the accountant, who's dead, but I still love Charlie.'

Despite the boos of the crowd, Sinead wasn't the only one to still love Charlie. In the *Independent*, the following day, one of the female feature writers devoted a whole page to her continuing loyalty to this man, now publicly labelled a liar, hypocrite and worse.

Much later in my journey, in the North, one of the many reasons advanced by Unionists against a United Ireland was the terrible corruption that was rife in the South, in all areas. The Establishment was venal, and the people tolerated it. Was this, in part, true? If it was, they certainly hadn't read Fintan O'Toole of the *Irish Times*:

> Haughey's fall is painful, not because a man who has had so much power deserves any sympathy, but because the rest of us have to take stock of the fact that we live in a society partly shaped by such a man. We are reminded of just how badly our public and social morality has lagged behind our economic progress. We are forced to look again at the history of the last 30 years, to wonder what seedy deals, what shabby bargains, have determined the direction of public policy. Whatever smugness we may feel about our success in joining the modern world is shaken. If the shock of his disgrace forces us to see the flaws in what we have become in his time, Charles Haughey may, at last, have done the State some service.

2

Green Eyes

I was glad to be leaving Dublin, with its tourist-packed pavements and its snarling summer traffic. Now I was going up, up into the green hills of Wicklow, always such a coolly beckoning backdrop at the end of these long, straight Georgian streets. It was raining now, and heavily, as the 44 bus trundled out past office blocks, council flats, more, but tattier, Georgian terraces, over a river and up a hill where clipped green lawns swept away from swanky executive bungalows with carports and topiary.

All too soon the green double-decker was chuntering incongruously down a leafy lane and into Enniskerry, which revealed itself as a village of almost unbearable picturesqueness, with a clock tower and surrounding rose-garden in the middle of its triangular central 'square'. Surely a big hand would descend from the sky and dismantle it into jigsaw pieces, or lift the whole scene and reveal the layer of Leprechaun Liqueur chocolates beneath.

On the corner by the bakery was Eilish's B & B, with red and yellow roses climbing the wall at the front and a yard out back where her two labradors, Hervey (one) and Benson (thirteen), scampered and lolled under the whirligig washing line. Eilish had apple-red cheeks in a face that looked altogether too young to be topped by her shorn grey curls.

So where was I from? she asked. London, yes. No, she didn't much like London. No, it was fine, but it wasn't what it had been, not at all. Oxford Street used to have some lovely shops, but now, especially down the end away from the department stores, it wasn't the same. She didn't like all those tatty ethnic stores, 'that kind of way'.

Before we got, as I felt sure we were about to, on to the

tatty ethnic people, I changed the subject to her. Oh well, the kind of tourists who lodged with her had changed over the years. They used to get 90 per cent English, who'd come over on the ferry, take the bus out to Enniskerry, and stay for a fortnight. 'They didn't have transport, anything in that kind of way.' But when the Troubles had started in the North, in 1972, or '74, whenever it was, the tourism had stopped – just like that.

Recently you'd got a younger type, who'd come for two to three days, then they'd jump in their car and be off somewhere else. They didn't know or care about any history, or anything in that kind of way; they just wanted to have a good time.

She showed me to a pink room with two pink single beds, green and pink curtains and a sign saying 'Thank you for not smoking' above the avocado sink. Unloading my books and papers, I confessed what I was doing. 'You can put us in the book, if you like, the tree of us,' Eilish said, as Harvey and Benson yapped at her apron.

'That's a nice yellow door,' said one of the two ladies dining in the window of Harvest Home, Snacks, as they gazed out over the empty street that evening.

'Yes, isn't it,' replied her companion.

But I didn't mind. Beyond the slate roofs and neat chimneys, up on the hillside, the rooks massed in the topmost branches of the haphazard green tumble of trees. The rain had stopped; the stillness was tangible.

In the morning, after another fine Irish fry-up (I was glad to see white pudding making a re-appearance), I strode off up the road towards Powerscourt House, the distinguished Anglo-Irish mansion of which Enniskerry had, since its construction in the early nineteenth century, been the estate village. In Dublin I'd been given a grand-looking invitation to its re-opening, twenty-three years after it had all but burned down on the eve of a party to celebrate the completion of an extensive programme of renovation. I hoped we weren't going to be treated to a fiery repeat. Surely not, because no less a person than the Irish President, Mary Robinson, was officiating. I was coming as much to see her as the house.

The drive was *very* long. Smart car after smart car whooshed past me as I paced along the tarmac under the tall trees, feeling decidedly underdressed and underconfident in my worn blue moleskins and non-matching jacket.

To my left the green Wicklow hills rolled out like a fantasy of what countryside should be (i.e., depopulated) towards the bizarre cones of Great and Little Sugar Loaf Mountains. They marked the edge of the Pale, the area of land around Dublin that had been, from Norman times, effectively subject to the English Crown. The Dargle valley below me, for example, had, post-Conquest, been 'granted' by Henry II to one of Strongbow's barons, Walter de Ridelesford (subsequently it had passed to the Anglo-Norman le Poers). Beyond the Pale dwelt 'wild Irish' clans like the O'Tooles and the O'Byrnes, who still laid claim to their ancient principalities.

Indeed, from the fourteenth to sixteenth centuries, the O'Tooles had managed to regain possession, being kicked out only when James I had confiscated the estate on the death of Felim O'Toole and replaced his grandson Tirlagh with one of the Crown's more outstanding servants, Sir Richard Wingfield, who had been Marshal of Elizabeth I's forces in Ireland. Like those other, less distinguished, Protestant soldiers who were given lands taken from the native Irish in Ulster, Sir Richard was, in the parlance of the time, 'planted'. (In 1618, James I completed the favour by making him the first Viscount Powerscourt.)

The story of the valley and its dominating dwelling, which had changed from a castle called Balytenyth to a house called Poer's (thence Power's) Court, was a fascinatingly illustrative microcosm of the broader movements of Irish history: the Gaelic O'Tooles, replaced by the Anglo-Norman de Ridelesfords and le Poers, usurped by the returning O'Tooles, removed again by the planted Elizabethan Wingfields.

In 1641, during the English Civil War, the risings against the newly planted Scottish Protestants in Ulster were matched in Wicklow by the O'Tooles. Powerscourt was 'burned out' (to use a favourite Irish phrase), and the next Sir Richard subsequently died in battle. Fortunately for the Wingfields, he had left behind young Folliott, aged three. By the time Cromwell had come and gone and Charles II's Restoration land settlement was complete, Folliott was in possession of the

Wingfield estates again, as Viscount Powerscourt of the second
creation. The O'Tooles, like other Celtic noble families across
the land who had supported Charles in the hope of getting
their lands back, felt entirely betrayed.

That was the end of the O'Tooles' attempts to regain the
'principality' they had once called Omurthie, described in John
O'Toole's family history as 'a sort of Irish paradise, whose
atmosphere was laden with the odours of perpetual Spring – a
land teeming with yellow corn and honey, where the herds
were all the year round knee-deep in rich pasture; a region
irrigated by sweet, fertilizing streams.'

Ah me! Those O'Tooles who lingered on could have been
forgiven for nurturing a deep sense of injustice against their
Protestant usurpers and the English overlords who had put
them there. There was a Captain Charles O'Toole in James
II's ill-fated 1689 parliament, who voted for the repeal of
Charles II's Act of Settlement. Denied, he subsequently fought,
alongside the O'Neills, O'Donnells, O'Byrnes, Maguires and
others on James's side, in the Battle of the Boyne, to be
defeated by William of Orange's army of Dutch, Danes,
English, French Huguenots and Protestant Ulstermen.

Other O'Tooles did as the dispossessed Irish had done
before and became expatriate 'wild geese' in Europe. Captain
Luke O'Toole was made a Knight of the Golden Spur by Pope
Clement XI; Colonel Count John O'Toole was considered the
handsomest man in France; Françoise O' Toole was a Captain
of the 73rd French Regiment of the Line. And so on down.
Doubtless Slugger O'Toole, who runs a pub near me in
Camden, is one of the clan.

Powerscourt, when it finally made an appearance, was splendid
enough, with oxidized-copper green domes above a grey stone
Palladian façade; but the grounds at the back were magnificent, sloping down in a series of manicured grassy terraces
with embedded jewels of rose gardens towards a lily-strewn
lake by the woods at the bottom, the Sugar Loaf view forming
a theatrical backdrop behind. Above, fluffy white clouds sailed
serenely across a clear blue sky.

The long terrace was thronged with a colourfully dressed-
up crowd, babbling at each other in a fine range of Dublin

accents. Here was a plump foursome of business suits; there two squealing little girls in pink, one barefoot; here a perma-tanned Hogarth caricature in a crisp, double-breasted blazer; there a swaggering trio of tweed jackets paying court to a gaggle of laughing young women, the ever-so-slightly chill breeze whipping at the white chiffon overdress of the most trendily dressed. Underneath, she had baggy, Indian-style white trousers. In her nose, a ring. Her hair was a startling chiaroscuro of orange and blond highlights against a dark base. She looked every bit the gatecrasher. It was only when I happened on her picture in the *Independent* the next day that I realized she was none other than Julie Wingfield, great-granddaughter of the 9th Viscount Powerscourt, the latest version of that long Wingfield line.

Recognizing nobody, I took a fizzy swig of sparkling wine and headed in, striking up a conversation with two cheerful ladies who worked for – well, well – Bord Failte. There were present, they explained, besides tourism professionals, country people, political people, social people. 'That's Lord Mount Charles over there,' said Catherine, pointing out the Hogarth.

We were just getting on to an interesting chat about Charles Haughey (Catherine had *worked for* Fianna Fail and she'd *never known* about the money), when there was a hush and it was the speeches. First was academic-looking Dr Slazenger, representative of the family that had bought Powerscourt from Julie's great-grandpapa in 1961. Having thanked the estate manager, the engineers, his daughter and the man who'd assisted in obtaining the grant from the European Regional Development Fund, he turned to the focus of everyone's attention, Mary Robinson, who stood beside him beaming like a marionette. She was leaving the presidency before the end of her term to become Human Rights Commissioner at the United Nations. 'Ireland's loss is the world's gain,' Dr Slazenger told us. 'If she can do for her new job what she has done for the one she is leaving, the world will certainly be a better place.'

She was, indeed, quite a phenomenon, this woman who now waited professionally for the applause to die down before launching into a speech that you really couldn't mock, combining, as it did, authority with accessibility, sincerity with

humour. She remembered, 'as so many here do, that terrible
night of November 1974, when Powerscourt burnt down'. She
had lived just down the road from Dr Slazenger, so had known
at first hand how devastating it had been. 'So on a personal
level it is a pleasure to be here. But it's also appropriate that I
be here as President of Ireland, as *Uachtarán*.'

It was perfectly pitched, describing the restored Anglo-Irish
stronghold entirely in terms of Irish heritage, managing to talk
about the estate workers' and local people's 'sense of joy and
pride in what is here' without sounding condescending or
bogus.

Even though there was, on the surface perhaps, something
almost too good to be true about Mary Robinson, the fact
was, to date, it was true. From a no-hope position, she had
taken on the two biggest parties in the land, Fianna Fail and
Fine Gael, and won, by a margin of 86,557 votes. She had
subsequently changed the Presidential office from sinecure to
world-recognized symbol, zooming around the world to meet
Yasser Arafat, President Clinton, the Queen, President Finn-
bogadóttir of Iceland, and in doing so had not forgotten,
indeed made a positive feature of, that oft-talked-about constituency of the less-fortunate. Her public engagements were
liberally sprinkled with visits to travellers' conferences, inner-
city organizations, women's aid refuges, gay and lesbian equal-
ity networks – you name it. And this wasn't just show. It was
an extension of the work she had done as the youngest woman
ever elected to the Senate. Having at first threatened to walk
through Dublin with a placard saying 'I am under-employed',
she had thrown herself behind the issues that had come to be
defined with 'modern Ireland', in 1971 calling publicly for a
removal of the divorce ban from the Constitution; two years
later publishing a bill to legalize the sale of contraception;
going on to champion the rights of unmarried mothers, homo-
sexuals and travellers. As the feminist journalist Mary Maher
put it, 'No one has shouted less and achieved more.'

It was an achievement, as I was to discover later, that more
than a few were unhappy with; but she had both symbolized
and actioned the change in Ireland from a country hand-in-
hand with the Catholic Church and its values to something
entirely new and other.

'I could go on,' she was saying, 'but if my husband Nick was here he would have coughed by now.' The cough was his signal, she explained, that she'd spoken for long enough. As the laughter died down, she switched deftly into Irish, a move that the crowd accorded an appropriate seriousness. 'I had to practise that,' she quipped, finishing with expert bathos.

By two the last guests had stumbled into the coffee shop for lunch and the gravel path along the front of the terrace was invaded by hand-holding Americans and loud groups of Continental teenagers with tiny, droopy knapsacks. '*Dario!*' they shrieked. '*À la fontana!*' I followed them down, round the lily pond and the Japanese garden, to where a steeply sloping graveyard had a scatter of tiny headstones with inscriptions such as:

TEDDY
THE FIRST PET OF MERVYN
AND WENDY WINGFIELD
DIED ACCIDENTALLY
AGED 2

The once-disputed landscape had worked a gentle magic on the descendants of the martial Sir Richard.

Enniskerry's other claim to fame was altogether more contemporary. The village was, with Arklow, just down the road, the location for the BBC's drama, *Ballykissangel*. Indeed, I'd been told that Father McCabe was 'the real priest of *Ballykissangel*'. Not that I dreamed of mentioning that, as the front door of the big square house swung open and Sheila, the housekeeper, let me in.

Father McCabe was waiting for me in the library, she said. And a very different sort of Irish priest he was from Father Clifford. Short, square-shouldered, with cropped grey hair, he seemed to exude, from behind those thin-rimmed gold glasses, a tangible air of calm. We'd just got over the initial civilities when the door opened and Sheila appeared with a huge tray of sandwiches and slices of fruit cake around a cosied pot of tea.

'You'll have a sandwich, Mark,' she said.

'Well . . .'

'You will, you will, you will, you will, you will, you *will!*'

No, not quite, but as she stood there, encouraging me not to 'make strange' with the goodies before me, I realized that *Father Ted* was mild exaggeration rather than outlandish fantasy.

I'd had no idea what I was going to talk to the 'real priest of *Ballykissangel*' about, but it turned out that Father McCabe had a subject, if not an agenda. Moving me rapidly from local to national history, he explained that he was a republican. He didn't mean by that that he was a supporter of the IRA, because he couldn't, of course, condone violence. 'Human life is much more precious.' But he was a fervent Nationalist, a strong supporter of a united Ireland.

He was tilted further in this direction than anyone I had yet encountered. Even Robert Kee's history of Ireland, *The Green Flag*, which I'd been happily regarding as admirably objective, was 'fine as a history, but he puts the British slant and construction on it all the time'. The slant that Kee put on it was, 'to say the least, not acceptable. The British are always accusing us of having too long a memory,' this softest-voiced of clerics went on, 'but the roadsides of Ireland are dotted with the evidence of British atrocities.'

What Father McCabe couldn't understand was why the British remained on. For seventy years they'd been supporting a privileged Loyalist group. 'They tell the world they're keeping the peace. I take that with a pinch of salt.' The British tried to convince the world that it was a religious divide, between Catholics and Protestants, but it wasn't. The divide was between Nationalists and Unionists. There were plenty of Protestant Nationalists, and quite a number of Catholics who supported the Union.

'I do take exception to the media drawing this line between Catholics and Protestants. It's Nationalists and Unionists,' he emphasized. He and his congregation, for example, had a wonderful rapport with the Protestants in Enniskerry.

If Britain decided to pull out tomorrow, Father McCabe went on, they'd find Ireland would be a better ally. It was time just to put an end to British messing with Ireland, and if there was a united Ireland the Unionists could fight their corner pretty well. The trouble was, up till now, they'd been fed privilege and supported in privilege, which had made them very arrogant. 'They have a heritage, yes, but they are a minority in Ireland.'

'Of course,' he concluded, 'I'm looking at it through green eyes. You go to the Six Counties, you'll see it through the orange glasses.'

His eyes, gentle and not at all green, fixed me in an altogether unaggressive fashion. 'No, it's my country, and I'd like to see it just one country and us all getting along.' Which would, he thought, be perfectly possible. In Rossnowlagh, Donegal, the Orangemen marched every year, as they did in Monaghan, where he'd grown up. 'And there's no opposition. People clap, and cheer, and all that.'

As a child in Monaghan they'd been surrounded by Protestants. 'And we were the best of friends. For 364 days of the year. Then on 12 July it was, "To hell with the Pope and his two white horses." I witnessed it myself, every year. Tom Dickinson, his name was, used to get up on the wall and shout it. I'm not quite sure what the two white horses were. I thought it was King Billy had the white horses.' Father McCabe chuckled. 'But surely we could live like that in the whole of the country.'

In the morning there was some excellent news. A new ceasefire was coming. 'This is more like it,' said the man at the bus-stop; but he was, of course, talking about the weather, which had reverted to bright sunshine.

The tiny bus wound down dappled lanes, lurched across the main Dublin to Rosslare N11, and then, via a scenic tour of a housing estate, into Bray, whose tourist leaflet described it as 'Gateway to the garden of Ireland'. Oh dear. I remembered other 'gateways' I'd encountered on my travels – Port Hedland, Western Australia, 'Gateway to the Inland Pilbara'; Ermelo, South Africa, 'Gateway to Hydro-Electric Country'. When a tourist board was reduced to referring to its product as a 'gateway', it meant the worst. I mean, would you describe yourself as 'gateway to a lot of interesting friends'? It was wise just to take them at face value – and head on through.

'Most of Bray's Victorian promenade and buildings,' the leaflet continued, 'are in the same style today as they were during the time Oscar Wilde may have walked in Bray.' Oh dear, oh dear.

I headed to the railway station, where a single to Wexford was £17, a return £10.70. 'Don't ask me why,' said the cheerful young guy in the booth. On the long platform two women holding a small boy between them were discussing a new film. '*Loads* of sex in it,' said the prettier of the two. 'Real raunchy stuff. It was *great*.'

When the train pulled in I slid into a seat opposite two white-haired old ladies in matching dark glasses, who were leaning so close that one had her lips virtually on the other's earlobe. From their whispery, gossipy tone you might have imagined they were discussing matters of highest state security, if not hatching a new revolution.

'D'you know what I *love*. Oven chips. They're very easy to do.'

'I've never made chips in my life . . .'

Inland, the steep green Wicklow mountains, a tunnel, then a dazzling flash of woodland, a glinting stream, a herd of Fresians at the bottom of a shimmeringly emerald slope. On the other side, in glimpses, the sea, neither snotgreen nor scrotumtightening today, more an unmetaphoric blue-grey. Greystones, Wicklow, Rathdrum, Arklow, Gorey. I got off at Enniscorthy, and found a quaint, conservatory-style waiting room hung with geraniums. Leaving my pack-cum-suitcase with the man in the parcels office, I headed off round the corner, past a sweet-shop, over the rushing, eddying, gleaming River Slaney, and up a steep pedestrian street to another triangular square, where a group of crop-headed teenage lads loitered by the tall monument to the 1798 rising.

Huzza!

Of the ironies that cram Irish history like currants in the richest fruit cake, perhaps the most commonly repeated is that the greatest rising against the British was led by Protestants. The 'leader' of that revolutionary group, the United Irishmen, who orchestrated much of the action of that disastrous year, was a young Dublin barrister called Theobald Wolfe Tone. He was a colourful, almost quixotically optimistic character, whose fondness for food, drink and good company went alongside, if not matched, his aspirations for an Ireland free of English influence, in which Catholics, who for the previous century or so had been subject to restrictive penal laws, would play a full part.

Here, for example, is his diary description of a visit to one of the Belfast United Irishmen, the industrialist ship-owner Henry Joy McCracken.

Walk out and see McCracken's new ship, the Hibernia. Hibernia has an English Crown on her shield. We all roar at him ... Gog and Mr Hutton called upon to give an account of the present state of Catholics. Mr Hutton makes a long and accurate statement, which meets with the unanimous approbation of all present. The Belfast men get warm with wine and patriotism. All stout; Gog valiant; also the Irish slave; also the Tanner; also Mr Hutton. Something will come out of all this. Agree to talk the matter over tomorrow when we are all cool. Huzza! Generally drunk. Vive la nation! Huzza! Damn the Empress of Russia! Success to Polish arms, with three times three. Generally very drunk. Bed. God knows how. To dine tomorrow with the Tanner. Huzza! Huz—

His journal is full of such delights, and is a most honest and revealing account of the American-and-French-Revolution-inspired feeling that was in the air in Ireland during that heady decade. On the anniversary of William of Orange's birthday in 1793, Tone noted, the Dublin Volunteers had not paraded as usual round his statue on College Green, and had worn 'national' green cockades rather than the traditional orange ones. 'This is a striking proof of the change of men's sentiments,' wrote Tone, 'when "Our Glorious Deliverer" is so neglected. This is the first time the day has passed uncommemorated since the institution of the Volunteers. Huzza! Union and the people for ever!'

The Union he was extolling was not, of course, the Union with Britain (which – irony no. 5492 – came into being less than ten years later) but the 'Irish Union', of all Irishmen, Catholic and Protestant, independent of Britain, for which the united Irishmen strove. The story of their failure and of those Catholic 'Defenders' with whom they formed a rough alliance is too long and complex to retell here. Suffice it to say that it was characterized by optimism, amateurishness and disorganization on the part of the Irish and the ruthlessness and professionalism with which the British authorities (employing a largely Irish militia) put it down. Its effective end had been here at Enniscorthy, just outside the town on Vinegar Hill, where the encamped rebel forces were decisively defeated by the Loyalist army.

Despite being offered pardons by Lord Cornwallis, the Lord-Lieutenant, if they surrendered within fourteen days, the fugitives were murdered by the king's troops, who, an eyewitness reported: 'never gave quarter . . . hundreds and thousands of wretches were butchered while unarmed on their knees begging mercy.'

Wolfe Tone himself was not involved in this gruesome Irish climax of the rebellion. Having fled for America in 1795, he had proceeded to Paris, where, under the pseudonym Citizen Smith, he spent the next three years trying to organize a French invasion of Ireland. Three fleets were prepared, two made it to the west of Ireland, and one actually landed. Had the weather been better, the Irish might have been liberated, or speaking French today, or even perhaps letting off bombs in the Champs-Élysées.

Tone died in ignominy in 1798. Sentenced to death and terrified of being hanged, he pleaded with Cornwallis to be allowed to be shot. His request was turned down, so he tried to cut his own throat with a smuggled penknife. Missing the main artery, he sliced through his windpipe instead. 'I am sorry,' he murmured to the sentry who found him in a pool of his own blood, 'I have been so bad an anatomist.' A week later he died. *Nil desperandum* is the epigraph attached to the front of his autobiographical *Life*.

Down the street from the 'square', in the old Norman castle – a certain Philip de Prendergast had built this one, early in the thirteenth century – was a little museum, presided over this Saturday morning by a blushing sixteen-year-old in a green V-necked jumper.

Wandering up the winding stair, past griddles, poteen stills, pig troughs and saddler's clamps, I discovered that Enniscorthy was famous, not just for 1798 but for a contribution to that other great date in republican history, 1916. The last surrender of that insurrection, which had famously begun with the taking over of the General Post Office in Dublin, had apparently been here, at the Athenaeum Theatre, just down the street. The day after, hundreds of Enniscorthy Volunteers had been arrested and deported to English gaols. 'The gallant Wexford men,' read an exhibit in the 1916 Room, 'had shown that the spirit of 1798 still lived.'

On another wall was an old photo of Michael Collins addressing a sea of Enniscorthy bowler hats, and alongside were pictures of the 1966 Golden Jubilee parade in the local *Echo*. 'In the foreground,' read the caption, 'are many veterans of the Rising and relatives of the 1916 Participants.' It had been as reverential an occasion as an English Poppy Day parade, but with Easter lilies, symbol of Irish freedom, instead of our remembrance flower. Further along 'For the Republic of Ireland. Wexford's Roll of Honour 1916–24' hung next to *Songs of an Old I.R.A. Man*. This military memorabilia was pure *Daily Mail* or *Daily Telegraph* territory – but with what a different perspective!

Downstairs I got chatting to the young curator and explained what an eye-opener it was for me to see all this stuff. Well, he said, there'd been about 3,000 of the local men involved in the 1916 Rising, but nowadays the Enniscorthy people didn't take great pride in it and only about seven or eight showed up every Easter to the 1916 memorial parade.

Was there anybody I could talk to about it, I asked. Were any of the original Volunteers still alive? No, he replied, the actual participants were all gone now. The last one had died a couple of years ago. He looked directly (was I imagining suspiciously?) at me, then down in thought. 'To talk to – who'd be handiest,' he muttered. Well there was Keith Doyle who ran Astor Electrics in town. 'He's a nice guy,' he said. His grandfather had taken part in the rising. He'd surely be happy to give me some help. Then, before I knew it, he'd gone. Had it been a mistake bringing my notebook out?

Keith Doyle was standing in a clutter of big cardboard

boxes at the back of his electrical goods store. As friendly a
character as you could hope to meet. Yes, he'd be happy to
help me with my research, in any way he could. His grandfather had indeed taken part in the rising. He'd been captured
after the surrender and sent to Frongoch.

'Fron . . .?'

'Frongoch gaol. In Wales.'

'How d'you spell that?' I was saying, starting to jot down
his testimony in my notebook.

'Just wait a moment, now,' said Keith. He'd see, in fact, if
he couldn't put me in touch with one of the best informed
people on the subject, a local historian who was also the
headmaster of the town's secondary school. He would be a far
better person to talk to. And he actually lived just below
Vinegar Hill, so if I wanted to see the battlefield it would be a
pleasant walk up there afterwards.

Before I knew it, my notebook and I were in an Astor
Electrics van being driven back through town by one of
Keith's employees. Past the youths still loitering under the
1798 monument, across the racing Slaney, up the steep street
on the far side. The local historian, unfortunately, was out.
But it would be no problem for Sean to bring me up Vinegar
Hill. I had planned a meditative walk. Never mind, I thought,
as the van sped between the honeysuckled hedgerows.

Where the lane came to an end there was another chunky
monument to 1798, this one with a lengthy gilt inscription. A
short stroll brought me to the scatter of rocks right at the top
of the hill. Below, the little town lay spread out in the sun; the
cars glinted as they purred to and fro over the bridge. Beyond,
the countryside rolled green and gentle towards the Blackstairs Mountains. It had, in fact, been a United Irishman,
William Drennan, who had coined the phrase 'the emerald
isle'. Looking at this landscape, it wasn't hard to see how the
gorgeously vivid colour of this rainy land could become associated with the fight for freedom.

To my left, two little boys played on the carefully preserved
ruin of the windmill, which had been, 199 years before, the
focus of the rebels' base camp. Here the 'green flag of defiance' had flown, while General Lake of the Crown forces had
fired eighty or ninety bomb shells into their ranks, 'carrying

death in a variety of awful forms to the terrified and wondering multitude.' An assault was then ordered and after a two-hour climb, during which the rebels kept up a sporadic fire on their attackers, the summit was stormed with shouts of 'Long Live King George!' and 'Down with Republicanism!' The rebel flag was seized and trampled underfoot. Cannon were drawn up and brought into action, and as the rebels retreated down the hill they 'fell like mown grass'.

This defeat, and the subsequent brutality described earlier, passed into Nationalist ballad and legend. But Vinegar Hill was important to the Loyalist myth-makers too. On the 1998 Orange Calendar, which I was to buy at the end of my trip in Armagh, it was one of only four colour images (the other three being Prince William, Prince Harry and the watergate at Enniskillen). For although the rising had been led by Protestants, the Catholic 'Defenders', who made up most of the rank and file and who ended up being so cruelly treated by the king's troops (many of them Irish), had themselves been famously brutal to groups of Protestants.

Just before the final battle on Vinegar Hill, a hundred Protestants had been massacred on the wooden bridge at Wexford, 'tossed writhing from the ends of pikes into the waters of the River Slaney below'. In a barn at Scullabogue, approaching 200 Protestant women and children were burned alive, while others were executed on the lawn in front with pikes. And by this very windmill where the little boys now played, thirty-five Protestants from Enniscorthy, 'suspected in the most general and haphazard way of Orange sympathies', had been put to death by an execution squad armed with pikes and guns.

The 200-year-old sectarian enmity, despite the best efforts of Tone and his high-minded friends, was already by then too strong.

Buzzin'

Sean, the man from Astor Electrics, had told me that Wexford was 'buzzin''. So after an hour or so loitering in the pub opposite the local historian's home (they reckoned he was on holiday), I decided to head on there. There was no train until twenty to nine, so I joined the little queue (two nuns, three backpackers) outside the newsagents for the early-evening Bus Eireann, which, despite the numerous jokes I'd heard to the service's detriment, arrived promptly enough.

It being Saturday night the B & Bs up the steep hill from Wexford's winding and narrow main street were all full. 'Sure, there's more at the top of the hill, you won't be stuck,' said one kind lady. Lacking Wolfe Tone's optimism I was beginning to despair.

Finally I found Tasmia, a spic and span little place, with the breakfast already laid on white linen in the room off the hall with the hunting prints, porcelain shepherdesses and cut-glass decanters.

'I've only got the little room at the top,' said Maureen, dyed-blond wave, five feet two inches in her Scholl sandals, showing me up to an attic-section that was not much more than a two-foot-six-inch bed and a window. She was sorry there was no hot water, but four lads had arrived at the same time and wanted a bath.

Half-refreshed by a tepid shower, I strolled down the hill into Wexford. The winding main street had been built by the Vikings and scarcely changed since (though obviously the shops were different). Parallel to that, the long quay that fronted the muddy expanse of the Slaney estuary was a veritable crawl of pubs. There were, it was said, ninety-three in town, but for some reason I was feeling distinctly unsociable and didn't fancy an evening of standing in the corner of some crowded bar with an enigmatic smile or making half-hearted attempts to talk to people who would undoubtedly assume I was trying to chat them up. So I avoided the merry crowd spilling in and out of the Bohemian Girl and dived into a little restaurant. I found a quiet table in the corner, only to be joined by a jolly Saturday night group who couldn't fit on one table, so split on to two, one on either side of me. Then, hilariously, they were trading insults, now burps, around me. 'That man's laughing at you, Kieran.' Thin smile from me. 'It was *him*,' goes Kieran. And so on. I gobbled down my Irish stew and swigged back my vinegary glass of house red. Oh dear. I couldn't even bring myself to call in at the place over

the road from Maureen's that advertised *craic* above a sign
that said: 'There are no strangers in this pub. Only friends you
haven't yet met.'

Up on my pallet I fell (half) asleep to the jabber of strangers
making wonderful friends with people with a whole lot more
energy than me. There was traditional Irish music in there,
too. I all but got dressed again and went down to join
them.

In the small hours, finally, there was silence. Then at 3.20
the *craic* came to me. The lads had returned. They were in the
next room, one laughing uncontrollably to accompany the
other's fockin fockin fockin fock. After about ten minutes of
this there was a loud rap on their door and Maureen's voice:
'Just leave the house, now. You're disturbing the other guests.'

The fockin and cackling were immediately silenced, to be
replaced by a pleading tone.

'No,' came Maureen. 'I want you out now. I'm not listening
to that sort of language in my house.'

A high pitch of apologies, but to no avail. 'Just pack up and
go downstairs and shut the door behind you.' She'd gone.

'You've done it now. You've fockin done it now.' Murmurs,
then more uncontrolled cackling. '*Stop* it, Seamus, she'll be
calling the Guards.' More cackling. Then Maureen was back.
A long begging male whine followed, then for some reason
she'd relented. 'I'll let you stay the night,' came her voice, 'but
I want you out first thing in the morning. I'm not cooking your
breakfast.'

'Just show us the door.'

In the morning Maureen was taut-faced as she brought in
the toast, tea and full Irish. 'Did you hear anything last night?'
she asked eventually.

'They came in a bit late, didn't they?'

Her upper lip trembled as she told me the story. She'd only
let them stay because if they'd been out on the street they'd
have been picked up by the Guards. One of them was sober
enough, apologetic. But the others had so much drink on them
they didn't know where they were. One of them had been
trying the handle of the wrong door. Never, in twenty-four
years of doing bed and breakfast, had she had any trouble like

that. Sure, she'd had people who came in after a few drinks, but they always went upstairs and were quiet. And these four looked OK – they didn't look like yobbos – but she'd never have anything like them in the house again. Never.

3

800 Years of Oppression

I had, I told myself, as I sped through the summery lanes of
Wexford the following morning, hired this absurdly expensive
car for a good reason. The next stop on my tour was Baginbun,
the remote creek where, on 1 May 1169, the Normans had
landed and the '800 Years of Oppression' had formally started.

> At the creek of Baginbun
> Ireland was lost and won

goes a famous – and surprisingly feeble by Irish standards –
couplet.

It would have taken me hours to work out a Bus Eireann
route down there, and days to make the journey. In this
gleaming machine, which smelled of fresh rubber carpet-
backing, I could do the trip in fifty minutes and, just for good
measure, take in neo-Gothic Johnstown Castle, with its reflect-
ing lakes and strutting peacocks; Kilmore Quay, with its rich
smell of fish and quaint floral mini-roundabout; not to mention
the host of spanking new bungalows, each with an exotic
garden, that appeared round every other corner of these
narrow back roads.

If anything was a symbol of modern Ireland, it was surely
the bungalow. Many had taken their design from a book called
Bungalow Bliss, which provided detailed plans for eighty styles
of house, thus removing the need for an architect. Anglo-Irish
acquaintances I'd met in London and Dublin groaned endlessly about them, saying they were destroying the beauty of
old Ireland and wondering why the Irish couldn't put up scenic
whitewashed stone hovels as they used to do. The answer was
given by the author of the manual, an Irish Senator called
Jack Fitzsimons, who wrote in the introduction:

For the first four years of my life I lived in a two-roomed thatch cottage rented by my father at two shillings per week. The floor area was about 300 square feet. The furniture consisted of a settle bed full of rubbish and rats, a table, iron bed and a few chairs. It had a front door and two tiny windows. Built in a hold on the side of a hill, if you can imagine such a situation, it blended into the landscape, surrounded by privet hedges, white thorn bushes and trees. I still have nostalgic memories of the cricket in the hearth and the high, thatched, smoke-blackened ceiling. But animals now would not be housed in such conditions.

Almost all of these Wexford bungalows were adorned with fluttering purple and yellow flags, the colours of Wexford county, whose hurley team was currently heading for the quarter-final of the All-Ireland championship.

Having arrived at the flat, muddy expanses of Bannow Bay, which my map had revealed to be 'the creek of Baginbun', I drove down a tiny lane to the very edge of the estuary and stopped the engine. The sun glinted on the bonnet. The fan died. There was nothing but the gentle rustling of the corn in the breeze, the buzzing of a wasp, the sky-high cries of gulls, the water-trickling, popping sound of seaweed drying on mud. Way out on the flats were the silhouettes of two men, standing talking, it looked like. I picked my way along a ridge of dirty stones towards them.

'Hello,' I began. 'Is this Bannow Bay?'

'This is it,' said the blond man, in the best of brogues. 'All round here.'

'Is this where the Normans landed?' I went on.

'It is.' He nodded towards the other. 'And he's one of 'em.'

The gentleman in question looked down, unsmiling. In comparison to his companion, who was neatly dressed in jeans and checked shirt, he was a mess. His grey suit trousers were covered in mud and wide open at the fly. Hanging loosely over this he had a stained white shirt, the sickly BO pong of which was just reaching my nostrils. His short black hair was greasy and unkempt. His face was shaved, but his neck was not, giving him the look of a werewolf. When he spoke, it was with the accent of an English public school.

It was true, he said, that the Normans had first landed at Bannow Bay. That was in 1169. A second party had come a year later, to Baginbun Head, but Bannow Bay was, strictly speaking, over the other side. Where we were standing was St Kearns. If I really wanted to see the actual 'creek' I'd have to drive back to Wellingtonbridge and round the other arm. There was a ruined Norman church on the point; the locals called it Oldchurch. It was an interesting spot because it had once been a sizeable town, and until 1800 had returned two MPs, even though, by then, nobody lived there.

The Irishman had wandered off, back towards the shore. The Norman carried in his hand two boxes, wrapped in black neoprene. He was just cross-checking a bog-iron site, he told me.

'Bog iron?'

Yes, this was a bog-iron site. They'd discovered it recently, and next weekend he had to go to Portsmouth. He was due to do some diving on the *Mary Rose*. It had gone well enough the last time except that their leader had held them up for two hours by locking everything in his car. He chortled with laughter and shook his head from side to side.

'So he was only joking when he said you were one of the Normans?'

'No, I'm Irish. Actually, I'm what they call Anglo-Irish.' His smile faded. He *certainly* wasn't a Norman. In fact, the other fellow was much more likely to be of Norman descent. It was a strange area round here, where over 50 per cent of the people had Norman names. No, he was probably more Irish then they were.

He stood in deep contemplation, then suddenly turned and marched off at speed across the popping seaweed.

'Got to go,' he called. 'Got work to do.'

I had a feeling that he was a manic depressive, at the 'high' stage of his cycle. It wasn't just his clothes, but the urgency, the awful desire to be getting things done – jobs, work, routine, normality, like everyone else – when clearly he had all the time in the world.

I drove up the coast road towards Baginbun Head. I'd decided that morning that one way of not getting fat on the huge Irish breakfasts I was being given every day was to skip lunch. However, it was now after three and I was famished. Seeing a sign saying Teahouse, I couldn't resist popping in. Just for a cup of tea, you understand. It was a sweet little Hansel and Gretel place, with stone walls that looked like crazy-paving and a table in the shade of a spreading apple tree, in a garden crowded with wild flowers.

When I called through the door a large woman in a pink apron appeared. She was inordinately welcoming. What could she get me? Tea, cake, a sandwich? Was Earl Grey all right?

Earl Grey would be fine, I replied. And, well, just a small round of ham sandwiches if she had them. Grabbing a trowel from the flower bed by the door she hurried back in.

I got out my notebook and started on a quick memo of my recent encounter. A shadow crossed me and I realized I was being watched, by a fellow with a big soft smile.

'Are ye on your hallidays?'

'Sort of thing. I was just looking for where the Normans landed.'

'Baginbun. It's up the road.'

'Your soup's ready, Paddy,' said the lady in the apron, appearing with a tray of tea and sandwiches, on which was also a huge slice of coffee cake. Paddy vanished obediently inside.

'He's supposed to be digging potatoes,' she said apologetically. 'If he once comes out here he'll be chatting all afternoon.'

She stood her ground, watching me eat. 'You're not from the Tidy Towns, are you?' she asked eventually.

'No.'

Her face crumpled in relief. 'Ah, they said it'd be a man or a woman on their own. We weren't sure which.' She'd been expecting someone for two days now, and some of the flowers were starting to wilt in the hot weather.

'How d'you make sure everyone keeps tidy?'

'Ah, there's five or six of us, we keep after them.'

Just in the lea of Baginbun Head was a pretty little bite of a beach sprinkled with family groups behind stripey windshields. 'Dere's not many places left like this,' said the white-haired fellow sitting on the rock where I was changing for a swim. 'Unspoilt like. How d'you get here?'

I explained that I'd hired a car. 'I started with public transport, but I wasn't getting anywhere.'

'Sure an' we found that out fifty years ago.'

Baginbun Head came complete with a Martello tower. In England it would have been a National Trust property, covered with cosseting little signs with acorns on them. Here, in a country marketed as empty and accessible, there was a gate marked 'Private' and a barbed-wire fence. It was probably some bloody Englishman's holiday retreat.

Approaching the headland from the other side, however, I found that it wasn't strictly private after all. There was a ragged coast path and, almost buried in the undergrowth, a discreet plaque. In AD 1170, it said, Raymond le Gros had landed here with a hundred men. 'The fortifications which they built, and which still survive, enabled them to defeat an army of 8,000 from the city of Waterford.' So my crazy acquaintance had been right. Tomorrow I would go round the other side and see where the very first Normans had landed.

Kevin and the Marquis

I'd been told about Dunbrody House when I was in Dublin. The ancestral seat of the Marquis of Donegall, it had recently been sold, the gossips had told me, to the chef from the Shelbourne – Kevin Somebody-or-Other – who was setting it up as a country house hotel. The marquis, now in his eighties, lived in a cottage in the grounds.

In the ochreous evening sunlight, my tyres crunched expensively up the gravel drive. There was a glimpse of garden past a tall hedge to the left, then the back of the house swung into view. Blue-grey brick, slate roof, two storeys of white sash windows, spreading away past a trio of smart cars. Through the open door, in the cool interior of the hall, stood a young guy in long shorts and T-shirt. He was, indeed, Kevin, and the dark-bobbed woman in the navy dress emerging from the office was Catherine, his wife.

'Pretty impressive place you've got here.'

'It's even better from the front,' Kevin replied, with a proprietorial chuckle. He showed me upstairs. My key was attached to a tattered beige card label. 'His Lordship's Guest Room No. 4' it read. It was a fine contrast to that sparse Wexford attic: a huge double bed, heavy brocade curtains in crimson and green, a desk with a TV mounted on it and a marble bathroom *en suite*. I was just starting to look forward to putting on the free shower cap and standing in the nude eating the gratuity chocolates, when . . .

'Are you coming for a drink?' Kevin asked. He led me down to the little ante-room that was now the bar. Outside, through french windows, two golden retriever puppies, Gin and Tonic, romped on the sunny terrace. There were white wrought-iron chairs around a fountain, whose centrepiece was a magnificent white heron, wings poised for flight. Beyond, the lawn swept gently down towards a perimeter wood. A bank of blue hydrangeas coloured the shade.

'So d'you own all this or have you gone in with somebody?' I asked, after we'd talked about Dublin and Wexford and Norman landings for a while.

'We own it,' said Kevin. Catherine smiled and looked down at her spritzer.

'And if I wanted to talk to the old marquis, d'you reckon that'd be possible?'

'No harm in asking,' said Kevin. But he was quite formal. Liked to be known as His Lordship. 'We call him "the Lord",' said Catherine, with a half-swallowed chuckle. He had gout, she went on, so it would probably depend on that. Some days he was very chatty, other days he just grunted as he walked round the grounds. 'You'd need to make an appointment,' said Kevin. 'He likes to do things properly.'

Despite the fact that his estate was in the Republic of Ireland, the marquis still had a seat in the English House of Lords. One of his titles was English, they thought. Catherine laughed about him saying to her, 'I have to be in the House tomorrow'.

'It took us a while to click what the heck he was talking about,' said Kevin.

'Have we got a menu yet?' said Catherine. It was quarter to

seven. They'd better get going. This morning they'd had three bookings; now it looked more like thirty.

They went in and left me to it, catching up on David Trimble's objections to the ceasefire by the trinkling fountain. One of the retrievers, Gin – or was it Tonic? – jumped into the pool and sat there eyeing me. An elegant middle-aged couple appeared, he suited, she in evening dress.

Changed and showered I took my seat in the splendid wood-panelled dining room (now 'The Harvest Room – Executive Chef: Kevin Dundon'). The elegant couple were next to a beautiful redhead, who was not being fully appreciated by her square-shouldered companion, and one along from an older pair, who chomped silently. Along from them three loud forty-somethings competed around a business-blonde in a lime-green jacket.

I was just sitting there, thinking that one definition of Hell might be to be eternally stuck in a such a lovely place, with the lightest of summer evening breezes off the terrace, the sun setting through the top branches of the trees beyond the garden, a half bottle of Nottage Hill in an ice bucket whose condensation just moistened the linen tablecloth, the difficult choice between duck *confit*, crab toes or seafood basket, two teenaged waitresses with discrete beauty in identical black trousers, but never allowed to step beyond your table, your allotted civilized space – when *whoosh*! We all looked up at the same moment to realize that one of the tall lampshades on the mahogany sideboard had caught fire. The flames were leaping up towards the ceiling as black smoke and a shower of sparks poured forth. Help! Not another Powerscourt! After a moment's hesitation the guests were on their feet. One had a jug of water. I had my ice bucket. With the smoke alarm now howling the sudden blaze was quenched.

Was there a tangible sense of relief that the over-formal country house dinner atmosphere had been broken? The male half of the elegant couple, Francis, was now standing by my table chatting as his wife Maire put ice on the slightly-burned hand of the older man. Catherine was running in with a first aid box; the Executive Chef was mopping and cleaning.

After dinner I sat with Francis and Maire on the terrace. He was from Co. Monaghan, she from Co. Galway. As we discussed the ceasefire Francis held both fingers crossed above his head. They were all mad up there, Maire said. Both sides. Locked into a situation that was going nowhere. She repeated what I'd heard from Sinead and others in Dublin: the South didn't want them now, anyway. 'We wouldn't want a situation where there were bombs going off in Dublin,' she said, with a frown.

I told them about the reception I'd got in Enniscorthy. Had I imagined that they were, albeit extremely politely, playing pass the parcel with me? Probably not, said Francis. As a matter of fact, he rather thought that the young lad who'd blown himself up in that bus off the Strand was from Enniscorthy. If not Enniscorthy, Gorey, or one of those little Wexford towns.

I remembered the way that incident had been reported at home. The young man's parents had been shocked and couldn't understand why their boy had joined the IRA. Lying in bed thinking about it later, I wondered whether he'd ever been to the Enniscorthy Museum. It didn't need the hugest leap of imagination to see how a young idealist could have got involved. Sure, but he hadn't been reading the *Songs of an Old I.R.A. Man*.

In the morning I drove round the other side of the estuary, through tiny Carrig-on-Bannow and up to the isosceles triangle of Bannow Island, now joined by a reclaimed isthmus of dunes to the mainland. Just before I'd left the Tidy Towns lady, Paddy had re-emerged with a local history of the parish of Bannow, which he'd insisted I take with me. It contained a vivid description of that May morning in 1169, when 'the inhabitants of Bannow and Brandane caught a glimpse of greatness and saw their little village leap into fame'.

There appeared on the horizon three magnificent ships, in full sail, riding proudly on the tranquil waters off the Keeroe islands. Slowly and ominously the first ship turned, and then the second and the third ... and made their way into the deep channel on the north side of the island. The stunned and petrified inhabitants must have felt that they were going to relive the horrors of the Danish raid so vividly described and handed down by generations of their ancestors as they looked on the scene before them. Drawing up beside the lowest point of the island, the first ship disgorged huge warrior-like men, clad in coats of mail, complete with shield, sword and helmet, on to the level strand. On and on they came, 120 men-at-arms, from each ship, archers and knights leading their horses, as they disembarked their tents, provisions and goods of every kind. The air was filled with a great babble of voices speaking in a foreign tongue, men shouting orders at one another and the neighing and snorting of sixty horses.

But there was no need for the stunned and petrified inhabitants to worry. The Anglo-Normans had arrived at the invitation of an Irish king, Dermot MacMurrough, who had canvassed their support on a series of trips to England (some, indeed, had already visited Ireland in 1167), offering them land in return for the military assistance he needed to regain his kingdom of Leinster. Led by him, they attacked the Norse stronghold of Wexford, which submitted after a short struggle.

The following May they were joined by more troops under Maurice FitzGerald and Raymond le Gros, who landed at Baginbun Head. Finally, in August 1170, Strongbow arrived and landed near Waterford with his bride-to-be, Aoife, Dermot's daughter, and a thousand men at arms. They immediately attacked Waterford and overthrew the occupying Norse earl, Sitric, who was beheaded, while Strongbow married Aoife in the city cathedral.

From there they headed north to Dublin, reaching the undefended south of the city in September. The Ostmen under their earl, Asgall, offered to negotiate, but Raymond le Gros and Milo de Cogan, like good impatient Normans, preferred to dive in and attack. The fortress was duly seized, Asgall fled to the Orkneys, and Dublin became the capital of 'English' power in Ireland.

Thus began the 800 years of oppression. With two Anglo-Normans seizing a castle from occupying Norsemen at the behest of an Irish king.

*

There was, interestingly enough, no indication whatsoever of the historical significance of this site. In the dunes a few cars broiled in the sun. The road up on to the little island was barred by another 'Private' sign. (It was owned, I was told later, by a farmer called Devereux. 'He came across the sea and he wasn't going any bloody further.')

I strode off down the beach to try the back way round. This was a mistake, as, after a mile or so, hard sand became shingle, sinking into oozing, stinking mud. I was glad I hadn't brought my chain mail. Eventually, a hundred yards or so from where, I reckoned, those clanking knights had landed, I could go no further. Parked out on the mudflats was a catamaran, on which stood a scraggy, nut-brown gentleman with luminous green speedos and long white hair. I hailed him.

'This is where the Normans landed,' I shouted.

'Beg pardon?'

Eventually I succeeded in explaining. He'd had no idea he was parked up on such a significant piece of Irish mud. He was a musician from Devon, who came over every summer for the festivals. There was one in Carrig-on-Bannow this week-end. I should stick around, he told me, for the *craic*.

I wandered back over the dunes to the ruined church that my mad friend from yesterday had mentioned. It had been built, my local history explained, by no less a person than Hervey de Monte Marisco, Strongbow's religious-minded uncle, after he'd failed to set up an abbey on the site. The 'sizeable town' that had grown up around it had eventually covered over thirteen acres, and was, in the fifteenth century, equal to Kilkenny in importance.

Now there was nothing but the wind in the long grass and the graveyard round the ruins.

Hervey had had more luck up the road at Dunbrody, where he had established a Cistercian foundation in 1188, ending his life as its abbot. The link from him to the man I had arranged to meet this evening was not complex. Dunbrody Abbey had stayed in Cistercian hands until the suppression of the monasteries in 1537. It had then been handed over to one Etchingham, a man who had endeared himself to Henry VIII by being nice, then nasty, about Anne Boleyn and helping him compose 'Greensleeves'. (Only joking, but doubtless something of that nature.) A century later, in Cromwell's time, the Etchinghams had been reduced to one male and one female, Jane, who had married, at the age of thirteen, a man called Chichester, son of the Earl of Donegall. His descendant, Arthur Spencer Stanley Chichester, had built the present house in the early 1800s, and given his name to the village below, Arthurstown. He had been the first Baron Templemore; the current marquis was the 6th.

All this I learned from Sean Pierce, Arthurstown's local historian. The Chichesters were held in great respect locally, he told me, as he sat in his green velveteen armchair chucking his cigarette ends into the pile on the grate. They'd been good landlords, paying the local farmers for their produce, digging a canal above the village and installing a sewerage system and a hospital. 'Which would be,' added Sean, with a curt nod, 'out of character with their class.'

'D'you want a drink?' asked the marquis, when I called on him, as arranged, at seven. 'I've got no soda, I'm afraid. You'll just have to shove it under the tap.'

With his two black labradors barking and pushing around us, I followed him through to his little sitting room. ' Did you have a good day in Dublin?' I asked, to break the long silence.

'No.' He sat firmly down in his armchair, his head a clipped silhouette against the windows, thick dark green braces pulling up tweed trousers well over his stomach. I had come to conduct 'an interview about the family history', but really, of course, I was just curious. To meet him and to get a feel of the sort of man who had traditionally been in charge in Ireland.

Sean had told me that he was 'totally straight', you knew where you stood with him, and that he liked him. Catherine had described him as brusque one day, talkative the next. I found him terrifying. Well, maybe not terrifying, but intimidating, certainly, as I perched opposite him on the peach-coloured sofa. His whole presence spoke of a lifetime of orders being given and obeyed.

We proceeded at a clip through the history that I'd already heard from Sean, albeit with a slightly different twist. 'Henry VIII sent over a man called Etchingham. I presume

Etchingham sent back such a lot of good silver plate that he gave him a grant of all the abbey's lands.'

There was a bit of a kerfuffle over the precise date of Miss Jane Etchingham's marriage, which involved the marquis leaving the room and returning with a huge, fat book with thick pages in which, as he leafed laboriously through, I caught glimpses of shields and crests and colourful coats of arms.

'Yes, here she is, married on 9 March 1660, being then but thirteen years old . . .'

'Right,' I said. There was a long pause. 'D'you think it was an arranged marriage?' I asked.

The marquis met my eyes with a firm look, as if I'd asked him a highly impertinent question about his private life. 'I don't know any more than you do.'

Things didn't get any easier. 'And I believe the Chichesters were pretty good landlords,' I heard myself saying. 'I mean, didn't they build a famine road?'

'The famine didn't exist in this part of Ireland.'

Five minutes later (oh, for the spirit of Jeremy Paxman) I was reduced to: 'You must have witnessed many changes?'

'Since I left the Army, which was in 1980, there've been a great many changes. In 1980 there was very little tarmacadam, they were all flint roads. Most of the by-roads would have been flint roads. There was nothing like the prosperity there is now.'

At the end, every last drop of whisky drained from my glass, I chanced: 'D'you think the Anglo-Irish have lost their role, as their estates have dwindled?'

'You mean like this family?'

'No, no, not specifically this family – but yes.'

He met my eye. It was a kindly, almost lost look. 'I don't know, your guess is as good as mine.'

'Back already,' said Kevin, pouring me a stiff double whisky. I sat down by the ancestral fountain wondering why I'd been so unnerved. Inside, Beethoven's 5th Piano Concerto pounded towards its conclusion. 'How did it go?' asked Catherine. I told her. She shrugged and smiled. You never knew with 'the lord'. It just depended on his mood. Once he'd taken her round the garden, gone through every plant there was, every shrub, every tree. 'We were there for two hours,' she laughed.

'If he met you in the garden tomorrow he might well come up and say, "There's something I forgot to tell you".'

That night Dunbrody was doing a roaring trade. In the Harvest Room the marquis's old tenants, dolled up in smartest evening wear, were sipping Australian Chardonnay and enjoying his view as they held respectfully muted conversations and waited to scoff Kevin's state-of-Temple-Bar cuisine. Catherine strolled among them taking the orders, charming, effortless, unflappable, like every waitress would be if she owned the £300,000 building in which you, her customer, sat. And did she pinch herself, just sometimes, and think, 'Am I really the châtelaine of this lovely place?'

4

A Rubens in the Bathroom

The next morning I was gone, up through the back roads with their yellow and purple flags and their handwritten placards saying 'British Queens for sale' (a 'queen' was a kind of potato) and out on to the N25, with the blue hoardings that read 'The European Community and Wexford, Working Together'.

These beautifully surfaced new roads had a broad main lane, and another, to the left, marked off with a thick yellow line, whose use didn't seem to have been generally agreed. Some vehicles, particularly lorries, would use it as a slow lane, pulling over into it as you approached, or just sitting in it, or half in it. Then, confusingly, others used it as a hard shoulder, parking in it, often just after a bend. Once I saw a family cheerfully having a picnic in it, complete with folding table and chairs. It was hardly a surprise that the spiralling rate of road accidents was such a preoccupation of the Irish newspapers.

I rang the doorbell of a slate-clad, ivy-covered farmhouse. A lanky bloke with black-rimmed glasses opened the door.

'She'll be here in a minute,' he said vaguely, wandering into a side room. He was one of the guests.

I loitered for five minutes or so in the hall. Suddenly Marigold appeared, in a wet, black, one-piece bathing suit, her sweeping blond hair held back in a band. 'I'm very cold,' she told me immediately, in a rather breathless voice. 'I've just come from swimming. In the river.'

Dripping slightly, she showed me upstairs. 'This is the bathroom. Towels in the cabinet. Help yourself to as many as you like. Or as few.' She led me on to a black-beamed attic room. 'Now I'll just change quickly and show you to the art studio, where you can make tea or coffee if you wish.'

The 'art studio' was a long, stone ex-barn with a half-glassed conservatory section in which lay a row of pink-cushioned wicker loungers. Up a flight of slate steps a mahogany table held a huge jug of purple flowers and two full candlesticks. On top of the upright piano was a stuffed sheep and an empty easel.

'D'you like beer?' Marigold asked suddenly.

'Sure.'

'There's a lot of beer in the cupboard that someone left behind. Help yourself.' She led me into a little kitchen cubby-hole at the end. 'And there's tea and coffee if you wish.' As we emerged she laughed nervously. 'I just slipped into these shorts and top. The top's black and the shorts are blue. It doesn't go together, does it?'

'Well . . .'

'We usually dine around 9.30,' she interrupted, and like an oversized sprite, departed. When she'd gone I slumped down in one of the loungers with my book. Twilight fell, and a girl appeared through the french windows and lit the candles. I sipped my beer and mused.

Marigold's home was one of a group of up-market bed and breakfasts that had been set up by a colourful Anglo-Irishman, John Colclough, whom I'd met in Dublin. Marketed under the name 'Hidden Ireland', they ranged from magnificent castles to unusual private places such as this. The idea had proved the saving of a number of fine Anglo-Irish houses, which would otherwise have struggled along with water pouring through the roof or, like so many of the dwellings of the Ascendancy, have been abandoned entirely.

When he'd started out, in the mid 1980s, John's charges, he had told me, had been 'wonderful in their innocence'. The nearest thing they'd got to marketing was B & B hand-painted on the gate. He'd had to gather them together in Dublin and lecture them. 'All of you went to college, all of you will have known somebody who's gone off and become a journalist.' No, no, they couldn't possibly. One's name should only appear three times in the newspapers. But when the guests and the money had started rolling in things had changed. 'Now,' he told me sadly, 'I've created a monster, which was never my intention.' He'd even been voted off the board, and 'Hidden Ireland' had been taken over by one of the very people he'd first encouraged.

At 9.25 I presented myself in the drawing room, where the assembled guests were studiedly leafing through books and magazines beside a hissing log fire. Apart from a middle-aged couple from a small Irish town, they were all English.

'Very profound comments in this book,' said a woman with a Yorkshire accent.

'Lost on me, then,' replied her stocky husband.

As the clock ticked on towards ten, there was a gathering chorus of low-voiced speculation about what time dinner would be. Guests who were not new arrivals chuckled knowingly. It might be ten, it might be ten-thirty, they told us. Marigold, basically, was completely scatty. Last night they'd still been eating at two. But this was clearly a recommendation.

Finally, at 10.10, the door from the hall swung open and Marigold swept in, resplendent in flowing pink and orange, a small brass gong in her left hand, which she now ceremoniously banged. We shuffled through and were placed around two tables. At mine were the Irish couple and a professional pair from the West Country, whose marriage was clearly heading at speed for intensive care. Roger had grey curly hair and was plump and genial; his wife, Sue, was skinny and nervous-looking, scowling down at the floor like an angry teenager.

'Of course, Sue travels a lot in her work,' Roger was saying.

'Oh God, please, Roger, we don't need to talk about that,' snapped Sue.

Roger tried not to look wounded, but as the meal progressed I felt terribly for him, bravely smiling as each new salvo sliced home. They'd come from Rosslare that evening, were heading to West Cork, which he'd known well as a child. Hadn't been back, in fact, for twenty years. Expected that he was going to be immensely disappointed. Ha ha ha.

Sue raised her eyebrows and puckered her mouth. 'Isn't he just the biggest bore in the world,' her face said.

Like me, the Irish couple pretended we were all having a

perfectly fine time. After starter, soup and main course there
was a long, long break. 'I'm going to bed,' said Sue, suddenly.
'Come *on*, Roger, I'm *exhausted*.' Defeated, he followed her
without a word.

Marigold reappeared with a tray of fresh raspberries and
cream. 'Sorry about the delay,' she announced. 'I was talking
to a fox.'

But where were Roger and Sue? Oh no, they couldn't go to
bed yet, it was barely one o'clock, there were fresh raspberries
and a selection of Irish cheeses. Dumping down her tray
Marigold rushed through into the hall. 'We have fresh raspberries and a selection of Irish cheeses!' we heard her shouting
up the stairs.

But the Irish couple and I were quite happy to sample the
Carrowholly, Cliffoney and Cashel Blue on our own. Somehow we'd got on to politics, the North indeed, and I was saying
that I was starting to understand the mentality of Republicanism, that the British knew nothing about Irish history and so
on. Husband Peter with the bushy eyebrows was nodding
along and going 'yes, yes', his face a mask of delight and
agreement. Although he didn't, of course, condone violence
and the sort of people who got involved with the IRA would
otherwise be criminals, nonetheless, he was a Nationalist; and
yes, no, the British *didn't* understand.

Now Marigold was inviting anyone who cared to to meet
the fox. And there he was, eyes shining in the skewed parallel-
ogram of light that fell from french doors to damp concrete,
his nose in a bowl of our leftover meatballs in soy-sauce-
flavoured spaghetti. 'You like that, Renard, don't you?' Marigold coaxed. 'You're a lovely thing, aren't you?' Once, she
said, turning, she'd had a Renard who would actually come
into the house.

As I lay in bed I could hear the Irish couple talking through
the wall.

'And what did you think of that writer chappie?' asked the
wife.

A low grunting from Peter, which, infuriatingly, I couldn't
make out.

'Oh,' came her voice. 'I thought he was a nice guy.'

Grunt, grunt. 'Well, let's see what he produces.'

I couldn't hear the rest, but it was clearly a contrast to the winning charm I'd had from him all evening. 'I do wish you the *best* of luck with your *book*,' he'd said, as we'd warmly shaken hands on the stairs.

I felt rather bad trying to wake Marigold with a loud double knock at 9.45 the next morning. But I had an appointment at eleven, and she had said breakfast was 'any time after nine, just rap on my bedroom door'. After a minute there was no answer. I knocked harder. Still nothing. I hammered.

'Who is it?' came a groan eventually.

'It's Mark. I've got to get on the road, I'm afraid.'

Ten minutes later she appeared, in fresh crimson lipstick and a black silk nightie.

'Good morning,' she said brightly.

'Good morning.'

'So was it tea you wanted?'

She hadn't got to bed till 4.30, she explained. She and Mairead had realized the raspberries were not quite as fresh as they might be, so they'd stayed up making jam. And then she'd ordered this hat from England, which she just *had* to try on, having left it in its box and talked about it for two days. But it wasn't right. She often wore a hat in the kitchen and people asked her why. Well, sometimes when she was cooking she needed to rush up the yard to the store, and if it was raining she already had her hat on. But this wasn't the sort of hat you could really wear in the kitchen. It was more the sort of hat you'd wear at a wedding. So it was going back. I imagined the Returned Order note: 'Not the sort of hat you can wear in the kitchen, I'm afraid.'

The Irish couple appeared just as I was leaving, fresh-faced, clutching the *Irish Times*. They'd tried to go to Mass, but there was no service locally on a Wednesday. 'I do wish you the *best* of luck with your *book*,' said Peter, with the warmest of handshakes.

Nesta

I was rather excited about my appointment. It was with Lady Nesta FitzGerald, a daughter of the Duke of Leinster and direct descendant of the FitzGeralds who'd arrived with Strongbow. Not that I'm a snob, but she did live barely thirty miles from where her Norman ancestors had landed in 1169. Best of all, she was called Nesta.

Described variously as 'the Helen of Wales', 'the paramour of every daring lover', 'the most beautiful woman in Wales', Princess Nesta, the daughter of Rhys ap Tewdwr, Prince of South Wales, had been a medieval legend in her own bedroom, spawning, in a sequence of liaisons, many, if not most, of the first conquerors of Ireland. Taken hostage by Henry I, after he'd defeated her father in battle, she became his mistress and gave him a son, also called Henry, whose two sons Meiler and Robert FitzHenry were both in the army that had landed at Bannow. She'd next married Gerald de Windsor, Constable of Pembroke, by whom she had three sons (one of whom, Maurice, was an invader) and a daughter, Angharat, whose son, Robert, was also in the fleet. Finally, she moved on to Stephen, Constable of Cardigan, by whom she bore Robert FitzStephen, another of the key knights of the expedition.

Raymond le Gros, who led the landing at Baginbun Head, was one of her grandsons; another grandson married Alina, Strongbow's daughter. Hervey de Monte Marisco married one of her granddaughters, as did our old friend Walter de Ridelesford, builder of Balytenyth, the castle that had been replaced by Powerscourt. If anybody was responsible for the 800 years of oppression, it was she.

Her many times great-granddaughter, herself a grey-curled grandmother, lived in small stone farmhouse at the end of a narrow lane. Her father's side was FitzGerald; her mother's McMorrough-Kavanagh, the royal line descended from that original King of Leinster who had invited the Normans in. It was good to see that eight centuries later the Normans were still marrying the native Irish. Despite her distinguished ancestry, there was nothing remotely grand or overweening about

her. Whatever your background – equine, canine, or human –
you felt you would be treated equally and straightforwardly.

'I'm not sure how I can help you,' she began, when her
daughter had brought us coffee, but immediately launched
into a colourful account of her childhood at Borris, the family
mansion just up the road.

Her grandfather had been slightly eccentric, she said, and
had hated mechanization of any sort. So she'd grown up with
eleven indoor staff, ten in the garden, fifteen on the farm and
estate. 'One old man was just employed to catch rabbits, which
we virtually lived on.'

The bathrooms had been full of oil paintings. 'There were
these remarkably hideous portraits of Thomas Cromwell,
which we threw sponges at. And then one day a young man
had come to stay and said, "D'you realize you've got a Rubens
in the bathroom?" So that was sold for something like £30,000,
which paid off the death duties.'

The tradition in the family was that the house and estate
were left to the eldest son, the contents to the widow. Two
generations of widows, Nesta chuckled, had emptied the house
of its contents. Her great-grandmother had even sold the
doors. Her mother had had no interest in the place. 'She was
totally amoral about the family effects.' She'd sold the dining-
room table and all the chairs, which had been specifically
made for the house. 'If she wanted money to buy a horse,
she'd sell something. She had no feeling for family tradition,
anything like that.'

In this gradually emptying grand house, Nesta and her sister
were always having parties. 'It was always going to be the last
party before we took the roof off,' she said, with a laugh.
Removing the roof meant, in those days, that the property
would no longer be rateable. To these parties came the
offspring of the other big houses of the area. Not many
remained now of these families, celebrated for, one might say
celebrating in, their Ascendancy eccentricity. At P——, of
course, there were still the D——s.

'As a child Gerald was *very* peculiar. He and his brother
were always made to wear saffron kilts and pipe jackets.' The
old boy, the father, had been one of those Anglo-Irish 'who
took to the myth of the Celtic World with a vengeance. With

the strange thing of being rabidly Protestant and wanting to be Irish at the same time.' In the winter they'd burned cowpats on the fire. 'When you visited there'd be this stack of dried cowpats by the front door.' At a P—— Hunt Ball one of the maids had fallen through the ceiling, landing on a pile of priceless china. Another time Gerald had walked into breakfast with a hatchet in his hand. 'That's thirty-two cats less,' he'd announced. 'Nobody knew whether he'd really been killing cats or not.'

But most of the other big houses were 'gone' now. Nesta went through them, ticking them off on mental fingers. 'Mount Juliet is an hotel . . . Oak Park's now the agricultural research station . . . Brownshole's gone . . .'

'When you say "gone"?' I asked.

'Pulled down, fallen down, burned down.' A lot of them had been burned in the Troubles, by which she meant the 1920s, the Troubles of the South, the War of Independence and the Civil War. 'But Borris wasn't. My grandpa and grandmother were very liked. It was "a friendly house". Things were *overlooked*. People on the run might be found in the kitchen, that sort of thing.'

'On the run from . . . ?'

'The British.'

Adventure in Borris House!

Borris itself was just up the road, a cut-granite edifice behind big stone gates up a grassy drive strewn with shaggy and rather yellow-looking sheep. It commanded (and 'commanded' was the word) a view across flat fields to the lovely emerald of the Blackstairs Mountains beyond. Nesta's half-brother Andrew McMorrough-Kavanagh was out on the estate, so his wife Tina showed me round. 'Having married in,' Nesta had said, 'she knows the history better than most.' I heard about 1798, when the house had been badly damaged, not by the rebels, but by the militiamen from Donegal who had come to defend it. I saw the private chapel, which had been built on in 1810, when the house had been restored. The gallery at the back led straight into the house, and the old story was that the family would only dress from the waist up. ('Come to Mass in their pyjama bottoms.') I heard about Arthur, 'the Remarkable Kavanagh', who'd been born without arms and legs but none-theless travelled from Scandinavia across Russia and Persia to India. While his two normally built brothers came down with TB, Arthur married and had six children. His saddle was on the children's rocking horse in the hall.

In the dining room the shutters were up and there was a strong smell of damp. A white tablecloth was still on the long table. 'Sorry about the shutters,' Tina said, 'but we have tinkers who steal the furniture.' Here were the very turf buckets they'd tried to pilfer. One of them had just walked in through the front door and taken them. 'When he saw me, he just screamed.'

'Oh no!' cried Tina. 'There's been a bird in here. There's feathers everywhere. It must have come down the chimney.' She stood in front of the grate examining a pile of fallen soot. 'Where is it?'

We hunted through the gloom until I found it, a big black raven, curled up on a pile of brown-stained tablecloths under an occasional table.

'Is it dead?'

'I don't know.'

She came over and poked it. 'It is dead. Oh feck it – it's shat on everything.' It had, too, even on the deep pink scagliola pillars.

There were portraits everywhere. Big, moulded oblong frames, little gold oval frames, tiny tempera miniatures in folding frames held royal Kavanaghs, of course, and Butlers, whom they were forever marrying. (The Butlers had been, from King John's time onwards, the royal butlers, and thus incredibly wealthy.)

'Look, look at this,' cried Tina, grabbing her thirteen-year-old daughter Romany, who was running past in her Nantucket sweatshirt. She held her up in front of one Thomas Kavanagh, who stood po-faced with another Butler. 'She's the *image* of her.'

'No, no, Mum, no,' Romany protested. But there was no denying it. Five minutes later she came running back. There was 'a tinker' outside looking for furniture, she said. Tina strode off. Through the door I got a glimpse of a short, swarthy-faced man in a flat cap. 'He's on the phone,' Tina was telling him firmly. 'No, no, he doesn't *want* any sheds painted.'

Their voices receded. Romany came dancing through. 'Mum says the man who's out there stole the turf buckets.' She grinned at me. 'Adventure in Borris House!'

Tina had reappeared. 'Show Mark up to the library would you.'

So I was escorted up the stairs away from the excitement, past yet more Kavanaghs and Butlers, to another gloomy room, lined with shelf after shelf of *Annual Registers*, whose floor was a magnificent overlapping collage of threadbare carpets. On a central table lay some large and dusty tomes. I leafed through *The Estates of Thomas Kavanagh in the Counties of Carlow and Wexford*. MDCCCXLV.

The land, the land. There it all was. Laid out and appropriated, down to the last stream and hedgerow.

'That's the estate map,' came Tina's voice behind me. 'This is the pedigree. These are muniments that trace the family back to two thousand years before Christ or something.' She laughed and wandered off. I leafed on through the thick and yellowing pages. Year after year after year of carefully detailed entries with little mini-biogs attached.

> Moragh or Maurice Kavanagh, King of Leinster 1327, taken prisoner by Henry Lord Traherne and confined in the Castle of Dublin, escaped therefrom 1329.

Tina was back. It was time to go. Exhausted by tinkers, she didn't need writers snooping around as well. Honking my way through the sleepy sheep, I slid through the electrified stone gates and passed out on to the main road, a long low terrace of pretty, slate-roofed stone peasant dwellings opposite the high estate walls.

5

The Ash and the Lime

Propped by the open gates of Stroove Castle was a small handwritten placard saying 'Guided tour of the House and Gardens £2'. I doubted that many of the cars and lorries that thundered past on the big new Euro-road outside noticed it. Or even the tiny sign just down the wall that read 'Castle Studio – Open'.

I swept up the granite-chip drive, to find a chunky grey castellated mansion set in a sweep of green lawns and mature trees. On an easel outside the step up to the front door was a brightly coloured, Matisse-like painting of flowers. I addressed myself to a bell-pull marked 'Bell'.

The door was opened by a plump, shortish man with receding grey hair tied back in a ponytail. A baggy cream shirt with thin red stripes hung over a pair of battered olive cords. His bare feet were in sandals.

'Hello,' he said gently. 'Hm, Mark?'

'Yes.'

'Come on in.' Adrian's manner, as he introduced himself, was gentle, almost diffident. His speech was punctuated by a reflective 'hm', delivered in a manner that was all but camp. His wife, Ruth, he told me, was in the kitchen, having brunch with the children. She'd been in bed with a cold. 'Hm.' Did *I* want anything to eat?

'Really, no. I've just had an enormous breakfast.'

'Oh. Well would you like a coffee?'

A coffee would hit the spot, I said. We paused in the hall. 'I'm not quite sure what you should be asking me,' Adrian began. 'I'm inclined to interview *you*. Where are you from?' He let out a barely suppressed giggle.

Inwardly raising my eyebrows, I laughed and told him. He

ushered me courteously through the hall to a gleaming mahogany table in a room overlooking an oblong lake, which was flanked on both sides by thick woodland. Beyond, over a fence, the cow-strewn fields rippled away to a low silhouette of mountains.

I sat quietly and looked around me. Adrian bustled back in with two cups of coffee and a plate bearing three huge slices of brown bread layered with smoked salmon. 'I don't know whether you want this. Don't eat it if you don't.' Putting it down to one side of me, he regarded his offering for a moment. 'You might want it later. Hm.'

'I'm so full I don't think I could.'

'We can cover it with something. Just so long as the cat doesn't get it. Hm.' He sat beside me and took a sip of his coffee. I sipped mine and wondered how to play it. I needn't have worried. Before I knew it he'd launched into the kind of history lesson a visiting English writer would almost certainly badly need. I sat back and enjoyed it. It was intriguing to hear the increasingly familiar story from a subtly different angle, like a favourite old tune put to a new orchestration. Once again I heard that it was very important not to get muddled between religion and politics. 'The Anglo-Irish were *inclined* to be Unionist,' but then, he, Adrian, was Anglo-Irish, and Protestant, and neither particularly Nationalist, nor Unionist. Hm.

The story of Irish history, really, was the story of the land. The friction between landlords and locals would always have been over land. Not so much religion. Hm. The landlords would have been making their estates; they'd have had great plans for their demesnes. They might, perhaps, have got rid of roads that had been public rights of way to make their own view nicer. 'It was the natural thing to do if you were a powerful landlord.'

Adrian got to his feet, hurried over to a sideboard to return with a pile of maps of Stroove. Here, for example. Did I see these right-angled roads that came right up to the estate and went nowhere? They would originally have been rights of way. Undoubtedly there'd been a road going right up to the old Norman church in the grounds. But the landlord had suppressed that. 'And obviously that created tensions.'

Now, of course, Adrian smiled, things were reversed, and
the County Council had recently taken a slice off the corner
of the estate to improve the main road.

'So you can't say it's to do with religion. It's to do with a
powerful person coming into an area. It's landlordism in
opposition to the earlier rights of people. Then things like
religion would get drawn into it.'

So anyway, Adrian asked, would I like to see the grounds?
The demesne, as it was called. As opposed to domain. What
was the difference? There was a difference. Hm. Did I know
what it was? Adrian chuckled lightly to himself. We crunched
out on to the gravel. Adrian wasn't at all sure about the grey
plaster rendering that covered the old stone of the house.
Ruth and he wanted to put back the plants, grow things up
the walls. But they were afraid of the damp. And of course,
they hadn't the money. Hm.

As we paused a few feet from the lake to study the missing
gnomon of the sundial, Ruth joined us, in something of a
flurry. She was waiting for the doctor to call. If he thought
that her infection was too strong she couldn't take the children
to the seaside and Adrian would have to go. OK, said Adrian,
he'd take them. He didn't want to, but he would. They *had* to
go, Ruth said. They'd been looking forward to it all week.

She was a striking-looking woman, some inches taller than
Adrian, with a figure like an ironing board and eyes of a
startling blue under her tied-back strawberry-blond hair. Her
lips puckered with the same wry humour as her husband's.
'Sorry Mark.' Then, 'I hope Adrian has told you about my
plans to have a ballet on the lake,' she cried, as she shot off.

Unperturbed, we strolled on. Hunched over a strimmer at
the far end of the narrow 'lake' (it was really more like a huge
square pond) was white-bearded, seventy-something Tom,
who was English, and had come over originally with the
BTCV, the British Trust for Conservation Volunteers. He
had been the leader of a group whose task was to clear the
lake. He'd loved the place and stayed. Now he came and
went, and was, Adrian lowered his voice, 'a law unto himself,
really'.

He got a good deal. In Ireland, courtesy of Charles

Haughey, old people had free travel, and here at Stroove, Tom was provided with free accommodation and telephone, and Adrian paid for his food and expenses.

'He does it for love. He's not the gardener. He gets perks. But he does what he wants to do.' Adrian's half-raised eyebrow quivered slightly. 'He runs the estate and I fall in behind him.' He laughed his light, giggly laugh. 'It's a good system, although occasionally I do wonder, Am I wise? I don't approve of everything he does, by any means.' He pointed to a small rockery we were passing. 'I mean this looks like someone's buried their dog here. Hm. But then I'll show you a photograph of what the lake looked like before Tom came. It was thick with weeds.'

Tom was strimming, just ten yards from us. 'No, I don't think we'll bother him now. He's clearly busy.'

At the end of the lake we paused and looked back at Stroove, reflected almost perfectly in the weed-free mirror. 'It calls itself a castle,' Adrian said. 'It's really a castellated house.'

We turned into the wood, which was a mighty tangle of trees and undergrowth. Nettles, ivy, purple-flowered thistles, a sprawling clump of hollybushes fought for space under the dappled green canopy of taller trees.

'The original layout would have been formal,' Adrian explained. 'An avenue of trees at the front. Then came Capability Brown and the fashions changed. These rough woods would have been squares with limes bordering them. Now they've been taken over by ash suckers. The ash is a very vigorous tree. There's a tension between the ash and the lime.' He paused and smiled. 'Just as there's a tension between the indigenous Irish and the landlords. Hm. This is a lime.' He pointed out a huge tree, towering above us, the fat growth of its lower trunk asprout with new branches. 'These younger trees are ash. And you see they just seed themselves. All these young trees have arrived against the original plan. But you can still see the old stock underneath.'

We strolled on and saw the ex-rose garden, the overgrown moated garden and the three walled kitchen gardens, the size of small fields, two of them now defunct: one a home for a row of apple trees, the other for a gang of startled-looking donkeys. Did I see that lighter patch on the far wall? That was where the greenhouses had been. They'd been taken down in the 1950s because of the rating system the government had introduced at that time. Rates had had no relation to people's incomes. 'Just to the size of their buildings, and the number of buildings they had. It was a very, very unfair system, which hit people with low incomes who lived in big houses.'

Musing quietly on the injustice, we came through cobbled yards and tumbling outhouses to the last walled garden, where vegetables were once again grown. 'Tom is the boss,' said Adrian. 'We all help ourselves.'

'But there's plenty to go round,' I said, surveying the beds – rhubarb, strawberries, asparagus, cabbages, a corner full of loganberry and blackcurrant bushes, and trained rows of raspberries. There was a central hooped walkway of apple trees, and down one long wall pears ripened in the sun. Scattered among the forty shades of green were red, yellow, pink and white roses, a spectrum of carnations.

'Oh yes. We'll never be fighting over the last apple.'

In the stable yard we found Pam, another volunteer, assiduously weeding a bed by the cottage in which Tom and his colleagues stayed. Round the corner was Dave from Balham, who normally worked as a maintenance man at a London hospital. And here, sitting up at a folding table in the sun was Eileen, Dave's mum, working her way peacefully through a book of *Sun* crosswords.

In another wood, jungled with vegetation, we came to the Norman church, ruined since the Reformation. Among the rampant tangle of weeds on the floor were the cracked graves of the original owners of the house, the inscriptions now neatly picked out in dark green moss. On one side a crumbling archway stood alone among the shoulder-high brambles, a plantation of five-foot nettles growing from it.

'We have plans to put walkways through,' Adrian explained.

Back in the dining room, he opened a bottle of white wine. 'Now perhaps you're ready for your smoked salmon. Hm?'

Ruth joined us, turning our rambling discussion into something altogether more immediate. 'We need more immigration,' she told me breathlessly. 'We're only three and a half million people. We need some of those blacks from Brixton to kick us into shape. No seriously,' she said, lips puckering with her excited amusement, 'I really think so. Especially in the North.'

Then, as had happened so often before on my travels with couples, they were both talking at once, overlapping, so my head was spinning from Ruth's vivid blue eyes to Adrian's grey ones, which became blank pools if he wasn't talking, his mouth suddenly a thin downward line, waiting polite-impatiently for his turn. Ruth calmed him, long fingers stroking back the wisps of white that strayed down over his ears.

Discreetly I pulled a single blond hair from my smoked salmon platter.

'Oh no!' cried Ruth. 'You can't eat that.'

'No, it's fine, really.'

But she'd grabbed the plate. 'No, you *can't* eat it. With a hair. I won't let you.'

'Really, it's fine.'

'I'll make you an omelette. I make a grand omelette.' We were tussling over the plate until I'd somehow managed to convince her that it was OK to eat a plate of smoked salmon that had one of her hairs in it.

Outside in the hall, the two children, and their tall French exchange Grégoire, were piling up the knapsacks and camping gear. Every twenty minutes or so they appeared at the door.

'Mummy, when are we *going*?'

'We have to wait for Dr Flowers to call back and say whether I can take you.'

'The truth is,' she said, when Adrian had gone off to organize the packing of the car, 'now you're here, neither of us want to go. But we've promised them this trip so one of us will have to.'

The phone rang. It was Dr Flowers. Ruth was well enough to travel if she wanted.

'I would *like* it if you'd take them,' she told Adrian.

Adrian was undecided. 'Well, you'll have to make up your mind soon,' she was saying, as they left me. I sipped my wine, gazed out on to the lovely demesne. Damn. I'd mistimed my arrival badly. It seemed a cruel shame to have to hit the road again, on to the doubtless touristy clichés of Kilkenny, and a dreary B & B.

They'd returned, standing framed in the doorway like a Van
Eyck. Ruth was going. 'You see I have to stand on the step to
kiss her goodbye,' Adrian said, hugging her affectionately.

'Come *on*, Mummy. We've been waiting *five hours*!'

When they'd gone Adrian and I had another glass of wine.
Outside in the sunshine Tom and Pam toiled with strimmer
and spade.

'That's the great thing about letting them do what they
want,' said Adrian. 'Hm. They'd never do all that if I was
down there telling them what to do.'

The doorbell rang. It was a group of Americans wanting a
tour. 'Damn,' said Adrian. 'Ruth must have left the gate open.
I'll have to do it.' So I became part of the household, shifting
back and forth to find the most comfortable position on the
yellow chaise longue in the formal drawing room with the big
orange carpet and the two huge, gold-framed mirrors, which
brought the fields and trees and sunshine and distant grey-
green silhouette of the Blackstairs Mountains in all around
me.

I leafed woozily through the newspapers (a million miles
away David Trimble had accepted the ceasefire) and gazed at
the mantelpiece, which held a porcelain figure of Britannia, a
tarnished silver candlestick, a yellow glass bowl, two small
gold and navy blue urns, some postcards of horses and a white
marble clock (stopped at 12.30.) Above, the plaster ceiling was
yellow-grey with age and cracked all over. Around me was an
assortment of furniture, a very old-fashioned stereo, a piano,
a violin out of its case . . .

The Americans were as taken by it all as I was. 'And this is
Mark,' said Adrian, 'who's writing a book about contemporary
Ireland.'

In the evening we sat outside in the drive drinking Pernod.
'I'm sorry,' Adrian said, 'I've got nothing else. I bought the
tonic but forgot the gin.' I sipped the cloudy-white liquorice
water and gazed happily down the twin rows of limes stretching away to the old, haunted gates of the estate, where even
now the locals wouldn't go. Adrian was very taken with his

new metaphor. 'Yes,' he said, rolling the words around his tongue with relish. 'The *ash* and the *lime* . . .'

At dusk we drove to a nearby small town for dinner. 'I don't like going,' Adrian told me. He owned a warehouse there that had been burned down a few months before. It had contained his valuable collection of French furniture. Was it just coincidence that a few hours before the fire Adrian had been discussing putting in a bid on an adjoining property? But the Gardai were useless in such cases. They didn't follow it up. Nor did they follow up burglaries. When they'd been burgled once, one of the police had said, 'Now what would you want all these old things around you for anyway?'

Over our meal my education in Irish matters continued. 'It's not *finer* Gael, Mark! It's *feena* Gael and Fianna *fohl*. Softly now, like you might "fohl" down stairs.'

'Fianna fo-hl.'

'Softer. I'll tutor you over breakfast.' And I mustn't pronounce Haughey as Margaret Thatcher always had, Hock-hey. 'You say the "Haugh" as if you're blowing on your glasses. Hoh,' he breathed, removing his own specs to demonstrate. 'Hee.'

'Hoh-hee.'

'Better. But you need to get these things right if you're going to,' he met my eyes with a mischievous look, 'pass muster.'

When we got back we found that Dave's mum Eileen (who slept in the house, in the bedroom next to me) had locked us out. We paced fruitlessly up and down the gravel trying to wake her. 'Eileen! Eileen!' But she was fast asleep, oblivious even to stones chucked at her window. 'Or she may be *frightened*,' said Adrian. 'She may not know who we are.'

There were lights on in the wing that had once been the governesses' rooms, which Adrian had rented to a local woman and her seventy-year-old Polish boyfriend. Adrian stood undecided in the dark yard. 'But I don't think I can really disturb them. They're supposed to be entirely separate.'

'I'm sure it'd be OK. In an emergency.'

'D'you think? Well perhaps we'll have to. They're not

fornicating or anything are they? All right then. Hall-*oh*! It's
Adrian! I'm terribly sorry, we're locked out.'

In the morning I was invited to stay on. Adrian would be
doing tours and I should make myself at home, just please
making sure the front door wasn't left open, as the cat got in.
'Door open,' Adrian gestured. 'In marches cat.' But apart
from three cyclists – who appeared, turned round in the drive
and departed – nobody else came.

'You see that lot had just one look and went away without
paying,' he grumbled. 'It probably doesn't look enough like a
castle. Sometimes I don't know why I bother. I probably only
make £1000 out of it a year. But it's extra income and, who
knows, it may prove a wise move in the long run, tax-wise,
when we come to do improvements.'

In the afternoon the bell rang and there on the porch was
a younger version of Betty Blue, flanked by two thirty-
something men. Adrian had wandered off, God alone knew
where. Did they want a tour, I asked. No, they were staying
the night. Sultry Helga, who was German, was coming as
an exchange. Oh, right. Somewhat uncertainly I let them
in. 'Please don't leave the front door open,' I said. 'The cats
get in.'

One of the men was German too, a Lutheran priest who
had come to officiate at a local wedding. He shot off in his
open-topped red car, and I left Peter and Helga to settle in.
Adrian had stacked up the table by my chaise longue with a
huge pile of books to read. All morning he'd kept appearing
with new ones, knocking politely on the door of his own
drawing room. 'Hm, Mark. Here's a book here edited by
Conor Cruise O'Brien. It was done before the Troubles, so I'd
say it would be interesting. You see his last chapter, "Deep
Sea Fishing".' His chuckle rose to a light crescendo.

Early evening the Pernod reappeared. Adrian had things to
do, so Peter and I sat in the drawing room getting quietly
stewed together. He was from Co. Louth, and, like Adrian,
one of those rarest of Southern birds, a Protestant. There
were, he confirmed, just 3 or 4 per cent left in the South now.

When they'd been growing up, Peter told me, his mother

had made them think they were the superior ones in the district. They weren't allowed to mix with Catholics, so they'd had hardly any friends locally. Then they'd been sent away to Protestant boarding schools, so all he'd known were other Protestants who'd ended up in Dublin. But his mother was very remote, like a lot of Protestants. 'They have a coldness about them.' When he phoned up, for example, to say he wanted to come and visit, she'd say, 'If you like.' It wasn't like, 'Peter, great, do come and see us.'

The light faded. Peter's features gradually became a soot-black silhouette against the lovely green outside. Behind his moving lips, the tops of the trees shone gold, then copper, in the last light. A tiny puff of pinkening cloud motored silently from one side of the peeling window frame to the other.

Catholics and Protestants, Catholics and Protestants. You couldn't escape it, even if, as they all kept telling me, the problems had nothing to do with religion at all.

At dinner we were a noisy six. Adrian, me, the Lutheran pastor, Peter, another friend of Adrian's who'd come to do some fishing and beautiful Helga, bemused, shy and giggling at the centre of us. The pastor had had an excellent wedding. 'Vat a grant affair it vass. Zey vere zis *ferry* upper-class rich family viss see hugest tent . . .'

'Rich doesn't mean upper-class in Ireland,' Peter observed.

Ruth seemed quite unsurprised to see me when she returned with the children on Sunday evening. She'd been hoping I'd still be around, she said, as she wanted to paint my portrait. And suddenly here she was, appearing with her open, almost childlike smile in a long paint-smudged brown coat. Five minutes later she was well into it, not insisting that I sit particularly still or not chat as she painted.

'I'm amazed at the way you just dive in,' I said.

'Painting's like that. It's a no-nonsense business. Painters are a lazy lot really.'

She was very lucky, she told me. She had a studio here in the house, a studio in Adrian's other house, and another studio. 'I would safely say I have the most space to paint of anyone in Ireland! Or England maybe.' But space didn't really

matter. 'When I was in London I had a bedsit. It was six foot
by ten. And I ate, slept and painted in it.'

At dinner the children were noisy and Adrian was upset.
Ruth had lost the lock to the front gate, and now anybody
could get in. Since the incident at the warehouse, which we
didn't talk about, security was a serious issue for Adrian. The
fire had had nothing to do with him being a Protestant, but
still, Ruth had told me, it had upset him deeply. He would
hate to feel he was unpopular with the people locally. He had
actually gone so far as to sue the Gardai, and until the court
case was over and there was some kind of resolution, he was
going to go on growing his hair.

The children wanted to get down. They wanted to watch
Keeping Up Appearances. Goodness! That Hyacinth Bucket
should be the hip thing among pre-pubescent Irish youth.

'Please, Mummy!'

'Josie, stop it! I'm going to get cross now. There's a thin line
between sanity and insanity and I'm on it!'

6

Hiberniores hibernis ipsos . . .

Whereas at the conquest of the land of Ireland and for a
long time after, the English of the said land used the English
language, mode of riding and apparel, and were governed
and ruled . . . by the English law . . . now many English of
the said land, forsaking the English language, fashion, mode
of riding, laws and usages, live and govern themselves
according to the manners, fashion, and language of the Irish
enemies, and have also made divers marriages and alliances
between themselves and the Irish enemies aforesaid;
whereby the said land and the liege people thereof, the
English language, the allegiance due to our lord the King,
and the English laws there, are put in subjection and
decayed . . .

Oh dear. Two centuries after Strongbow and things had gone
badly to seed. When Lionel, Duke of Clarence (Edward III's
third son), arrived in Ireland in September 1361 to put things
straight he found the Anglo-Irish less than eager to support
him against their Irish neighbours. They had become, in the
medieval phrase, *hiberniores hibernis ipsos*, 'more Irish than
the Irish themselves'.

So in February 1366 he summoned a parliament to Kilkenny
to come up with a solution to *his* Irish problem. Thirty-five
acts were passed (of which the above is the preamble). The
English were forbidden by the severest penalties, 'to make
fosterage, marriage, or gossipred [*sic*] with the Irish'. They
were no longer to use Gaelic Brehon law, nor entertain those
influential troublemakers, Irish minstrels, poets and story-
tellers. They were banned from selling horses or armour to
the Irish in peacetime, and in wartime, food. They and the

Irish who lived among them had to use English surnames,
speak English and follow English customs. And so on.

The Statute of Kilkenny was an early form of apartheid. Its
thirty-six clauses remained in force for over two centuries, and
had the effect of dividing the land between the 'obedient
shires' of the English, and the rest. Outside the 'English land'
(about one-third of the island) the Irish stuck with their own
language, law and customs. 'The question was solved,' said the
historian Edmund Curtis, 'in a way fatal to the union and
fusion of the two races.'

In November 1366, less than a year after passing this
stringent legislation, Lionel did as more than one or two other
disgruntled English overlords were to do in the future and left
Ireland for good. Despite being Earl of Ulster and Lord of
Connaught, he yearned for France, where 'chivalric glory and
rich booty were to be made at every battle' and besides, the
weather was better. He left behind such 'chieftains of the
English lineage' as the Burkes, Roches and Geraldines, and
our friends the Butlers, who in 1391 acquired Kilkenny Castle
(which had been started by Strongbow's son William in 1213)
as their main base.

Six centuries later, the fortress was in better shape than ever.
The Butlers had finally packed up in 1935. Unable any longer
to afford both Kilkenny and their London house, they had
chosen to abandon Kilkenny. Later, Lord Ormond, the 30th
Hereditary Chief Butler of Ireland, handed the place over to
the Irish government for a nominal £50.

The Free State authorities had done handsomely by it,
restoring exterior and interior to the state it had been in in its
heyday. Under the hammer-beam roof of the long gallery the
rows of Butler faces dramatized the history. (They had clearly
been a shrewd and diplomatic lot, having had both William of
Orange and James II to stay.)

Over the road you were back in modern Ireland – with a
vengeance. Having had your obligatory helping of history and
culture (and perhaps a nice portion of Bailey's and coffee
gateau in the tea room), you could shop till you developed
pointy ears and turned green in the Kilkenny Design Centre.
Guinness ties and baseball caps; Magee tweed jackets; T-shirts

saying 'I've got Irish roots'; Waterford crystal ('the Powers-court suite'); the Claddagh Silver Collection; Celtic 'love toasting' flutes; sacred spiral stones; Irish whiskey truffles; Butler's Irish Handmade Chocolates (so that's what they were up to these days); Irish Morning Mist Soap – the whole astonishing cornucopia of shamrockery was here.

Down from the hill on which the castle was set, Kilkenny town had streets full of houses painted in a range of bright colours alongside carefully preserved traditional shop fronts. There'd been a bit of a rumpus, I was told, when Supermac's Pizzas and Ices had managed to get the site opposite the stone-columned Old Town Hall, the site of the city's other great claim to historical fame, the 1642 Confederation of Kilkenny, when leaders of 'all-Catholics in Ireland' had allied themselves against Cromwell's Puritan parliament, which had decreed the absolute suppression of their religion.

Cromwell's 1650 desolation of the town was still in evidence. His troops had razed the roofs and smashed the windows of the Dominican Black Abbey. In beautiful St Canice's Cathedral, they'd uprooted tombs, dragged bodies out of graves, used holy water for their horses, which even my 'lapsed Protestant' guide Ian (aged twenty) found 'pretty shocking stuff'. At the time I thought these stories were unique to Kilkenny. As I was to discover, there was barely a church in Ireland that Cromwell's troops had not 'used as a stable'.

'God, I love it here!' exclaimed the man with pink shorts, as we stood at the almost-top of Slievenamon, which was, he assured me, one of the most sacred mountains in Ireland. Above us, a chilly swathe of cloud obscured the summit, its wispy fringes blowing around the tall crucifix that could, on special nights, be electronically lit.

He was an English 'blow-in', who'd moved from Gloucester-shire in 1964. 'It had all become too prettified. Everything painted and clipped. It wasn't the real country any more.' The only alternative was somewhere like Suffolk, but there they'd torn out all the hedgerows. No, England was largely spoiled now. Whereas here . . .

Below us, the huge plain of Tipperary stretched out, green, hedgerowed, empty and unspoilt. 'Every time I climb up here,' he went on, 'I just think, God I'm lucky.' When he died he was going to have his ashes scattered at the summit. His girlfriend Penny had said, 'Why don't you take some fire-lighters up with you and spare yourself the return journey. God she's funny!'

Yet even in his garden of Eden there were problems: an immigrant German who'd apparently been trying to block off one of the local rights of way. And then, horror of horrors, there'd been a suggestion that Slievenamon would make a good site for wind-turbines. They'd sent some bloody woman over from London who'd got neighbourhood hackles seriously up by saying, 'When I get my windmills up . . .'. *My* windmills indeed! One of the locals had told her, 'If you get them up it'll be over dead bodies.' That had shut her up. But the arrogance of it! Thankfully, the District Council had voted the scheme down 36–nil. 'I've only been here thirty-five years; I can't imagine what people who've been here thirty-five generations must feel.'

And now Lord Lloyd Webber had bought the castle I could see there in the middle. He'd once kept some local hosts waiting for over an hour. 'When they give people titles they should send them to some sort of charm school, don't you reckon? They could call it Knight School.'

But these were minor bugbears. The Irish were wonderful. They had 'the best manners in the world'. And every day you got these 'wonderful shafts of humour'. In all his years of being here, there'd been no problem about his being English. Even in the early 1970s, when the Troubles were at their height. Once he'd had an anonymous telephone call. 'Have you been getting any threatening letters?' asked the voice.

'No.'

'I'll make sure you don't.' And the phone had gone down.

Yes, he wore pink every day – pink shorts and a faded maroon T-shirt. Why? It was easier. In the morning you didn't have to think about what to wear, you just put 'em on. And when he was walking, which he did a lot, often quite long distances for charity, he took a pair of his girlfriend's tights and a supply of disposable paper pants. 'You can just chuck

'em away.' And if he stopped to call in on anyone that was
OK too. Wearing tights under shorts was 'perfectly acceptable
court dress'.

I drove south, crossing the Knockmealdown mountains by way
of 'the Vee', a pass which yielded, at its top, another fine,
wide-angled panorama of Tipperary and Limerick. There was
nobody up there but a lone German cyclist, buffeted by the
rainy wind. The sun appeared. Winding down through dripping, dappled woodland arches I came to the little town that
is the home (or one of the homes) of another Englishman, the
Duke of Devonshire.

He wasn't in residence at Lismore Castle just then, so I took
a stroll round his Alice in Wonderland gardens, with their
ankle-height miniature hedges and neat rose trees against a
crumbling pink brick wall. It wasn't a bad holiday cottage, this
nineteenth-century imitation of a Tudor castle built around
the Norman fort that had originally stood here, but by all
accounts the duke could rarely use it, being both a target for
the IRA and, because of his extraordinary wealth, for ransom-
seeking kidnappers.

On the radio there'd been an item about the famous moving
Madonna of Cappoquin. Somebody had seen her budge yet
again, yesterday evening. And here I was, just three miles
away. I hurried thither, expectantly.

There were twenty cars, at least, parked over the road from
the Grotto where the beautifully painted statue stood at the
top of a bracken-covered slope in the deep green shade of a
thick canopy of trees.

At the bottom, by numerous bouquets of flowers and signs
saying 'Silence' and 'I am the Immaculate Conception', an
assortment of pilgrims sat quietly on the painted green
benches: a woman in an orange top, with three daughters in
lime green; a grey-haired fellow in an open grey cardigan with
a walking frame; a man in a red Reeboks sweatshirt with a
gaggle of shaven-headed kids. All were immobile, staring up
at the statue, as if it might at any moment oblige them.

There were, the leaflet I had picked up at the gate informed
me, numerous witnesses to the supernatural goings-on that

had previously last occurred during an incredible week in August 1985, when, little expecting the chain of events they were setting off, the O'Rourke family had come, one Friday evening, to pray at the Grotto.

Having recited the rosary the family started to leave the Grotto, Ursula taking up the rear. As she looked up at the statue she noticed that Our Lady was moving. First she thought that it was her imagination, and she looked away several times before she finally realized that she was looking at the Blessed Virgin Mary.

'A strange feeling came over me which is very hard to describe. Tears came to my eyes, and I pulled my hands up from my sides, joined them and blessed myself. I said to the Lady. "You are the Queen of Heaven." She smiled. I kept exclaiming, "Why me? Why did you pick me, why?" She smiled again, and then I said, "Please bless all my family." She smiled even more. She did not speak to me during this vision.'

How the news of Our Lady's manifestation got out the leaflet didn't say, or perhaps what happened the next day was just a coincidence, or maybe the statue, after tedious years of immobility, had decided that turning into a person was much more interesting. Whatever. The very next afternoon, a local woman, Breda Coleman, went to the Grotto to pray, with her daughters, Sandra (aged thirteen) and Carol (aged six).

In Mrs Coleman's own words: The whole statue was glowing white and the blue sash disappeared, then the face changed to Our Lord's face – bearded and dark hair to shoulders – also glowing. Sandra saw the same. They left somewhat confused.

And who can blame them, both seeing the same vision like that?

All returned to the Grotto at about 5 p.m. Mrs Coleman, who now had with her her six children, saw the statue glowing as before and the face changing to Our Lord periodically. Sandra saw several interesting visions – the background become dark and she saw St Joan of Arc and other saints in full length appearing one after another. She then saw Our Lord, who floated upwards out of her vision as if heavenwards.

But Sandra and her mamma were not alone. The next day yet more witnesses came forward. A local farmer, Michael Cliffe, and his son Tom, aged twelve, saw 'Our Lord's face on the statue'. Mrs Breda Lyons saw Our Lord dressed in a white robe with a black belt, and Our Blessed Lady, head turning towards the road. She appeared to be sad.

Later that day, clearly bored with just manifesting, Our Lady of Melleray started speaking, first off to little Tom Cliffe, who heard her say, 'I want you, too', or possibly 'I want two'. Tom and his mother left the Grotto in a very distressed state.

By the evening the Madonna was getting more outspoken. 'Preserve Sunday for prayer,' she told another local farmer, Michael O'Donnell, from a set of steps that had magically appeared, down which she walked to within feet of him. In his vision her face was 'lightly tanned'. Shortly after that, a neighbour saw Michael transformed into 'a very old man, completely deformed and with a bald head. He thought I was about to die'.

Fortunately, Michael was fine. But the visions accelerated. The next day Tom Cliffe returned with his cousin Barry Buckley (aged eleven). They were privileged to see Our Blessed Lady with a crown on her head. Suddenly she cried to them, 'Behave!', but when the people around ignored this injunction she started, according to the boys, to cry. Her tears splashed on the ground. 'I want prayer!' she shouted.

Heeding the boys, the people in the Grotto started to say the rosary. It was clearly what Our Lady wanted, for the boys then heard her say 'Thank you'.

I wish I had the space to detail the rest of the happenings of that extraordinary week. Suffice it to say that Our Blessed Lady got more and more talkative and took an increasingly special interest in Tom, who by now had started having full-blown visions – of Our Lord at a table, beggars in a street, dogs barking. Our Lord also took unusual notice of Tom, at one point 'giving out' to him so sternly that he was reduced to tears. At this point Our Lady reappeared. 'Tell Tom to stop crying,' she said, and as he was shivering in his T-shirt, obliged him by sending down 'a warm breeze'.

Barry was now privileged to see visions too. The steps on which our Lady appeared were soon 'of brown clay with multi-coloured roses of all sizes' on both sides. 'God is angry with the world,' she told both boys. Then, 'I love the Irish people'. Then, 'If the people would improve and pray God would save Ireland'.

By the end of the week Our Lady had been joined by Satan, who had, the boys said, 'a pock-marked face, bulging eyes, big teeth, pointed nose and jaw, little stumps of horns and big ears' and who was threatening a Noah-style flood 'unless the people improve within ten years'.

It now being twelve years later, the people had clearly heeded her warning, or perhaps Our Lady had waited a couple of extra years and now it was time for a repeat of the events of the week that had had the Grotto so packed with people listening to Barry and Tom's visions that the crowds outside could not get in to see for themselves and had to rely on secondhand reports. Or even a Noah-style flood. Help! I hurried off.

That night I stopped at a pub whose host was a rural Dave Allen. This part of Ireland, Ted explained, was *inundated* with English expats, or, rather, with expats of British origin. You'd hear their accents and you'd say, 'Are you from England?' and they'd go, 'God no! Dreadful place!' They'd be from Rhodesia (as they still called it) or Australia or Argentina.

There was a place just down the road called Villierstown where just about everybody was Lord this or Lady that. But local people didn't, by and large, mind the landlords. The Duke of Devonshire was, in fact, very popular in Lismore – after all, he provided employment for 400 people, and when they'd finished in the Duke's service they might retire to the town and open up a flower shop or something. That was the sort of place it was. The next big estate over belonged to the Duke of Westminster, and he was popular enough too.

But these people were colourful. There was a man called Sir Richard Green, who was the landlord of Cappoquin and who, in effect, owned the village. He'd been caught speeding recently and had been up in court. His name was read out: 'Richard Green'. 'It's *Sir* Richard,' he interrupted, 'not Richard.' The magistrate looked sternly at him and said, 'You may be Sir Richard at home but here you're Richard Green like anyone else – that'll be £75.'

'Well, that gave us all a good laugh,' Ted said. No, he actually liked these English expat types. They were all characters. There was definitely a part of him that enjoyed a bit of the old forelock-tugging. He liked putting on the act. 'If Sir Richard came in here now and said, "Eh Ted, could you get down on your knees and polish my shoes, there's a good man" I mean I'd probably do it. Just to keep the sort of Disney-world-thing going.'

He'd rather – to be honest – have them in his pub than the wild folk who came down from the mountains on a Saturday night. 'Hillbillies, I suppose you'd call 'em.' They were the descendants of locals who'd been evicted in the 1850s by a landlord who had built a huge pair of gates and then hadn't had the money to build the house to go with them. The gates were still there, standing alone in the middle of nowhere. They were incredible, these hill people, intermarried and interbred beyond anything you could imagine. 'Hello, I'm John, and this is my brother John, and this is my sister John – she's also my wife.'

In the two centuries after the Statute of Kilkenny, the Gaelic chiefs outside the English counties had continued more or less as before. The English Crown continued to assert authority and achieved nominal success. Henry VIII, in particular, got the leading Irish earls to acknowledge 'no other king or lord on earth except your Majesty'. Elizabeth I was more aggressive, forcing the chiefs to surrender their lands and receive them back 'regranted'. Resistance was dealt with fiercely. The lands of people who stepped out of line were confiscated and 'planted' with settlers from England and Scotland. This process took place initially in Counties Laois and Offaly, which were then re-named the King's and Queen's counties; later, and more successfully, it was done in six of the nine counties of Ulster, the one-time lands of Hugh O'Neill, Earl of Tyrone.

O'Neill had sought help from Philip II of Spain but had

been defeated decisively at the battle of Kinsale on 24 September 1601. Not for the last time, 'the whole fate of Ireland hung upon a single battle'. A victory for O'Neill would have led to further aid from Spain and 'a great flocking to his standard'.

However, the Spanish-Irish army (including 900 Scots) was routed by the English Lord Deputy (ably supported by Richard, Earl of Clanrickard, O'Brien, Earl of Thomond, Cormac MacCarthy of Muskerry and St Lawrence of the Pale, good Irishmen all). O'Neill retreated to his stronghold in the North, where on 30 March 1603, he finally agreed to submit to Elizabeth I (who had died, unbeknown to him, six days before). He renounced the title of O'Neill, his authority over his former subjects, and resigned all lands and lordships except those the Crown might see fit to grant him.

Four years later, after a failed series of attempts to regain authority, O'Neill and his ally the Earl of Tyrconnell sailed from Ireland for ever. This was the celebrated 'Flight of the Earls', and it marked the end of Gaelic and feudal Ireland. Ulster, the last unconquered province, was thrown open to English law. The poets, Brehons and chroniclers of the Gaelic world were usurped by 'planted' Englishmen and Scots, whose religion was, of course, Protestant.

So was the seed sown for the Ulster of today. Had O'Neill waited another day (as he favoured) my ancestors might never have found a home in the North, Gerry Adams might be a greengrocer in Glasgow and ... and ... and ...

Enough of that! I'll be writing ballads next.

> THE FLIGHT OF THE EARLS
> To other shores across the sea
> We speed with swelling sail;
> Yet still there lingers on our lee
> A phantom Innisfail.
> Oh fear, fear not, gentle ghost,
> Your sons shall turn untrue!
> Though fain to fly your lovely coast,
> They leave their hearts with you.

Now, just short of four centuries later, the little port of Kinsale, at the head of the steep, well-protected Bandon estuary, had become a prettified town of international blow-ins and gourmets, catered for by streetfuls of fine restaurants and with a famous October Food Festival. To aid the digestion there were art galleries galore, featuring everything from colourful watercolours of local scenes to installation art and the work of Australian Aboriginals.

Having failed to check in to a B & B run by a rather crisp South African lady, whose vacancy sign was, she said, an oversight on the part of her Irish maid, I had better luck over the road with an ex-policeman from Cork, who sat me down with a pot of strong tea, shoved a plateful of fruit cake in my direction and told me how glad he was to be out of the big city. When he'd started thirty years ago they'd had a few drunks in Cork and that was about it. Recently there'd been increasing problems with drugs.

'I'd heard west Cork was where they all came in?'

'Even near here, near Kinsale.' A French fishing trawler had netted some bales of cannabis just off the Old Man only a few months back.

I strolled down the street, past the tizzed-up, brightly painted houses. White with navy blue woodwork stood next to canary yellow with orange (Favourites); green with white (Hurley's TV and Video); salmon with turquoise (Kinsale Crystal); and midnight blue with cream and red (O'Neill Auctioneers). So not all the clan had fled.

How futile had been the attempts of the English overlords to silence the Gaels. Irish music and singing *still* rang out through the door of the wine bar on the corner. I took a table by the wall and watched a noisy group of eight work their way through 'Forty Shades of Green', 'The Fields of Athenry', 'In the Valley of Slievenamon', ending with a spirited rendition by their oldest, most elegant female member of Andrew Lloyd Webber's 'Memory'. (Did they know, I wondered, that the musical English lord now had his own demesne in the Valley of Slievenamon?)

'You've got a wild bunch in tonight,' I said to the waitress.

'That's the owner.'

Before I knew it, that boisterous blond lady had invited me over. The menfolk had left. 'We're wondering who you are,' she said, 'the Lone Ranger sitting over there in the corner.'

There were four of them: Lesley the owner; her raven-haired

sister Noreen, recently returned from Canada, where she'd 'stayed ten years for a man'; the elegant singer, whose husband of thirty-five years had just died; and her niece Angela, who'd just been chucked by her boyfriend. They were having a high old time.

The niece wanted to set up a club called the 4B Club, but sadly I couldn't join, because it was open to women only. You had to have balance, boundaries and balls, she said.

'Then it's the 3B Club,' I pointed out.

'No. Then you become a butterfly! You have to have balance, boundaries and balls – then you become a butterfly!' So many women were caterpillars, didn't I think.

'Well . . .' I began.

The world would be an altogether better place, she interrupted, if women discovered their masculine side and men their feminine side. She, for example, was strong but also vulnerable. The point was, anyone who tried to manipulate someone else was insecure. For sure. Didn't I think?

Well no, I said, I thought there were undoubtedly people who manipulated others who were entirely secure.

No, no, Angela argued, they were insecure. She knew because she was just starting a psychology degree at Cork University.

The widow had been manipulated too, she told us. For sure. Although her husband had been a perfect gentleman, in thirty-five years of marriage they'd only been out, what, ten times. She'd never really known him. Only in the last four years, when he was ill and she'd nursed him, had she really got to know him.

'Now he's gone to meet his Maker. And I loved him. Of course I did.'

The sister had stayed in Canada for four or five years longer than she should have done, more maybe, because of the material stuff that had gone with her man. 'I used to drink out of hand-painted glasses,' she sighed.

So the widow got to her feet and sang another song, a deep and haunting ballad about Donegal. And over the applause, she cried, 'I could have been professional. But I got married, and now I've been married thirty-five years, but I could have been a professional!'

7

Rebel Cork

It was a great little eyrie, my attic room in Cork, at the very top of a tall Georgian house on the steep slope that rose up from the canal-like River Lee. Directly below, the houses on the other side of the street were pocket, three-storey affairs, painted green, white, brown and grey. Beyond them, a hundred yards of rooftops faded through the rain to the silvery glint of water beneath.

Central in my private panorama was the scruffy Bus Eireann terminal, with ten or more red and white buses drawn up outside, surrounded by a forever-shifting struggle of passengers. To the left, rust-red cranes rose against a grey, silo-style warehouse; in a broad V to the right, toy cars crowded the three-lane, one-way streets of the central island, champing in tiny movements to cross the bridges and get out past the stark, five-storey blocks of the city to the softer swathes of the suburbs with their rooftops, blobs of dark green trees and dark windows in grey walls. Here a canary yellow chapel, there a bulbous oxidized-copper green dome. Here a bright pink rectangle of a house end, there a crimson strip of industry. Over the top of these, no more than three miles away, rose the washed-out hills, green and paler green into the misty sky. Which gnarled and eccentric old lime still hung on in that hillside mansion? Which upshooting ash sprouts had just put up that fine row of Bungalow Blisses?

In this smudged, rainswept landscape I knew nobody. The long list of contacts I'd had in Dublin was here replaced by a couple of unlikely numbers. So I gazed out at my view. I lay on my bed and read more history. I smiled aimlessly at Clare, my mumsy blond landlady, who seemed to be forever working her way through a vast pile of ironing in the TV room just off the hall. 'Now with all this rain,' she'd apologized on my arrival, 'the water's been coming out brown. It's better now, not black-brown as it was, but you'd better make tea rather than drink it.'

By the evening the rain had called a temporary halt. I came down past the pool hall and over St Patrick's bridge into the criss-crossing streets of the city-centre island. There were any number of pubs, many with the sound of traditional music and *craic* ringing out through open doors. But, bar a McDonald's, there were no places actually to sit down and eat. Finally, through a window, I saw a black-tied waiter bending to a table. Deep purple carpets, black and white marble tiles, a pianist tinkling – Clouds Restaurant at the Imperial Hotel.

There were lights in brass Chinese-hat-style shades hung midway between ceiling and table. Grey walls with pastel screenprints of Cannes and Nice. There were navy blue napkins, pink carnations and plates with airbrushed rims of salmon pink and grey.

I was seventeen again! Enjoying my first-ever meal out in the mid-1970s. The large laminated menu offered *Fresh Prawn Cocktail 'Riverdance' (excellent fresh prawns topped with brandy-flavoured cocktail sauce); Provence-style Pâté; French Onion Gratinée (soup); Goujons of Cod and Salmon 'Jaipur'.* Now when had I last had a good goujon of cod? Aeons ago, in another life.

For the main course I was faced with a choice between *Breast of Chicken 'Cordon Bleu'* and *Crispy Roast Duckling 'à l'Orange' (glazed with Cointreau and orange caramel).* For pudding there were *Pear Belle Hélène, Vienna-style Chocolate Gateau,* and *Parfait 'Amour' (homemade log of Cointreau, toffee-flavoured almonds and butterscotch sauce).*

O tempora! O mores! O homemade log!

But there was only one option really, *Imperial Sundae – a combination of ice-creams, fruit, nuts and luscious sauce.* I prayed for pineapple chunks, tinned mandarin segments, thirds of almost-rotting tinned strawberries, slightly stale, criss-cross-decorated wafer triangles, a scatter of triangular chopped almonds in sickly whipped cream. My prayers were answered.

All around me were hilarious tablefuls of women of a

certain age and a certain hairstyle, the age being between forty-one and sixty-five, the hairstyle being that clipped, tightly waved perm that sits like a helmet above an exhausted face. They had lived and loved, these women, borne and raised families, and tonight, earrings-a-dangle, they were bloody well relaxing, plucking homemade logs from butterscotch sauce, scooping in huge mouthfuls of Baked Dutch Apple Pie. What were they all celebrating, I wondered. Only later did I discover that this was the first Tuesday of the month – Child Allowance Night.

'Hello' came a call from the TV room, as I let myself in at 11.20. Clare was still at the ironing board in front of a late film.

'Enjoy yourself?'

'Lovely. Had a wander round Cork.'

'All the convenience of a big city without the size.'

'You're doing your ironing.'

'A month's build-up, and no slaves, you see.'

In the morning I phoned Irene, Features Editor of the *Cork Examiner*. It was that or suicide. Yes, she could meet me for lunch.

As she led me down packed St Patrick's Street and up into the English Market (James I had granted the charter in 1610), she stopped about once every thirty seconds to say hello to somebody. On the balcony, above the crowd of stalls specializing in bacon, fish, olives, cheese and pâté, we paused at every other table. This tousled freelance was writing a novel, that one would deliver her piece by Friday. It was a friendly little city, if you knew somebody.

So what about Cork? I asked.

Well there was food, of course. Cork was big on that. And people now had this idea of Cork café society, which was quite new, in the last five years these café-type places, where people just hung out. The club scene was quite something. Of course, they were terribly proud of their soccer.

There was snobbery – people to the north of the river were considered rougher and known as 'Norries'. Very posh Corconians lived up on the hill in Montenotte and spoke through their noses, like this, 'It's awfully snotty in Montenotte.'

There wasn't much emigration from Cork. People wanted

to stay close to their mammy, their auntie, their nanny. The mammy ruled Cork, in fact, and would be very keen to see her children get on. There was the joke about the Cork mammy and her son who'd fallen in the river. She rushed to the Guard. 'Help! My son, the engineer, is drowning!'

I laughed. Now where had I heard that before?

'But it's *true*,' said Irene. Her neighbour had eleven children, and every one was a doctor or an architect or an engineer.

Provos

In London I had spoken to the actor Kenneth Griffith, an unashamed supporter of Irish Republicanism and, controversially, the IRA. So it was with some nervousness that I drove down along the Bandon estuary to call on his contact Jim, who had once been, he'd said, 'a great figure locally'.

Jim strolled towards me down the echoing corridor of the spacious ex-convent where he lived, face creased up with smiles.

'You're Kenneth Griffith's friend?'

'Well, yes . . .'

Jim wasn't quite sure what I wanted, he said, as we stood uncertainly by the yellow formica table in the big kitchen. I held my ground, still in my jacket, not forcing it, talking in general terms about what I was trying to do.

After a minute or two he gestured to a wooden chair, offered me a cup of tea. We sat down. His wife, Glynis, appeared, bringing tea and a piled-up plateful of biscuits and cake.

'One thing you should gather from me,' said Jim, 'is that the fight in the North isn't sectarian. Here I am, married to a girl who's a Welsh Baptist!' In and out of the kitchen danced two little girls and a crop-haired lad in a grey tracksuit.

Jim had now started to talk about 'General' Tom Barry, the legendary leader of the West Cork Flying Column during the Anglo-Irish 'War of Independence' of 1919–21. Having served in the British Army during the First World War, Barry was one of those returning soldiers who had been converted to the

Sinn Fein cause, which had been going from strength to strength since the executions of the leading rebels of 1916, and the subsequent General Election of 1918, when it had won 73 out of the 105 Irish seats at Westminster, refusing famously to take them up. His book, *Guerrilla Days In Ireland*, had become, Jim chuckled, compulsory reading for the SAS. 'What I'd really like to have seen,' he added, 'was the letters the British generals wrote him after the fight.'

'I've got his watch,' Jim went on proudly, and sent off one of his girls to find it. 'And bring his walking stick now,' he called after her.

As we talked, Jim was emerging not just as a Republican and supporter of the Provisional IRA, but as one of those hardliners who thought Adams was making a mistake negotiating at all with the British. There'd been a split in the local party when the ceasefire had been mooted, and Jim had been the first man to walk out. 'In my opinion,' he told me, 'one bomb at a financial centre in London is worth more than twenty years of talking.'

He'd been trying to explain this to somebody the other day. The only way he could do it was to put a bottle of orange squash beside a bottle of water. 'The fight's getting watered down,' he'd said. 'I'd be against any concessions,' he went on now. 'Our freedom is non-negotiable, and until Gerry Adams and Martin McGuinness prove otherwise . . .' His sentence tailed off in a shrug. 'I'd be saying that to their faces, even though I'd hope to be proved wrong.'

The general's watch had arrived, strapless and reverently offered in the palm of his little girl's hand. On the reverse it was engraved, 'To Tom, with love from Leslie May'.

'That is actually her signature,' Jim said reverentially, running his finger over the inscription. Leslie May Barry, messenger for Michael Collins and Patrick Pearse. He'd named his own little girl after her. Now the children were sent off to look for a video that Jim had made of the general. It would be good for me to actually see the man talking. He was a great fighting man, Jim said, but never a politician. The night after Bloody Sunday, in 1972, Jim had organized a meeting in Cork City Hall. Barry had stood up and said, 'It's not good enough that the Paras are sent out of Ireland, they must pay the price.'

He grinned. 'There was uproar. You see, he was a soldier to
the last.'

Now a thick tan file had appeared, whose contents were
spread open on the table before us. Letters, papers, an orange
booklet, price 2d, printed in the Charing Cross Road, entitled
Bombs – and their Reverberations. This was the first page of a
journal the general had intended to keep in gaol. Here was
the article in the paper on his death, 'The Passing of a Legend'.
And here was a letter from an American congressman who'd
helped get Jim out of gaol when he'd been held with his wife
at Heathrow under the Prevention of Terrorism Act. They'd
strip-searched Glynis in front of male officers and she'd only
just had a baby. 'That wasn't nice.' But the congressman
had put pressure on the British government and succeeded,
'where Jack Lynch couldn't'. Jim laughed. He was relaxing
now.

'If you ask what makes a Republican tick, Mark, it's very
hard to explain. But,' he gestured out of the window at the
rain, still lashing down outside, 'even now there's fellows out
there in the fields training. And it's cold, and it's raining, and
they're not doing it for any personal gain. It's for the love of
their country.'

He shook his head slowly and looked into the middle
distance. 'I don't know what it is. I've probably given most of
my life to the Republican movement. I could have been a
multi-millionaire by now.' Instead of which – he laughed – he
just had the one million. But Republican business had always,
would always, come first.

He'd started in 1956, when he'd joined the Fenian Scouts.
'From young boys we were trained' – he looked at me sideways – 'not brainwashed.' Out of forty or fifty scouts, only
four or five had carried on as 'very active Republicans'. What
this had meant in practice, Jim obviously couldn't tell me in
too much detail, but his commitment to the cause had been
such that even in the late 1950s, when support for the IRA
had been at rock bottom in Ireland, he'd been out on the
street, selling the Republican newspaper *An Phoblacht*. In the
1960s he'd been gaoled for selling an Easter lily. 'The money
would go to the IRA, so you'd be banned from selling them
without a permit.'

'They sought no permit to fight for freedom,' he intoned. 'We seek no permit to honour their dead.'

Jim's little boy Stephen had found the video. He stood beside us holding it proudly.

'As sure as day follows night,' his dad was saying, 'and night follows day, when the likes of me go, there'll be ten to take my place.' He looked down at his son. 'I'd pity the British soldiers in fifteen years time if it's not over then. He's so stubborn, this one.' If the goal of a united Ireland wasn't achieved by negotiations, the British would regret it, 'because the fight'll get dirtier. And the sorrowful tale about that is, more lives could be lost.'

We got up from the table and went through to the television, by way of a room where, starkly alone on the wall, hung the tricolour that had lain on the general's coffin at his funeral. As I stood there on the bare boards by the window, nodding and admiring, ten-year-old Stephen ran back in with a camera, snapped a flash photo of my head and shoulders. 'Got him!' he cried, and ran off, laughing, with his sister.

In the TV room the Mickey Mouse cartoon characters that the children had been watching were replaced by the shaky home video, in purplish monochrome, that Jim had made one day when General Tom Barry had called round for tea. There he was, an old man, sitting bolt upright in a square-backed armchair, while around him the eldest three of Jim's children squealed and played, much as the youngest three did around me now.

'Give Mr Barry a kiss now,' said Glynis, and the children lined up to pay homage to the old man. 'Hard to think,' said Jim beside me, 'that he planned an ambush with 104 men that wiped out 1,500 British.'

He was talking of the celebrated attack on the British forces at Crossbarry on 19 March 1921, when Barry and his West Cork Flying Column had successfully ambushed a convoy of nine military lorries and then fought their way out of an attempt to encircle them afterwards. At another of his ambushes, at Kilmichael, in November 1920, some of the Auxiliaries' bodies were found to have wounds that had been inflicted after death. (The first British officer on the scene after the fight said that though he had seen thousands of men lying dead in the course of the First World War he had never before seen such an appalling sight as met his eyes there.)

Tom Barry's accounts of this engagement don't mention this aspect, dwelling instead on the dreadful behaviour of the Auxiliaries in the weeks leading up to the ambush, 'driving into villages and terrorizing everybody. They'd beat people and strip them and shoot the place up, and then go back to their barracks, drunk on stuff they'd looted.' After the fight, which had involved, in Barry's account, the dishonourable trick of a false surrender, Barry's main concern had been for the discipline of his 'shaken' men. He'd drilled them in the road, which he describes as 'a strange sight, with the lorries burning in the night and these men marching along, back and forth between the blood and the corpses'.

Now, on the flickering screen, Jim conducted a rambling interview with the old soldier, going over – I might almost say gloating over – the famous old war stories.

'Did you actually march the men over their bodies?'

'I did.'

'Did you hear that,' Jim said, leaning forward excitedly at one point. '"I never had one failure."' He repeated the phrase, shaking his head slowly from side to side.

When General Barry had gone up to Dublin to meet Michael Collins he had, by chance, got into a carriage with a British officer. 'He was,' Jim chuckled, 'at that time one of the most wanted men in the country. Four times they searched that train, but because he was talking to a British officer they didn't question him.' Jim laughed delightedly.

'This is where he claims the watch,' he cried. Before our eyes his son was given the general's watch. Then the old man was joined by three women, Jim's young wife and two others. 'Tom Barry and his gun-runners!' joked Jim.

'Did they bring in guns from Europe?' I asked.

'No!' Jim replied with a wink.

On screen now there was solemnity as Glynis stood to sing the Welsh national anthem, then a song about the hunger striker Joe McDonnell. The children ran into frame again.

'There's the connection,' Jim pointed out. 'From the old to the new.'

Suddenly, in the manner of the best home videos, we'd jumped to footage of Tom Barry speaking at the monument that had been erected at Crossbarry. The video quality was dreadful, but you could just make out a few of the words. 'The same prayers are being said for the men who are being crucified in the H-Blocks ...' Barry was telling the crowd. 'Long Kesh ... railroaded by the same British ...'

Another man got up: 'The men who died on this spot died for the complete freedom of Ireland – not for the twenty-six counties,' he shouted.

When the tape was finished Jim showed me round the rest of the ex-convent. Here, in a corner by the stairs, was the board with the row of handwritten cards indicating which nun had lived in which room. If he turned the place into a hotel, or apartments, he told me jovially, he could clear half a million easily. But he wanted it to be a nursing home. He wanted to do something for his home village.

'Not bad,' he said as we stood outside, admiring the rows of white-framed sash windows in the long red brick frontage, 'for someone who once lived in the smallest house in the village.'

Now he wanted to show me his metal workshop on the quayside. He had fifteen people, sons included, working for him. These here were the balconies for a new hotel, those there were railings for a new roadbridge.

Outside stood my hire car, still dented from a rock I'd run into at Baginbun. While I waited for Jim to finish talking to his son I had a sudden idea. When he came out I was on my knees, trying to push the dent out from the inside. Seeing me struggle, Jim had a go, then, 'Drive it round here, up that ramp.'

Five minutes later the corrugated sliding door to the workshop was open and the whole lower bumper had been taken off, screw by screw, by Jim and his mate Sean, who'd appeared from nowhere. Oh hell, I thought, I've truly gone and lost my £200 excess now. How little faith I had. A few skilled hammer blows later the wing was all but back to normal, nothing that a dab of paint from the shop in the showroom couldn't fix.

Flat on his back with the final screw Jim laughed. 'Don't tell 'em two old Provos fixed your bumper, eh?'

Now, enthusiasm undiminished, Jim wanted to take me out to Crossbarry, to see the actual site of the famous ambush. So we swept round the south of Cork on gleaming new double-track roads, over the shopping centres and industrial areas, Jim pausing in his flow of Republican argument and reminiscence to point out railings, balconies and fences supplied by his firm.

Eventually, way out in the countryside, we found the monument. It was decorated with the crossed guns of the Irish Republican Army. A long inscription about the ambush concluded with the words: 'Pray God that Ireland in her hour of need will always have sons like these to fight and die for her.'

On our way back into Cork we stopped at the little country pub where Tom Barry had spent his honeymoon. Jim went up to the bar and spoke in a low voice to the beefy triangular-headed youth who was serving. Was his father around?

He was.

'Your father was a good friend of Tom Barry's,' Jim went on. The young man nodded, glancing sideways at me.

No, Jim wouldn't have a Guinness, he'd have an orange juice. He'd never drunk alcohol in his life, he told me, as we sat down on a bench by the wall. 'Careless talk costs lives,' he added.

As it happened we were sitting right by another interesting piece of history. A framed blow-up of a document relating to the execution of two rebels just over the road from here in 1798. 'This morning,' Jim read out, 'Sherry and O'Neil, soldiers in the Wexford militia, were escorted from this City to Ballyteague-hill . . .'

The good friend of Tom Barry's had appeared: lean, white-haired, shuffling towards us in slippers. No, he wouldn't have a drink, he was just about ready for bed. He carried with him, in a plastic bag, a faded, framed, black and white wedding photograph: 'Eamon de Valera at the wedding of Tom and Leslie de Barra on 22 August 1921.'

'These icons they carry!' I was thinking. The general was

next to Eamon de Valera in the front row. Countess Markiev-icz, who had started life as an Ascendancy child, one of the Anglo-Irish Gore-Booths, was at the end. The two men studied the picture with murmurs of approval. 'What I've been trying to tell this fellow,' said Jim, 'is how it's handed down, father to son.'

Our white-haired friend nodded, looked at me sideways, not fully meeting my eye at first.

''Tis all the same cause, all the time. I can't see it's any different now.'

'What I've been trying to get across to him,' said Jim, 'is what makes a Republican tick.'

Again came the sonorous, elegant, almost pre-formed reply. 'A cause like that is never dead. Every country likes its own freedom. 'Tis only that, you know.'

Driving back, I felt confident enough to ask Jim about the blot on his idealist's landscape, the people from whom I had sprung, the Unionists. What about their freedom?

Jim didn't think the likes of Paisley should actually *go*, but they'd 'have to learn to live as Irishmen'. As for the Ascendancy Unionists, Tom Barry had always said: 'You'll have to get the landed gentry out. They must be driven out.' If all the landed gentry, all along the border, were burned out, he had said, the British would sit up and take notice.

And nowadays, I asked (keen to find out whether these strictures would apply to, say, Adrian and Ruth in Stroove Castle).

'If anybody got ground wrong,' Jim said, 'it would have to be put back in the Irish nation.' No matter how long ago, if they had burned Irishmen out of their ground, they were going to have to go. Time made no difference. It was like those old Nazis being hounded out of retirement to face trial for old war crimes. 'I always cheer when I see that,' Jim said.

Back in Cork he was just going to take me quickly to see another fellow he wanted me to meet. We came off the main road and stopped in a cul-de-sac of small, modern, detached houses. A short, neat man in white shirt and red tie came to the door. He and his wife had American guests with them, and they were just back from a trip to England; nonetheless, I was taken in, down the corridor and into a small side room that was a shrine to Republicanism. One wall was entirely taken up with framed prints of the 1916 rising. Another had a Roll of Honour of West Cork's Heroic Dead.

Denis didn't approve of what the Provisional IRA leadership were up to either. The British had to go, completely. 'As long as there's any trace of the British,' he told me, 'even if they keep just one county, we'll fight.'

It was late. We arranged to reconvene at the Imperial Hotel at 8 p.m. on the Friday night. There was another man they wanted me to meet.

The Corncrake and the Skylark

So I stayed on in the city, getting to know the difference between the River Lee and Southern Channel, so that I no longer got hopelessly lost on the central island.

In steep Shandon I found elegant Georgian St Anne's, with its salmon weathervane and tall bell tower, which cost £1 to climb. On the first floor was a sheaf of simple tunes set out for numbered bells. Having performed a fine rendering of 'Abide with Me' and handed over the ropes to a pair of excited Japanese, I wondered how the inhabitants of the picturesque cottages all around put up with the racket.

I walked west through increasingly tatty streets to find the Cork Public Museum in Fitzgerald Park, another shrine to Republicanism. Among other trophies were a 1798 Commemoration Bowl; a casket presented by members of Cork Young Ireland Society to their president; Daniel O'Connell's rosary beads (not the last set I was to see); and a jewelled brooch presented by Robert Emmet to his sweetheart, Sarah Curran.

Alongside was a detailed history of the long struggle, from the Cork point of view. The visiting American or Australian backpacker could learn how, in 1920, the Black and Tans burned much of the city and murdered Thomas MacCurtain, the lord mayor and Commandant of the No. 1 Brigade of the Cork IRA, and how the next mayor, Terence MacSwiney, also a Sinn Feiner, had been gaoled for possession of a Royal Irish Constabulary cipher and had died in Brixton prison after a hunger strike lasting seventy-four days. His strike had been in protest at the British government's interference with elected civic functionaries; the government, meanwhile, had announced that it would not surrender to moral blackmail. Now where had I heard that again?

In the marbled foyer of the Imperial Hotel I waited on a red plush chair under a portrait of Michael Collins in full uniform. 'Who's that man?' asked a little boy in a frilly white shirt. His mother explained that he was a famous general from the past.

Denis appeared down the lobby, polite, smiling, but obviously nervous. Then Stephen had joined us, a younger man with tousled dark hair and round specs, which he kept pushing up the bridge of his nose. He, too, was visibly ill at ease. A teacher from a little town in the Cork countryside, he had driven up specially for the evening.

We found the 'quiet place' they sought at the far end of the empty bar, which ran into Clouds, the very restaurant where I'd had my 1970s-style pig-out three nights before. Even on a Friday evening they were both on soft drinks. My glass of Guinness made me feel almost decadent.

So what was this book about?

I explained that part of my intention was to get across a rough outline of Irish history, about which the English were, in general, largely ignorant. Few, for example, had even heard of Wolfe Tone.

Denis shook his head sadly. Even in Ireland now, he said, among the young, these great national heroes were not so well known. It was, he thought, due to the advent of television. When they'd been younger, he and Stephen, they'd been almost entirely concerned with local or national issues. The Irish newspapers were all they'd ever read. Then TV had come along, so 'we were opened up to the influences of the wide world'.

Now, Stephen said, the kids didn't even read newspapers. If they did, they were 'of the tabloid variety, not dealing with serious issues, just sport, scandal, or sensations of various kinds'. 40 per cent of the papers over here were from Britain anyway now. It was no wonder the youngsters knew so little.

A colleague of his had been driving some young lads from his school up into town and they'd passed the spot of the

Bealnamblath ambush. ' 'Twas there Michael Collins was killed,' he had said.

'Was it in a car crash he was killed?' one of the lads had asked. Stephen shook his head in bewildered amazement. 'And he was a reasonably typical product of his time.' But recent history wouldn't have been taught in the schools. It was actively discouraged.

'The idea for that being,' said Denis, 'that it was too close to the bone.' The Civil War was still too recent. When he and Stephen had been at school in the 1950s, history had stopped in 1916. You see, the chap next to him in class might have been from the opposite side of the fence. It wouldn't do any harm now, Stephen said, for them to know more. Politicians had been using the sensitivity of the subject as an excuse for too long. There was a dreadful lack of knowledge, particularly about the current situation in the North.

'That lack of knowledge,' said Denis, 'is deliberately propagated.'

But the Civil War, said Stephen, had been an awful thing. Both their fathers had been involved, on the IRA side.

'They weren't very proud of it,' said Denis. 'I think they were sorry that it had happened at all. When they mellowed in later years.' When they had met their opponents in the 1940s they would almost be fighting. But afterwards, in the 1960s, men who had fought on opposite sides had been reconciled.

'People that my father had shot at forty years before,' said Denis. 'He'd stand up and buy them a drink.' He took a long sip of his mineral water. 'But I'm very much afraid,' he continued, 'that it's going to repeat itself again with the current talks.'

Stephen agreed. Adams and McGuinness going to London to negotiate. It did look very much the same as Griffith and Collins in 1921. On that occasion, when the Anglo-Irish Treaty had been signed between the British government and the representatives of the Republicans who had been fighting the War of Independence, the President of Sinn Fein, Eamon de Valera, had stayed behind in Dublin. When Griffith and Collins had returned with the agreement, which they'd reached (under considerable pressure) with Lloyd George, de

Valera and other Sinn Feiners had refused to accept it. Bitterly divisive debates in the newly recognized Dail had followed, and the Treaty was only finally ratified by sixty-four votes to fifty-seven. The refusal of the defeated section to accept its terms, which included, controversially, an oath of allegiance to the British Crown, a British governor-general, the separate Northern Irish state (borders to be finally decided by a boundary commission) and continued British use of key Irish ports, led to the Irish Civil War of 1922–3, which split Sinn Fein and the IRA down the middle. The anti-Treaty forces, known as the Irregulars, were eventually squashed by the new Free State Government with a ruthlessness, some observed, that matched their one-time British oppressors. But once again in Irish history, nothing was ever simple, for it was the pro-Treaty Collins who died in ambush at Bealnamblath, and the anti-Treaty de Valera who lived to set up Fianna Fail, become Prime Minister and, eventually, President.

'I hope it won't happen,' Stephen said now, with a sad, thoughtful shake of his head. 'But I'm afraid it will happen.' Adams and McGuinness would sign a partial solution. Then you'd have the diehards, and Adams would turn out to be a second Collins. In his view, any settlement short of a united Ireland would only last for a few years. 'That's my honest belief.'

Denis agreed. Anything less and the Republican trouble would still continue. They were talking about it almost as if it was an intractable problem created by someone else. But then, 'If the people of this generation,' Stephen said, 'accept anything less than a united Ireland they're betraying past generations. And future generations. Have the people living now the right to decide for all those who have gone before, and all those yet unborn?'

'I hate to say that we'd have more bloodshed in the North,' said Denis, slowly.

'Which you would support?'

'Reluctantly. Reluctantly. Because it would still be unfinished business.'

But what, I asked, about the Unionists. They were on the island, one million of them, and they wanted to stay British. You couldn't deny them their aspirations.

'The Unionists,' said Stephen, 'say they were part of the United Kingdom, and then they say they're Irishmen as well.' The problem was that they'd never integrated into this country they'd been put into. 'The thing is this,' he went on. 'They're always being told there is a place for them in this country. I'd agree.' There *was* a place for them.

Nobody was asking them to leave, interjected Denis.

'And if there was one government,' Stephen continued, 'ruling the thirty-two counties, they'd have huge influence. How many seats would they have in an all-Ireland parliament? I could see them producing fifty at least. They could hold some key ministries . . .'

Actually talking in practical terms about that promised land, a united Ireland (as opposed to the slogan that he'd lived with all his life), Stephen was visibly excited. Having removed his steamed-up glasses, he leaned closer, hands windmilling to make the point.

'The other thing is, they'd be allowed to keep their identity. In one sense it would defuse the situation. If the Unionists would come in we'd bend over backwards to accommodate them. In fact, if we had the united Ireland we could sit down and have meals with them. If it were pointed out that we're not trying to dominate them. They probably have a legitimate point there. But we're *not* trying to.'

Denis brought up – as Father McCabe of Enniskerry had done – Rossnowlagh in Donegal. 'There's an Orange march there every year, watched by thousands of Nationalists, and nobody interferes with that.'

The other point, he said, the Unionists were always making was that the Protestants hadn't been treated well in the South. But no fewer than two of the presidents of the Irish Free State – Douglas Hyde and Erskine Childers – had been Protestants. And that was from a 3 per cent Protestant population. And there had been umpteen Protestant deputies.

So what about the Protestant gentry, I asked, and Jim's opinion that anybody 'who was on the wrong ground' should be moved. Oh, Denis chuckled, he thought Jim was being a bit hardline there. 'If they behave themselves, they'd be OK.'

Even the Duke of Devonshire, in Lismore?

Yes, he'd be OK. And they had no objection at all to individual British people coming to live here.

Stephen was nodding thoughtfully. A large part of the problem, he said now, was the attitude of the Free State government. 'We always blame the British, but in a way we should blame our own government. They should be more assertive. Quite honestly, the British fought their corner well.'

'The government,' Denis agreed, 'which is supposed to be our voice, has done sweet damn all . . .'

Bertie Ahern, Stephen said, had recently said that the aspiration for the united Ireland was still there. 'But they're putting it all the time on the long finger . . .'

'Even commemorations,' said Denis. The government positively discouraged the remembering of the Civil War anniversaries. 'The likes of Stephen and myself have been involved in committees that defied the thinking of the Irish State . . .'

'The thinking is, that there's a connection between that and what's happening in the North . . .'

'They're dead right . . .'

At one commemoration Stephen had applied for shots to be fired over the graves. The minister at the time had refused. It was too similar to the North. But this was wrong, Stephen said. In every country you would find commemoration committees.

'You observe your Remembrance Day,' said Denis. 'And rightly so, and rightly so.' In Devon, where he and his wife had just been for a summer holiday, for example, even in the tiny village he'd been staying they'd had a monument to the British dead. 'And it was lovely to see, and yet we're half ashamed to do it here. Officially.'

'We're a peculiar race in that respect,' said Stephen.

And then, quite suddenly, the conversation had turned to birds. Wasn't it sad, said Denis, how you no longer heard the song of the corncrake in Irish fields. He had heard it only last week in Devon. And the skylark – when did you hear that now?

There were only a couple of places, Stephen agreed, where you could hear the skylark now. In fact, he'd heard it recently on the way to Dublin.

Had he? Now where was that?

''Twas just outside Dublin, on the motorway. 'Twas on the radio.'

Came the gentlest of Irish chuckles from the IRA hardliner.

8

Puck

Opposite me, on the train from Cork to Killarney, sat a crazed-looking young man with eyes that met mine and held them, but offered no expression at all. I looked away. Outside, in the empty green countryside, stood a ruined tower on a hill.

After a while the young man brought out a roll, which I could tell he was eating slowly with his mouth wide open. Trying hard not to look up, I looked up to find his blank stare fixed on me above a mouth full of half-chewed white food. Jesus. What else did he have in that bag of his? It was a relief to escape into the midday sunshine at Killarney.

The little town was crowded with tourists, many in bright green baseball caps with messages in Gaelic on their brims. What they said was anybody's guess. 'This man knows no Irish,' perhaps, or 'I am an eejit from Minnesota'. Having narrowly avoided purchasing a Celtic love flute in one of the numerous 'craft' shops, I headed off to my rendezvous at the Great Southern Hotel.

Astrid, the producer of the radio programme I was here to present, was slumped with a gin and tonic on a sofa in the splendid foyer. She was, she apologized, exhausted. She'd been doing a vodka-tasting tour of Poland with Vitali Vitaliev and had barely had time to *turn round* before flying on here.

I did a double-take. She was a breath of London air and London preoccupations in my slowed-down traveller's mind-set. The quaint traditional fair we were going to – where they crowned a goat and hoisted it fifty feet above the town square – was suddenly 'a piece'. The questions they'd been framing in the BBC office for me to ask the locals seemed alarmingly metropolitan and cynical. 'What makes a good goat?' They'd all been laughing their heads off about that one.

There was a little mix-up with the hire car. The girl at the reception desk hadn't managed to pass the message to the Avis man that we'd moved from the foyer to the bar. For Astrid, it was incompetent and annoying. Then on second thoughts, and second drinks, all very Irish.

Right, having waited so long we were going straight out there to have lunch with some local dignitaries. No, it didn't matter that I was unshaven and still wearing the T-shirt I'd run through Cork in this morning. We didn't have time to go to where we were staying. It would be 'really great', Astrid said, charmingly but firmly, to get some stuff 'down' today.

I'd been uncertain about doing this programme at all, worried that it might somehow interfere with the 'authenticity' of my journey. But arriving in the crowded little room above the pub, with the windows open to the fast-flowing river outside, I appreciated the upside. The BBC microphone was a magic wand that threw a place open to you. How else would I have been sitting here, dressed like a backpacker, at the same table as the Puck Fair's chairman, the Guinness representative and the Irish Minister for Justice, no less?

Opposite me was the managing director of the local Japanese pharmaceuticals factory, which was, he told me, one of the two major employers in the town. The other was FEXCO, a large financial services company, which handled the cashback business for Harrods and the Bank of Scotland among others. In the era of IT, Killorglin was no longer merely a sleepy agricultural Kerry town. We were just getting on to this being the shape of the future and how great it was that children now had a prospect of staying in the area, when the chatter hushed and it was time for a few post-prandial cracks from the Minister for Justice. Then the handing out of awards in the shape of pottery goats by the Puck Queen, Breda, as Celtic-looking a ginger-curled twelve-year-old as you could hope to find. Finally, a jig by two more little girls who'd been fidgeting round the corner by the bar all lunchtime. They flew around the room on pointed toes, in deep blue velvet dresses embroidered over with a gorgeous kaleidoscope of multi-coloured darts.

Presently we were outside, standing by the river with Declan Mangan, the chairman of Puck. Astrid had found him comic and irreverent on the phone from London; now, faced with the microphone, he'd switched into formal, not to say pro-motional, mode. The lovely green ranges behind us were Macgillicuddy's Reeks, Ireland's highest mountains. The river that rushed so attractively under the eight arches of the old stone bridge was the Laune, which flowed from the Lakes of Killarney and down into Dingle Bay. 'You couldn't have,' Declan told me, 'a more romantic place for a setting for a town.'

Nobody quite knew how Puck had come into being, but it was probably a mixture of a pagan and a Christian festival. It had certainly been going since before 1615, when the local landlord, one Conway, had got an official charter from King James I for the fair that was already in existence.

As chairman of Puck for many years, and, in the winter, Killorglin's perennial pantomine dame, Declan seemed more practised at interviews than me, rookie radio presenter that I was, hurriedly getting used to the fact that I needed to nod rather than go 'mm' and 'yes' as you usually do. 'You said "this is",' said Astrid tactfully. 'Maybe it's nice to say, "I'm with." No, you don't have to do the whole river bit again, just say "I'm with," and I'll edit it in.'

Declan smiled gracefully. 'And I hope that your programme will make wonderful listening for the world at large,' he concluded, putting us, in the gentlest possible fashion, firmly in our places.

Having interviewed one key personality of the fair we were now off through bunting-bedecked Killorglin town to talk to another. Frank Joy, the Official Goatcatcher. If only we could get past John Mulvihill, the landlord of the Red Fox, who was eager as anything to promote, not just his pub (conveniently situated on the Ring of Kerry) but the Kerry Bog Turf Museum, a cluster of old whitewashed stone cottages that John had gathered together 'to keep alive the traditions of our ancestors'. There was a traditional turf smoking in the grate, and at the rough wooden table were a traditional white enamel plate and mug. 'It was,' John told the radio audience, 'from little houses like this that way back in time Ireland got its name as the island of saints and scholars. I felt that there was so much progressiveness in the country that it would be nice to hold back a bit, put these houses up as a show, the past has such an important part to play in our future.'

Indeed. And the very finest of three-course meals is to be found at the Red Fox afterwards.

In wider Ireland, the Kerryman is the butt for the kind of jokes the English make about the Irish, the Americans make about the Poles, the Australians make about the Tasmanians. 'Did you hear about the Kerryman who climbed on the roof of the pub? He'd heard the drinks were on the house.' And so on. But this was way wide of the mark. Far from being slow or stupid, the beady-eyed Kerrymen we were to meet around Killorglin proved actively to be the opposite. So 'cute' (to use a Kerry phrase) they'd leave the average London wideboy standing.

Astrid was an old hand at this, slicing through the tourism puff to get to what she needed. Having let John have his sadly-to-be-cut say, we moved swiftly on to the man we really needed to talk to, his friend Frank. Now this was more like it! Soon we were speeding down a back lane and into the lushest of Kerry fields to inspect the future monarch of the fair, a handsome two-tone beast with splendidly curving horns; to embark on those questions that had caused such hilarity back in the striplit cages of Portland Place.

'So what makes a good goat, Frank?' I heard myself asking, aware that Astrid's rapid nods and broad toothy smile were concealing the fit of giggles she would let free later in the car. Luckily, despite its Pythonesque overtones, it was a fair question, deserving of a sensible answer from Frank.

'A good coat. He's got a nice fur, a good pair of horns. And colouring, you know, age as well, he has to be old. It takes so many years to be a Head of State, or a king in other words.'

This would all edit down to a nice pithy introduction, suitably alien in Frank's richly lilting Kerry accent to entertain the breakfast-time listeners of Radio 4. Though being here now, with the breeze on your face, and the mountains right behind, it was you that was strange, with your big furry mike and metropolitan attitudes.

Prepared for charges of cruelty from the visiting townies, Frank was keen to tell us that he'd be personally looking after

the goat all week, before, on the last evening, taking him back
to the herd of which he was the leader.

'D'you feel sad when you leave him?' I asked.

'I do, in fairness, yes, I do.'

There was no guile about Frank. 'We don't see him any
more,' he continued sadly. 'He's never captured for a king
again, we move on to different areas.' And I was left ponder-
ing the paradox that the person directly responsible for whatever cruelty the poor goat experienced was the one who really
understood him best.

Astrid was at last satisfied. We were free to decamp to our
rooms in our very own Bungalow Bliss, two miles outside
Killorglin, one of a number of ordinary family houses opened
up for the duration of Puck. Sheila, our new hostess, had
blond hair in corkscrews, fingernails painted ten different
colours, and a high, singing Kerry voice that was hard at times
for us strangers to follow. But we were very welcome.

And this was her twelve-year-old daughter Jacqueline. 'Now
I've told her you're from the BBC and she's all excited about
it.' Did we know the people from Channel 5 Sport, Jacqueline
wanted to know. Not personally, Jacqueline.

We were up early the next morning. Astrid had a tight
schedule of soundbites to pack in, starting with the neighing
and whinnying and hoof-clattering of the horse fair. 'Wouldn't
it be great to have a camera here,' she cried, as we pushed
nervously through the animal throng, talisman microphone to
the fore. 'That man hasn't washed his neck for three days.'

The ruddy faces under flat tweed caps would certainly have
merited lingering footage. Now at last I knew what a cauli-
flower nose looked like. And Irish eyes are smiling? Forget it.
At Puck Fair they were bloodshot.

The old boys were much keener to make Astrid's acquaintance than mine. 'What's your first name again?' they'd ask
her, as I stood lemon-like alongside.

'Astrid.'

'*Ass*-trid, is it?'

'Yes. And Mark.'

'Mark, yeah. And what d'you tink of t'fair now, Ass-trid?'

'I don't exist,' she whispered, holding a finger to her mouth.
But to no avail.

Around one o'clock we stopped for a glass of Guinness and a grated cheese sandwich. Ass-trid loved the fact that the bar was full of old men and children. 'You don't see this in pubs in London, do you?' As she sat beside me, confessing to an unfashionable broodiness, an extremely plump woman in coloured leggings lurched up to us. Her hair was tied up in pink and yellow hair bands and she was holding a bunch of huge multicoloured balloons. 'One pound,' her lips mouthed extravagantly, but no sound came out. She was dumb.

Outside in the square, up on the Puck Fair stand under the huge Guinness banner, Declan, looking relaxed in a yellow polo shirt, was in full unstoppable swing. The sun was shining from a glorious blue sky and it was the biggest entry in the Bonny Baby competition they'd ever had. 'I've just had a word from the judges,' crackled his voice above the cries of the assembled crowd of tinies. 'They would like to compliment the mammies and the daddies ... very, very difficult to pick ...'

Getting thoroughly into Dimbleby mode, I was attempting, over this, to wax lyrical about the outfits. The matching dress and bonnet combinations. This contender (dribbling) in navy blue with white spots; that contender (pushing at Mammy's hair) in simple pink; this one (trying on Mammy's huge sunglasses) in a lime green that matched Mammy's daringly cut-away outfit.

Astrid tapped me on the shoulder, pointing out the row of young daddies at the back with the pushchairs. Perhaps I should just hand the reportage over to her. 'They're just so cute,' she added, excitedly. 'I bet they pick a Celtic-looking one.' Damn it. Not only was she more observant than me, she was psychic. The overall winner, Breda Fleming, from Midtown, was as Celtic as they come, with a flaming mane of curling ginger curls.

Down the street we went looking for vox pops. 'In Holland we don't have such events,' said a dry Dutchman outside the Bianconi Inn. 'Of animals getting crowned and married to a girl of twelve years old. So it's new for us.'

'We don't get anything like this in Britain,' said Brendan from Finchley. 'It's all theme jobs. But this is the real thing.'

'It's so vibrant,' said a Chinese-American lady. 'But you

worry when you find a thing like this. It's like a gem, but its own success may spoil it eventually.'

Down the hill there were stalls selling everything from Gerry Adams's autobiography to Spice Girls gift packs. In a display of colourful pots sat a gentleman in leather trousers and boots whose expansive white belly, framed by a sheepskin coat, was wide open to the sunshine. He was a Celtic potter, making exact replicas of Stone and Bronze Age pots for the National Museum in Dublin and the Ulster Museum in Belfast. He was also, it emerged, when we started discussing his 'Viking' leather shoes, a 'time traveller', which meant that 'there was no limit to where you can go, you can take a chance and go into the future, or you can go back and visit Ancient Egypt. Actually in about a hundred years' time things are really good . . .'

This was all wonderfully eccentric material for the programme, of course, but as I knelt beside him, eyes fixed seriously on his, lips tight against my teeth, not looking anywhere *near* Astrid, I wondered whether he was just a fabulously straight-faced pisstaker or if he actually believed all this stuff.

'D'you know what happened when the Normans landed in Waterford?' he asked now.

'At Baginbun?' I replied intelligently.

He ignored me. 'They were rough and ready, they didn't come to please anybody, they didn't come to scratch the local dogs behind the ear or borrow a pint of milk, they just *arrived* – 300 armour-clad knights and 700 Auxiliaries. The Viking and Irish citizens of Waterford said, "We're going to move these people off, they're not a friendly presence," so 4,000 of them went out armed to the teeth to dump these lads in the water. Well the Normans thrashed them . . .'

'And you saw this?'

'I was there at the battle. You didn't see what happened after?'

Or perhaps it's all true. Perhaps it's the rational consensus smiling at the weird that's in error. Perhaps if I threw aside my reservations and went up to New Grange and joined Iain in his time-travelling machine, a fifteen-inch-long ceramic Celtic boat ('with spirals in the front and back, which are the source of power, like outboard motors, when they start to run low on energy they grow extra tentacles and then you heave them over into the water and they become squid or octopus'), I too could meet the Normans, interview Hervey de Montemarisco in person, ask him in a one-to-one kind of a way whether he realizes he's the start of the 800 years of oppression . . .

Then again, perhaps not.

At five, the opening parade was gearing up in the little carpark opposite the fishery. Breda, the Puck Queen, was there, surrounded on her float by a gaggle of junior Fianna warriors, in turquoise and orange cloaks, richly decorated with plum and cream. Breda's older sister stood beside her, with King Puck's crown on a cushion.

'What are you going to do, Breda, tell us?'

'I'm going to crown the *gooot* . . .'

She's so excited she can hardly breathe. Next to her, the goat seems almost placid on his bed of crimson-belled fuchsia in the 'friendly cage' that's been designed by Frank's son Francis, and is so constructed, Frank explains proudly, that the puck is free to move about inside without being 'cuffed', as was always the tradition before.

Then there's the Kerry Rose (from the Rose of Tralee contest) who's the grand marshal of the parade; three beefy guys from the local sailing school hanging off a windsurfer; another bunch of studs, in yellow, from the Peak Fitness Multipurpose Sports Club; some girls in blue T-shirts with red bandannas on their heads carrying a huge portable radio; Killorglin Country Market, in an open horse-box containing a lady playing the harpsichord surrounded by geraniums; Vincent Prendergast, Building Contractor, whose van pulls a float full of cyclists in the Kerry colours of electric green and yellow; bagpipers from Newmarket, Co. Cork, in dark red tartan kilts; Morris dancers from Herefordshire, with blackened faces under top hats covered with feathers and ties.

'We're Welsh border Morris dancers,' they tell us. 'It's not your average hanky-wanking club dancing . . .'

'I've always wanted to know,' interrupts Astrid, 'what are the tattered shirts for?'

'It's to keep big wobbly women away because they're scared they'd have to iron them.'

'But you like big wobbly women, Dave.'

'This is true.'

But enough of this holiday ribaldry – we're off! At a lick down the Tralee Road, only to get held up on the bridge by an opposing jam of traffic, which includes tourist coaches, cars, tractors, horse-boxes, lone horses, small boys on bicycles. Under the massed criss-crossings of the Guinness and Smethwick's bunting the steep main street is five people deep on either side. Astrid and I, clutching our magic microphone, are marching right beside the parade and are actually now part of the parade.

Arrived in the main square, high above the crowd on the Puck stand, clever Breda welcomes her subjects in four languages, Irish, English, French and German. The crown, donated, as Declan now tells us, by a fan in Memphis, Tennessee, is lowered on to the bemused goat's head.

'Three cheers for King Puck!' shouts Declan. The crowd, packed in, children on shoulders, others watching from windows above, applauds enthusiastically. Then, under Frank's careful supervision, the new Monarch of Killorglin is raised up fifty feet to the tiny platform atop the four tall poles. 'They're used to heights,' Frank has told us. 'When they're on cliff tops, they're at home then.'

So now it's off to the pubs, each with its different crowd. At this one we've found at the top of the town the *craic* is mighty. There's a music session crammed in one corner of the bar (the band ranges from a little girl of ten squeezing the harmonica, to a boy of seventeen with a guitar); in another, a man with a leather waistcoat above a sweat-dripping naked torso throws his arms around a plump, motherly soul in a neat blue and green floral dress. His head slumps as he's overcome with inebriation. Here, in the middle, a visibly blushing teenage lad dances with an upright-backed sixty-something lady with tied-back grey hair.

Astrid has been trying to record background music and has got herself buttonholed by an Englishman with thick black-rimmed glasses who's in charge of marketing, licensing and merchandising for a British TV company. He gives me his card. He made a documentary about Puck four years ago, he tells me. Against the uproar, his voice is the flattest monotone as he succeeds in making the entire West of Ireland sound like a theme park for documentary makers. On Valencia Island there's a boatman called Des Lavell, who's 'a documentary in himself'.

Really?

'You know who comes here a lot?'

'No.'

'Ian Hislop.'

In her green crop-top Astrid is a liability. Now she's gone and got herself picked up by a tall engineer from Dublin who is visibly throbbing with energy having just got off the plane from Hong Kong. He bobs around her, his face one big welcoming smile, his talk an unstoppable patter. For a while he thinks I'm her boyfriend, that I've come over to stake my claim, then he realizes I'm just her colleague and gets absurdly keen. When she wanders off to record some more sounds of *craic*, his I've-just-crossed-the-world-and-now-I-can-do-anything stamina collapses into a wave of exhaustion. He's slurring his words as he tells me that his grandmother runs a pub in Ballykissdolphin or somewhere and if I ever happen to go there I must call in . . . it's the first place a mink whale ever got washed up on the beach . . . did I know how Puck had started when Cromwell's soldiers had arrived . . . the goat had come running into town foaming at the mouth . . . so they knew something awful was up and ever afterwards they've crowned him as a thank-you . . .

I wake to a poster of Joe from *EastEnders*. Where am I? Oh yes, Jacqueline's room.

Breakfast is ready on the table even though Sheila and her family were out till after three. Sheila insists on letting us have the main, front room of the house to work in. 'We're after having our breakfast in the kitchen,' she says. She clears the table of its cloth and brings in tea and biscuits.

Astrid wants to get out of the fair today, to do something contrasty – we got more than enough music and *craic* last night – so we trundle through horse-box-crammed Killorglin and out into another world. Barely five miles away, on the shore of moody Lake Carrig, there are a hidden string of elegant country house hotels, each with its fine or not so fine view of the lake and Macgillicuddy's Reeks behind.

Caroline had bought her place from an English judge who'd retired there with his wife, but during the hunger strikes of 1984 the IRA had turned up and poured petrol through the front door. The judge and his wife had escaped, but the place was burned out. Deeply shocked, he'd died within the year; his wife had returned to England.

After she'd shown us around the lovingly restored bedrooms, each with a different flower arrangement, and done a rather nervous taped interview about Puck (to be honest, she kept away from it these days; she was nostalgic for the old times, for the 'real' travellers and tinkers, in their colourful barrel-topped wagons), she insisted on treating us to 'a platter of wild smoked salmon' and cold Australian Chardonnay on her terrace. She was sorry, but she just couldn't eat farmed smoked salmon any more.

Down the road we escorted the magic microphone around another fine country house establishment. Yes, said Peter, the courtly owner, Caroline had bought that place off a man who was 'burned out'. He used the expression quite matter-of-factly, like an Englishman might say 'went bankrupt'. It was the action of 'local hotheads' and not popular roundabout, as the judge had done a lot for the area. But what could you do? You didn't want the hotheads harassing *you*. You'd certainly not want to get involved with speaking out against them or getting threatening phone calls, and then who knew what might happen next. So mostly people would just keep quiet about what they thought. Though, of course, they'd talk privately among themselves.

When we were finished, he invited us to dinner with his compliments. Oh dear, it was far too nice in these comfy armchairs by this log fire, with film theme tunes trinkling out of the CD, to go back into noisy over-crowded Killorglin. But we had everything we needed now, and next Saturday morning the Radio Four audience would get a thoroughly convincing impression of me having fun alone at a boozy Irish fair.

*

When Astrid had gone I stayed on at Sheila's. She was adamant that I use the front room to write. 'You're working,' she told me, as she moved the phone out into the corridor and made her husband go round the side of the house and through the front door to answer it. At hourly intervals she offered me tea, then, around lunchtime, a huge plate of lamb chops and vegetables appeared. 'I'm after bringing you a small bit of lunch,' she told me.

In the evening I wandered back up to the Fair. It was rather lonely without Astrid and the Radio 4 audience. Even in mid-afternoon there were music sessions going on in most of the corners of the pubs. Here was one in the street, a little children's band in a doorway; a boy of eight playing violin, two girls of six on squeeze box and flute, a three-year-old lead singer dancing beside them.

Up against the clear blue sky the goat looked almost sedated. How had he coped with the thunderstorm that had crashed around us last night? Did he know his ordeal was about to end?

Declan Mangan was still going for broke on the PA. 'And her goat won – sorry her *duck* won – the Puck Duck Race – I'm getting all mixed up here . . .'

The square filled up. The parade of floats reappeared. Breda was publicly congratulated. The goat was hoisted down and decrowned. The crowd dispersed, wandering away past the packing-up stalls.

'Fifty pence each to clean 'em up!' shouted a man with some fluorescent dangly things on sticks. The Spice Girls gift packs were reduced to £1. For a fiver you could buy a T-shirt saying, 'BEEN THERE, DUNNE THAT, BOUGHT THE TAOISEACH'.

I sat with a long cold pint of your only man outside the pub at the top of the hill. There was a tangibly gentle, released feel about the groups of people drifting past.

'It was the best *craic* of all . . .'

'The Guards were after taking her down . . .'

Here comes a young woman with a gold cross dangling over her ample bust, seven under seven around her, six of them with pink and white ice-cream smeared around their mouths. Then a young boy with a ball on a pink spiral cord; then a ginger-haired ten-year-old with two identical younger sisters in identical blue denim dresses. So much for the strange death of Catholic Ireland.

Did I know how Puck had started, asked a man next to me. There was this fellow who didn't realize that Cromwell had banned gatherings of more than four people and brought his goats to the fair. The locals thought he was defying Cromwell, so they hoisted the goat up a pole and danced around it . . .

At Sheila's invitation I hung on another day, writing quietly at the table in the main room. Outside, beyond the tiny patch of lawn and the bright pink wall, the grass and trees and swathes of purple and yellow flowers receded to the cloud-shadowed backdrop of the mountains, their jagged outline like the graph on a heart monitor.

Both Sheila and her husband were out working. Around two little Jacqueline knocked on the door.

'Would you like a cup of tea, Mark?'

'Well, that would be lovely, Jacqui.'

Five minutes later she reappeared.

'D'you take sugar?'

'I do. Thank you.'

Five minutes later she came back again, with a tray on which were teapot, milk jug, sugar and cup. 'Would you like a sang-wich?'

'Only if you're making one.'

Twenty minutes later, just as I was wondering if she'd forgotten, she tripped around the corner. She'd only gone out specially to fetch ham from the shop up the road.

9

The Foundling

The road west along the Iveragh peninsula, part of the celebrated 'Ring of Kerry', was not, unfortunately, at all like those roads pictured in the postcards and Bord Failte literature, blocked only by a 'traffic jam' of sheep. It was nose to tail with cars and tourist coaches. Over a hundred of the latter went round the Ring every day in the season, each packed with punters gawping through tinted glass windows at the undeniably gorgeous mountain backdrops on all sides.

Why couldn't they just build a huge audio-visual 'Ring of Kerry Experience' in Killarney, equipped with intravenous Irish coffee dispensers, Guinness drips and an Irish crafts hypermarket? This poor seaside track was never made for such a pounding. It was narrow, hilly and twisty, and the frequent road-widening schemes looked both pointless and self-defeating. Why widen a road so you could speed on to a narrower bit? And who wanted to journey miles to the 'wilds of western Ireland' only to find the same row of traffic cones they could get at home?

Ducking and diving through this traffic-jam-with-the-finest-view-in the-world were the poor cyclists, for whom you had to feel most dreadfully sorry. This was not the fantasy they'd bought at all. Rained on, weighed down by panniers, cut up by passing coaches, passing another of their kind every hundred yards or so – it was so sad it was funny. The faces on the tarmac slopes ranged from stoic young backpackers to the kind of bespectacled fifty-something you can be sure is taking a few days off from running an international company in Brussels, Munich or Chicago. As he puffs along, he's looking restlessly round at his holiday landscape as if it should somehow *yield* more.

Approaching Cahirciveen we all came to a total halt. Helen's Bakery, M. C. O'Shea, West End Video, C. O'Neill, Tom's Tavern. I wondered idly which of these were the Sinn Feiners. The town had polled handsomely for that party at the last election, and was, I'd been reliably informed, the local Republican stronghold. Then, suddenly, I'd taken a right turn and was off the Ring. The narrow lanes had reassuring 'No coaches' signs, and the hedgerows were even thicker with deep pink fuchsia and orange montbretia.

I was an hour early for my appointment so I stopped at a cosy-looking roadside B & B with a large 'Open' sign outside. The front door was locked, but eventually I found a side entrance and ventured in. It was an echoey, pine-tabled, farmhousey sort of place. Eventually a ridiculously cheerful ginger-haired man appeared, humming loudly. Could I have a cup of tea, I asked. No problem, he sang. And a sandwich? He'd see what he'd got in the fridge. 'Just get my bread out of the oven,' he cooed.

When I told him where I was going he sat down opposite me. Oh, Noelle was a lovely woman. A fascinating woman. A very clever woman. 'She'll baffle you,' he said, nodding slowly. She had the kind of brain that could do fifteen things at once. And her energy just *transferred* itself to you. It was incredible what she'd done in this little place. The woman was, in fact, responsible for bringing him down here.

His girlfriend worked at Noelle's Cill Rialaig gallery. A job had been advertised back in Dublin and they'd decided to go for it, move down here. He'd been a taxi-driver in the city for fourteen years and now he didn't miss it at all. 'I said to Avril the other day, "D'you miss Dublin?' and she said, "Not one bit."' He missed his friends, of course, and being able to collar them for a drink, but apart from that, no. Anyway, a bunch of them were coming down next week for the weekend.

And now, as a result, he was starting to appreciate art. 'In Dublin, if I'd seen someone standing back from a painting' – he scratched his chin illustratively – 'like that, you know, I'd think, "What an awful gobshite".' Now he was doing it himself.

There was a show at the gallery at the moment that was, what was the word, *sublimeral*. You looked at the pictures once and they were just bits of colour. Then you looked again and they were witches' heads or animals or faces. He jumped up and ran over to the corner of the room, returning with a circular *objet*. It was about ten inches across and an inch thick, bubbled-looking transparent blue plastic.

'See this,' he said. I prayed that he hadn't taken up conceptual art; that these swirling facets weren't meant to recontextualize my world.

He'd gone home recently and his mother had had it on the sideboard. 'I said, "Mam, this is lovely, where did you get it from?" "I made it," she replied. "You made it?"' He'd had no idea his mother was an artist. 'Yes,' she'd said, 'and I could make you another if you wanted it.' It was only a blue plastic fruit bowl she'd put in the microwave.

I'd already met Noelle Campbell-Sharp, the *éminence grise*, or rather *blonde*, of the Cill Rialaig project. I'd called on her at her gallery in Dublin, which showcased, and sold, the work of the artists who spent time at her brainchild, this remote retreat built in the ruins of a village that had been deserted since Famine days. Walking me round the eclectic range of paintings and sculptures, she had talked enthusiastically of the incredible atmosphere they had 'down there', the principle that there was no money in the village, that artists stayed for free, nothing was bought or sold. Some felt, she'd told me, as if they were returning to pre-money values, so were freed creatively, did amazing amounts of work in comparatively short stays. With the Dublin traffic rattling outside I'd been intrigued, had hoped I could take up Noelle's generous invitation to come and see for myself.

My curiosity had deepened as I'd heard a little about her. She had quite a reputation. She was mad; she was wild for younger men; she liked to dress up as Napoleon; she wore leather suits. 'Be careful,' went the gossipy line.

Now I found her snatching a hurried lunch in the oblong, glass-roofed tearoom-cum-restaurant that formed the centre of the gallery. She looked older than I'd remembered. Her face, under the white-blond mass of curls, was more lined, the blue-grey eyes were wearier. Perhaps it was just this dazzling Kerry light; glimpsing myself in the lavatory mirror I saw that I looked pretty haggard myself.

They were frantic, she said, preparing for the opening and a 'fund-raiser' tomorrow night. Nonetheless, soup spoon in hand, she launched immediately into a breathless continuation of the story she'd started in Dublin.

Creating Cill Rialaig had been like dropping a stone into a pond. There was a ripple effect outwards. First, the colony, which we'd visit later. Then this gallery and centre here, which showcased the work, not just of the international artists who stayed in the colony, but local Kerry painters, sculptors and craftspeople also. The third ripple was just in the planning stage. That would be the international gallery planned for Waterville, up the road on the main Ring of Kerry. The aim was to make it like the Tate at St Ives, housing a permanent collection of work from Cill Rialaig.

In return for their month's free stay, artists donated one painting each. Sometimes they gave more. Sergei Sviatchenko, the well-known Ukranian artist, had left six works. Aurelio Caminati, an Italian who was actually in Cill Rialaig at the moment, had left twenty. In one month he'd produced eighty-one paintings, and had still found time to fish every day. So many of the artists talked about this tremendous energy the place gave them – the landscape, the scenery, being away from the concerns of the world. The only rule in the village was that money was never mentioned. 'You don't sell a painting, you don't buy a painting, you don't pay rent.'

'So what do they live on?'

'We provide them with food for their arrival. We put stuff in the fridge. Then they're on their own.'

How did it work, I was wondering. Did they live off fish and gulls eggs? But Noelle was racing ahead. The one thing she wanted to do above all was make sure any development was brought about in a sensitive way. For so long this particular part of southwest Ireland had suffered from neglect. There were few people, so few votes, so no political action. When she'd first come down and built her holiday home here there'd just been this terrible air of neglect. 'I could feel this dreadful waste,' she remembered.

In 1834, she told me, before the Famine, the census of population had revealed forty-five dwellings housing 290 people. Now there were fifteen houses with forty-five people. 'Up

Mark McCrum

on Bolus Head it's even more poignant.' Once there had been ninety-nine people. Now there were just three, one in each house.

When she'd first come it had been as if there was 'this very faint cry, that wasn't being heard in the seats of power in Dublin. In a way I became an articulator of that cry.'

To give a practical example. The Ring of Kerry had become so saturated with tourist traffic that there was a plan to make a second ring. They were going to crash through the existing village and drive a road right over Bolus Head. 'Of course it would have given a wonderful view of the Skelligs, but it would have ruined this beautiful cul-de-sac.' She'd actually had to march the local councillors up there, on to Bolus Head, to persuade them not to do it.

The local community seemed to have really taken to the artists, although their view of them would have changed. When artists had first come to this area, perhaps in the 1960s, they'd been hippies. 'So they'd have seen them as poor people.' They'd left gifts of bread or apple pies on their windowsills.

Now, Noelle continued, the local people saw artists coming down in brand new Volvos and they realized that they were not so poor after all. So instead of apple pies they'd leave found objects, for them to use in their works. One of the artists had been talking to her about the extraordinary hospitality of the locals, the genuine feeling of wanting to *give* stuff. But it had, Noelle said, been a long tradition in these parts. When Isaac Weld had journeyed here at the start of the nineteenth century, he'd woken up every morning to find his tents surrounded with gifts of eggs and butter and poultry and fish. She had his book at home. I must see it. I was going to stay, wasn't I? It would be interesting for me to meet the artists who'd be coming to the opening tomorrow night, the blow-ins who lived in the mountains of Kerry.

In a moment she had another meeting, but she'd just quickly show me round. So we saw the long side gallery, where tall bog-oak sculptures awaited the opening of Bog Language the following night. Köning, the Dutch-born sculptor, was incredible, Noelle said. 'He yokes himself like an oxen to the bog-oak and just pulls it out.'

We saw the round main-gallery shop, packed with an extraordinary range of stuff, from Alexander Sokolov's *Female Relief*, a powerful set of buttocky curves in dark Kilkenny limestone, through John Shaltz's *Night Garden* (acrylic tree branches against a spooky moonlit landscape – was this the *sublimeral* stuff, I wondered), to cheerful landscape watercolours with titles like *Onto a Kerry Beach* and *Ox Mountain, Sligo*. In among these were ceramics, glass bracelets, flower paintings, candles, handmade cards and even a basketweave hare.

Noelle's promotional touch was everywhere. 'Gere is hung up on art,' read a cutting. 'Hollywood heart-throb Richard Gere has taken a shine to the work of Kerry-based artist John Shaltz. London-born John, living near Waterville for the past 20 years . . .' Beside it was a photo of 'world-famous singer Donovan', who'd opened Shaltz's exhibition.

The one thing Noelle did want to say was that the Irish Arts Council had been no help to her at all. Loud as she'd shouted, she'd got no funding from them. One of the big disappointments about the whole thing was that in three years they simply hadn't visited. They had come once, before the project had got going, and that had been that.

What she *thought* they thought was that here was somebody who had a reputation for being a shrewd businesswoman, and this colony was like a whim. She didn't have an 'arts background', so for her to even *attempt* to do something like this was almost unbelievable. But they'd been proved wrong. She now employed nineteen people, many of them locals.

And here was one of the artists in person! Felipe. An Italian from Genoa, in his early to mid-thirties, I guess, from the grey temples tingeing the thick black quiff, the two deeply-receding darts on each side of his forehead. He's carrying a large painting of a cow, which he's donating to the project. It's an impressionistic, semi-abstract study with a bright orange skeleton at its centre.

We stand admiring it. Why the skeleton, asks Noelle. Felipe shrugs. 'I imagined it like this, like a skeleton.'

Noelle is intrigued. In the little cottage where Felipe is

staying and working, cows would have once lived alongside
the people. 'They would have come through one way and out
the other.' Maybe Felipe has picked up some atmosphere in
there. 'The sacred cow, if you like.'

Now moustachioed Ger is here, offering to make a frame
for the picture. 'He couldn't believe it!' says Noelle enthusiastically, of Felipe. 'He thought it would have to be sent away.'
But Ger is one of the local employees she was talking about.
Starting with odd jobs, he's now moved on to being a frame-
maker.

Felipe is one of the lucky ones. They've looked after 140
artists to date at Cill Rialaig, and that is out of 3,000 candidates. As we sit for *lattes* and *espressos* in the café area, Noelle
hands round a thick file of letters and transparencies. 'This is
how they apply. Take a look. This is interesting,' she adds,
holding up a slide sheet, 'an application from Bangladesh.'

'How did you hear about this place?' I ask Felipe.

'From Caminati – the other painter.'

'These are good,' I say, finding a page of strong portraits by
a candidate called Kat O'Shea. But Felipe isn't impressed.
'This is academic style,' he says.

'Let's see,' says Noelle.

'Typical paintings from the academic school,' says Felipe
dismissively.

Noelle nods. 'This is probably why she wouldn't get through
the selection process – because it's too academic.'

I pick up another application. 'My work over the last decade
or so,' it reads, 'has addressed issues of language, memory and
anonymous commemoration, but in the last two years it has
related more specifically to issues and places of erasure related
to the Famine.'

Goodness! To be honest, I'm not sure I know what an issue
of anonymous commemoration is when it's at home. I wonder
how well that will do in the selection process.

I follow Felipe's battered Fiat out to the colony. The single
track road that leaves the little crossroads at Ballinskelligs gets
tattier and tattier as it pushes round the side of the mountain
which drops away steeply to the ocean on the left. It's grey
and windy today, but the view is still spectacular, the lower tip

of the mountainous peninsula sweeping left to right across the horizon. In the foreground the wide bay is strewn with islands.

Felipe's studio/living space is one of a cluster of ruined grey stone cottages, rebuilt and cunningly converted, so that what would have been the tiny cowshed of the dwelling is now the studio, with a clear glass roof supported by crimson girders. The central dividing wall has been knocked out, and the fireplace replaced with a stylish cast-iron stove with a polished chrome flue.

Felipe has a deep blue abstract set up on the easel.

'I am painting some dicks,' he tells me.

'I'm sorry?'

'I'm painting some *dicks*,' he repeats.

'Dicks?'

'Dicks, yes, you know, *dicks*.' He points them out, and I laugh as I see them, tiny blue and green male genitalia buried here and there in the abstract. They are crudely drawn, in every sense. As a teenager, he explains, he used to draw dicks all over his schoolbooks. Now he's incorporating the motif in his grown-up work.

One of the dicks appears to be wearing a hat. Is this symbolic? I refer to the artist.

'Is that a hat there, Felipe? On that dick?'

He comes out from the little kitchen where he's been brewing up some tea. 'What?'

'Is that a hat?'

'A hat.' He shrugs. Because it's an abstract, he explains, you can see many things. So maybe it is a hat.

'Did you go to art school?' I ask him.

No, he hasn't trained. 'I tried for a week but it was boring.' The teachers wanted to show they were artists. Before, in the old days, if a painter was good, a student would ask him to give lessons. Now the teacher had to be from the academy. 'So the circle is very closed.'

As we sit down to tea Felipe laughs and says, 'I would die to create a myth about myself, but I don't know how.'

We sit and sip Earl Grey and eat biscuits and dates. Felipe's cottage is well stocked with pasta, salad and even a large bottle of extra-virgin olive oil.

'Do they supply all this?'

'No. I got it from the supermarket in Cahirciveen.'

'You bought it?'

'Yes.' Clearly the artists have to think a little about money then.

Before I'd arrived, the phrase 'artists' colony' had conjured up quite a picture. Would they be with partners or alone? Were there terrible jealousies? Would one artist privately slag off the next or were they one big groovily supportive family, nurtured by the incredible atmosphere Noelle had talked about? But it turned out now that there were only two cottages complete and therefore only two artists in residence, Felipe and Caminati. Two's company, three's a crowd. It was the ideal size for a spite-free group; especially if they were rivals from the same North Italian city. When he'd first arrived, Felipe said, Caminati had been put out, cross; now they were the best of friends.

But before we went to visit him, how about a walk up to Bolus Head? It was a mile or two, but beautiful up there. We could just leave a note for Noelle and—

But it was not to be! For here was Noelle already, nosing round the corner in her big red car, with a young woman in a crimson jogging outfit beside her – Martha, an American friend.

'Oh you don't want to walk to Bolus Head!' Noelle told us. 'I'll drive you up there.' So we climbed, obediently, into the back seat and headed off down the increasingly scary, cliff-hugging road, with Noelle giving us a non-stop guided tour. That was the concrete sheep dip that one of the artists had wanted removed, it was so ugly. But then another had said, 'He's got to do his thing'. So anyway, they'd decided that next time he dipped his sheep they were all going to be present, make it into an 'event'. Maybe put some dye in the dip, dye them all orange.

This cluster of ruins was Upper Cill Rialaig. There was a stone cross in the bracken there somewhere, marking a ruined monastic settlement. But look at the field patterns on the hillsides. You could see the devastation left by the Famine. These three houses at the top here were all that was left. This one at the end had been featured in a photo-book called *A Day in the Life of Ireland*. Had I seen it?

Back down the hill the celebrated Caminati was, fortunately, in. He was a dapper little man, with flowing white hair above a dark jacket and neat bow tie. He was working patiently away in the clear north light, on a piece that featured a slice of Irish log mounted on a canvas. This he had collaged over with variously painted paper.

Ah, Martha! Where had she sprung from? Unable to speak a word of English, Caminati greeted her with gestures that enthused his meaning.

'What's he say?' asked Martha, with a pleased smile.

Felipe smirked. 'He is saying how beautiful your breasts are.'

Martha jumped back. 'Aw!' Then laughed loudly.

'You're just a tit and bum man, aren't you, Caminati!' cried Noelle. 'Look!' She reached for one of a row of sculptures on a nearby shelf, of the woman Caminati had brought with him the last time he'd come to the community, who had clearly been amply endowed with both of these features. 'He's just a tit and bum man.'

Noelle's house was high on the mountainside, a row of four ruined cottages that had been knocked into one splendid holiday home by the architect Alfred Cochrane. Noelle showed me to a 'minstrels gallery' above the dining room on which was a huge double bed.

Back through the house, beyond the drawing room with its loungey sofas, and the 'sky room', where the original stone walls were the inside surface of the house, the last of the ex-cottages was the 'pub' Noelle had talked about. There were real beer taps serving Guinness from a barrel. There were bottles of red wine on a long wooden table. There was a smouldering log fire in a big slate fireplace. On the walls were framed maps and old photos of the area. But it wasn't really a pub because all the drinks were free.

It even had a name, the Anchor. It was called that, Noelle explained, after a famous shebeen in Cahirciveen, where Brendan Behan used to drink. The landlady, pictured in a photo on the wall with an inebriated-looking Behan, had given her permission to use that name (though why you needed permission to call a room of your house 'The Anchor' wasn't clear).

Felipe was doing supper. While he got going in the kitchen, Noelle and I sat sharing a bottle of red wine. Or two. Martha came back and forth. Then Caminati joined us, an ever-polite, graciously smiling, non-English speaker. Noelle talked twenty-nine to the dozen, about Cill Rialaig, her wider ambitions for the project, the big fund-raiser tomorrow night, herself. The myths started to deconstruct.

She did, it appeared, genuinely have an interest in Napoleon. One of the rooms in this house was a Napoleon room. The interest had started because she had been an 'attic child', spending all her time in the loft reading. There were all these books up there about Napoleon she'd got interested in, 'this little man who conquered Europe'. As a young woman she'd taken *Irish Tatler* and made it into *IT* magazine. *IT* . . . it. She'd done things that people weren't doing then, twenty-five years ago, certainly not in Ireland. Why shouldn't men wear skirts and be feminine? So she'd put a heterosexual man, in full make-up, on the cover of *IT*, in the early 1970s. Now everyone was doing such things.

She'd eventually sold her magazine group to 'a man called Robert Maxwell', but she had, unfortunately, only got an advance. When it emerged that that was all she was going to get and she realized how much money she'd been swindled out of, she'd come down here, to the country, to think things through. And that's when she'd started to question all the morals of that money-based world in which she'd previously been involved. It had been that mood that had been the inspiration for Cill Rialaig and the rule that artists didn't talk about, or use, money.

As we drink more (get more 'jarred' in Noelle's phraseology), I sit there looking into these big blue-grey eyes and think, 'You are one complex subject, Noelle.' For under the blarneying, go-getting side, there's this vulnerable, affectionate side to her too. She wants you to like her, approve of what she's doing. She reveals things to you, becomes your friend. 'I feel I know you well enough to show you this,' she says now, bringing over a huge profile of herself from the *Irish Times*.

She's always wanted to be a writer and artist herself. She

dives off and returns with a cutting from a magazine she edited when she was just eighteen. It's a story in Dublin dialect, and why am I surprised that it's good? The sort of thing that if an eighteen-year-old showed you, you'd say, 'Stick at it, you've got real talent.'

At one point during supper out slips the phrase, 'my passion for younger men'. I shift in my seat and catch Felipe's eye. He smiles. Her first husband, the English photographer Campbell-Sharp, was younger; as was the boyfriend who followed him, and died tragically of a heart attack at the age of twenty-nine. Her current boyfriend is in his early thirties, almost twenty years younger.

Later, she tells me that I really ought to get to meet some of the local Kerry people, listen to their stories. 'But the only way they'd really accept you would be if you were my lover,' she says. She's joking, of course.

At around eight, two comely young women, Angela and Dervla, arrive from the Dublin gallery. 'Go and get your glad rags on and get *out* there,' cries Noelle. With barely time for a welcoming sip of whisky after their seven-hour drive, they're off down the lane again, dolled up in evening gear, to the famous golf club round the bay in Waterville, which will be packed with prosperous punters who have to be lured to the opening of Bog Language tomorrow night.

We're still boozing and chatting when they get back at two, giggling triumphantly at their snaring of a string of likely buyers. The flickering *craic* ignites again. At three the phone rings. It's the sculptor Sokolov, seemingly suicidal in Cork. Noelle counsels him for a while, then slams down the phone. He may be about to top himself, but that's no way to talk to her. The phone rings again. And again. Until with each new call we're taking turns to talk to Sokolov, his unhappiness, serious or not, turned into a party game. He's now threatening to drive up and see Noelle in person.

Then there's silence. It has all been a great joke, is still probably a great joke, but what, says a tiny serious voice inside my inebriated brain, if he really has killed himself?

*

In the morning it seemed best to make myself scarce. Noelle was in a white towelling dressing-gown, hair up, shouting orders into, it seemed, several telephones at once. The Dublin pair were charging around in tight jeans with sheaves of paper and cups of coffee. Outside the cloud had cleared and the view down over the panorama of scattered islands on the wide, sun-dazzled sea sang of every landscape cliché ever used by a hung-over travel writer.

I treated myself to a medicinal brunch at the gallery, then headed off up the long lane towards Bolus Head. Felipe was out, doubtless doing in-depth studies of the anatomy of cows, so I parked the car outside his cottage and continued on foot. There was nothing up there but sunshine and breeze and the trickling of water from the hidden streamlets that flowed down through the peaty hillside. Turning a corner, I found an eight-year-old girl feeding a sheep with a milk bottle. It was her pet, she told me.

The man who lived in the house from the photo-book was out in his garden but didn't greet me. The sign at the end of his drive said 'Privit', and he'd clearly had enough of cheery international walkers wanting to bond with a real native. I skirted up through the tussocks in the company of his two bounding collies to the very top of the great promontory that was Bolus Head. Only it wasn't. Bolus Head was stretched below me, a good half mile further on, etched grey against a sea that looked like the silver floor of a huge open-air disco, dappled with 300 separate pools of light, receding ever smaller to the horizon. Just below this, two steep blue-grey silhouettes, a pair of faery castles on the sea, were the Skellig islands.

Whatever you thought of the colony and gallery, you had to take your hat off to Noelle for preserving this view.

The *éminence blonde* had not yet arrived when I appeared at Bog Language that evening. My companion was the great Caminati, whom I had found pacing up and down her house in bow-tie and velvet jacket. He had no English, I had no Italian, so we waved straws of goodwill at each other in appalling French. Yes, he had *travailled très bien aujourd' hui*. He was *content*. And me, too, *après un – une – un promenade magnifique à Bolus Head* …

We strolled around the sculptures. Bog Bird, Stalks, Lady in High Heels were all tall arrangements of polished bog oak, some on marble stands. *Sign Language (no. 1)* demonstrated more traditional skills, a series of hands with different gestures – two fingers, one finger, a clenched fist – all carved from a single chunk of yew.

'*C'est bon*,' said Caminati.

Unable to communicate my complex reaction, I nodded. '*Bon*,' I replied. We smiled.

Ger the frame-maker came to join us. He stood beside Caminati and smiled. 'We can't exchange a word,' he said. 'But we understand each other perfectly.'

I was whisked away by one of Noelle's gallery assistants to meet Pieter the artist. He was Dutch, as tall and lean as his sculptures, with the addition of a little half-beard.

Could he explain *Sign Language (no. 1)* to me, I asked. Of course. It was about the Northern peace process. He had started it during the first ceasefire – that was the two-fingered peace salute on the left. But then had come the bomb in London – that was the finger up. Then the fist; and the empty hand outstretched; and the finger nervously touching a thumb; and the thumbs-up.

Of course. Now I liked it unreservedly.

But here was Noelle! Blond curls down, power-dressed in a blue satin number with padded shoulders. 'Mark McCrum!' she cried, embracing me warmly. Then, before I could reply, she'd shot off. I was left nodding at a pair of grey-haired blow-ins, he from Belfast, she from the north of England. They were potters, and David had nothing but praise for Noelle. They might have had their disagreements (indeed he'd once had a *dreadful* row with her), but she was the only one who could make a place like this happen. Truly. There was some young girl over from Cornwall, looking to see if the same thing could be done over there. 'You need to find another Noelle,' he'd told her.

On cue, the room hushed. Noelle was before us, admitting to particular pleasure in introducing Dr Joe Carr, the distinguished amateur golfer, to open the exhibition. He had brought some of his associates over from Waterville and he just loved Pieter's work; the Dutch government had commissioned

Köning to do sculpture outside their wonderful public buildings, he told us, and the people of Kerry should be very proud.

But Noelle wasn't going to relinquish the microphone that
easily. 'People often ask me this question, why, why do you
allow yourself to do it? It's an embarrassing thing,' she told
us, 'to say that you do something for love.' But it *was* for love,
and it wasn't just the people here. '*You*, but it's love for
people like Sean' – she smiled at one of the flat-capped locals
– 'I want them to share in something that is time-defying . . .'

Before she'd finished, twenty minutes later, I had been
presented to the mixed throng of artists, golfers and locals, as
had Felipe and Caminati. Why was I so English and bashful?
On the mention of his name and work Felipe strode proudly
to the front of the crowd, and stood there like a preening
goose.

Martha and Angela were driving over to Waterville for dinner.
Would I join them? I was all set for a merry evening *à trois*
but then, well well, who should be here but Noelle, now well
away and very touchy-feely. We arrive at Waterville, and now
Noelle wants to show me the site for Phase Three, the
international gallery. It's an absolutely terrific location right
on the front, looking out over the bay where, now, in this
windy ten o'clock twilight, huge charcoal-grey clouds race
across the oyster sky.

'It reflects the four elements,' cries Noelle, into the buffeting
gusts, as rain starts to spatter her headlamp-lit cheeks. 'The
wind to drive its generators the sun to illuminate its halls the
local earth to build its walls the sea its moat and all that kind
of shit,' she adds in one breath.

Then we are being shown into the Huntsman, which is the
finest fish restaurant in Kerry, or Ireland, or Waterville anyway, run by a short, dark-haired gentleman in black tie who,
although he is full, absolutely appreciates that he must find,
somehow, a table for Noelle.

We have a fine meal – oysters and fresh bass and three
bottles of Sancerre – and then, oh my God, it emerges that
none of the ladies has any cash or indeed credit cards or
cheque books on them, so I'm having to be a gentleman and
pay for the whole thing. Of course, Angela and Martha will

pay me back tomorrow. 'Thanks, Mark,' says Noelle. It's £150, but *pff*, what's that among friends? Especially in this community, where you get freed up creatively because the rule is you don't talk about money. Shit, what am I being so mean about, Noelle's already put me up for two nights, I can just kid myself that her house is a ferociously expensive hotel.

We sail on to the Butler Arms, and mysteriously some cash appears, which isn't mine, which is a relief. The bar is packed with prosperous golfers. Everyone is buying everyone else drinks and there's money just lying around on the side shelves by the bar. I contemplate helping myself, just to redress the balance, but decide that that really wouldn't be good form at all.

'This bar is wall-to-wall millionaires and multi-millionaires,' shouts Noelle in my ear. The red and white pinstriped shirt fellow who is singing now is one of the richest Irishmen in the world, his company's just bought Sandy Lane in Barbados, they own London City Airport . . .

'And I think to myself,' croons this gentleman into the microphone by the piano, 'what a wonderful world!'

By the time we get to 'The Fields of Athenry' the *craic* is beyond mighty. There's a huge, inebriated joy in the place. There are smiles everywhere you look. And tears from the golfing millionaires, whose ancestors, 150 years ago, would have been cursing the blighted potatoes in these very fields that are now fairways, as the British ships laden with corn and cattle continued to sail on to the mainland.

'Yeehah!' they're shouting now.

'She'll baffle you,' the man had said, and he was right. You never quite knew what facet of this extraordinary woman was going to be revealed next.

Crawling back from a long walk the following afternoon, I found her brightly entertaining two genteel couples from Cork whom she'd got chatting to in the gallery.

'Where *does* she get these people *from*?' muttered Martha, heading through to the kitchen. But it turned out they were architects. Noelle wanted their opinion of the plans for Phase Three, the Waterville Gallery.

'You have *such* enthusiasm,' said one of the very polite wives, sipping wine at the long table in the pub.

'Yes, but I can be an awful bitch sometimes,' Noelle replied, laughing.

When they'd gone she suddenly swung into confessional mode. She had been a foundling, it emerged, born on Christmas Day in Wexford, given away on St Stephen's Day, fostered, then adopted by another family. Once she'd realized this, she told me, learned that she was, as it were, a cuckoo in the nest, she began to feel a burden on those people and she wanted out. So though her Reverend Mother had been 'exceedingly mad', she had left school at fourteen. She had just had this total eagerness to *get out*, into the great university of life, which teaches you, of course, to use your wits, and you learn the behavioural sciences, you have to study people more, you have, in fact, to get by, to survive.

When she talked about her real parents being dead, there were tears, and, sitting over from her with my notebook, I felt suddenly very sorry for her. I felt like going over to her and holding her, but perhaps that would have sent out the wrong signal and I'd have ended up trussed up in leather in the Sky Room dressed as Josephine.

I wasn't going to mention this moment of intimacy, when she appeared so lost before me for a moment, and I felt in a flash that I understood her powerful and dynamic restlessness. But half an hour later she was making light of her own tears with Martha, sending herself up at the very moment I'd started to feel a serious empathy for her.

As we talked on, it seemed that she was much more of an Irish celebrity than I'd realized. Now she was regaling me with stories of how she had outraged an audience 'full of feminists' on Gay Byrne's famous *Late Late Show*. Another time on TV she'd been asked what she'd do if she was Minister for Health, and she had said she would prescribe a glass of champagne to everyone over fourteen. 'And ever since then, when I walk into shops, people say, "Are you Noelle Campbell-Sharp?"' Then they either berated her or congratulated her. Another time she'd had to judge a music competition and there'd been this really rough-looking band of *gurriers* and she'd held up her 1 card with her 10 card ('you know 101'), and she'd said she was doing it because she was worried she might get beaten up if she didn't give them a good mark. The uproar there'd been about that! The Guards had had to be called to escort her back to her car after the show. There were photos of her in all the papers, with two huge policemen on either side.

'But you just do that, don't you, because they invite you on, and you want to do something to liven it up.'

10

The Truth Ever Dawning

The famous Rose competition, the taxi driver who drove me into Tralee told me, was supposed to be more about personality than looks. Last year one of the judges had stood up in front of the assembled guests and said, ' 'Tis not a beauty contest,' and some wag from the back of the tent had shouted, 'We can see that.'

On my last day in Killorglin, Sheila's husband Michael had taken me aside and told me that Tralee was 'awful dangerous now'. There'd been a murder at last year's festival, a man had pulled a woman down a lane and knifed her, and then there were muggings and stabbings, and it was mainly because of the drugs. So as I headed out of my hotel and down Tralee's narrow main street, I looked cautiously around me. The usual loud music rang out from the pub doorways, and there were a number of rather over-refreshed jaywalkers, but it was hardly Alphabet City.

In a narrow town house opposite the Festival 'Dome' (a huge plastic marquee by the main road out of town) I found the press office. Liam, the press officer, had a grizzled salt-and-pepper beard and looked as if he'd been hammering out pieces with two fingers on an old typewriter since the late 1960s. The *Rose of Tralee* was still RTE's number one programme of the year, he told me, attracting a million viewers throughout Ireland, worth £20 million in passing trade to Tralee. From an idea to generate a bit of business for the town it had become possibly Ireland's premier festival, financed by companies that were entirely blue-chip, Guinness, Eirecell, Ulsterbank . . .

He broke off the PR spiel to let out a deep yawn. Sorry. The problem they were all fighting, him included, was lack of sleep. In the last few days the Roses and their entourages had progressed from the Curragh Racecourse outside Dublin, to Waterford, to Lismore Castle, to the opening ball here in Tralee. They were all exhausted.

Liam picked up a press release containing the Roses' individual details. They had to have Irish backgrounds, of course, but it could be from four generations back. Last year they'd even had a *black* Rose, from Paris. This year there were all the usual Australian and American Roses, six British Roses, and one from Dubai! As we leafed through, we went off-the-record. This one's claim to fame was being at college with Clinton's daughter ('who fecking cares'), this one had *great* legs . . .

But it was – Liam's enthusiasm suddenly seemed genuine – a pretty incredible event. The Dome was basically a concrete carpark with a tent on top, and tonight they were producing a fashion show with clothes from the House of Rochas in Paris, and tomorrow the programme that would top the year's ratings . . .

I saw what he meant that evening, when, freshly accredited with a press pass whose photo made me look like the booziest of Irish reporters (surely I wasn't that fat already; tomorrow I gave up white pudding), I attended the opening fashion show. On the concrete under the rows and rows of plastic chairs you could still see the white car-space lines.

Above us the TV lights swayed precariously beneath the flimsy-looking blue plastic sheet that was the roof. But never mind! The place was packed. The cameras would never see the floor, the Exit arrows, nor yet the dress-sense of the crowd. The Roses, in two glamorous rows by the catwalk, were enough of a feast for any lens.

The evening began with four guys in sharp suits doing a not half-bad imitation of a black dance troupe. We moved rapidly on to a parade of costumes from Ireland's top boutiques and designers. Please put your hands together for Carraig Don, Bridge Street, Tralee (Quality Fashions and Knitwear); Chic Boutique, Listowel (Fashion House, Designer Outlet); Brenmar Jon Knitwear, Kenmare (Made-to-order Coats, Suits and Separates).

The posse of gorgeous females modelling these creations

came from a Limerick agency, and what they lacked in haughty, dead-eyed stares and heroin-chic pallor, they more than made up for in natural good looks. Give me Maire from Irishtown over Stella Tennant any day! In addition to the girls, there was one stately lady of middle age, representing perhaps the aspirations of the majority of the women in the hall. Sadly, there was no one to offer a realistic fashion fantasy for the two pug-like old dears on my immediate right, their lips set in a downward grimace that could have been envy, approval or a stoic nostalgia.

For some reason our genial DJ host took great delight in taking the mickey out of the two male models, James and Walter, who, unlike the girls, never ventured out on to the catwalk without a prop. First, they came with mini-bottles of Perrier, then with a book (which was half-heartedly perused), now they sauntered past, each with a mobile phone. Reaching the end they tapped out a number, stepped back as they instantly got through and stood chatting. Then – *hey!* – bumped, bottom to bottom, into each other. Well goodness, what are *you* doing here?

This little vignette brought howls of laughter from the crowds and an all but straight line on the mouths of my two neighbours.

'D'you think you might just give them a round of applause, ladies,' gurgled the DJ, 'they're ever so shy.'

Up by the bar the Roses' escorts jostled like colts in their identical black dinner jackets with their identical shorn hair, sipping crème de menthes as their eyes followed the return of the lovely young models (now in combination yellow and grey trouser suits from Fashion World, Castleisland). 'Where would you wear an outfit like that to now?' observed Eamon, who was a pig farmer from Adare, Co. Limerick.

How had he got to be an escort, I asked him. The first year, he explained, you just applied. The second, if you had behaved yourself properly, you got asked back. The interview was pretty informal. As long as you had two arms and two legs. He laughed.

Behaving yourself properly, I asked, presumably meant sticking to the rules, not getting involved with your charge? Of course, said Eamon. It also meant – look, there was one of the American escorts who just *didn't* know how to do it. He was smothering his Rose on the first night. Like, he was standing outside the girls' toilets waiting for her. Eamon and his fellow escorts had told him to ease off a bit, and he'd gone apeshit and complained to the organizers. Said he was behaving like a perfect gentleman and what were they talking about. 'Typical Yank,' said Eamon, contemptuously. 'He was right, and the rest of us were wrong.'

Eamon's Rose was from South California. That was her over there, with the tan. She was half-Indian, in fact. She was beautiful, wasn't she? But he didn't think she'd win because she wasn't doing the right things. Like, last night at the dinner with the judges, she'd been sitting opposite Gay Byrne – I knew who Gay Byrne was, right, OK – so she'd been sitting opposite Gay Byrne and she hadn't even talked to him. That sort of thing.

In the interval, wandering around the vast tent with my camera, I spotted, over the far side, a young woman who looked spookily like an old friend from London. (By which I mean I hadn't seen her for four years, even though she lived only half a mile away.) But surely it couldn't be *Leah. Here*. I followed her round the catwalk at a distance. No. It was just an Irish teenager who resembled her. But, as I got closer, she returned my stare.

'Mark?'

What in the name of frivolous fornication was Leah doing at the Fashion Show for the Rose of Tralee? We repaired enthusiastically to the bar. She was researching a film, a thriller, which was going to start with a scene at the Rose.

So the second half of the show (a parade of increasingly extravagant evening wear) became just a backdrop to our gossipy catch-up. How excellent it was to have someone from home to laugh at James and Walter with! And afterwards, to swan into the mini-dome, where the VIP reception was being held and Peter O'Brien, Irish-born designer of the House of Rochas, whose Parisian Haut Coutre [*sic*] had been the climax of the show, was dancing wildly across the empty parquet floor with a barefoot blonde in a black slip, and later the Roses would almost certainly join us.

*

The fun continued the next day, as we sailed together in a cab to the Golden Rose lunch at the Earl of Desmond Hotel, there to mingle with such heavyweight dignitaries as the chairman of the Leeds Rose Committee (originally from Co. Meath) and his vast-bellied English insurance broker pal, who was also a sponsor. A scarily switched-on lady who was something big in Eirecell Telecom was a former Rose and now one of the judges.

'What are you looking for?' I asked.

'A winner.' No, she went on, when the laughter of the chairman had subsided a little, she was looking for a girl who could talk to me one moment, then turn and talk to the Taoiseach the next, then turn and talk to a child. 'Because that's what they're going to have to do for a year.'

As we sat at twenty round tables with seating for ten in the spacious panelled dining room the speculation as to who might win was hotting up. Liam had already tipped Sinead, the Tipperary-born French Rose. Now David, who was a PR man with Waterford Crystal, told me to watch out for Yvette, the Sydney Rose, and Skye, the South African Rose. Somebody else, Leah said, had mentioned Michelle, the New Zealand Rose, and Alexi, the Queensland Rose. Niamh, the Dubai rose, might prove a dark horse, said somebody.

That evening the first bunch paraded before us, one by one, in the screaming supporter-packed Dome. 'Good luck Amy, Chicago Rose' read one of a forest of banners. Our genial host, Marty Whelan (receding TV hair, bushy brown moustache, more than a touch of the Wogans), put them at their ease with a gently held hand and few easy questions, until they were ready to perform their 'piece', which ranged from the highly competent to the deeply embarrassing (generally with an Irish theme).

There were blooms for all tastes. Here, to kick off, indeed, was Sinead the Paris Rose (Liam's favourite), who looked elegant, almost maternal, in the white top and long pink skirt given to her by Peter O'Brien of the House of Rochas. She was sweet, and a bit nervous, and gave us a fine rendition of 'The Galway Shawl'.

Now here was Raelene, the Darwin Rose, whose dad had fallen in love with the Northern Territory on a trip from India, and he'd been there ever since. She shimmered on stage in an appropriately antipodean turquoise and sang an Indonesian song, 'because Darwin is closer to Indonesia than Melbourne'.

And here was Sorca, the Boston and New England Rose, glamorously American in her silver glitter top and tight black skirt, whose dad had had to shop for winter clothes when they first arrived in the US, because they weren't accustomed to the cold weather. She was a medical student, studying psycho-biology 'which is another term for neuro-biology and I'm studying infectious diseases on the side . . .'

'As you do,' gurgled Marty, 'as you do . . .'

She recited a four-line long 'Gaelic pome', which (oh dear) she still managed to fluff. 'That's it,' she beamed, to huge applause.

Ann O'Sullivan, the Jersey Rose, was clearly under instruc-tions from both her home tourist board and the AIB Bank, for whom she worked as a portfolio manager. Jersey was the most beautiful island she'd ever seen. It was safe, clean and wealthy. *Whoops!* 'It's friendly,' she hurried on, with an embarrassed giggle, 'an extremely friendly island, you can do so much there no matter what age you are, the beaches are beautiful, the water's warm, the walks, the scenery . . .'

'Grand,' interrupted Marty. 'And there endeth the lesson.'

But oh no it didn't. Quizzed about her boyfriend, Niall, Ann managed to steer her emotional life on to the fact that he headed 'the export package, which is a new service, offered by AIB . . .'

'I'm getting a headache,' groaned Marty.

'It's a new service,' Ann ploughed on, 'offered by the Channel Islands AIB for Irish people living abroad . . .'

Having reached its thirty-ninth year, the pageant's format had, let's face it, long since blossomed. Once these young women would have been near-virginal creatures without jobs. Now some of them had careers that made Marty look like the dumb blond. ('So what's occupational therapy?' he asked the Ulster Rose.) And as for boyfriends, far from being hushed up or skated over, this was now one of the set questions. Followed by a frank little quiz as to how it was going.

The general rule was that they had one and it was going fine. Judging by the applause, it was a plus if the squeeze was

Irish. Frankly admitting, like Siobhan, the Manchester Rose, that you were single and looking for a man ('with rhythm') seemed to be a mistake. 'And he's got to be able to do the housework,' she added.

'No wonder you can't find a man,' crowed Marty, to big laughter from the mostly female audience.

It left the official escorts, who were sitting in six rows of identically cropped heads, right in front of the press section, looking more than a bit otiose. Although Michael, who was escorting the lovely Sydney Rose, Yvette, told me it made it all very simple. 'She's got a boyfriend in Sydney. The first day she made it very clear she was here for a professional purpose, and that was that.'

A professional purpose! Don't the young people know how to have fun any more!

The only one who seemed to be getting anywhere with his Rose was Eamon the pig farmer, whose close relationship with Soraj from South California was now the talk of backstage. Marty had picked up on this and now, naughtily, brought it front stage.

'Tell me about Eamon from Adare,' he teased.

'His name is Eamon,' said Soraj. 'He's from Adare. He's a pig farmer.'

There was a cheer from the escorts at this concise statement of the facts, and the farmer rose, blushing, to his feet. Marty knew well enough not to push it further.

Our press passes were getting Leah and me everywhere. In the interval we were whisked backstage to see the dolled-up assembly of Roses gathered earnestly round the TV monitor, like something from a contemporary Degas, with added fragrance. Now, show over, we sauntered through the crowds packing the foyer of the Brandon and straight into the RTE reception. I was a trifle nervous about my 'black tie' ensemble, which consisted of worn blue jacket, tired blue moleskins, exhausted brown Timberlands, set off with a ready-made bow-tie, purchased with great difficulty that afternoon. (Nu Gent is the place, if you're ever stuck in Tralee without a bow-tie.) But it was OK. There were others in worse. Two of the younger press corps, indeed, were in jeans.

They were from the local rag, the *Kerryman*, it turned out: the assistant editor and one of the subs, Donal, who told me with some force that he wouldn't approve of anything I wrote about the Rose unless it was cynical and denigrating and reflected the reality of this room full of gobshites. He was only there for the free bar. His other pal, Niall, was a genially cackling ex-journalist, who had reached that stage of inebriation where this coinage seemed preposterously comic. 'I'm an *ex*-journalist,' he kept repeating. At one point he tried to tell us a joke but couldn't get the punchline right. 'That's why you're an *ex*-journalist,' said Donal. 'Because you could never get the story . . .'

Niall's sister Christie was the colour-writer for the *Cork Examiner*, up to do pieces with titles like 'Everything in good taste as 17 sweet girls help Marty come up Roses'. How on earth did we end up on a sofa arguing passionately about the North? It went something like: I was English. The Irish were better informed about England than we were about Ireland. (True, but inevitable.) The English didn't care about Ireland any more. (Any *more*?) As far as the North was concerned the British had to go, it was as simple as that. (Was it?)

They didn't talk about the North usually, she said. It was just like such an old, old problem, and beyond their control. But if they started to think about it, it made them mad. Passionate at any rate. 'It's only a small island. What *business* do the British have here?'

I wasn't disagreeing, just chipping in with devil's advocate points like, What about the Protestants? What *about* the Protestants, said Christie. Nobody wanted them to leave, but they just had to accommodate a little. Had I ever met a Northern Protestant, Niall interrupted. They were the most dogmatic, intransigent bloody people in the world. 'Sometimes,' he said, 'I just feel like going up there with a machine gun and wiping them all out.'

Take the marches they were forever going on. Why? Nobody else in the world marched as much as the Protestants. Celebrating ancient, *ancient* victories over Catholics. Even recently, when they'd let that bomb off that killed all those Catholics, they'd been out there with their drums and their songs.

'Some of them,' I pointed out.

Christie nodded. But still, some of them.

It was 4.15. The party was still going strong. Nobody trying to make us drink up. No sense of things tailing off, the *craic* ever becoming unmighty again.

'I think I'll call it a day,' I said.

What kind of an expression was that, scoffed Niall. Why did people say 'call it a day'? It wasn't a day any more. It was a night. In fact it was the beginning of the next day, how in feck could you call it a day when it was *the beginning of the next day!*

He let out his wildest cackle yet, and I called it a day.

I Meet a Trivia Question

When I surfaced it was almost lunchtime. Outside, the rain lashed the gleaming paving stones; the wind flicked my throw-away umbrella inside out, had blown over a news-stand in the little square. Down at the Dome the blue plastic roof was flapping thunderously. The lights swayed and creaked on their mounts. 'They're talking of cancelling it,' said Colleen, the reigning Rose of Tralee (last year's Toronto).

We reconvened over the road in the Brandon foyer, perched politely on two of the maroon sofas that had seen that sprawling political argument only a few hours before. After a year of Rosedom Colleen was highly practised at her quotes. It took a few minutes to push beyond the huge honour it had been to win, the most important thing about winning being the pride on her parents' faces.

Dad was 'a tradesman', a tool and die maker from Dublin who'd emigrated to Canada when he was twenty-one. Mum had hated it, but stayed because 'she was the housewife, you know, woman stands behind her man kind of thing'. And Dad could earn two to three times more in Toronto than at home. They had planned to make money and go back, but it never happened. 'The way of life was very good, much better than here, they stayed.'

Now she regarded Canada as home. Ireland was a great place to visit, 'maybe even come back to for a few months,' but Canada was home. Even though there was a romance associated with this country you couldn't get away from.

Yes, as a child she'd been aware of her Irishness. Comparing herself to other Canadian friends, there was more of a social aspect to her family. Her mum and dad loved to have company over, to entertain, to go out to the Irish club on Friday and Saturday for their pint of Guinness, at Christmas to have a party in their house, 'which no one else does'.

The important thing for her about coming back was not to find the culture, but to get to know her relatives, 'get to know my blood, because we have no one in Canada, so when you come back it's important to be able to hug your grandmother because you've never hugged her in twenty-six years'. For other girls, whose ancestors had gone over in the Famine ships, they would want to go and find 'these small little parishes' their family had originated from. 'That means a lot to them, especially in this day and age where in Canada, for example, we're a melting pot, we don't seem to have our own culture, it's just a mixture of all kinds of cultures'.

As the reigning Rose, she was hardly going to knock this festival that had brought her back, that meant enough to her *émigré* family for them to stump up the costs of taking part, flying over. But underneath the practised platitudes I was surprised at her passion, both for the event and the values (albeit with its jokey, Martyesque, post-modern flavour) it represented.

The media, she complained, were forever taking a poke at it. The *Independent* last Sunday had said, 'Where's all the girls with the nose rings, where's the girls with the tattoos, where's the girls with the funky haircuts?' 'And I mean,' Colleen protested, 'I actually think the women here do represent our generation: they're well-educated, they're intelligent, they're charitable, they're honest, you know, these are the women of our generation; I really think the punks, the nose rings, that's a minority . . .'

Indeed she had been approached one afternoon in Tralee by 'a local girl' who said she wished she was like her. 'She had the nose rings and the earrings and a baby – which would have ruled her out.' But she wanted to be Colleen, she wanted to be the Rose of Tralee.

Colleen just wished that one of those journalists who liked to take a stab at the whole festival would come in for a luncheon with the girls, sit down and talk to them. 'They'd be talking to some extremely intelligent women.'

So it wasn't just beauty? And being able to put on a good performance?

Absolutely not. Colleen had helped pick the Washington Rose this year, she'd been one of the judges, and although, yes, there was a column on appearance ('I myself have a hard time with that, what do they mean, face, eyes, hair, you know appearance is how you present yourself'), there were also columns on intelligence, personality . . .

'In the end the judges usually say they try to find a girl that matches the song. What they mean is, there's that line that goes, you know, "the truth in her eyes ever dawning." If you read that line they're looking for someone who's an honest, sincere person like us.'

It was an opinion echoed by the stately group of ladies I hurried through the rain to meet for lunch at the Imperial – the old Roses.

'You don't call us old Roses,' said Sheila (Galway, 1980). 'You call us "former Roses", don't you Betty?'

'Just Roses,' said Betty (Ulster, 1963). 'Once a Rose, always a Rose.' But yes, they agreed, it wasn't just physical beauty, or intelligence, or even the quality of the performance, it was the eyes, that line about the eyes.

Despite that, I didn't imagine that the squat, plump, slightly spotty teenage waitress, who dropped the dish of garlic mussels and covered her mouth goofily with her hand, would ever be a Rose. Though if you got to know her, I guess you might well see the truth ever dawning in those narrow forget-me-not blue eyes of hers.

'Did being a Rose change your life?' I asked Julie (Birmingham, 1985). No, it hadn't changed her life, 'but it was a good year'. She laughed.

'We still gloat,' said Sheila, 'all these years later.'

Shock horror! Having crashed out for three hours, and spent another hour trying to neaten my appalling evening outfit, I strode out through the howling power-shower that was the weather to find that the final selection had been cancelled. In a corner of the empty press office bar, Liam, face as grey as his beard, chattered urgently into his mobile. It was the first time in the history of the competition that such a thing had happened, he said. But they just couldn't take the risk. It was wild in there.

Leah appeared, dressed to be disappointed. Other members of the press, including new big shots from the nationals, drifted in, shouted and cackled at each other, ordered and devoured a Chinese take-away, got to their feet to flick on *Batman*, the Rose's replacement, agreed reluctantly that since there was nothing better to do they'd attend the Guinness Reception at the Brandon, which was continuing regardless.

So all too soon we were a noisy press table at the centre of another grand party. The gang had all filed their disaster stories and were in merry mood. Besides myself, Leah and Christie, there was Dermot, the gossip man from the *Evening Herald*; Deirdre, the star colour writer from the *Independent*; Niamh, the lovely young trainee from the *Munster Express*, and David, the tall, laid-back fellow from National Radio.

Deirdre, a large forty-something in jeans and untucked blue-checked shirt, was right next to me, but not interested in talking. Clearly bored, she leant forward and tapped her fag out in the centre of Dermot's trademark hat (he wore it everywhere, as in his photo byline).

'This is like a bad wedding,' said the guy from National Radio, looking round at the middle-aged couples sashaying to the antediluvian cover versions. Then Deirdre got us all to link fingers and sway round satirically to the music.

It was important that we weren't really enjoying ourselves. As Colleen had said, the Rose was universally looked down on by the insiders of the media, despite – perhaps because of – its huge TV popularity. It represented the grossest, most sentimental aspects of an old Ireland that the pace-setters of Dublin believed had been swept away. The *Irish Times* called it, 'a carnival of naffness ... this jamboree of ersatz Celtic wholesomeness, Kerry's answer to Osmond family values.'

'It continues,' went on this correspondent from beside his Dublin TV set, 'to wither, and at this stage very serious pruning is required.' The Dome, 'let's face it', looked more like a shed. Allocating six hours of prime-time TV to what was, in effect, a local festival, was 'highly questionable. As it all bears such scant relationship to the real Ireland any of us experience, it has increasingly become more cult than culture.'

So although Christie was forced by her newspaper to take the event at least half-seriously, filing tonight a piece to be headlined 'Tears as disappointed Roses wait another night,' on the national record the consensus was total. It was our duty as aware, postmodern 'meeja' cynics to show that we were above it and all that it brought with it.

'Let's go!' cried Dermot now to Niamh and her pulchritudinous pal from Waterford Radio. Brushing the ash from his hat, he was off, out into the real world of rain, crowds and drinks the *Evening Herald* had to pay for.

Being altogether lazier, less cutting-edge (and *sans* expense account), I lingered where the sausage rolls were free. Colleen was there, wholesomely radiant as ever, doing her unfashionable bit with the aunts and the grandmothers. And this elegant lady in black was the 1961 Rose, in extremely fine shape for one who'd had eight children. She flew immediately into promotional mode. Had I seen the parade on Saturday? For young children it was better than Disneyworld. The Guinness float had been two huge pint glasses, out of which Colleen had stepped. (The physiotherapist leaps out of the beer-froth, splendid.) 'It was just magical,' sighed this former Rose.

But here was Niall the ex-journalist! Once again having broached security. It seemed a mere moment before he, Christie and I were slumped back on our sofa in the foyer, thinking up hilarious puns for Christie's diary piece tomorrow. 'The girls rose to the occasion.' 'Thorny times as show is cancelled.' 'O Rose, thou art sick.' We were at our very wittiest. Was it really 3 o'clock?

'Mark!' shouted Deirdre the colour writer as I headed back to the loo. I double-took. Now she was my best friend. 'Are you all right?' she asked.

'Yes. And you?'

'No. I've got a lot of bother on me.' She came to join us on the couch. The wife of one of the local VIPs had told her off for wearing jeans at such a formal reception. 'She really lit into me,' she cried, pulling hard on her cigar.

A man stumbled past in a colourful bow-tie, announcing himself as an Irish queer. An Irish queer, he elaborated, was a man who preferred women to beer. Ha ha ha!

'D'you think there's something sad about Irish people?' asked Christie.

'What d'you mean?' I asked, gazing at the sofas full of drunks all around – laughing drunks, arguing drunks, glassy-eyed drunks, sleeping drunks.

'They drink so much,' she replied. 'They drink to hide their feelings. English people suppress things in one way, by being reserved. The Irish just drink.'

Marty Whelan was on winning form the following evening, when the rescheduled competition reached its climax in the Brandon ballroom. 'It could have been the very first topless Rose of Tralee,' he quipped to the delighted crowd. Tickets to the solid, weatherproof, but much smaller new venue were 'like gold dust', but having been warned that there would only be room for us to stand at the back, Leah and I suddenly found we'd got seats right at the front, within sniffing distance of the trembling Roses.

Was it just fortuitous or had they deliberately saved the most unusual blooms till last. Yvette, the black-maned Sydney Rose, was an undercover cop.

'You normally carry a gun?' said Marty.

'I do.'

'You do. Have you ever used a gun, if I may ask you that question?'

'Only for training purposes. I've actually pulled it out, but I've never had the unfortunate experience of using it. God help me if I had to.'

'You won't ever have to, let's hope not. But you do, I know, embroil yourself in secret surveillance work. What are you working on at the moment – can you tell us?'

'I can't tell you that, unfortunately – it's secret.'

Marty's ambition, it transpired later, was to travel the world and meet people.

Skye, the glamorous South African Rose, was a rock star,

with a band called LED. Why LED? Because it was originally formed by a lawyer, an engineer and a doctor. The name didn't mean too much any more because Skye had switched from law to finance, the doctor had left South Africa, and the engineer was in a mental institution. Cue laughter.

The final Rose, the Midlands UK candidate, was undoubtedly the hippest and most cutting-edge of all. I shifted in my seat, wondering whether I'd been transported to a *The Day Today* style satire.

'You're into mass murderers?' asked Marty, chirpily. She was. She liked reading about them, and the person she most wanted to meet was no, not, like 75 per cent of the others, Mary Robinson, but Denis Nielsen.

'You need to get out more,' quipped Marty.

Speculation continued right to the end. Leah, who'd been favouring the Ulster Rose, now liked the New York Rose. I rated the Kerry Rose (fond memories of Puck), and was rather sold on the Australian Roses, in particular the dreamy Perth Rose, although whether that light in her eye could be described as the truth ever dawning was anybody's guess.

Colleen came out to announce the winner, embracing Marty and pointing out that she was now a trivia question, 'Who's the longest-reigning Rose of Tralee?'

And the winner was ... oh my goodness, no not really, Liam what did you know that we didn't, Sinead, the French Rose, who'd been the very first on. Now she was crowned in front of a million-plus viewers, over one-third of the island's population. Then, more intimately, in the Brandon foyer, the press pack got to ask her if it would change her life, what was her best memory, who was her escort, did she have a boyfriend, if she hadn't won who was her favourite?

'If I said something now I'd be killed,' she answered, truth ever dawning appropriately.

'Any marriage plans?' asked the man from the *Kerryman*.

'He always asks that,' muttered Deirdre.

Then it was out into the crowds to watch Sinead from a pavement perspective, being brought over to the Ashe Hall by coach, then crowned by the mayor on the balcony in front of her floodlit, distantly glamorous peers.

'Look at them,' said the man with the microphone, 'they're absolutely beaming.'

'Absolutely beaming,' repeated the tall man in the leather jacket in front of me to his mate; and raised an eyebrow.

Back inside the Brandon holy-of-holies, now that the winner had been announced the losers were letting rip. One poor Rose, whose family had had to fly home early that morning, was lavishly locked. Wine stained her teeth as she lurched towards us, wondering what we'd thought of her jig. Another loser, whose hopes had been very high, stood by the food table in her pyramid of green satin, stuffing cocktail sausages into her mouth like tranquillizers. As for the escorts, relieved of duty, they'd abandoned their personal blooms and struck out into the wider garden. Eamon and Saroj, the gossip of long-ago Tuesday, sat to one side holding hands like an old married couple.

Round the corner, Dermot, the man with the hat, had, despite his trademark bottle of champagne, been abandoned by the lovely Niamh from the *Munster Express*. You'd want to sleep with a Rose, he told me, just so you could sing the last line of the song, 'And I rode the *arse* off . . . the Ro-ose of Tra-lee-eee.'

And then tell them in the morning.

11

At Home with John B.

Leah was driving north to spend some time with her boyfriend
– another Dermot – so I hitched a lift with her as far as
Listowel, a little market town in north Kerry, which I thought
would be a good place to hole up for the weekend, get some
sleep and catch up on my notes.

The square was everything I'd hoped for – wide enough for
a very large market indeed, with shops, banks, a ruined castle
and two churches, one crumbling and weed-covered in the
centre (ex-Protestant) the other repointed with a neon Ave
Maria sign at the side (Catholic). In a sunlit corner, just twenty
yards from the curve of pavement where Leah had dropped
me, solid red letters on a quaint cream frontage announced
the Listowel Arms Hotel. The fine tubs of purple hydrangeas
out front completed the collapse of my resolve. I lugged my
bag into the green-carpeted foyer, which smelt of all those
wonderful provincial hotel things like sunshine on wood polish, piles of laundered linen waiting half-way up the stairs,
shepherd's pie being served in the panelled bar off the hall.
And yes, they had a room; for tonight, at any rate. Tomorrow
might be a problem, as they had a wedding party.

The bar off the hall turned out to be a Writer's Bar, with
large pencil portraits of local authors: Bernie O'Connor, Maurice Walsh, Brendan Kennelly, George Fitzmaurice, Maureen
Beasley, Sean McCarthy, Bryan MacMahon and, peering out
from narrow almonds of eyes under high, thin brows, the most
famous of all, John B. Keane, author of *The Field*, *Sive* and
The Buds of Ballybunion as well as works well known only in
Ireland, *Letters of a Love-hungry Farmer*, *Letters of a Successful T.D.* and *The Gentle Art of Matchmaking*, to name but
three.

Walking out into the sunshine that afternoon I discovered that Listowel, not content with just a Writer's Bar, had designated itself a 'Writer's Town'. There was a modernistic Writers' Well in the middle of the square, and in the crumbling ex-Protestant church (now the St John's Art Centre) was a Writers' Museum, with manuscripts, ephemera, photographs, memorabilia and a mildly frantic man in a black T-shirt trying to organize a dinner to celebrate ten years of the St John's Art Centre.

'If he is unable to honour us with his presence himself his invitation can, of course, be passed down the line,' he was saying into the phone, as I emerged from the spiral stairs, 'or he'd be more than welcome with his wife, partner or whatever ...'

Or whatever. John B., it turned out, had already refused, 'due to ill health'. The man was struggling heroically to fill what was clearly going to be a jamboree of subs, secretaries, office juniors and dogs, and all the more fun for that, doubtless.

'Why does the County of Kerry produce so many writers, playwrights and poets?' Dr Seamus Wilmot, Registrar, National University of Ireland, had asked at an address opening the annual Listowel Writers' Week (established 1971). 'Is there something in the air or in the blood that brings forth the gift of words in abundance? ... The town of Listowel with some 3,000 inhabitants has produced playwrights, poets, novelists, scholars, actors and some of the best story-tellers in Ireland. Is there any town of comparable size that can match this – anywhere in the world?' (Was Seamus a distant relative of Liam McShane of Dublin's, I wondered.)

In another of the exhibition cases, Brian MacMahon, 'one of Listowel's most renowned literary figures', had attempted to answer 'this conundrum' with a detailed list of factors, a 'combination of circumstances that put the area to the forefront of the literary world'.

The tradition of Gaelic Bardic Schools had lived on in the region long after it had vanished elsewhere. Traditional poets, writing in Irish, had practised their trade locally until a century ago. When Catholic education was banned in penal times, hedge schools had been widespread in north Kerry, and students had often travelled to the Continent in search of further education. The establishment of St Michael's College had 'created a love of literature that became a marked characteristic of the area'.

It was no surprise that Brian MacMahon was also the local schoolteacher. But I reckoned this prosaic summary was closer to the truth, about Listowel, and Ireland in general, than any of the myths of wild, inebriated genius people love to attach to writers, Irish writers in particular. Having said which, there was also clearly something in the air. Where else would you find such a perfectly-worked gem of inconsequence as this?

> SONNET TO A COW DUNG
> To-day ('twas from a friend) that first I heard
> You had a beauty and a homely grace,
> Poor cow-dung! Playground of the passing bird
> That seeks refreshment, or that loves to trace
> A claw-print pattern on your soft dark face
> You held a rich potential, 'tis averred,
> For grass and tillage fields – shall I construe
> Bucolic poets of great Rome's ancient day
> Mused as I do, trod and smeared the shoe
> In pastoral walk beyond the Appian Way,
> Yet murmured not but spoke nice words to you;
> Horace or Virgil, in long-forgotten lay;
> Cow-dung, all nature greets you with a smile
> Your blending essence made our Emerald Isle

That evening, intending to raise a quiet glass to Robert Leslie Boland, the poet-farmer of Farnastack and author of the above, I came down from my room to find the Writers' Bar already packed with the threatened wedding party. They were English, enjoying themselves as the English do when abroad – noisily. Although I knew none of them, I felt I knew them all. They came from the Home Counties, and they lived in Clapham and Battersea or perhaps Islington and Notting Hill, and they worked as lawyers and money-men and doctors and record-promoters. I knew how delighted they'd been, racing to the airport at lunchtime; what a laugh they'd had landing at Shannon an hour later and picking up the hire car; how great it was to be with their chums in this funny little bar in this anonymous little town in the west of Ireland, where their friend, relation, beloved daughter, was getting hitched to a local man, an Irishman.

Having eavesdropped my way through a pint of Guinness and found out enough about Fiona, Jeremy, Russell and Charlotte to make myself the target of a successful libel suit, I retired to the peace of the dining room. It was empty save for a couple watching the sun sink orange over the huge green oval of Listowel racecourse, the racing, bubbling River Feale in the foreground shadows.

'What did you think of the Rose last night?' she asked him. 'She was great now,' she answered immediately to his murmur. 'Very level, very natural. Everyone I spoke to mentioned the French Rose ... she's living and working in France now ... she's from the west ...'

Just as I was wondering where else in the country Sinead was being fêted and appropriated thus, there was a crash. The English had joined us! Or at least a selection of the older members of the party, clicking noisily over the parquet in their polished brogues and settling back to bellow at each other as if from one end of the Empire to the other.

'That's how the Irish *work*,' opined a half-bald fellow in a navy blazer. 'That's why I've ordered the coach so early. We'll be bloody lucky if it gets there at all.'

Ha ha ha! was not a sound I heard emanating from the quiet Listowel teenager serving them. Over the table Navy Blazer's toothy daughter whined nasally, a half-heard descant above the braying chorus. 'I think personally ... I just thought it was ... yah, OK, but they *gave* me the *reservation* ...'

At breakfast the theme was continued. 'Was your water hot?' 'Nor mine.' 'Absolutely nothing's changed,' said a white-haired skull who'd clearly last visited the island sometime before Partition. Navy Blazer was now telling us about the groom's family. 'Father likes his pint of Guinness ... fairly typical ... eight children ...'

I marvelled quietly at the providence that had brought Dan and Caroline together, one weary evening in the pub, perhaps, round the corner from the London teaching hospital where they both worked. They married, and I had a quiet day alone. At the plastic pine-style tables in the Coffee Nook most of the women were waiting on a toasted sandwich. 'Clearing up nicely, isn't it?' one observed. I spread something called *Move Over Butter* on to two slices of fare that could well have been marketed as *Move Over Bread.*

With time on my hands, I had my hair cut by a wry-lipped blonde who looked as if she'd been chain-smoking since she was thirteen. In three weeks' time, she told me, they had the famous Listowel Races, which everybody in town would be saving up for. Not much else went on in Listowel. There were a couple of race days in April and that was it. Writers' Week was not mentioned, but (surely I'd misheard) in August there was the All-Ireland Rentboys Competition. *All-Ireland Rentboys*? Yes, Rentboys from all over the country competed for the All-Ireland title 'King of the Rentboys'. Well, well, you live and learn. (It wasn't till I got to Limerick that I discovered what Wren Boys were.)

The celebrated John B. Keane had an ideal day job – or rather, night job – for a writer. He ran a pub. You could just walk in there and meet him, I'd been told. But I had a problem – I'd never read a word he'd written. I'd seen the film of his play *The Field* and that was that.

Had I known what a treat was in store for me I'd have run out and bought his complete *oeuvre* and sat in the Writer's Bar speed-reading it. But dim memories of *The Field* and a flick through *Irish Short Stories* in Listowel Library had led me to the idea that John B. was a revered master of some worthy, agricultural school of writers. His characters would be tragic peasants trudging through rain and mud, and I would struggle to enjoy him.

In fact, John Bosco McLane, the hero of *Letters of a Love-hungry Farmer*, and his conspirator, the professional match-maker Dicky Mick Dicky O'Connor ('Courtesy and Civility assured at all times'), are wonderfully accessible comic characters (quite apart from telling you more about the reality of rural Ireland since the Wyndham Act than any number of history books could do).

More fool me that I didn't appreciate the kind of truthful humorist John B. was. After dinner in the hotel I paced round town, passing the John B. Keane frontage twice, telling myself that it would be at best rude, at worst embarrassing, to attempt to interview a writer whose work you hadn't read. Then I succumbed to curiosity and went in.

It was nine o'clock on a Saturday night and the place was empty. There were four girls up at the little bar and three old fellows opposite, in a dense cloud of smoke on the shiny green banquettes under the TV, which was on. In a writer's pub!

'That's an odd combination,' said the neatly curled lady behind the bar, serving me a Guinness and a Kit-Kat. I took a stool at the bar and perused my *Irish Times*. No, I decided, I wasn't going to ask for him ('Hello, I'm a great admirer of your ... your reputation'). I was just going to sit there and observe. John B., I'd been told, got many of his ideas for his stories by sitting listening to his customers. I would do the same.

The girls left ('G'night Mary') and were replaced at the other end of the bar by two tweed-jacketed chaps giving Mary a long earful about how John B. had given someone at the Tralee Races his autograph. This fellow had been so delighted it was John B's. John B. ... John B. ... John B. ... they gabbled on.

'That's John coughing now,' said Mary. Around 9.30, quite quietly through the side door, he appeared, the living image of his pencil portrait, in a loose V-necked jersey and slippers. He took a seat with the two enthusers, who quietened down visibly and treated him as an old and not at all unusual friend. Congratulations were in order as John B. (and yes, Mary *was* his wife) had just had a grandchild.

Perhaps I should go over, I thought, and introduce myself. No, I'd leave it a few minutes. Suddenly the place was packed, and John B. was surrounded by a noisy crowd of friends and admirers. Ah well, I'd blown it now. But just as I was finishing my drink, I was pushed up against the bar by a motherly lady who was buying a round of drinks for her family and it was a sin that I was up here on my own. Would I have another with her? They were right by the door, her long-haired son in a wheelchair, his young wife in white top and black skirt beside him, then a skinny sister in pink, with her huge farmer husband in broad pinstripes. 'She's so tiny,' said the widow, whose name was Susan. 'But she loves him.' Her son Conor, she went on, was also after writing a book, about his experiences, his life story. Would I talk to him?

It turned out that Conor had been the press officer for Sinn Fein in London. Now he was strongly of the opinion that Gerry Adams was making a mistake. There should be no surrender on British terms . . . until the British left . . . etc, etc.

I was not looking for these people! But with a bit of chat about English ignorance and Irish injustice it seemed you found them everywhere.

Susan had come in, she told me, to see John B. She'd been a neighbour of his and Mary's in Listowel many years ago, but she hardly knew if she dared go over. Go on, I encouraged. So she went and brought them back, and we were introduced round the group. I think John B. thought I was an English friend of Conor's.

It had been an interesting snapshot. The Irish will often tell you that they're unimpressed by celebrity, that the reason Peter O'Toole and John Hurt and Mia Farrow and Julia Roberts and the gang like the place so much is that they're treated like ordinary people. This may well be true, but the Irish, I realized that night, cared just as much for celebrity as anyone. Like everything else, though, they were better at hiding it.

Back at the Listowel Arms it hadn't taken long for the wedding party to become *hiberniores hibernis ipsos*. They were going wild to the *ceilidh* band in the ballroom, chatting away enthusiastically to the various locals and strangers who'd joined in. In Watford, I felt sure, they'd have asked us to leave. Here, I found myself at some small hour of the morning in the middle of the party, dancing with widow Susan and her daughter-in-law around the wheelchair-bound Sinn Fein hardliner son. 'Thank you, thank you,' she kept repeating, after I'd attempted a couple more with her alone. 'Thank you, thank you.' What could I say?

'I'm sorry about Princess Diana,' said the taller of the two lads at the newsagent's in the morning.

'What about her?'

She'd been killed last night, he said. 'In a car crash in Paris. Her and Dodo.'

What? There was nothing of it in the headlines. I looked from one to the other uncertainly. 'You're winding me up?'

'No,' the boy said, his eyes sincere. ''Tis true.'

Now his friend was laughing. At the idea that I thought it was a wind-up? Or because it was a wind-up and they'd decided to see how many of the English wedding party they could kid?

'Of course it isn't true, you *eejit*!' Princess Diana killed! It was even more ridiculous than the whole silly-season affair, with its ghastly 'Di & Dodi' loveheart logo. But back at the hotel the TV was on in the foyer and a few of the early risers among the wedding party were watching the news disbelievingly. I was surprised how strongly the abrupt extinction of this contemporary icon affected me, as I phoned girlfriend and brother and parents at home, one after the other.

By lunchtime it was the talk of the bar. ''Tis truly a tragedy,' said the waitress. 'Such a lovely girl,' said the lady at the table next to me. 'She was,' agreed her friend. 'The poor girl had such an unhappy life,' they were saying at reception. 'And those two boys . . .'

By the evening every pub in town was showing a retrospective of the Princess's life on the TV. 'What's the news?' said the barman, emerging from the back room.

'She's still dead,' replied the beefy bloke in the shiny green sports shirt.

12

Fab City?

'It's a kip, it's a kip, it's a kip!' Sinead from Dublin's words rang in my ears as the pretty little fields of Newcastle West and the tizzed-up cottages of Adare gave way to Bungalow Bliss suburbs, then red brick terraces facing 1930s semis, finally the grime-stained pebbledash frontages and concrete roads of a dreary grey estate. Limerick.

The bus terminus was a sequence of queues waiting wearily in the drizzle. A white-haired man with a grimy flat cap, two blue-uniformed schoolboys with hurley sticks, a cluster of backpackers, an ash-faced cigarette smoker with a tight auburn perm. I hoisted my case-cum-pack up on my back and trudged over the busy main road, past the stained curtains of the Railway Hotel, to a street full of grubbily beckoning B & B signs.

I chose the smartest, a brown and cream plastic frontage, which belied its dingy front hall. The lady of the house appeared from behind a door that let out a gust of old bacon fat; showed me up past a sign saying 'Thank God for our Pope', to a gloomy cell with two narrow beds and a fuggy stench of old sweat.

'It's a bit stuffy,' she told me. 'I'll open the window.'

Oh shit, I thought, closing the door, sinking back on the bed in an instant depression. I didn't want other people's prejudices to be true; I wanted to think well of Limerick. And why had I let her take my money off me already?

'Look,' I fibbed, going downstairs. 'I hope you don't mind if I head off to a hotel. I really wanted an *en suite*.' She smiled and took me by the arm. 'I'll show you another room.' It hadn't been available five minutes ago, but it so happened that an American lady had just checked out.

The room had a shower in a cublicle off a space that was almost entirely filled with double bed (which is not to say that the double bed was large). Through the tiny aluminium-framed window the view took in a grey brick wall, a flat roof (with a well-rusted Coke can), a tiny backyard with an empty clothes dryer. No, no, no, I didn't want to stay. But there was no escape from this lady's grimly determined smile.

Hair and Beauty Salon; Mustang Sally's Restaurant; Leavy's Ladies' Footwear – the shops along main O'Connell Street seemed out of some lost decade. The prices in the windows were half of what I'd seen elsewhere – Photocopying 5p; Sandwiches and tea £2; Shoes £8.99. And crossing the circular, zigzag brick, pedestrian area by the river, I was accosted by two American missionaries, something that hadn't happened since I'd been in a South African township.

Now here was something nice about Limerick – the Shannon, foaming yellow-white over a long gash of rapids. Below, a forty-strong rake of swans circled and preened themselves in the strangely luminescent surface of the deeper pool; above, there was a picturesque grey stone castle. At each end of this central section an elegant stone bridge. It was a river vista to put Cork, or indeed Dublin, to shame.

It cheered me as I lay in my cell that night, unable to sleep for the whirr of the extractor fan outside the window, the rattle of rain on the metallic roof, the streetlight shining eerily bright through threadbare curtains, the shitty stink that rose from duvet, yes, and mattress, yes, worse. A thousand and one inebriated travellers had sweated heavily into these fibres – Australians, Americans, low-budget commercial travellers from Dublin, Belgians, I could smell every last one of them.

I sprayed my neck with deodorant, jammed earplugs in my ears and sat up in bed reading *Angela's Ashes*, the Pulitzer-Prize-winning memoir of an impoverished childhood in Limerick that was high in the best-sellers at the moment. Reading it in a lush Updikean suburb in the States you would, of course, chuckle and be delightfully appalled in turns at its sharp, humorous recollections of Irish poverty. Here, a few streets from its setting, it seemed altogether too close to home.

The fleas in Frank McCourt's mattress were 'a right bloody torment an' I should know for didn't I grow up in Limerick, down in the Irishtown, an' the fleas were so plentiful an' forward they'd sit on the toe of your boot an' discuss Ireland's woeful history with you. It is said there were no fleas in ancient Ireland, that they were brought in be the English to drive us out of our wits entirely, an' I wouldn't put it past the English. An' isn't it a very curious thing that St Patrick drove the snakes out of Ireland an' the English brought in the fleas.'

Mother o' God, but those weren't the same bloody Limerick fleas that were itching me now, were they? Nose down to the stinking mattress I searched for culprits. But none of the black specks amid the exotic melange of brown stains actually jumped. I was a neurotic English softy, even if I couldn't sleep for scratching.

In the morning the sun had come out. In my groggy state, the old centre seemed prettier than ever. It was nicely tatty too, with broken windows in the Bishop's Palace and a hideous prefabricated building ('De 'Ting,' the locals called it) lowered bang into the historic centre of King John's thirteenth-century castle. Up a backstreet in Englishtown I found Michael, the gentleman who led the walking tours of the city. He seemed somewhat surprised to be disturbed, and positively alarmed that an Englishman already knew a little of the outline of Irish history.

Before the battle of Clontarf, he told me, the Danes had frequently made it up to the 'falls'. The Shannon was navigable thus far up, hence the city's position. In due course the Normans had put in an appearance, King John building his castle on the edge of Englishtown, and removing the Irish over the river to Irishtown. In the 1650s Cromwell's son-in-law, Ireton, had personally taken charge of the assault on Limerick, and in 1690 the city had famously rallied to the Jacobite cause under Patrick Sarsfield, Earl of Lucan. From the far side of the river you could still see, very clearly, in the castle walls, the brick in-fillings of the holes made by the cannonfire of the Williamite forces. The final surrender of the Catholics to the Protestants, a year after the Boyne, had taken place right here, on Thomond Bridge.

'This surrender,' Michael told me gravely, waving his rolled-up umbrella at the castle, 'was the destiny of two *nations*, not just two armies.'

And here, on the far side, on Clancy's Strand, where sea-gulls swooped over pretty little houses with long front gardens, was the very stone on which that irrevocable Treaty of Limerick had been signed. I ran my finger over it and thought of Mo Mowlam, that patient nanny-figure, still trying to put the pieces together to this day.

In exchange for their surrender of Limerick, the Jacobean military men had been allowed free passage to Europe, where they continued the war as other 'wild geese', fighting for France in the 'Irish Brigade'. (Sarsfield himself died at the battle of Landen, in Flanders, in 1693, with, according to legend, the words 'Would it were for Ireland' on his lips.) The local civilian Catholics were promised the religious and property rights they had had, briefly, under Charles II, but within months, the English had reneged on this part of the treaty and enforced anti-Catholic penal laws of such severity that the city gates of Limerick were locked, Michael told me, to keep out the angry Irish, every evening for sixty years.

These penal laws, which survived throughout Ireland in some form until O'Connell's Catholic Emancipation of 1829, excluded Catholics from all public life and much private social activity. They could not join the army or navy, vote, be elected to parliament or hold any offices of State. Any form of Catholic education was made illegal (leading to those 'hedge schools' so popular near Listowel – schools assembled literally in fields and hedgerows). Catholics were forbidden to buy or mortgage land, rent it at a reasonable profit or even inherit it in the normal way. If they were found owning a sporting gun or horse worth more than £5 they could be whipped. The Catholic priesthood had to leave the country, under threat of being hanged, drawn and quartered if they returned. Mass had to be celebrated in bog, field or forest as an outlawed conspiracy. The temptation to 'take the soup' and accept the different version of Christianity now enshrined in the fabric of the central State was powerful, and many succumbed.

Such is the version of history you may hear on the ground. In fact, as always, the reality was considerably more complex. The penal laws were not always strictly enforced, there were numerous evasions, and not all classes of Catholic suffered equally, the interests of the gentry being harder hit than those, for example, of merchant and tenant classes. But even those two sentences would get me into a fierce argument in many a pub, not to mention a campus, on the island.

Back at Merchant's Quay history was simple again. This place was, Michael told me, a focus of one of the other major catastrophes of Irish history – in his words, 'the most devastating tragedy ever to befall any nation', the Great Potato Famine. We stood there together on the very spot where the emigration ships would have left, and Michael, with skilful use of the rolled-up umbrella, painted a vivid picture of the starving sailing away to America in ships run by captains whose previous experience had been in the slave trade; of 'people dying in their droves'; of absentee landlords (he tactfully left out the word 'English'), who continued to demand rents and force evictions.

Ruminating on all this my eye fell on a long queue, snaking out of the groovy pink 'n' blue, steel 'n' glass construction that was the new City Hall. They were waiting patiently to add their signatures to the Book of Condolences for that celebrated republican, Diana, Princess of Wales.

In the rest of Ireland, the casually cruel nickname they have for Limerick is Stab City, and although there are doubtless as many individual incidents of knifing in Dublin or Cork, this reputation for violence has stuck. Even in the empty bar of Hanratty's Hotel (to which clean and comfortable little establishment I had now escaped) I heard them discussing it, quite at random: 'It's a phrase that's done us a lot of harm . . . it was mentioned once in that article by that lady . . . it's because it flows so easily off the tongue . . . Stab City.'

'It's crazy, like,' said Billy, the taxi driver who agreed to give me the alternative Limerick tour, an insider's view of the city's less prosperous districts. 'There's plenty of incidents, yes, but if something happens in Limerick it'll be on the front page of the paper, but the same thing's probably happened in Dublin the same day and it doesn't get in at all.'

On this dreariest of wet Irish days the estates we drove round were so grey that they looked like deeper shades of the lowering sky. The only colour in the whole drab collage was an oblong square of green grass, along the edge of which a (very) young mum pushed an off-white pram.

The roads we were coming to now were 'stickier' than those we'd just been through. They'd left 'scumbags' in these houses, Billy said, 'and they just wrecked 'em and wrecked 'em, in the end they just wound up knocking 'em down.'

The next area was better, these were 'the good old people'. But now we were coming down to where the younger folk lived, and I could see the windows boarded up with huge rust-red sheets of metal, the only other splash of colour against the monotonous grey.

What did he think was the problem, I asked him; why did the young people behave less well than the older?

Personally, very much off his own bat, this mightn't be true like, but, Billy thought, the way it worked was that you'd get kids whose parents 'weren't worth a hope in hell, who didn't rear their kids right. So the daughter then is fifteen and she winds up becoming pregnant by this other fellow. Now how are they supposed to rear *their* kids right? They haven't a clue because they haven't been brought up right themselves. That's how the circle starts.'

And while other children might have an obsession with hula hoops or disco boots, up here it was robbing cars. The road we were on now, in fact, was just perfect for that, 'because it's a big circle, it's like a big race track'. That's why they had put those short pillars in by the pavement there; to try and stop them joyriding up on to the grass.

We passed two altogether neater houses. One had been done up, Billy explained, because someone had been murdered there; the other because Mary Robinson had visited. It was sad, he said, because if you were never used to this, you'd hate it. Then, if you moved in, after a year you'd put up with it. And after another year you'd become like it. 'Don't get me wrong,' he added, 'it's not a ghetto, there are people here with excellent jobs. Ninety-nine per cent of the people have excellent jobs, like.'

Father Joe Young, the priest of one of these areas we'd visited, South Hill, was, initially, similarly eager to be upbeat.

Limerick, he told me, was a city he was very proud of. The
developments that had taken place in the city centre in the
last few years were a phenomenon – I should find out how
many millions of pounds had gone into buildings alone.

Having said that, the community that he worked in (and
where he lived) had an estimated 80 per cent unemployment.
'Which I've always felt was totally unacceptable.'

The major problem they faced was alcohol abuse. 'Which
we've been in denial about for so many years, not just in
Limerick, but across the nation.' Second to that was the abuse
of prescribed drugs from the medical profession. Finally, there
was cannabis, which he could not understand being promoted
'as a soft drug'. (Cocaine, crack cocaine and heroin had not
reached them yet.)

'The casualties that I have seen have been quite phenom-
enal. It's frightening, the paranoia cannabis creates. I probably
wouldn't be too good at spelling it,' he chuckled, 'but I can
tell you I've seen it. Two dogs on the far side of the road
doing what dogs do, you think they're talking about you.'

Addiction flourished in this community. There had been so
much unemployment for so long that people had become
'casualties of the Welfare State'.

'It's a dangerous kind of ethos to develop, when people
believe that somebody else may be responsible for looking
after them for the rest of their lives.' When that was passed
on to children, it was 'nothing less than a haemorrhage and
mutilation of people's spirit'.

He told me about the cycle of addiction that he had seen,
repeatedly, develop: children growing up in households with
addictive parents would have no trust and nobody to talk to,
and a 'reversal of nature' would take place, with kids 'as young
as five' having to respond to their parents' needs rather than
vice versa. The children would end up with what he called
'low-grade chronic depression', which led in turn to 'a
smouldering rage'.

'Now maybe around twelve years of age, such kids will
themselves end up experimenting with alcohol for the first
time. And what then happens is they have a highly intensive
experience with alcohol and they confuse it with intimacy.'
And if they had never had an intimate experience with another

human being, when that confusion took place it led to what Father Joe liked to call 'addictive logic'. So inevitably, as time went on, every time these young people experienced conflict or pain they'd go back to that original object, 'with a view to having their intimacy needs met. And this is the beginning of the love affair.'

Most of the time he got no chance to do anything much about this dreadful cycle other than speak about it, which he'd been doing for so long, 'and a lot of it has been falling on deaf ears'. Otherwise he was just reacting to crises, of which there would be several a day. It was now eleven in the morning and already he'd taken seven calls. The one big step he had been able to action was to set up the Soccer Academy, which was attached to Limerick Football Club, of which he was chairman. He had been greatly helped and supported in this venture by the late Bobby Moore, who had been here with him in Limerick until his recent death. The vision they had had was to give some opportunity for children 'who didn't have the feeling for the traditional education system'. It would be like a carrot, to 'bring them across the bridge away from the addictive cycle and into some sort of normality'.

And, however unlikely Father Joe's metaphors, his methods were definitely working.

'I've seen them coming down at nine o'clock in the morning with their tracksuits on them and that sense of dignity. You take dignity away from people, you destroy their spirit. One of the greatest poverties that exists is the poverty of spirit. When you don't aspire to anything. When you've no reason to go to bed at night. And no reason to get up.'

Sometimes, he went on, he felt the Welfare State was like a way of stopping people from revolting. 'Or maybe from making a mission statement about what they want; and what they'd like for their kids. I just find that obnoxious. It goes against everything that I've given my life to as a priest.'

Would this desperate cocktail of welfare and addiction (which I had last seen close-up on the far side of the world, among people with a very different reason to despair, the Aboriginal 'communities' of Far North Queensland) lead to violence, I asked. 'Course it does,' Father Joe replied. When one was carrying all that excess baggage, there were moments of insanity, when people just went out of control. In any case, violence was another form of addiction.

But the Stab City label was 'crazy, just a myth totally'. This was 'one beautiful city'. There was no part of it that he wouldn't walk in day or night.

Bishop Eamonn Casey, who had fathered a child by a secret mistress, and Father Brendan Smythe, who had abused boys in a string of foster homes, and other holy men who had failed to live up to their vocation, had got all the publicity and were endlessly held up in pub arguments as examples of why Catholic Ireland was going to seed, was no longer relevant, was the architect of its own downfall and so on, but Father Joe (about whom of course few outside Limerick had ever heard) could have reinspired disillusioned Catholics by the score. I had found him, as Hollywood might have set him, a ruggedly handsome forty-something, saying Mass in a church full of disabled people (signing off with a prayer that they might be 'reasonably happy in this life and supremely happy in the next'). Sitting talking about his faith, it wasn't just pompous ritual or angels on pinheads we were discussing. 'People always talk to me about callings and that kind of thing,' he told me. 'But nobody called *me* in the middle of the night. I just always had a fascination with this whole God thing.' For him, the Divinity was 'the higher power that I choose to call Jesus Christ'. It was essential for 'all human beings, if they're to get equilibrium, balance, sense of place, belonging, to believe in something greater than themselves'. He didn't even *like* the word 'church'.

'The church that I belong to is about people, and it's about quality of life, and I try and do whatever I can, just one day at a time.'

After my day in the estates, central Limerick seemed alarmingly cheerful and vibrant, and although the Celtic Tiger was hardly parading triumphantly down O'Connell Street, once you started looking you found touches of the modern Ireland wand. Here was a Temple Bar-style café called Nestor's, with maroon velvet chairs, bare floors and every type of Continental coffee and beer. Tucked away down a side street was the funkily decorated Green Onion Caffè, with a Salad of Poached Pear and Prosciutto with a Cashel Blue Cheese Dressing, run by two chefs who had trained in London and Germany and the States and had now returned to Limerick to settle. Things had certainly changed, Diarmuid told me. Two years ago, 'if I'd asked someone I'd consider a worldly friend of mine, "What exactly *is* an espresso coffee?" it'd be, "You got me there, you know." But now . . .'

Making a gentle evening tour of these hot spots – I ended up in a crammed dive called the Wicked Chicken – I felt remarkably ancient, marooned at the bar among the sociable teenagers. At my age, in Limerick, these would be my kids.

I amused myself by trying to think up a catchy replacement label for this city of which the locals were so very proud and which, visibly, if you knew people or were under twenty-two, was a cracking place to be. But the rhymes were not auspicious – Grab City, Jab City, Drab City, Rehab City? Fab City seemed to be the best the tired sub could think of at this time of night.

In the morning, seeing a sign in a travel agent's saying 'London rtn £89' I succumbed. Shannon airport was just a cheerful taxi ride away. By early afternoon I was stuck in traffic near Hyde Park Corner, listening to Billy's East End counterpart grumble about his recent holiday in Turkey. The extraordinary reaction to Princess Diana's death had created a surreal field of cut flowers outside Kensington Palace, cellophane wrappers glinting to distant railings in the ochreous September sunshine.

The wealth of the Union's capital was tangible – the cars, the jewellery, the restaurants, the clipped and perfumed *people*. Where were all the mums pushing prams, where were the old men? A tide of perpetually youthful international singles had pushed them to the margins, were gossiping and flirting like there was no tomorrow.

In my local bookshop in Primrose Hill Jessica had had some Americans in, wondering whether it was possible to fly to Limerick for a weekend. They had read *Angela's Ashes* and 'reelly wanned to go there'. What a shame I'd missed them, I said. I knew the perfect place for them to stay, if they wanted a real, contemporary flavour of that wittily captured poverty.

13

Moonlight Roses

Back at Shannon, ten days later, nothing had changed. It was still raining. Things were still 'grand'. The Guinness-pouring was still a laid-back two-part process. The young lady who brought my sandwich over still said 'now' as she put it down. There were, it appeared, no taxis to be had. A disconsolate-looking German stood by a trolley full of luggage. He'd never been to an airport where you couldn't get a taxi, he told me.

A kindly, white-haired security guard explained the problem. Clare were just after winning the All-Ireland Hurley Final and the celebrations had brought the place to a standstill. I should try the taxi desk in the corner of the building. Only now did I notice that half the people in the airport were wearing yellow and blue strips.

But the taxi desk was unmanned. There was a list of likely numbers on the wall. Colum, Joe, Frank, Donal . . . I was just about to try one when the telephone rang. I answered it.

'Is that the taxi desk?' came a female voice.

'Yes,' I replied, explaining the situation.

'And *you're* waiting for a taxi!' There was a loud laugh and a click.

Over at Information the desk was deserted and the receiver was off the hook. The genial security guard loped past. 'Try phoning Information,' he told me. But I was *at* Information, I said. 'Try dialling 0 then.' I picked up the Information phone and dialled 0. Two minutes later it was answered. By a sad German voice. It was my pal at the taxi desk, as bewildered as I.

Some time later I caught a bus. I was lucky it was running, Paddy the driver told me, but they'd put on a special trip for the people who wanted to meet the victorious team, who were due in to Shannon from Dublin at any moment.

The road north to Ennis was full of cars with blue and yellow flags waving, horns honking. '95 and 97 – Well done boys it's heaven,' said a sign stuck in the top of a tree. In Ennis, the narrow central street was a solid jam of cars under a criss-cross mass of bunting. I checked into the youth hostel right by the bridge over the swirling River Fergus and went in search of a cup of tea.

'Clare strikes again,' said the legend on the big mirror above the bar of the Queen's Café. An impromptu music session was in progress, at four on a Monday afternoon, while on the wide-screen TV they were replaying the famous match. 'It's my sixth time hearing it,' said the waitress. 'I could almost give the commentary myself.'

I sat over my tea and watched the culmination of a contest that seemed almost to have been following me around. The game was a bizarrely skilful mixture of football, hockey, rugby, cricket and the egg-and-spoon race, with its own language of clearances and hooks and cut-ins, and the Aussie Rules advantage of frequent 'scores', even if actual goals seemed to be few. Clare had recovered from a disappointing start to equalize a third of the way through the second half. Then they were ahead, Clare 13, Tipperary 12, 'in this magnificent all-Ireland game'. Then Tipp scored and surged ahead. Clare equalized; and just three minutes from the end pipped Tipp 20–19. You could see why they were all so extra-excited.

That night the *craic* in Ennis was up in the three hundreds. Unable to get through any of the bar doors, unable to fake the joy, I retreated to the quietest place in town, the TV room in the youth hostel, where a lean Canadian with a gingery-blond moustache under long gingery-grey hair was watching Jack Nicholson turn into a wolf on the flickering screen.

He was touring round 'the British Isles', he told me, looking for his roots, which were, he reckoned, in the North of Ireland, or possibly Scotland. He'd done some research in Glasgow and discovered that the Gilmours had originated from Lewis, but the weather had been so bad he'd only got as far as Skye. Coming across to this island he didn't understand at all why you had to use pounds in the North and punts in the South. It was crazy. Why?

I gave him the briefest of history lessons and he looked suitably baffled.

'This all goes back four hundred years, right?'

'Right.' (I was keeping it simple.)

'To King William or somebody.'

'Or somebody.'

'And *I'm* part of the problem.' He nodded and chuckled delightedly over his attachment to this quaintly real bit of European history. I had told him that the Gilmours, if they had settled in the North from Scotland, had most probably been planters.

In the morning it seemed less chuckle-worthy. The ceasefire had been broken. With a bomb in Markethill, Co. Armagh. The IRA had denied responsibility, and the attack, two days after the start of 'the most significant talks on Northern Ireland's future for seventy-five years', had outraged Dr Mowlam, who declared it 'the work of sinister people'.

Sinister people indeed, not to want to *try* for peace. But at the end of the bridge over the Fergus was a rough stone on which was carved a dagger and the dates 1916–66. And in the little square, a tall column held up the noble figure of Daniel O'Connell, MP for Co. Clare from 1828.

The man known variously as 'the Great Dan', 'the Liberator', 'the uncrowned King of Ireland' had devoted his life (1775–1847) to peaceful and constitutional efforts to settle Irish–British differences. His first big fight had been for 'Catholic Emancipation', a repeal of the last of those penal laws that had stayed in place since the Treaty of Limerick. (It was more a matter of principle than anything else: the rights being campaigned for – to sit in parliament, to hold senior government offices and to be a member of the privy council, a judge or a king's counsel – hardly being of direct interest to the ordinary Catholic.)

O'Connell had taken his non-violent ideal to magnificent heights. The huge public meetings organized by his Catholic Association had rattled the British rulers of the day to the core. Robert Peel wrote of the 'fearful exhibition of subdued and desperate enthusiasm' at O'Connell's election in Clare (the first time a Catholic had stood for parliament for 150 years), and after he had won noted, 'Such a scene we have had! ... no man can contemplate without alarm what is to follow in this wretched country.'

When O'Connell had won the Catholic Emancipation battle the 'Monster Meetings' he then organized to try and bring about the Repeal of the Union were the biggest peaceful democratic protests the world had yet seen. Facing ever huger crowds (1 million turned out to the Hill of Tara in 1843), he rang every patriotic note in the scale:

> there is not a lovelier land on the face of the earth – a more fruitful or fertile land the sun never shone upon [hear, hear, hear, and cheers]. I will repeat that the sun never shone upon a lovelier, or greener, or brighter land [hear, hear, hear, and great cheering]. Oh, it is a land to fill one with patriotism – its picturesque beauties please and delight the eye – its majestic mountains rise to the heavens – its limpid waters irrigate the plains, and its harbours are open to the commerce of the entire world, asserting for Ireland the great prerogative of being the first nation on the earth; and the period is coming, when standing forth in their native dignity, the people will be prosperous and free [cheers].

In the end, as was the norm for Ireland's heroes, there was disappointment and defeat. The British banned O'Connell's most ambitious anti-Union meeting, set to be held at Clontarf (symbolic scene of Brian Boru's victory over the Danes) on 5 October 1943. O'Connell, non-violent in the crunch, backed down. He was subsequently prosecuted by the authorities and found guilty (with six others) of conspiracy. For a man who had determined above all to work within the law, this was a severe blow. He was gaoled for a year. Although the governor of Bridewell gaol in Dublin vacated his own house for O'Connell's use and he was allowed as many visitors as he liked (dinner parties of twenty-four and more were frequent, sometimes in a dining tent in the garden from which a French tricolour was flown), it was the end for the Liberator. The limited measure of Irish autonomy that he had sought had to wait seventy years, and the life's work of another 'uncrowned King of Ireland', Charles Stewart Parnell. In 1845, the Repeal of the Union was overshadowed by the catastrophe of the Famine. In 1847, O'Connell died, in Genoa, on his way to Rome.

Though O'Connell remained (and remains) an inspiration and hero for moderate nationalists, the failure of his peaceful attempts to achieve some measure of Irish autonomy is perhaps an explanation of why others felt that violence was their only way forward. Down the street, indeed, in Ennis's little Museum (alongside a letter O'Connell had written in 1828, seeking support for his candidacy: 'It really seems to me that the approaching election for the County of Clare may decide the liberties of the Catholics of Ireland') were local memorabilia that charted the continuation of the Irish fight by less peaceful means. Here was a blood-pact between O'Connell's one-time associate, William Smith O'Brien, and Thomas Francis Meagher, 'written in their own blood at Clonmel Gaol, October 21st 1848', after their unsuccessful rebellion of that year (presented by Miss Mary Maguire, Spa Hotel, Lisdoonvarna). Here were autographs of men and woman of the Easter Rising, 1916. Here was a poem, 'Invocation to the Sacred Heart', written by leading local participant Eamon de Valera, as he awaited execution in Kilmainham Gaol on 28 May 1916:

> Thou, Sacred Heart, has known the prison cell,
> The pangs of hunger, Thou hast known as well,
> The soldiers rude assault has torn Thy frame,
> Their ribald speech blasphemed Thy Holy Name.

And here was the telegram he received on his release from Pentonville in 1917, telling him he had been nominated to contest Ennis for Sinn Fein (he defeated the Irish Party candidate by 5,010 votes to 2,035). Here were the autographs of hunger strikers of that same year – Frank Gallagher, Clare Brigade IRA, Meelick, Co. Clare (Mountjoy and Dundalk Hunger Strikes 19 November 1917); Paid Na Braenan, Commandant Clare Brigade IRA, (Hunger Strikes 2 years, Dublin 18 November 1917).

Let cowards mock and tyrants frown
Ah little do we care!
The felons cap the noblest crown
An Irish head can wear:
And every Gael in Innisfail
That scorns the serf's vile brand –
From Lee to Boyne will gladly join
The felons of our lands

ran one of many handwritten poems. O'Connell, de Valera, Frank Gallagher, Bobby Sands – the connection was not hard to make.

Beyond Ennis the countryside started to roll, ever greener and prettier. It was mid-September and the bus was full of locals, not a backpacker in sight. We rattled on, through quaint Ennistymon and down to the sea at Lahinch, which was a building site of holiday bungalows in pastel shades.

From the coast road all I could see of the famously scenic Cliffs of Moher was just a giant tarmac carpark in a field, a parade of tiny black silhouettes climbing slowly against the lightening sky. Then, after a lumbering detour through Doolin, we reached the little spa town of Lisdoonvarna, on the eve of the biggest weekend of the month-long Matchmaking Festival.

Originally, this had been a serious-enough event, with prosperous landowners and farmers congregating after the harvest for a bit of *craic* by the sea. Then, the matchmakers – Dicky Mick Dicky O'Connor and his like – had seen it as a good source of likely husbands. So the women had started coming, and in due course men had come specifically looking for wives. Now, I'd been told, it had gone seriously to seed. Plane loads of American women flew in from New York to be sorely disappointed by the John Bosco-like characters on offer. Comic set-pieces were clearly going to be available round every corner.

For the time being, though, the main figure of absurdity in the neighbourhood was me. Having cunningly contacted the festival organizers and sorted myself out with free accommodation I now discovered that this was a considerable way out of town. There were only two taxis in Lisdoonvarna, said the over-stretched lady at the front desk of the quaint, wood-panelled Imperial Hotel (why wasn't I billeted *here*?). They'd most likely be busy and I'd have to call them myself from the public box in the hall.

An hour later, having had a progression of ten-pence chats with the sleepy-sounding wife of Sean, who would be back for sure in fifteen minutes, watched an episode of *Coronation Street*, and been vacuumed and mopped around by a sequence of skinny young Europeans with bad skin, I let out a loud snort of frustration, hoisted my over-heavy pack on to my back and strode off down the hill, past a party of over-excited Scottish pensioners and out into the dank green country-side. What the heck am I doing, I wondered, as I trudged along past field after field of gloomy-eyed, recumbent cows. I was deeply grateful to Mr Jim White, head of the White Hotel Group and king-pin of Lisdoonvarna, for giving me a complimentary room for two nights. But here! A mile and a half at least from the action. I was going to get awfully familiar with this Statoil garage, this crossroads, this up-turned water butt.

The façade of the Burren Castle, when it finally swung into view, did little to raise my spirits. It was a bleak-looking stone fortress built around a huge black tarmac carpark. By the road wall a long double row of powerful motorbikes was drawn up. There were sixty at least. Great! The Burren Castle was clearly where the Hell's Angel contingent of matchmakees hung out. Maybe I could get a lift into town with them.

I got my key from a skinny girl from Birmingham in a shiny satin top and retreated to my gloomy ground-floor room. It had salmon pink walls, a narrow *en suite* bathroom and a splendid view of the carpark. I showered, drew the curtains and fell into bed. Outside the bikes revved intermittently.

'Table for one?'

'Thank you.'

In the restaurant that evening the massed bikers (they were English, on some kind of cross-Ireland race) were enjoying a surprisingly sedate end-of-week dinner. 'I've got to do fifty-seven Irish coffees!' cried the young waiter, rushing through. Besides them there was just one old couple and a pair of dolled-up forty-something females, whose rattling laughter revealed a nervousness that was contagious. Did I really want to head out alone into that town full of hormone-soaked singles?

Then Ned, the rotund and ever-smiling hotel manager, appeared, a wonderfully on-the-case character, with a thoroughly upbeat spiel about the festival for the visiting writer. Yes, people did still come looking for wives, and it 'was amazing, it really was an amazing place'. So I had no car. Not a problem. He would drop me in, introduce me to Jim White, and, whenever I wanted to return, be it three, four or five in the morning, I had only to phone and someone would collect me.

Jim White had once, Ned explained, been an elected representative of the Dáil, for Donegal. Now, leaning against the reception desk of the Imperial, the white-haired General of the town-wide matchmaking battle paused to give me five minutes of his time. A hurried history was followed by a more leisurely description of the present state of affairs. It was, he told me, a hugely successful festival. Tonight, there'd be between five and ten thousand people, and you wouldn't get a bed within four miles. Tomorrow you'd have fifteen thousand and you wouldn't get a bed within ten miles.

Outside, the bars were indeed heaving. No New York singles that I could see, but John Boscos everywhere. Here he was in Mary Maguire's (not the same Mary Maguire who had presented the Smith O'Brien blood-pact to the Ennis Museum, surely?), solid as a rock on his stool by the bar, as down the room a couple of his younger helpers on the farm stood eyeing a lipsticked blonde and a permed chestnut, who were having a *very* animated chat to each other. Engaging them in some kind of conversation was clearly the thing to do – or was it, as a staggering fellow from down the bar decided to cut out that whole tedious courtship business and go straight for what he wanted. The young ladies didn't seem to mind unduly, pushing him off as if he were an over-frisky colt.

In the car back to the Burren Castle after a long evening of similar vignettes, I was squashed in with two loud men of murderous aspect sharing a vinegary-stinking bag of chips.

'Where you from, you *cont*?' asked the one next to me.

'Erm, London.'

'Fucken gypsies, that's all we get. Fucken travellers and gypsies and *conts*.' His tone softened suddenly. 'Wan' a chip?'

No, I have to report that sophistication was hardly the name of the game. At the 'first dance of the day', at one o'clock the following afternoon, under the V-shaped wooden beams of the Spa Wells, I met a cheerful gent from Kildare who surely hadn't changed that polyester-cotton shirt since he'd left home. His breath was none too fresh either. But the 'girl' (fifty-five, minimum), whom he'd met last night at the Ritz, didn't seem to mind. 'I'll have the next,' he cried, as she glided past on the arm of a skinny dotard, who'd economized by keeping the remaining strands of his hair in place with lard. She flashed him the warmest, yellowest of smiles.

He worked in a soft drinks factory himself, but some of these people (he winked theatrically) who called themselves farmers had as much of a farm as he had. 'You take a piece of ground out there.' He gestured towards the Burren. 'Twenty acres and a couple of cows, that's a farm. Or a strip of flowers at the front of your house.' He laughed. 'That's a farm.'

There were bumbling amateur amorists everywhere, but up the hill and through the altogether grander doors of the Hydro, I found a slick professional. *The* slick professional, in fact – Willie Daly, Lisdoonvarna's official matchmaker. He had longish grey hair and a brogue soft enough to voice-over the corniest of stout ads. As for the twinkle in his eye, he was clearly the original for that expression. He had an ease of manner that would have made the awkwardest, most hopeless bachelor boy or girl feel relaxed.

Cupped in one pink hand was a large glass of Jamesons; under his other arm was the bulky matchmaking book, inherited from his father, with the names, addresses and requirements of a huge range of seekers after love, from Offaly cattlemen to Josie Esparago, PO Box 60437, Riyadh 11545, K.S.A.

'Is that Russian?' he asked me, sliding over a photo of a bikini-clad bird, who would have brought the Spa Wells to a frenzied standstill.

He showed me the form you had to fill in if you required his services. 'It's very simple, there's only about four or five questions.' He didn't have more, he said, because he was an awful believer that in the west of Ireland you wouldn't find a wrong man anywhere. 'You'll find 'em full of love and romance, looking for someone to share their life and love with.' Most of the men he'd be working for would have small local farms, which was 'a marvellous environment', looking out over the Atlantic Ocean. 'But there'd be a huge absence of women.' The girls, you see, went off to Dublin, England or America to work, and the farm would be left to the boy. Way down in the west, it was estimated, there were twenty-nine men to every one woman.

A lot of these men were very good-looking, well-educated, 'quite refined in a number of cases'. The biggest problem they would have would be shyness. A farm was a beautiful place, but very isolated, 'and they actually become bad mixers. Now when they have a lot of drink on them they overdo the mixing, so again they don't appeal.'

I had, I said, seen a couple of examples of that only the evening before.

'All of a sudden,' said the matchmaker, 'they have the courage, but it isn't the right courage. And when the music comes up what they want to do then is grab a woman – but again that doesn't work.'

Which is where Lisdoonvarna came in. 'It's kind of called the love-capital of the world.' And the reason for that was the opportunity it afforded people to enjoy themselves. 'It gives people ... the music lends itself to ... quicksteps sometimes, but a lot of waltzing, and a nice amount of slow dances where people get a chance to talk nicely to each other.' Then in the evening they might go out to the coast. There were some beautiful drives out there. 'And again, it enhances romance if they're in a car together. If you meet a girl and drive back by the sea it's a lovely thing, you know. It does a lot for them. That and a few pints of Guinness.' Willie clearly had the mechanics of romance sewn up. After the dance and the drive and the Guinness then you could make the grab. So where did he fit in?

My question was answered by four women who tumbled down the corridor towards us.

'Are you Willie Daly?' they asked, in strong Northern Irish accents. 'What do you do?'

'It's a good question,' he replied, chuckling and turning his Southern twinkle full beam in their direction. With effortless good manners, he rose to his feet and held out a hand in their direction. 'It's a pleasure to meet you.'

'We keep watching you and you were sneaking about and we said, "What is this man about?"'

Willie explained. The men came to him, the women came to him, he made the match. Otherwise a fellow might be asking twenty of the wrong girls to dance and in the end he'd give up. 'For 'tis embarrassing to be refused too often, you know.'

The ladies knew all about that. 'You come to a certain age, and you've worked, and you've let life slip by, so we're trying to make up for it now.'

'You'd have an awful lot of time left for doing that now,' Willie reassured them. 'In my calculations.' He gave them each a form. He was delighted to make their acquaintance. And he'd see them this evening in the foyer any time up till half past nine.

'And what d'you do then?' the tallest of the ladies asked nervously.

'Well, I'll be introducing people around that period.'

What did he charge, I asked, when they'd gone. He didn't charge women anything, he said, due to the shortage. But men would pay between thirty and forty pounds.

'And what happens if they don't like the match?'

'Oh, if they don't they just tell me.' The women were not too shy about that. Fellows, on the other hand, would almost like any person you introduced them to. In his thirty years' experience men's needs were much the same – they wanted a companion, someone to share their life with, maybe their love with, definitely their farm with. Looks wouldn't come into it, only a very little. Women, however, were pretty particular. 'They're looking for a fellow that looks nice, dresses nice. I said to people recently they might have a very big amount of land or cows, but there should be big interest put on personal appearance. Ten years ago it wasn't necessary, but it is now. Hygiene is a factor. I'd say now to a fellow who's got ninety cows, "Did you ever think of spending the price of two of them on yourself?"'

But was it really always for marriage, I asked. While he'd been chatting to the ladies my eye had drifted down over the famous matchmaking book. One of the entries read, 'I will ride everything and you'.

Originally, of course, Willie replied, it *was* all marriage, but it had, in fairness, changed slightly now. There were young people who'd walk up to him and say, 'Will you get me a woman for the night?' Even a man of eighty years of age had approached him three days earlier looking for a partner. 'Now I assumed his wife had died, but then he said, "She's not interested in much now." And all of a sudden I knew that his wife existed at least. But he said, "It'd be nice to meet someone for a couple of days." Which is a fairly honest statement – I mean, 'tis a marvellous age to be like that, although I'd say his mind had gone a little bit ahead of his body all right . . .'

And as for him, I wondered, did he, Willie, ever meet a beautiful woman who might lead him astray?

For a moment the matchmaker looked almost taken aback. 'Well, I could have . . . One would be open indeed . . . You meet some lovely people now.' But it was, he decided, regaining his composure, a bit like a doctor or a teacher. There was 'kind of a little barrier. And if I was to pass that I think people'd be very surprised.'

I was to discover no more. I wasn't the only one after the matchmaker's tale. A four-strong TV crew had been waiting in the corridor for some while, looking ever more impatient as this mere writer hogged the man of the moment. They were from the Irish-language TV station, Teilifís na Gaeilge – T-na-G – it transpired. They had with them a pretty, dark-haired young actress from Dublin in high lace-up boots and a short navy skirt. Willie's services were to be employed to fix this metropolitan vision up with an appropriate man. I left him looking like one very happy matchmaker indeed.

In the little lounge round the corner I found two of the four Northern ladies who'd interrupted us earlier, Maureen and Noreen, trying to fill in their forms. They were from Belfast, and, despite their bantery tone with Willie, they were in deadly earnest. They weren't looking for moonlight roses, they said, but at the same time it would be nice to meet a decent man who would respect them for what they stood for, who wouldn't just be in it for the physical side of things.

If you were in your late thirties, early forties, as they were, there was not one place you could go, Maureen said, in the North, if you seriously wanted to meet someone of the opposite sex. Most of the dance halls had been blown up. Those that remained were for the over-sixties. The disco scene was for the under-twenty-fives. In England, she believed, there were singles clubs, but not in Belfast.

'The Troubles were responsible for so much,' said Noreen. 'As for the ceasefire, I don't even *listen* any more . . .'

By the time I left them Noreen had tears in her eyes. 'If anybody says they're coming to Lisdoonvarna Festival for the *craic* and they're not looking for a man they're lying.'

'Whatever they say,' said Maureen, who was a primary school teacher, 'there's a wee hope that Mr Right might be standing in the corner.'

It was a terrifying thought to hold, as you walked up and down the main street of the little town. All these hundreds of people, young, middle-aged, old, very old, very very old, secretly looking for the *one*. Surely it couldn't be true?

Early evening, near the guy selling hats in the little central square, I ran into Willie, still clutching his big matchmaking book, casting greetings here, there and everywhere. Half the town, it seemed, were using his services.

Had he found a match for the Belfast ladies, I asked. He was working on it. And the Dublin actress? Oh, Therese, he chuckled. A lovely girl, a lovely girl. He thought he might have done. 'Twas an American fellow, a computer programmer from New Jersey. He was tall, like, and well presented. Who knew? If I came to the Hydro later I could see how it went off.

'Are you looking for wives?' I asked two tweed-jacketed chaps up at the bar of the Ritz.

'We got 'em! One's enough.'

'They drive us hard enough!'

'We couldn't manage another!'

Now and forever till the eh-eh-ehnd of ti-i-ime. Between the deep orange-red walls of the Hydro's main bar they'd been bopping and twisting all day. In the corner of the crowd I noticed that the lipsticked blonde and her permed chestnut mate had found themselves a couple of attentive bearded gentlemen. I slumped down next to a nurse from Dublin, who wasn't, she said, particularly looking for anybody. 'It's a weekend,' she said succinctly.

Through the foyer, beyond the dividing doors, two huge women in their sixties were propped up in velvet armchairs.

'Are you hungry for a meal?' asked one of the other, eventually.

'No, no.'

'Nor me. Not for a big meal I'm not.'

I looked up to find – well I never – the Gaelic TV crew: Sonya the producer, Leslie the director, Paddy the cameraman and Therese the performer.

'Oh hello,' I said, as casually as I could. They were after somewhere quiet to plan their shots with the computer programmer from New Jersey.

'I'm available,' I joked, 'if it doesn't work out.'

By eleven the bar was so full you could barely move. I was trapped against a radiator, talking to a man from Co. Limerick who was up for the festival with three mates, two of whom were 'definitely on the pull'. The bald one with the black eyebrows was knows as the Bull, he told me. In the little town they came from there wasn't a woman with a marriage in trouble whom the Bull hadn't... Thankfully, the noise drowned out the details of the Bull's horrid activities. My new friend ended with a shrug and a smile. 'They'll pull,' he yelled in my ear. 'They're not fussy.'

We were just getting on to politics (he was for a united Ireland, the British *had* to leave the North), when Therese suddenly appeared, weaving her way delightfully through the contrastingly hideous crowd.

Look, was I serious about doing this TV thing? It would only be an insert. You couldn't *believe* the men Willy had set her up with. It was a *panic*. The guy from New Jersey looked like a spider, and the other fellow, a farmer from Tipperary, was so stupid he could barely speak.

So I played an Anglo-Irish farmer from Kilkenny, in the

absolute certainty that nobody I knew watched Gaelic TV. It was a *panic*.

Around 4.30 in the morning the Guards appeared in the back bar of the Imperial, where the Teilifis na Gaeilge crowd, the spider-like computer whizz from New Jersey, Ned from the Burren Castle, the lipsticked blonde and the chestnut perm, the Bull and his mates (still trying to pull) were all to be found.

The authorities' assault on this last-chance saloon was slow, as every time they asked someone to drink up now please and move on, they'd find themselves, it appeared, falling into ever such an interesting conversation themselves. By five, having finally shifted everyone into the front bar, they sat down for a well-earned rest, and were promptly set upon by two young females with cropped tops, one of whom had one of their caps perched jauntily on her head. 'Sure, but you've got lovely eyes,' her friend was saying.

14

Cúpla focal

If I were trying to write about contemporary Ireland, Sonya
the producer told me, one thing I should definitely check out
was the set of Teilifís na Gaeilge's Irish-language soap opera,
Ros-na-Rún, which she and Paddy the cameraman were moving on to on Monday. I'd be welcome to come along.

So I missed out on a closer look at the bleak beauties of the
Burren, the limestone plateau that covers 100 square miles of
northern Clare and famously supports a huge variety of Arctic,
Alpine and Mediterranean flora, all, by some freakish botani-
cal enigma, growing alongside each other. Instead, I squashed
into the back of the battered little Polo with Paddy and the
camera equipment and wound off the escarpment down a
narrow, drystone-wall-lined road towards the shimmering blue
and deeper blue of Galway Bay.

In the following morning's sunshine we were out early down
the coast to Spiddal, the seaside village on the edge of the
Irish-speaking region, the Gaeltacht, where the Gaelic soap
was made. While Sonya and Paddy did technical things with
the Lisdoonvarna footage, I toured the *Ros-na-Run* set with
Fran, the production manager. It was, I discovered, 'a typical
west of Ireland village', with a pub owned by a sinister and
calculating landlord, a café run by an openly gay couple, and
a radio station that played host to a vexed love triangle.

Just to keep things realistic, there was a young hunk in love
with a much older woman, an ex-nun with a shocking friend-
ship, and a B & B landlady with a stormy marriage to a
husband who lived in Boston. That they all spoke different
regional dialects of the Irish language (an aspect of the soap
I'd heard about in Dublin) wasn't a problem. That was how it
was, Fran protested, in real life these days. Their crew, for

example, were from all over – the sound mixer was from Belfast, the cameraman from Connemara, the costume designer from Dublin.

But would the inhabitants of a real Ros-na-rún really all speak Irish? Oh yes, Fran said. Right here in Spiddal, for example, it would be people's first language. Some of the local children wouldn't speak English until they went to school, and even outside the Gaeltacht, in wider Ireland, it was now quite trendy to speak Irish, which it never used to be. You could get a little badge reading *fáinne Gaeilge* which meant, 'I speak Irish', or *cúpla focal Gaeilge*, which indicated, more approachably for most, that you spoke 'a bit of Irish'.

Down the street in the centre of Spiddal it was certainly true that many of the shop signs were in Irish – *An Droighneán Dunn*, *Eamonn O'Fatharta* and *An Cruiscín Lán*, the pub. In the playground of the little school with the wonderful view of the sea the kids squawked around bilingually. And when we called in for a coffee at An Cruiscín Lán, and Sonya ran into a couple of mates who played in an Irish reggae band, no less, they greeted and spoke to each other entirely in Irish, to the total exclusion of me and Paddy (coming from Belfast he had not a word of the language) who sat beside them like dumb, English-speaking lemons.

But there was no gay café, there were five B & Bs, the chemist was Walsh's Pharmacy, the garage Burmah Petrol, and the woman in the newsagent was from Stockport.

Sonya and Paddy had a little filming to do in the large white building that had once been a convent and was now a residential centre for people with cancer. So I sat down against a rock in the garden and looked out at the three Aran islands, basking in Galway Bay. The sea, stretching out towards them under the early afternoon sun, really was, I decided on consideration, a burnished gold.

The TV pair emerged, rhapsodizing about candles, incense, the gentle atmosphere and a great piece of footage. We sped north, through the most bizarre, yet most symbolically Irish, landscape I'd seen to date. On the rock-strewn ground to either side of the road, the criss-crossing limestone walls formed a vanishing perspective to the high horizon. In among these tiny plots were the ruined stone cottages deserted in the

Famine years, and then, cheek by jowl, the bright Bungalow Blisses of modern Ireland, seemingly oblivious of the picturesque antiquity around them.

On our left, just beyond a large square pub that was straight out of Father Ted's Craggy Island, were the squat hi-tech headquarters of Teilifis na Gaeilge, where our frantic pair had yet more business.

While they got on with that, I snatched a coffee with the equally busy PR guy, Padhraic, who, despite the timeless tranquillity of the landscape through the windows, was torn between a meeting he couldn't avoid at 2.30 and wanting to fill me in on the history and purpose of T-na-G: the growing disillusionment in the Irish community from the mid-1980s onwards with the national broadcaster RTE; the awareness that they weren't fulfilling their remit to provide some sort of special recognition of the Irish language; the development of a focused campaign for a major initiative, culminating in the demand for a dedicated channel . . .

As I picked at my baked potato and listened to this enthusiastic mission statement, I was wondering about these phrases that get bandied about in such situations. What did 'growing disillusionment in the Irish community' actually mean? Did one shepherd in Dingle turn to another and say (in Irish, of course), 'I don't know about you, Tadgh, but I'm increasingly disillusioned with RTE's failure to fulfil their remit?' I doubted it. Somewhere along the line a few educated movers and shakers had stirred up the situation, just as they always had.

Ever since the arrival of the Scandinavians in the ninth century the status and health of the old Gaelic tongue had been an essential, latterly symbolic, part of the Irish struggle. From the Statute of Kilkenny onwards, English attempts to put down the vernacular had repeatedly met with failure. When Poyning's parliament had re-enacted the Statute in 1494, they'd had to skip the Act against the Irish language, so prevalent had its use become during the fifteenth century. Subsequent measures by Henry VIII and Elizabeth I, the downfall of the old Gaelic order after Kinsale, the rise of the Ascendancy after the Boyne – all had taken their toll, but Irish remained the speech of the majority until the mid-eighteenth century.

It was the very badge of Irish identity. The traditional Gaelic bards ('who by their ditties and rhymes in commendation of extortions, rebellion, rape and ravin do encourage lords and gentlemen') played a major part in keeping it alive, identifying the language with the 'Golden Age' of the ninth century, before the Norsemen had arrived to spoil everything. For the native nobility, use of Irish was a matter of pride; English was the hated officialese of the middle-class Army officers and other State servants who arrived to confiscate their land.

Only in the nineteenth century was this identification between language and nationalism broken, when O'Connell told his loyal masses that Gaelic was a barrier to progress (and a new system of national education made English the standard).

This was temporary. Even before O'Connell's death, Thomas Davis was filling the columns of his Nationalist newspaper *The Nation* with enthusiastic articles on the Irish language (alongside others on Irish poetry, music and art). 'A people without a language,' he wrote, 'is only half a nation.' He urged a revival until 'the brighter days shall surely come, and the green flag shall wave on the towers, and the sweet old language be heard once more in college, mart and senate'.

The recovery took another bound forward with the Irish literary renaissance of the 1890s. Yeats, Standish O' Grady, Æ, Lady Wilde, Lady Gregory and others made Irish folk tales, myth and language central to their work. In 1892 Douglas Hyde (like Yeats, a Protestant Anglo-Irishman) delivered a famous speech, 'The Necessity for De-Anglicizing Ireland', and a year later he founded the Gaelic League, which, within fifteen years, had enlisted a quarter of a million Irish men and women, and introduced the teaching of Irish to 3,000 schools. (The League was also a central force behind the 1916 Rising.)

After the Free State came into being in 1922, the Gaelicization of education became a central policy. The first Minister of Education, Eoin MacNeill (who had, incidentally, been the Chief of Staff of the Irish Volunteers when the Easter Rising took place), wrote of his belief in 'the capacity of the Irish people ... for building up an Irish civilization ... I hold that the principal duty of an Irish government in its educational policy is to subserve that work.'

There was plenty more where that came from, but after all the centuries of ups and downs it was, ironically, the compulsory instruction of Irish in schools that had led, as Padhraic told me now, to very negative feelings towards the language, a negativity that was currently, he went on, 'actually one of the main areas of baggage that we have, at T-na-G, to try and break through. Because even though teaching approaches have changed, an awful lot of people still associate the Irish language with old Ireland, retrogression, narrow political and religious and social attitudes.'

T-na-G was doing that breaking through by telling people 'that this is just a language, not a whole set of values. It's like, if you wish, a computer language, which buys you an alternative view of the world. It doesn't demand you ignore the vision you already have, it complements and augments it.'

Indeed, as Fran had told me, Irish was 'quite trendy' once again. Gael schools throughout the island were oversubscribed, and if you saw someone with a *cúpla focal* badge in An Cruiscín Lán, you might go over and say, '*Dia dhuit?*' if you were from Connaught, or '*Dé mar atá tú?*' if you were from Donegal.

Man of Aran

The one o'clock coach from Galway to the ferry at Rossaveel was a swishly modern double-decker, and it seemed to be entirely full of boisterous, adolescent schoolgirls. An assorted foursome opposite me was teasing the prettiest of their number about which of the Bungalow Blisses along the road was her home.

'Is it that *shed* there?' one of them crowed.

Eventually it appeared, a long, low building (plan no. 59) with a sea view and a crimson saloon car parked in its gleaming black driveway.

'Oh, it's *nice*,' the girls murmured, mockery modulating into polite or actual approval (it was hard to tell which).

Then we were passing the Craggy Island pub and the headquarters of Gaelic TV.

'Teena-gee!' the girls chorused, giggling, before launching into an in-depth critique of the station's programmes, which my PR friend from yesterday would have found most interesting:

'What was that one with the man in the hat, it was *deadly* . . .'

'No, no, some of them are quite good, what was that one about the snowman . . .'

On the little ferry's deck I sat in the sunshine with my newspaper flapping on my knees. 'Trimble to lead his Party into Stormont to "confront" SF' read the headline, but my eyes had wandered lazily away from the small print of this latest twist to the immaculately hairless, caramel legs of a plump American woman in a tight pink checked shirt opposite. Next to her, her husband's fat purple money belt nestled snugly against his expansive navy belly.

We docked at Kilronan, the little harbour-town of Inishmore, the largest and most developed of the three islands. Parked at the end of the stone pier was a long row of maroon minibuses, each containing a driver offering an island tour. At the end, where the pier became the sand-dusted, dung-scattered road by the beach, was a new row of persuaders, standing picturesquely by their pony buggies – jarveys, as they are known. I trudged on, up past the big hostel above the pub and the café on the corner, to the little square by the Spar shop, where the yellow 'island bus' was just being loaded up prior to departure.

It was driven by a man from Leeds with a colourful biceps-load of tattoos. We bumped along the tiny 'upper road', stopping here to drop off an old lady, there to leave a parcel of groceries or pile of fuel blocks on a wall. At the little school a fat-faced nine-year-old ran out. 'Beat him,' he shrieked to our indulgently smiling driver, 'by *far*!' He was followed thirty seconds later by a ginger-haired lad who would turn your ambitions to parenthood overnight, so thoughtful and expressive were his young features. He smiled, nodded and said nothing.

Just above the little white-sand curve of Kilmurvey beach,

where a blue flag fluttered proudly above a squawking mob of seagulls, was a long double-cottage, the Man of Aran, which had been recommended to me by an guidebook compiler from home. I'd already had a intriguing chat with Joe, its landlord, on the phone from Spiddal.

He'd sounded dryly good-humoured down the line and although he was altogether larger and more lumbering than I'd imagined, he was dryly good-humoured in person. 'Did you stay sober?' he asked me when I told him I'd come from a weekend in Lisdoonvarna.

'No.'

'Well, then you're human.'

He hadn't been to Lisdoonvarna himself in a long time. Living out on the island, he spent most of his spare time these days in London.

The Man of Aran was about the quaintest-looking dwelling I'd yet seen on the island, with its long, thatched double-roof and its terraced garden running down to the turquoise sea. I should have guessed it wasn't entirely authentic. It had been built in the early 1930s for the film *Man of Aran*, by the Canadian director Robert Flaherty. 'It only featured in a couple of frames,' said Joe, 'but there you are, money was no object.'

Joe and his wife always used to show the film after dinner, he said, but his son Patrick had done for the video and gone off to Cork, so that was that. There were daily showings in town, though, at the tourist centre. 'It purported to be about the life of the island,' Joe continued, loitering by the door to the little kitchen, as I sipped the tea he'd made me. 'He got a few things out, but it wasn't bad. They went out on the headland and caught a shark, which they hadn't done for a hundred years or so. But he was trying to make a point.' Joe chuckled and raised an eyebrow. 'Man against the elements. Rousseau had the same idea. The noble savage.'

But he couldn't be standing here idly chatting. He had vegetables to dig for dinner. If I wanted a walk there was a nice one up to the old prehistoric ring fort of Dun Aengus.

'On fine Saturdays and Sundays in summer,' (wrote the Englishman Tim Robinson, in a book I was to dip into that evening, by Joe's toe-scorching peat fire) 'a line of slow-moving coloured dots slants across the hillside west of Cill

Mhuirbhigh – tourists climbing the path from the village to the
famous prehistoric fort of Dún Aonghasa. The intentions of
thousands of their predecessors have prepared a way for them
that channels their own intentions, in a self-perpetuating process. ... The ancient remote fort is a cog of a worldwide
machine, hauling up a chain of expectations almost as predict-
ably as a ski lift.'

Now, on this late September's evening, the day trippers had
gone back to the mainland, leaving just one jarvey-load from
the sightseeing tribes – a perma-tanned walrus in grey slacks,
white trainers and yellow baseball cap, and his plump, oven-
baked consort in shell suit and wraparound shades. They were
just leaving, so I paced alone along the well-worn path up the
steep, stone-strewn hillside. At the top rose the three wide
circles of 'fortifications', one inside the other. The first, outer-
most, was five feet high and six feet thick; the second, 150
yards up through a field of jagged spike-like stones, eleven
feet high and eight feet thick; the innermost ring was much
more solid and carefully built, a beefy wall of precisely cut,
unmortared stone eighteen feet high and thirteen feet thick,
with one entrance, just three feet wide.

Not that I was measuring at that moment. I was in a daze,
enjoying the silence of the evening, quietly stunned by the
yellow-pink glow of sunset that shone, primevally, through this
narrow oblong eye. Inside the inner ring there was an eerie
hum from the wind in a ragged wire-netting fence. The well-
trodden lawn led over to what looked like it might be a cliff
edge –

JESUS!

I cowered back and sat shaking on the grass. It wasn't just a
cliff edge, it was a precipice! An absolutely sheer drop of
what, 200, 300 feet, down to tiny white waves outlining toy
rocks far, far below. But there was no fence, no sign, nothing.
Only when you turned did you see a small placard on the wall
behind you: '*Aire fan siar ó bharr na hoillte* – Danger. Keep
back from the edge of the cliff.'

It would have been a symbolic enough place to go, for the
limestone rings of Dun Aengus swim mysteriously out of the
very earliest Irish history, long before the unjust arrival of
English, Norman or Dane. The 'fort' is named for Aengus

(also Aonghas and Engus), the leader of the Fir Bolg, the short, dark people who, in legend at least, occupied Ireland before the Celts.

It's a misty, exotic, rather Tolkienesque era, the early historical period, peopled also by the semi-divine Tuatha De Danaan, who travelled through the air in dark clouds to Ireland, and slew 100,000 Fir Bolg at the battle of Mag Tuired, the plain of towers. Present as well were the Fomorians, a race of one-legged, one-armed, one-eyed demons, led by Cichol Clapperleg, whose stronghold was a castle in the sea.

Eventually, all three tribes were swept away by the Gaels (or Goidel), a race founded, according to the *Lebor Gabála Erénn* (*The Book of the Taking of Ireland*) by Goidil, the great-great-great-grandson of Japhet, Noah's third son. The Goidel invaded from Spain, whence they had arrived after a journey that took in Egypt (where, like the Israelites, they were oppressed), the isle of the Sirens (like Odysseus they filled their ears with wax and sailed on by), and a battle with the Amazons. According to *Lebor Gabála*, it is from the invading Goidel leaders, Heremon, Heber and Ir, that all the royal clans of Ireland are descended.

Still shaking slightly, I headed back through the narrow door and down to the outer fortifications. From this height, looking back over Inishmore, you got a clear idea just how freakishly barren the place was. Even on this late-summer's day, the grey limestone base had just a flecked covering of green.

On the right of the picture, to the south, the cliffs continued so sheer that they looked as if they had been cut with a giant cake mould. Apart from two small farmsteads I could see in the centre, the houses of the island were all straggled along the main east–west road, from which, to the left, the coast sloped gently down to the low northern shore.

Back at the Man of Aran, Joe's wife, Maire, had risen from her daily nap and was busy in the kitchen preparing dinner. Unlike her husband, she was an islander, and her skinny frame, dark skin and clear, far-seeing eyes in her pinchedly handsome face spoke of a very different breed from the comfortably padded Joe.

He, having dug his vegetables, was lurking by the fire with a pile of books for me to read. It was his intention, he told me, one day to produce a bibliography of everything ever written about Aran. To be going on with, he gave me the Robinson pair, a battered biography of the local lead actor in the *Man of Aran* film (entitled *Man of Aran*), and a travel book by one C. C. Vyvyan, *On Timeless Shores*. She had arrived at Kilronan on a whim from Galway and had no sooner set foot inside the house in which she was staying before she'd been invited to a funeral.

'That wouldn't happen today,' I said to Joe, looking up from this passage, with its atmospheric description of the huge procession following the bright orange cart on which the coffin had been laid, the mourners bowing down to the earth 'like Muslims'.

'We don't have time to go to funerals,' he replied. 'We're so busy with the tourists we're getting to the stage where we'll have to vaporize 'em.'

He had started his adult life at Trinity College, Dublin, it emerged, though he'd never finished his degree, a source of wry disappointment to him, it seemed. ('Now I must do my chores,' he said, as he headed off later towards the washing-up. 'This is what becomes of a man who couldn't even get a degree out of Trinity.')

After Dublin he'd moved to London, where he'd worked as a builder for years, playing rugby for Ealing in his spare time. There he'd met Maire, and now, having moved back to her island, he spent most of his time breaking stone in the one-acre organic vegetable garden he'd hewn from the intractable soil. I asked him about the criss-crossing stone walls that ran like a web all over Inishmore. Were they anything to do with the Famine? No, he replied. 'It's just so fecking hard to make a piece of ground where you can grow something – you've got to put the stones somewhere.'

In the morning I took the bus into town to see the famous film for which my lodging was named, and in which, for all of two seconds, it featured. Although no big deal by the standards of today, you could see how this early documentary had been received as a masterpiece, with its wide-screen depiction of gnarled, black-clad islanders struggling to wrench a living from the harsh shore by the perpetually roaring sea. You watch these lurching 1930s figures bringing up seaweed by boat, fishing by line over the cliffs, then hunting a shark and almost drowning in the process. 'Two long days of struggle to win the shark's oil for their lamps,' read one of the sonorous titles that interspersed the action.

'Every year school upon school of these monsters migrate along the western coast,' read another. Mr Robert Flaherty, the hyperbolic director, had had similar luck to C. C. Vyvyan. No relation to the Aran O'Flahertys, he had visited the islands by chance in November 1931, and, 'as they got off the steamer they were introduced to Pat Mullen, an islander who had spent many years in America and who, since his return to Inis Mór in 1919, had been supplementing his small income from kelp by driving tourists around the island in pony and trap.'

It was the perfect symbiotic relationship. Flaherty got his reputation-winning documentary about remote poor people; and Pat Mullen and his mates got to star in a movie, become celebrities and eventually write a book. The autobiography takes us from 'Early Years' and 'School', through 'Family Friction' and 'Better Fortune' to 'I Meet Mr Robert Flaherty', 'I Become Contact Maker' and 'Selecting a Cast'.

The picture of the island before the corrupting blessing of tourism is one of extraordinary hardship and poverty. When Mullen was a boy, the family lived, like many of the other Aran islanders, by gathering seaweed, which was dried and burnt for kelp (from which iodine was extracted). This seaweed gathering was no jolly or noble community activity, but a competitive struggle, with every family foraging for itself.

After a storm, Pat and his brothers would be 'rooted out of bed' by their father, at 'one, two, three, or four o'clock in the morning' and hurried down to the shore. 'At such times my father was like a tiger. He yelled at us and cursed at us as we gathered the seaweed in the tide and filled our buckets, which he would carry up the beach and then come running back for more.'

The best wrack would then be dried on walls from August till June or July of the following year, when it would be burned in kilns. Thirty tons of wet seaweed would produce one ton of kelp, for which the asking price was around £5. It was hardly surprising that the half of Mullen's family of ten who didn't die in childhood emigrated, like him, to America – 'America! How I used to sit by the sea and watch the sun sink in the western ocean, beyond which that great country lay!' – or that Mullen himself, when he discovered that he 'wasn't built for America anyhow' and returned, took to tour guiding.

I looked on the maroon minibuses in a different light now.

The most dramatic part of the film, the shark-hunt, had been made at the far western tip of the island. The next day, although it was thick with mist, I walked up there. It was the weirdest place, the rocky fields gradually giving way to a great pavement-smooth plateau of metallic grey limestone, in whose fissures a few blades of grass struggled to grow. The drystone walls continued to criss-cross the landscape, so that it looked eventually as if the entire scene had been petrified, cast in a spell perhaps by one of the wicked spirits of Celtic legend.

Eventually, a wash of blue sky appeared through the mist. The sun, no longer just a flickering white-gold disc, began to give form to the mightily receding slabs of cliff. The sea, swirling and heaving around the brittle-looking rocks, gleamingly reflected the powerful, if still diluted, light. It was easy to see how Flaherty had been inspired.

I gazed out west, hoping to see the outline of the mountainous Hy-Brasil, a meteorological mirage that featured in Aran folklore as the Island of the Blessed, visited by saints and heroes, and actually marked on maps until the sixteenth century. But there was nothing there, just sea and sky and the prospect of America.

That evening I was joined in Joe and Maire's little dining room by two Germans, a jolly, grey-bearded father and his lean, black-bearded son, who quizzed Maire earnestly about the organic 'wegetables' we were eating, of which he thoroughly approved.

It turned out that the father wasn't German at all. He was an 'ex-Rhodesian', had only moved to Germany when Mugabe had taken over. Standing with a glass of claret in his hand after dinner, Gerald remembered the old colonial days with fondness. Frankly, he couldn't believe there wasn't something good about that system, when you could clap your hands and Jackson would bring you two perfectly done eggs. It was a matter of pride to Jackson that they were perfectly done, and in return . . .

Anyway, now – Gerald nodded towards his son, who was discussing cucumber frames with Joe – he was trying to get used to a more egalitarian way of life. His son was staying on a religious commune near Kilronan, and they were having an 'interface week', sharing a tent and trying to work out things between them. Attending the University of Pietermaritzburg, 'mixing with blacks', had changed the son's life for ever, and now he wanted to return and become part of the future of South Africa.

The fact was that, like so many fathers and sons, although they were wrestling mightily with the differences between them, they were two of a kind: intense, passionate, serious – albeit the father had developed a surface modicum of humour. When we repaired to the pub with Joe and Maire, Gerald told me about an experience he'd had when visiting the Black Abbey in Kilkenny.

There was a wooden figure of Jesus in there, with no arms and no legs. The inscription nearby read 'Defaced by Cromwell's soldiers'. Gerald was staring at this, with tears streaming down his face, because he was half-Cornish and half-Irish and the two sides of him were forever at war. He thumped his breast. The Irish rebelling, and the English – he made a fist – punching the shit out of them.

He'd been standing there, weeping in this fashion, when an old Franciscan priest ('in the white cassock, you know') approached him.

' 'Tis lovely weather we're having,' he said.

After talking like that for a while, Gerald decided to broach his problem. 'Oh,' said the priest, 'I wouldn't worry about that, I'm half-Norwegian myself.'

Now Gerald laughed and raised his eyebrows. But he'd still wanted to sort out this problem, so he asked the priest if he'd give him absolution for what his English forefathers had done to his Irish forefathers. He felt all this so strongly that it was tearing him apart, he said.

What religion was he, asked the priest. Well, he was Lutheran, but he'd been taught at a Jesuit school.

'You were taught by Jesuits?' said the priest. That was good enough for him. So they knelt together by the defaced Christ and said the Our Father together. But still Gerald wanted more. In the end the priest agreed, and knelt with him and they intoned together an absolution for the sins of his English fathers. And since then he'd been at peace. In here – he thumped his breast again.

When they'd gone, back to the tent where the son was going to try and persuade the father not to return to his marketing job in Germany, but to 'drop out, stay and experience something real', Maire and Joe and I had another little drink, and all kinds of island secrets came out.

It wouldn't, sadly, be fair to repeat such private gossip in detail, but what came through very strongly was that being an islander was one thing and being from elsewhere was another. If someone was unpleasant and an islander, they could get away with far more than if they were from the mainland. That was the only problem Joe and Maire had ever had between them: that her family was working-class and from the island and that his was middle-class from Dublin.

Maire had once had long, ash-blond hair, but in her years in London she was always pursued by the wrong kind of man. Men who would take her out and try and take her to bed. She was asked everywhere – to the theatre, to the opera – then, one day, she'd grown sick of it and cut her hair short. The wrong kind of men left her alone after that, and a little later Joe had happened along. Beside her, the ex-builder raised his eyebrows and made a face.

C. C. Vyvyan had found Inishmore hard to leave, and so did I. 'I do not now remember the early stages of our absorption,' she wrote, 'nor how and when we cast all our daily habits aside, nor at what moment we began to feel that we had always lived on that timeless island. We were very soon convinced that there was no other sane way of living.'

I had only been there three days, but I could have sat reading in front of Joe and Maire's fire for a month. You had to go no further, it seemed, to meet most of the the interesting people on the island. Here was a bulky man with glasses who ran the Irish School. Soon he and Joe were ensconced by the fire discussing the finer points of vegetable growing.

'This year was bad for pumpkins – why?'

'It's cold, too cold . . .'

'Courgettes were all right . . .'

'I think the mistake we're making is trying to keep heat in . . .'

Luckily my mind was made up for me. One evening I returned to find the front door of the Man of Aran blocked by a huge pile of straw. The chocolate-box roof had been stripped down by two thatchers, revealing battered green corrugated iron beneath. Making a bonfire with some of this old thatch, Joe had managed to burn through the main electricity cable to the cottage and now there was no light or oven.

'So this is how a prop forward ends his days,' Joe said, leaning on his garden fork by the thatch, as I headed off to catch the yellow island bus to the harbour.

Kenny Live

It was paradoxical that all the tourists went to Inishmore, because the old Ireland they were seeking was preserved in aspic on the next island along, Inishmaan, which had, if not turned its back on visitors, certainly done nothing to encourage them.

There was an infrequent boat service to the 'Middle Island' and I got out there only through the good offices of the ferry captain, a neatly uniformed Englishman, whose haunted eyes, pockmarked skin and pukka accent made him seem like a character out of a black and white adventure movie from the 1950s, almost certainly starring Kenneth More.

'I'll see you inside in a minute,' he'd said, as I stood on deck with the straggle of islanders who were returning from the mainland this Friday evening. I thought he might be about to tell me that he'd once murdered a man, that things had never been quite the same since 'Nam or even invite me up to the bridge for a shot or two of fine old navy rum, but it was only the fare he wanted, a cash payment of £6, which he trousered efficiently.

The flashing lighthouse of Inishmore receded and the scattered lights of an altogether squatter silhouette appeared. I stood outside in the chill twilight wind. Someone had made a little silver cup with a piece of chocolate foil, which whipped madly this way and that in the airstream by the green gunwale. It was a very different reception at Inishmaan's stubby little pier. There were no pony and trap operatives, no minibuses, just a couple of tractors holding a group or two of welcoming friends and relatives. A spattering of English words amid the unselfconscious jabber of Irish; there was no need for any artificially constructed language revival here.

A row of incongruous orange streetlights lit the pier and fifty yards along the dusty track up into the island. Drawn up along the stony shore were an upturned row of black curraghs, the first time I'd set eyes on these traditional Aran boats, except, of course, in the *Man of Aran*.

I followed the gaggle. Which way was Faherty's, I asked a pair of lads loitering under one of the streetlamps.

'Angela's,' they replied. She was up the hill and right, a stumbling walk along a pitch-dark lane under the brilliant stars.

In the morning Angela Faherty cooked me a fine breakfast. 'Are you a writer?' she asked.

I owned up.

'That's all we get from now on,' she told me. 'Writers, sitting in the front room with their laptops, condensing their books.'

Hoping my occupation wasn't too obvious, I headed up into the middle of the little island. It rose, in terraces of limestone-strewn fields, from the curved shore on each side of the pier to a ridge along which straggled, my map told me, seven villages, although to the untrained eye it would be hard to tell them apart.

It was astonishingly quiet. On the long lane that was the main street of all the villages a bee buzzing past was the noisiest thing. Even the little mopeds that people used to get around seemed to whoosh silently past. I wasn't the only visitor on the island, yet everyone stopped to greet me. In Irish. I cursed myself for forgetting the phrase of acknowledgement that Maire had taught me, replying, rather lamely, 'Hello'. This brought the reply, 'It's a nice day.' 'It is,' I replied, 'lovely.'

Yes, here indeed were all the things that you see in the postcards and brochures, the Ireland of dreams. A woman with four teeth in a traditional shawl; a Madonna and child in a niche of wall, surrounded by a vivid green tumble of orange-flowered nasturtiums; dogs and cats lolling in the sunshine by open doors; a group of five men on two ladders rethatching a whitewashed stone cottage. Bungalow Bliss had not reached this shore.

In the village shop the goods were stacked up on high shelves like something out of the 1930s. A blind man and his dog lurked just inside the door of the church. And what should have been the island's prime tourist attraction, Synge's cottage, had nothing but a tiny sign, 'Teach Synge', pointing to the derelict dwelling. Anywhere else this would have had an interpretative centre and audio-visual at the very least. Here, pushing through a creaky door under the rotting brown thatch, I found a strong smell of damp, bare stone floors, blue and rose flowered wallpaper peeling in yellowing strips from wood-wormed pale blue board. There were a packing case, an old stove, a broken fishing rod and, above the fireplace, a blackened and rusted cooking pot. In the end room were a Madonna on a shelf, a lopsided sink, a stack of paint cans beside a great pile of rye. 'It's in a sore state,' said the man in the shop next door, but I found it wonderful – a fittingly unfurbished shrine.

It had been Yeats who had encouraged John Millington Synge to come to Inishmaan. A Trinity-educated, Anglo-Irish Protestant, Synge had, after some years wandering the Continent, drifted to Paris, where he had been leading the bohemian life of what Yeats later called 'the Tragic Generation'.

'Give up Paris,' Yeats had told him. 'You will never create anything by reading Racine, and Arthur Symons will always be a better critic of French literature. Go to the Aran Islands. Live there as if you were one of the people themselves; express a life that has never found expression. I had just come from Aran, and my imagination was full of those grey islands where men must reap with knives because of the stones.'

So in 1898, this 'gentle, shy fellow' with the bulky figure, heavy black moustache and 'that deep sense of humour that is sometimes found in the quietest people' set sail from Galway in 'a dense shroud of mist'. He spent a short while on Inishmore before moving on to Inishmaan, 'where Gaelic is more generally used, and the life is perhaps the most primitive that is left in Europe'.

Many writers had written of peasant life before, but never from the point of view of one who had lived among them. Synge had already won prizes for Irish at Trinity; here he enlisted a local teacher and listened. The result was the plays that were subsequently performed at the Abbey, the theatre that Yeats and fellow littérateurs had recently opened in Dublin, as a deliberate part of their literary renaissance. 'We will show,' he had said, 'that Ireland is not the home of buffoonery and of sentiment, as it has been represented, but the home of an ancient idealism.'

Riders to the Sea was set on Inishmaan, and *The Playboy of the Western World*, Synge's most famous play, had characters drawn from his continuing close study of Ireland's country people. When *The Playboy* was first shown in Dublin in January 1907 it provoked riots, with the first-night audience breaking up in disorder at the shocking use of the word 'shift' (to describe a night dress). This was not the idealized image that the middle-class Catholic audience wanted of traditional Irish life.

'Anyone,' Synge wrote in the preface to the play, 'who has lived in real intimacy with the Irish peasantry will know that the wildest sayings and ideas in this play are tame indeed, compared with the fancies one may hear in any little hillside cabin in Geesala, or Carraroe, or Dingle Bay.'

On the last night the play had to be performed under police protection – seventy stood inside the theatre and 500, according to some newspaper reports, kept order in the streets outside. Such was the artist's reward for his honest portrayal of the life that had never previously found expression.

Having drunk in the unpolluted atmosphere of Teach Synge I walked on, up past another Dun and out beyond the last little hamlet of Cinn an Bhaile and over the blue-grey fields of stone to the cliff's edge. Here was Cathaoir Synge, the play-wright's chair, a horseshoe of piled stones with a view over

Gregory's Sound to Inishmore. The only noise was the splashing of sea on the rocks below, overlapping with the distant echoes of waves thumping into blowholes.

I paced on, hearing only the occasional seagull against the breeze, the heaving of the sea, the brittle clink of the hard limestone under my shoes, the low wail of the wind in the walls.

Right out beyond Ceann an Bhroibh I found two men fishing with bright orange lines on wooden reels (larger versions of those we used to use in Cornwall as children) with stones for weights. This had been one of the scenes of *Man of Aran*, still quietly thriving here.

I asked if I could take their photograph and they stood before me like Victorians, holding the two fish they had caught and already gutted.

'Will you be in the pub this evening?' the older asked.

But when I went there – expecting what? A game of dominoes, a music session, some of the faery stories Synge had heard? – I found instead the ruddy-faced gentlemen of the island (not a woman among them) lined up in a row on a long bench, their dark pints before them, watching a large-screen TV above the bar. It was broadcasting *Kenny Live*, an Irish chatshow almost as celebrated as *The Late Late Show*. Throughout this programme there was a most respectful silence, almost as if Pat Kenny and his guests (Gaelic footballers from tomorrow's All-Ireland final) were larger-than-life figures at the end of the bar.

15

Latte, is it?

James Harrold, the Galway Arts Officer, had initially been labouring under the misapprehension that I was my elder brother Robert. He must have misheard the message I'd left on his answerphone, because I had to stop him in full down-the-line flow as he enthused about how he'd read all my (his) works, it would be a *great* pleasure to meet me for a drink etc.

Now, single malt in hand, perched tubbily on a stool at the bar of Tigh Neachtain's ('the best bar in Galway'), he seemed to be making the best of his mistake. So it was a *travel* book I was writing? Yes, I replied, and a piece for the *Sunday Times*. At the mention of that newspaper, whose specially recon-structed Irish edition is one of the more popular Sunday reads, James's eyes regained their sparkle. So what sorts of things was I looking for in Galway?

I began on my standard explanation. That I tended just to go with the flow, follow up—

Well, in Galway, James interrupted, there were simply *loads* of people I should talk to. The Druid Theatre company, of course, was a must – they had an *amazing* production of Martin McDonagh's *Leenane Trilogy* on at the Town Hall Theatre at the moment. Then there was a season of new short plays in the studio upstairs, might well be worth checking out. It was a *dreadful* shame I hadn't been here during the Festival . . .

His flow was interrupted by an edgy-looking character in round glasses, to whom James now introduced me with all the flowery formality of an Edwardian dowager duchess. 'This is Mark McCrum, who's writing a book on contemporary Ire-land, and a series of articles for the *Sunday Times*. And this is Eion O'Connor who . . .'

Eion, it seemed, read scripts for Druid, among others, and was working on his own plays. No, Martin McDonagh wasn't bad for someone who lived in Camberwell.

He'd taken his holidays in Leenane, that was how he knew it, said James.

But the characters were terribly stage Irish, said Eion.

The Lonesome West was the best one, said James, without a doubt. But in his opinion Druid's acting actually transcended the writing. I should really look into the whole Druid success story from the 1970s onwards. They had, interestingly, first become famous internationally. In Australia, the States – but they'd never been to Dublin. And in the end, Dublin people realized they had to come down West and see them.

Had I seen *The Weir*, Eion interrupted. No, I replied (not quite sure which of the two I was talking to), but I'd met Conor McPherson, its young author, briefly in Dublin. *Had* I, said Eion. He was only twenty-five or something and he'd got the most incredible reviews in London, the *bastard* . . .

It was said as a joke, of course. But Eion's whole skinny thirty-something frame trembled with feeling at the word 'bastard'.

But before we could attempt a satisfyingly begrudging analysis of that youthful success story, we'd been joined by Justine, a shimmeringly lovely masseuse whose husband worked as a designer for – well, well – Teilifís na Gaeilge. She'd just dropped in to Tigh Neachtain's for a pint or two on her way home from swimming. Our conversation ground to an abrupt halt as I discovered a sudden deep interest in aromatherapy oils.

Now here was Kate, a short, neat, dark-haired law lecturer at University College, Galway, in a state of upset because she'd had a row at work over the marking of a student's papers, and had got caught up in faculty politics. The anger in her intense blue eyes mellowed to breathless laughter as she swigged back bottle after bottle of Holsten Pils . . .

Now here was Kate's American friend, Molly, who was an actor and working in a secondhand clothes shop between jobs and . . .

Here was a man from Mayo . . .

Tigh Neachtain's was just that kind of place. By ten o'clock James was the plumply twinkling centre of an ever-shifting crowd of writers, poets, performers of various kinds and levels. As Arts Officer he had control of the Galway Arts budget and, therefore, the funding 'yes' or 'no' over any number of projects. Here was a gaggle of long-haired poets who wanted him to come to a wine bar to hear their reading at midnight. James nodded and smiled and promised to do his best, before leaning forward and, in his soupy, lilting, almost camp Galway accent, saying behind his hand, 'They're dreadful, absolutely *dreadful*, there's no way I'm going to their reading.' I sympathized: midnight was clearly beyond the call of even the most committed arts administrator's duty . . .

At quarter past we have to drink up and leave. James and I have been sitting on the same stools since five, and I've had nothing to eat but half a packet of peanuts, but I'm still just as keen as he is to go on. The vexed question is where. The wine bar is clearly out of the question because of the dreadful poets, but it's OK, your man from Mayo is sorting it, his cousin has a pub just down the road, a call is put through on the mobile, and in a moment we're sating our hunger in Supermac's on the corner, where the soggy burgers take no longer than ten seconds to arrive in your hand, and in another we're standing at the side door of your man's cousin's establishment while your man's cousin gets rid of the legitimate customers from the front.

I'm not quite sure whose friend your man from Mayo is, but he's from Mayo, and he's wearing a suit and tie, and the main thing about him is he's still seriously depressed about Sunday's result when Mayo lost to Kerry in the All-Ireland Gaelic Football final. It's not something to tease him about, because he really is terribly upset about it, and he's powerfully built and even more powerfully boxed, and the only thing that's going to cheer him up tonight is Molly, the American, who has an open, pretty, Goldie Hawn-style face, albeit under dark hair, and the man from Mayo is going to take her home with him, which is why we're all being allowed in, I guess, to your man's cousin's pub.

Now the side door opens. With a rapid glance up and down the street for the Gardai we're hustled in. The lights are dimmed, curtains drawn, we're served, the *craic* goes on.

Mayo man is quite convinced that Molly is going to spend the night with him. He's pushed right up against her by the window, his hand clutching out vaguely in the direction of hers. A less-boxed man might have noticed her body language, which is not encouraging. She arches away, like a ballerina, makes discreet faces sideways at us, and moves her non-drinking hand out of range behind her back.

Meanwhile, the cousin and the other barman have wished us goodnight and let themselves out. We're left in charge of the glistening barful of bottles and taps, and the etiquette seems to be that if we want another drink we help ourselves and put the money in the till. We're to lock the door behind us when we go.

The stories roll on. We roll out. Mayo man goes home. 'What a turn-off,' says Kate. 'Please don't drive,' begs Molly. Mayo man stumbles off towards his car.

There's nothing for it but the wine bar and the poets. But the lights are up, the chairs are stacked by the window and it's utterly closed. The drinking is over. James, Kate and I repair reluctantly to Apostasy for a hot chocolate. Apostasy was set up by an Australian who had travelled all over the globe before settling in Galway. On the wall are shelves containing *objets* from fabulous destinations: a trio of buddhas, an espresso machine, a model of the Taj Mahal, a copper-wire Arabian teapot, a Celtic cross. 'Old endgame lost of old,' says a legend on the wall. 'Play and lose and have done with losing. And may these characters remain when all is ruin once again.'

The Australian is not the only settled traveller in Galway. The place, even now, at the start of October, is a buzzing hive of them. On the wide grass oblong of central Eyre Square, they sit, this lovely autumn morning, loosely dressed, stripped to their narrow waists, strumming a guitar, nodding, chatting, strolling up towards Eamonn O'Donnell's bizarre public sculpture, whose rusty 'sails' are supposed to evoke a Galway hooker and thus the city's proud nautical history as the third most important port (after London and Bristol) in the British Isles.

This I learn from yet another blow-in, Michael, a writer from Chicago, who's leading the Galway City Tour to pay the rent while he finishes his book on the Irish Civil War. Michael has the weirdest accent – American, but with powerful touches of Irish ('grand', 'tink', 'dat' 'your man') thrown in. The 'grand' is fine; even I have started saying 'that's grand' rather than 'that's great' when the white pudding arrives each morning. 'Your man'? Well I have started thinking it if not saying it. But 'tink'? What's your man tinking of?

Michael speaks of his adopted city with warm Irish pride. As the open-top bus chunters past the Lawn Tennis Club, he tells us that tennis had initially been reviled as an English game, 'but now we're awfully glad it's here'.

Most of historical Galway, sadly, appears to have been pulled down. Michael enthuses about the lone seventeenth-century doorway that stands in Eyre Square. ('It would have once graced a building that would have stood two or three blocks back.') He asks us to imagine 'the great tower' that 'would have risen' by what is left of the city walls. He shakes his head sorrowfully at the destruction of the Claddagh, the old fishing village that predated Galway City, where the people had lived in thatched cottages, spoken Irish and given each other Claddagh rings, which had been torn down as a health hazard in the 1950s. What a misjudgement! For what a tourist mecca it would be now, I thought, gazing down at the homogenous streets of dull brick council housing that had replaced it.

With plenty of time to spare after our look at the remains of old Galway, the tour bus chuntered adventurously up the hill, past washing-festooned tower blocks that made Limerick's South Hill seem like an up-market residential area. That yard of battered caravans was 'the travellers' halting site'. And here was 'a development of new bungalows'. You had to admire Michael's resourcefulness as he drew our attention to 'a patch of blackberries, which are now,' he added helpfully, 'just coming to the end of their season.'

From here you got a splendid view down over the little city, dominated by the mighty limestone cathedral that looked as if it might have dated from the Middle Ages, but was actually completed in 1965. Just about time to pull it down, then.

*

There was a lot of smartly kept housing in this panorama, which was clearly not lived in by boho drifters; the hordes of tightly buttoned old ladies who drank tea at the formica tables of the Galway Bakery Co. on Shop Street were clearly not all struggling with their first novels; but it was the students from UCG, the backpackers and James's constituency of the would-be artistes that gave the place (for me, at any rate) its stay-awhile charm.

Though I was actually sleeping in a pristine B & B up on College Road, it was down in the Cross/Quay nexus of streets that I hung out. Here, just along from Tigh Neachtain was Kenny's Bookshop, an old town house chock-a-block with every Irish volume under the rain. Up the narrow stairs in the Poetry Room a young man with long dark hair and a black velvet waistcoat sorted slim volumes into tall piles.

A contemplative stroll away was the Café du Journal, where, under a bust of Shakespeare, they served *mocha* and *latte* and you could sit at the little marble tables by the dark green and purple walls and gaze up at bookshelves full of books that no one would ever read, or listen as the man with the fey accent and baggy blue jeans complained about his croissant. ('I'm not being *fossy*, but it just wasn't *hot*.') Around you groovy singles and couples got on with their mellow days, read a paper, did a crossword, flicked through a playscript, studied the manual of the new laptop they'd just bought. For the first time since Dublin I felt both mildly pretentious and at home, catching up on my journal in the corner.

'Too Much Bohemian Coffee Shop Layabout Types and drug-induced bilge from crusty hippy type shites (also begrudging graffiti artist types)' said a scrawl in the Gents, and who was I to disagree? Another read 'Beware the ceasefire'; another 'The Next Race To Conquer Ireland Should be the Irish'. Why, the place was educational.

And who should I find when I emerged, sitting smoking in a white jersey in the sunshine by the window, but Kate, who had recommended the place to me, and usually dropped in for an hour or so at some point in the day. She was still furious about the case of the wretched student, but laughed in that now familiar breathless fashion about the details of last night, some of which I'd completely forgotten: out by the loos of

Tigh Neachtain a man had been throwing up next to a woman talking on her mobile phone; and then, in the ladies, the woman had been saying, still on the mobile, 'He's not very well, but he'll probably make it.'

But UCG really were the pits. The fact that they had given Ronald Reagan an honorary degree said it all. None of the other universities would touch him, but Garret FitzGerald and the President of UCG had dreamed it up between them. So outraged were certain junior members of the faculty that they'd gone out on to the streets of Galway and conferred honorary degrees on passers-by, asking them questions and only giving them a degree if the answer was sufficiently stupid.

Goodness! Who should be floating in now but American Molly, just finished her day at her clothes shop, and would anyone like to come to a play this evening at the Town Hall Studio Theatre – it was supposed to be quite good and she had a friend in it.

Recalling the Arts Officer's recommendations, I seized my opportunity, remembering too late (when I was actually squashed on a hard wooden bench at the back of the studio) that much fringe theatre is a firm proof of the essential goodness of human nature. Why else would twenty people sit through a 'black comedy' that was more black than comic but wasn't even that black? Certainly not to admire the loud hum of the lighting system.

Afterwards Molly and I and Maggie, another supportive actor friend, stopped behind (as you do) for a glass of wine in the empty bar. We were joined by the two actors and then the lanky grey-haired playwright. Congratulations were clearly in order for the actors for endurance beyond the call of duty. Having seen a fringe play of my own performed, I felt like anything for the playwright, who sat, genial but uncomplimented, on the edge of the group. But I still couldn't bring myself to utter the comforting lie.

When he'd gone, the actors let rip, as actors who've agreed to take part in a dud show always do. 'When you're doing it it feels like it'll go on for ever,' cried Dan. 'Then you've done it and it's a *blip*!'

The Fields of Athenry

What do people do in a little country town like this, you think, as you step off the gliding train, push up a crimson throwaway umbrella against the drizzle and stroll, comfortably baggage-less, up the empty road over the railway bridge.

There are heads bent in the classrooms of a big school on the right. Here, ahead, is a curving shopping street, with a steamy-windowed tea-shop where they have Van Morrison on the sound system and two plump women in overalls behind a tempting glass-fronted cornucopia of cream-filled pastries. 'Queen Cakes', says a hand-written card on a row of pink ice cubes, '10 for £1'. Yes, oh yes! If it weren't for the coffee (a heaped teaspoonful of Maxwell House powder) I could grow fat and happy in Athenry.

I have left my luggage in Galway and come out here vaguely hoping that some relatives of a London friend might put me up for a night or two. Peter's sister Angela looks, to my tired traveller's eyes, just like him. It's uncanny. As if he's had a sex-change, got considerably prettier, and moved to the west of Ireland to become a housewife. He is a successful London journalist, forever flitting from launch to opening to launch to opening. And here she is, knee-deep in toys in an Athenry kitchen. She's as good company as her more-famous brother, though, and our first, somewhat nervous coffee, turns easily into a second, relaxed one, then a mutually confessional bowl of soup.

Angela's husband Dick is a vet, indeed, I guess, *the* vet in Athenry. He arrives as we're on our third cup of coffee, bringing with him mud from the celebrated fields, and Cousin Dan, the reformed alcoholic American poet cousin whom Angela has warned me about in advance. Dan's been staying in the spare room for *months* and they just can't get rid of him. Originally he'd been funding his poetry by driving a cab in Boston, but he'd lost his permit. His plan, Angela laughs, was to come over here, get an Irish licence and then drive a cab in Galway. But first he has to take his test and really she doesn't see why they should have to wait around all winter while that happened.

Cousin Dan has obviously sensed the pressure a *little*,

because now he's taken to going out with Dick on his rounds, 'taking the numbers' as Dick inspects cattle. But quite honestly, Angela says, Dick's happier on his own. Dan doesn't really know what to do, he makes mistakes, he's more a hindrance than a help. But it's clear that Dan reckons he's done a good morning's work. He sighs loudly as he removes his muddy boots. He sits hungrily at the table, shakes his long black hair out of his face, wipes his mouth with the back of his hand. Behind him, Angela raises her eyebrows and makes faces as she prepares him yet another meal.

On Angela's suggestion, after lunch, I head out with Dick for the afternoon. I've heard 'The Fields of Athenry' so often that I'm rather taken with the idea of seeing the reality.

By the lonely prison wall, I heard a young girl calling,

First stop is an abbatoir. As we walk in they're killing sheep. I stand and watch as the dark-haired fellow with the Sweeney Todd face does the honours in the high-sided metal pen in the corner. The live sheep, trusty-eyed, is stunned with an electric tool that leaves a bloody hole in its woolly head. It's chucked out, still kicking, on to the concrete floor, which is awash with gore as thick as whipped cream.

'Even though they're kicking they're stunned,' Dick assures me, as the butcher slits the animals' throats with a big knife and the red liquid arcs out in a spurt. One, two, three of them lie in the crimson pool, legs writhing, throwing up splash-patterns on the green stone wall behind. As the blood drains out of them they grow stiller.

'Out with him for the day, is it?' asks the butcher genially, as he sets about removing the fleece from the first corpse, shoving his balled fists deep down between skin and carcass. The whole thing peels off like a lady's coat, albeit a lady's coat matted with red blood and green faeces and brown mud.

'Michael, they are taking you away',

Half-stripped, they hang the carcass on a hook, drag the rest off with the slow tug of a powerful chain-drive. Inside, the white surface of the body is almost plastic in texture. In the old days, my butcher friend tells me, they just used to slit 'em down from the throat and tug 'em off by hand. But the buyers won't take 'em like that now. If there's any knife marks on them all the fleeces get sent back.

Where do they go, I ask.

'A lot of them goes foreign,' he replies. To Russia, he thought. Europe. For sheepskin coats. Some, I shouldn't wonder, end up in the souvenir shops of Killarney and Kilkenny – genuine Irish wool fleeces. Lovely.

For you stole Trevelyan's corn, so the young might see the morn,

While Pat slits open the sheep's belly, chucks the grass-filled stomach into one trolley, and the long coil of guts into another, Dick is round the back, checking a row of stripped corpses on hooks for BSE. He's looking for a clean carcass, he tells me. He stamps each body with a little purple triangle: 'Approved 32 GY.' Then he's checking the livers, which are hung on a rack nearby, slicing into each with a sharp knife. 'A little bit of an abscess there. That's OK,' he says. The high-risk spleen goes into a bucket, to be burnt. Spleen is a specified risk-area for BSE.

Now a prison ship lies waiting in the bay,

Set back from the abbatoir is, not a Bungalow Bliss, but a Detached House Ecstasy, a spanking new double-storey mansion in a Versailles-style layout of gravel paths and potted trees. 'He's doing well,' Dick agrees.

Driving on, I ask about Cousin Dan. Dick is considerably more circumspect on the subject than his wife. 'These artists and writers,' he says, raising an inclusive eyebrow in my direction. Then, keeping it very general, there was, he adds, a kind of American who came to Ireland who was 200 per cent Irish, if I knew what he meant.

Low, lie the Fields of Athenry,

Next stop is a little farm, where we're going to test some cattle for TB. Outside a battered corrugated-iron shed a dark-haired lady with a fringe is beating her small herd of five into a narrow pen. They're whipped along with a length of black hose; then, lined up and jostling, a patch of hair is shaved at the neck and they're stab-injected with a brisk sideways movement. If they have TB they'll get an allergic reaction. They make noisy attempts to kick their way out of the pen, pissing and shitting on the front of the one behind.

Where once we watched the small free birds fly,

I'm surprised that it's worth keeping a herd that small, I tell

Dick as we rattle on down the little lanes in the grey semi-
drizzle. There are plenty of farms like this, he says, of forty or
fifty acres. A lot of the farmers would have other jobs too.
Increasingly, the women work. They have to, Dick says, to
keep up with all the expensive things people need nowadays,
cars, televisions, videos. The world is changing.

Our love was on the wing,

And indeed there's another woman waiting alone at the
next farm.

'There's no men around,' I say.

'Because we're the better gender,' Katrina replies with a
matter-of-fact smile. We spend a drizzly hour stabbing heifers
in the backside.

That place of Katrina's was unusual, Dick says, as we drive
off, the farmhouse still being on the farm. In the old days it
was the norm, but now you'd find the farmer and his wife
probably lived up the road in a new bungalow. Maybe the old
mother would live in the farmhouse. So when Dick pitched up
at a farm, he'd then have to drive on somewhere else. It was a
time and motion study; to be honest, a pain in the arse.

We had dreams and songs to sing.

Our last call of the day is with a dashing-looking gentleman
with blond hair and moustache. No muddy green waterproofs
for Rory. His gear is blue, above matching blue denims, which
are tucked into shiny blue wellingtons.

He's after certificates for three of his horses. One, the black
three-year-old, he's already sold to a dealer from Limerick
with more dash than cash. Your man had hair down to his
shoulders and champagne boots, and he arrived at seven in
the morning knowing exactly what he wanted. The second, the
grey, is for an English lady from Tipperary with plenty of
money. The third is headed to the Ballinasloe Horse Fair,
which starts on Saturday. He's a magnificent specimen, cream
with chestnut patches, a skewbald as opposed to a piebald,
and Rory will be looking for a handful for him.

A handful?

Rory holds up five fingers. Five grand. He nods, smugly.
He'll be there on Sunday around 12.30 if I'm going.

When will he sell it?

Around seven, he guesses.

'Nasty old evening.' I turn to find we've been joined by Ian Paisley, in a thick coat and flat tweed cap. 'Yes,' I reply, and out of politeness refrain from asking him why, as a reverend Christian minister, albeit of his own church, he won't come in on the peace talks.

Down the muddy track Dick tests the creatures' hearts. In the damp gloaming they canter round the ring on a holding rein as Rory stands proudly central, cracking the whip. Behind, across the celebrated fields, the smudged blobs of trees fade into the darkening mist.

'Magnificent horse,' I say to Dick.

'Flashy,' he replies. 'Like a fellow with a platinum blonde.'

It's so lonely round the fields of Athenry.

Dick has a dog and a cat left to see, then a meeting of the Hunt Committee (the famous Galway Blazers), so he'll join us back at the house later. Which is now full of children, behaving very naughtily indeed, running into the kitchen behind the resident poet and humming, 'Goodbyee, goodbyee . . .'

Behind the bulky Bostonian, Angela looks exasperated as she cooks him bacon and eggs for his supper, meanwhile loading the washing-machine and dealing with the endless questions and demands of her children. Cousin Dan offers not a smidgeon of help, just chomps away, between, and during, mouthfuls engaging me in pro-to-pro *chad* about *riding*.

Around half-ten Dick is finally finished. We go for a drink. Dan, who has come along for the ride, sticks manfully to Coca-Cola, as our cream-topped, lip-smacking pints arrive. We're joined at the bar by Malachi, who's a local antiques dealer and, would you credit it, the town's resident Republican. Before I know it, I'm caught up in another passionate conversation about the North. One of those rising, eloquent, detail-packed tirades that makes you wish you were permanently wired for sound, but if you were, you'd have half a book by the time he'd finished.

When Peter was last over, Malachi tells me, he offered to drive him, personally, up there. So that he could see for himself how working-class Protestants abuse working-class Catholics, how shop owners abuse their customers, how South Armagh is the most militarized zone in Europe. I have to see it, the place is bristling with hi-tech equipment. He'll take a weekend off and personally drive me round.

In the morning Angela walks me through the town. Athenry reminds me of Fethard, in Tipperary, full of unkempt important ruins. The Priory (built 1240) is the only surviving example of a priory within city walls, which are themselves the 'best preserved in Ireland'. The old Protestant church, which rises picturesquely from the crumbled remains of the collegiate church of St Mary's, is now derelict itself.

Only the three-storey tower of the Norman castle of the de Berminghams has been restored. The authorities have done a good job, refurbishing the interior with 100 per cent Irish oak. Angela is passionate to do something about the rest. She wants to turn the little wilderness at the heart of the town into a formal garden, the ex-Protestant church into a heritage centre, and then pinch some of Galway's tourists, which she would surely do, for this place is a trove. How can I tell her that I prefer it as it is, with the cigarette ends of the school smokers and lovers littering the ground under the sprawling brambles.

Athenry has another big issue, too, which it shares with numerous towns across the Irish Midlands. Travellers. Many of them stay out on the edge of town, by the rat-infested dump; others have beaten-up dwellings along the Galway Road. One caravan is parked at the end of a neat street; a settled woman who lives there chucks a bucket of Dettol-filled water on the pavement whenever the two little traveller children run by.

Sister Leo, head of the local convent, whom we meet by chance in the market place, does a lot, Angela tells me, for these much-reviled people. But when I ask her if she'll take me round the sites she refuses. It's very controversial in Athenry, she tells me. Come to the convent and she'll give me a book.

So I go to the convent and wait by a vase of fresh flowers in the echoing hall, which smells faintly of furniture polish. Sister Leo appears with the book. 'It's a deep-down *racial* prejudice,' she all but whispers. If I want to know more, I should go to Tuam, where a third of the town are travellers, and, for the

first time in history, a traveller has been elected on to the
town council.

Passing the steamy-windowed cake-shop where the queen
cakes are still ten for a pound, I feel I know Athenry better
than I did twenty-four hours before. I have almost enough
characters for a *Ross-na-Rún* style soap for the English-
speaking rural population of Ireland.

16

Holy Mother of God

City Styles, Dolan Electrical Supplies, Hogan's Pharmacy, Xtravision Video Films, Cakes 'n' Creams, Simply Red Hair Fashions, Beatty Jewellers – another country town whose secrets I shall never know. The Athlone local bus, speakers blaring Michael Jackson, chunters out of Loughrea and on past Aughrim to Ballinasloe.

The Battle of Aughrim (12 July 1691) was both strategically more important and bloodier than the Boyne, marking the final defeat of the Jacobite forces before the Treaty of Limerick. The gable-ends of the Shankill Road could as easily read 'Remember Aughrim', but the empty fields have forgotten all that now, and Bungalow Blisses sprout where once the Marquis of Saint-Ruth had his head taken off by a cannon ball.

We grind, in a jam of horse-boxes, Land Rovers, lorries and picturesquely trotting loose horses, into Ballinasloe, where I alight opposite the focus and main meeting place of the International Horse Fair, Hayden's Hotel. The name had led me to expect something much grander and more nineteenth-century, not this grey motel lookalike. It's of no account anyway. The place was booked up months ago. As were all the other hotels and B & Bs in town. Only by ringing round desperately have I managed to get a room in a private house in Harmony Park, which I realize, as I dodge a couple of frisky piebalds and trudge round the corner, is in fact Hymany Park, not the leafy cul-de-sac of my imagination, but a Limerick-style council estate, with grey pebbledash houses in long terraces, each with a handkerchief of garden out front to express its tenant's personality: flower lover, grass lover, paving-stone-lover, old-car-parts lover, alcohol lover. Children fool on the concrete road. Dogs yap from behind fences. Here, on the corner, a horse tied to a shed whinnies magnificently.

Reaching my appointed number (neat green lawn and elaborate window boxes, good), I sling my pack off my shoulders and ring the bell by the frosted glass door. As I do so a man with lank black hair, greying beard, wobbling belly, limp and accompanying stick, appears behind me with a key. But he won't let me in. It's not his place, he tells me, in a whining (English) accent. He's only the lodger.

Oh for goodness' sake! I'm staying here, I know the name of the landlady, I have a piece of paper with this address and phone number on it. What more does he want?

That's as maybe, he replies. But he's only the lodger. He might get into trouble if he let me in. Anyway, am I after the single or the double?

I'd booked a single room, I said.

Oh well, he replied, there was only one single room and that was gone. He'd paid, up front, for nine days.

We'd sort it out, I'm sure, I said, when the landlady returned.

Well, he wasn't sharing, he replied. He'd paid, up front, for nine days.

Look, I said, could I just leave my bag inside. Then I'd go off into town and come back later.

'It's not my place,' he whined. 'I can't.' And with that he pushed the door firmly shut, leaving me and my bag on the concrete path. It had started to rain again.

Fifteen minutes later Pat appeared. She was a skinny lady in her sixties, squeezed dry by life. Her bright, nervously flickering, grey eyes shone out of a crumpled parchment skin. Her hair was short, permed, pensioner ash-blond. You'd imagine she'd had the butt end of a cigarette between her lips since the last war.

Wouldn't he let you in? Oh, that *man*. Pat shook her head and lowered her voice. She'd known as soon as she'd seen his face he was going to be a problem. She headed upstairs, purposefully, and returned, shaking her head some more.

In the tiny kitchen at the back she was apologetic. She was stuck, she said. She'd taken on too many and the thing was, would I mind sharing? He was a very nice man, the other man who was staying, 'a gentle-man like yourself'. As soon as she'd seen his face she'd known he was a gentle-man. She'd never put me in with the likes of *that* man. He'd come over from London. He was from Ballinasloe originally; now, she whispered, he lived in Streatham. He was here for nine days and she didn't honestly know how she was going to put up with it.

I didn't mind sharing, I said.

Oh *thank* you. As soon as she'd seen my face she'd known I was gentle-man. Now would I like some tea and sandwiches?

She and her husband, she continued, flicking on the kettle switch, were already going to be sleeping on the floor of the kitchen tonight. Nine days. She didn't know she could face it. Last year they'd had two ladies who were a bit loud when they came in but otherwise no problem. And a lovely Swedish fellow. She'd given him the key and said, 'See you next year.' But he wouldn't take it. And then, d'you know, after he'd been up to look around Connemara he'd come back to stay with them.

Her husband had joined us. Joe was diffident and mild-mannered. His aim in life was, clearly, to avoid saying anything that might upset anyone. Had I been to the fair before, he asked. No, I replied. Well, the weather was looking hopeful, he said, nodding through the window at the drizzle.

Now who had appeared, brazen beast, but your man from upstairs, freshly changed into a shirt with fat blue and white stripes under an off-white windjacket. His grey flared trousers and white shoes completed the ensemble nicely. Banging his stick on the yellow lino floor he stomped over to sit on the chair next to Joe, addressing him loudly, man to man direct, as if Pat and I weren't in the room. Didn't they have a cousin in common, he began, launching into a catalogue of Ballinasloe names.

Pat stood tensely by the sink, hands curled back with irritation.

'D'you come to Ireland often?' she tried in a pause.

He ignored her, rattling on at Joe. Pat looked over in my direction. But I was looking studiedly, ever-so-politely (being a gentle-man you see), directly at your man. She tried again. Was ignored again. Now when I looked over and met her eye she flash-raised her eyebrows, made a jabber-jabber gesture with her hand.

I addressed my lips firmly to my mug of tea.

Poor Joe! He was so well-mannered he had to be polite to the Streatham monster. Yet you could see he was simultaneously trying not to upset his wife, who had a huge workload this weekend, all these guests in addition to her regular job nursing a lady in a private house in the country for cash. *And* they were spending tonight on the kitchen floor.

I gulped down the dregs of my tea and took my leave. Joe seized the opportunity to escape from his awful dilemma, literally leaping across the kitchen floor on the pretext of showing me the short cut into town, which involved turning right and going straight ahead into town, rather than turning left and going right round the estate first. Thanks for that tip, Joe.

Ballinasloe was pretty miserable in the drizzle, so after a quick nose round Main Street and Society Street, I did what everyone else was doing and pushed past the dinner-jacketed bouncers into Hayden's. The hotel was well-prepared for a weekend of agricultural roistering. The floral carpet and halfway up the walls being covered with thick polythene. Already this was overlaid with a muddy scattering of boot tracks.

The long bar was packed with red-faced chaps in fifteen shades of green keeping the noise level at a back-slapping din. I sat with my pint in one corner, feeling decidedly out of it. Having made all this effort to get here, and to find somewhere to stay, I clearly couldn't run away now. And look, already I'd seen a young traveller ride bareback down the main street. That had been quite colourful. Tomorrow, doubtless ...

'Mark!'

My lonely musings were interrupted by the voice of – surely not! – Frank the Goatcatcher. What on earth was *he* doing here? Well of course. Puck and Ballinasloe were two of the three ancient fairs of Ireland and kept up a twinning arrangement. I had even spoken to a couple of the Ballinasloe organizers back in those summer days in Kerry.

Frank, accompanied by his wife and son Francis (inventor of the 'friendly cage'), was on the most relaxed possible form. No, I wasn't to buy him a drink; he would get me one. So how did I find Ballinasloe? And where was I staying? They were at Hayden's, which was comfortable enough.

Now what was I doing tonight? There was a reception here in Hayden's, which Frank was sure I'd be welcome at. If I met them in the foyer at 8.30 he'd introduce me to the town clerk and then, he winked, we'd see what would happen.

So it was that I ended up having dinner under the stained-glass dome of the Hayden's ballroom, seated next to the Chief Superintendent of the Ballinasloe Gardai. The person on my left had not turned up, and there were quite a number of empty seats around the room, but who was I to complain, tucking into Melon Fan with Kiwi and Peach Sauce, Cream of Vegetable Soup, Salmon Darne Bonne Femme and a pudding entitled Sweet Melody, with which feast we were offered a single glass of wine.

'No, they won't come round again,' said the chief superintendent, with a knowing gurgle. He was a most genial fellow, coming up to retirement age, I guessed, but in no way high and mighty. Ballinasloe, I discovered, was not such a quiet little backwater as you might imagine. They'd had a murder four weeks back. The assistant manager of the amusement arcade (Fun World) had been found first thing in the morning with his throat cut. Their prime suspect had fled abroad. 'To your country, we think,' said the chief superintendent.

After the meal there were, of course, speeches. A dour-voiced gentleman from Ballycastle told an off-colour joke (which brought hands to the mouths of many of the ladies present) before presenting the council with a bottle of whiskey from the Bushmills distillery. A large lady in crimson from that same Northern town celebrated the fact that the Three Fairs connection was going from strength to strength. No mention was made, of course, of the fact that Ballycastle was, technically, in a foreign country; in this kind of context, they just seemed to gloss over all that.

Then Frank was called up, on behalf of Killorglin. 'I am delighted to be here,' he said. 'We like it so much we keep coming back and I'd like to thank you all very much. Thank you.'

Sadly the chairman of the Ballinasloe Council, who followed, was not so succinct. He was delighted, he began, to have office again nineteen years after he'd had it before . . .

No, it was clearly going to be water for some time yet. Now there were presentations, to representatives of companies who'd made a significant contribution to the town: Dubarry Shoes, Western Post-Form Fitted Kitchens, then it was my dinner companion's turn to take the stand, for the 75th Anniversary of the Garda Siochana was being recognized. The chairman extolled them for their skill in operating in difficult times. 'No matter what town or village you visit, there is the name of a Garda written in indelible ink across it . . . they have always been there to talk to you, to help you out, they have always been fair, they have always been good . . .'

If only there'd been more to drink we'd have all been in tears.

But we weren't going to be allowed near the bar yet. Encouraged by Frank, I'd mentioned to the town clerk that I was doing a travel piece for the *Sunday Times*. Now, suddenly, I was being welcomed in front of the whole hall as 'The *Sunday Times*'. As I looked down blushingly at my coffee cup I thought of the two or three paragraphs I would be able to allot to Ballinasloe, if I included it at all (and if Christine, the editor I'd never worked for before, liked and decided to run my piece in full). Clearly, I should regurgitate my Salmon Darne right now.

Now at last a band had appeared and the bar was thrown open. The policemen were up by the optics in a flash. What was I drinking? Well, I wasn't one to refuse a chief superintendent if he was buying.

Some time later I found myself at a large table by the empty dance floor. Did I know, said the woman on my left, that at least two Presidential candidates were coming to see the parade tomorrow. Dana, Frank Nally (the only man running), and possibly even Mary McAleese, the current front-runner.

'We don't need a president in this country,' said an orange-faced man on my right. 'It's a cabbage patch.' Paying for yet another politician was ridiculous. What did they do? How much did all this campaigning cost?

Behind us, the band played all the old favourites of the popular music repertoire and struggled mightily to get the grandees up and grooving. 'Let's get it moving now!' cried the raven-haired lead singer, but to little avail. Only the merest sprinkling of waltzing couples obliged, two of them all-female.

At midnight I stumbled back to Hymany Park to find the other bed in my little room occupied by a shadowy dark-haired man whose snores started up the moment I laid my weary head on the thin pillow. One rasping, gasping, wheeze-futtering hour later I summoned up the energy to fetch wax earplugs from my washcase in the bathroom. Even with these making my head hum it sounded like a Continental moped rally was taking place on the concrete road outside.

'Did you get a good night's rest?' asked Pat in the morning.

'Er, yes,' I lied, smiling thinly across at the destroyer of my sleep, a skinny fellow called Pascal, who'd come to the fair for a number of reasons I couldn't understand, his accent was so thick. When he rose from his last slice of toasted Move Over Bread, who should appear but your man with the whiskers, scrubbed pink and ready for the fair. He was a fascinating specimen of humanity, one of those people who are totally unaware of the appalling effect they have on others. Now, spluttering over his cornflakes, he regaled the company with the details of his evening out. He'd gone into town and had a pint; then he'd come back and watched TV. Well I never.

As she fried up the eggs and bacon, Pat's parchment face was even more pallid and drawn than yesterday. She'd clearly had a bad night on the kitchen floor, and you got the feeling that the hovering Joe was suffering for it, under his ever-upbeat chitter-chat about the weather. We were lucky with it, he observed, nodding out past the aluminium window-frames at the damp grey blanket that was the sky.

Nonetheless, the huge square of green below the tall stone church on the hill was already a wonderful jumble of horses and humans of every description. Chestnuts, greys, blacks, duns, pintos, piebalds, skewbalds, palominos; the blue of jeans, the red of windjackets, the green of tweeds and padded waistcoats, the cream of coats, the black of a polo-necked jumper, the purple and yellow of a football shirt. Here ambled an ebony-haired youth on a handsome bay stallion; there a red-ribboned roan mare was being carefully led by a tightly-jodphured blonde. This dappled grey foal appeared to have no owner; this very frisky sorrel filly pulled hers twenty yards across the throng, to a vociferous chorus of protest (from him, too).

Now the sun had slid out. The muted colours of the scene lit up, the vivid green of the grass base dwindling by the minute.

Directly below my vantage-point (at the top of the steep slope by the main road through town) was the narrow concrete pen where the travellers raced their horses bareback, whipping them till they drooled and foamed at the mouth, skidding like kid cyclists on the mud and shit at the end of a run, leaning so far back from their steeds' necks they were almost horizontal.

Beyond that, the massed rows of stalls sold everything anyone who had ever set eyes on a horse would ever need, including kettles, ferrets and dogtooth jackets. Over the far side were the 'amusements', spangly circles and curves of coloured lights against the grey and white house backs of Society Street. To the left, the horse-packed green led, over the road, to the showground; to the right, the hill was crowded with a muddle of travellers' caravans.

'Once again, ladies and gentlemen,' rang a crackly voice from the tannoy, 'we're taking entries for the Supermac Horse of the Fair Lunging Competition.'

After a fine – albeit entirely dry – lunch with a selection of the less important functionaries from last night (Ballycastle councillors, Frank and his wife, me) I found myself being ushered through the crowds on Main Street and up on to the Guinness Gig Rig to join the chairman of the Council, my old friend the chief superintendent and the Presidential candidates for the viewing of the parade. No fewer than three had turned up: Dana, the ex-pop singer, yes; Frank Nally, the ex-policeman, yes; and Mary McAleese, the academic, in a deep sienna suit that all but matched her layered chestnut hair. From the way she was mentioned first and seated regally between the other two it seemed almost taken for granted that she was the one being taken most seriously. (Nonetheless, when she stood up to wave at the crowd she didn't look as if she was entirely used to it yet; from behind she seemed like a little girl waving goodbye because she'd been told to.)

The parade rolled splendidly past. It was a mightier and
altogether more seriously agricultural affair than Puck. Kellco
Plant and Tool, Ollie Colohan DIY, Value Tile ('a new
business here in Ballinasloe, a beautiful selection of tiles'),
Dormac Plant and Tool. Aer Lingus had a pipe band and
Gullane's Hotel a splendid living tableau of elegant gentlemen
and ladies in top hats, tails and crinolines, laid on by the
forthcoming production of *My Fair Lady* by the Ballinasloe
Musical Society.

There were more speeches, of course: the chairman of the
Council, Alan the Guinness rep (no Irish festival complete
without him) and a junior minister who wasn't nearly as
glamorous as Mary McAleese but then, how were they to have
known she'd be coming when they'd booked him. The future
president smiled with a distant politeness as he rabbited on
about what a welcome change it was that all the horses bought
at the fair were now used for equestrian events, not warfare.
A welcome change indeed, from Napoleonic times.

A bishop blessed the fair and the whole crowd crossed itself.

'Give us back our country!' shouted a wild-eyed gentleman
at the front of the crowd. (Oh dear, had nobody told him?)

As the party broke up, Frank the Goatcatcher rushed over
to shake hands with Mary McAleese, who was already being
led off, flanked by suited minders. I made my way to Dana,
whose only companion was the smart-hatted young female
reporter from North Shannon Radio. I felt rather thrilled to
be one-to-one with this woman who was definitely the wacky
card in the presidential line-up. 'Were it not for what it tells
us about the state of Catholic conservatism in Ireland,' the
ever-waspish Fintan O'Toole had written a while back in the
Irish Times, 'the notion of Dana coming to the Aras from
Alabama with a banjo on her knee would not be worth talking
about. The very absurdity of the idea is significant, though, for
it arises from what must be desperation on a heroic scale. The
conservatives have seen what Mary Robinson has done for
liberal Ireland. They have had to sit and watch as a woman
who opposed them through all the battles over contraception,
divorce and abortion has become the acceptable face of Ireland. And they want to seize back the symbolic high ground.
And they pick . . . Dana?'

At that stage he, and other pundits, had assured us that she'd never be a candidate, but she had read the Constitution, knew that the president was technically the direct choice of the people and had managed to get herself nominated by five county councils, one more than she needed, to become the first-ever presidential candidate not put forward by one of the major parties. From his Dublin eyrie, O'Toole and the others might scoff, but the councils hadn't denied her, out here the crowd was still crossing itself, and the revelation that today was Dana's nineteenth wedding anniversary had brought a great cheer.

I'm afraid I managed to squeeze nothing startling from the ex-Eurovision winner. She was, she told me – fixing me in professional fashion with her big brown eyes – speaking for those who hadn't got a voice, and having really tremendous support from people of all ages and backgrounds, cross-party support of every denomination and no denomination, basically she was standing on the grounds that Ireland was a country that could have economic security but also retain values that had sustained them as a people through centuries.

Before I could find out precisely what those values were, and how she, as a long-time resident of the USA, felt she represented them, she was whisked away by her minder from RTE, pausing only to squeeze the hand of Frank the Goat-catcher, who was waiting politely to one side.

Who should I find in the mud-thick foyer of Hayden's (well, I knew he was probably coming) but James Harrold, the ever-ebullient Galway Arts Officer, now in the company of his 'chum Dolores' (by which he means, I think, his girlfriend), who returned to Ireland only yesterday after a year designing theatrical costumes in London.

We stroll à trois through the fair, making the kinds of self-consciously dry observations educated thirty-somethings do in these situations. 'See where they get their tarp from?' says Dolores, pointing at the plastic roof of a stall reading 'Channel 5 – Tuning now for Britain's fifth TV channel'. James says how good it is to see the travellers in such a relaxed frame of mind, their dormobile doors open, mum and the kids piled inside. On the horse-packed green I look for Rory from

Athenry, with his five grand skewbald, but fail to see him. Dolores, meanwhile, has more luck, running into a friend from Co. Cork with a string of tiny grey ponies for sale.

Rebecca Townsley TV Personality; Madame Zelda, Mystic, Palmist on Tour, Choice of the 90s, Advice and Help in All Matters; Madame Lee, Business as usual, Different caravan . . . On a whim, I decide to have my fortune told, for a laugh. And who knows, maybe Madame Lee will know something about the rest of my journey. Will I be kidnapped and murdered when I get to the North? In her lavishly decorated caravan I let her take £20 off me. She looks deep into her crystal ball, which sits in the middle of my palm refracting light from the rounded oblong windows. She knows everything, she reassures me; there is nothing about me she doesn't know.

I'll have a long life and be happy and have good luck in the future. I nod. Sounds good. Now what? She studies me closely.

'You drive a car,' she tells me; which I reckon is a fair guess for a thirty-something guy in a newish brown jacket from GAP. But as it happens I got rid of my car four years ago and am currently proceeding by public transport.

I shake my head. 'No,' I tell her. She shrugs practisedly and looks back in the ball. She looks up. No, there is a car there for me. In the near future. And I won't need to pay for it, it'll just come to me.

'Right,' I say. (I'm still waiting.)

She stares deep again at the multi-faceted reflections of her state-of-the-art caravan. There is somebody in my family on a sick bed, she says eventually. But as it happens, just at the moment, there is nobody in my family anywhere near a sick bed. A year ago, five years ago, that would have been true, but not now.

'No,' I say.

And on it went, the worst fortune I've ever been told, beating even Lincoln from Mysteries in Covent Garden for spectacular inaccuracy. There were two women in my life, Madame Lee told me, one with dark hair and one with slightly lighter hair. The one with dark hair would make me happy. Only one problem there, Madame Lee. There aren't two women in my life.

I was very independent, I wanted to work on my own. Soon I would be in a position to do this. Oh dear. But I already do work on my own, have done, off and on, for sixteen years.

Outside, James, ever the contact maker, has someone he wants me to meet, Cathal, a Ballinasloe 'character', who could be useful to me, being very well connected in Befast on 'the green side of the game'.

We find him eventually in Minnie's bar, which James introduces to me, with his usual formal flourish, as 'the best bar in Ballinasloe, actually one of the best bars in Ireland'.

He's rather magnificent-looking is Cathal, tall, pony-tailed and with a long and bushy blond moustache, highlighted along the bottom with a well-worn nicotine stain. James has described him as, 'a good friend, actually', but I fear the 'actually' gives him away. Like me, he would like to be looked up to, or at least, along to, by this guy who you'd think had just strolled out of *Easy Rider* and would be on matey terms with Clint Eastwood, were Clint Eastwood here.

He has a bookshop in Ballinasloe and acts, and his red-haired wife Leslie is one of the leading lights of the Ballinasloe Dramatic Society (they're currently casting for a production of *Little City* to be performed at Hayden's in December). She has no time at all for the Festival Committee, who entertained me so royally last night. It may well be that I enjoyed my meal, but there's an argument over £300 for something she did for the parade in 1994. She's still bitter about it. Oh dear, oh dear.

Cathal, meanwhile, has no time for the Protestants of the North. On a cross-community theatrical visit they brought down twenty guys from the Shankill Road, and sang 'The Sash' with them, right here in the bar in Ballinasloe, but when they went back up there, they wouldn't let them say the rosary at the end of the play they were doing.

The malty black pints go down in gulps. Three, for these thirsty Galway men. James is in his favourite position, twinkling on a bar-stool with two drinks in front of him. The other is hot port. The 'actually' has left him now, he's back on form, giggling like a Bacchic Bunter at his magnificent fund of gossip. Filtering through the din, music is provided from the corner by a man with a tambourine, and another man with clacking spoons, and Pat, who has bloodshot eyes under a black plastic cap, a single silver flybutton prominently undone on his jeans, and is so totally boxed he can barely stand, yet the flute at his lips is a twittering songbird.

Pat sleeps, says Cathal, either at the police station or the big mental home down the road. He goes out busking round town and brings his money back to Minnie, and she feeds him, takes his drinks out of his busking money. He may be permanently locked, but he doesn't have a mean bone in his body.

The next afternoon, as Cathal, Leslie and I stroll through the thick of the fair, someone lets off a banger and there's a great surge of horses, a whinnying and rearing-up all around us and the three of us are running for our lives. It's all over in a few seconds, but Cathal and Leslie are shaking visibly. 'I'll tell you the truth,' Cathal says, 'I'm frightened of horses.'

We pace hurriedly up the hill to the church, through the mish-mash of travellers' caravans. I stop to take a photo of five or six traveller kids, with their baggy clothes and their hair teased and long on to their shoulders. How quaint and friendly they are lined up, but as we turn there's a couple of loud bangs. Cathal's jumped and I'm smelling singed hair – my own. Cathal has a burned hole in the back of his blue T-shirt.

At the top of the hill, by the low wooden barrier fence, there's a gang of maybe fifteen, twenty traveller youths watching us and talking among themselves. 'Go on,' I hear one of them say, 'just for the laugh. Go *on*.'

I pull my camera to me and we quicken our steps, back towards Minnie's.

By the evening the green is a wide sea of chocolate brown. Close up, it's a slurried collage of dark mud and tan horseshit, pocked with a thousand hoof prints. It's been raining hard since lunchtime, and the competitors taking part in the gig, cart and horse-drawn implements competitions at the showground have all got spectacularly drenched.

Wandering back from this entertainment I am hailed by name. Well, well! It's Rory from Athenry. He's had a good weekend, sold two horses at a profit (not the beautiful skewbald) and bought a fine English saddle from some knacker.

He shows me the price tag, £160, and asks me what I think he got it for.

Um, £100, I reply.

'Seventy pounds!' He's delighted and gives me a short dissertation on the virtues of an English saddle.

'Good luck!' he cries, as I leave him.

I'm going to need it, for tonight I take the eight o'clock bus on to Tuam, and it's not entirely clear where from. Normally you pick it up outside Keller's on Main Street, but on Friday Citylink told me it'd be Hayden's carpark, what with the fair and all. But then, when I phoned to double-check this morning, I was told, no, not Hayden's, I should wait outside Supermac Two.

There are three Supermacs in Ballinasloe and it took a while to establish which was Supermac Two. (It doesn't say Supermac Two outside, or inside; it just says, as on Supermacs One and Three, Supermac. You just know it's Supermac Two if you live in Ballinasloe.) Now I pace around the green in the gloaming, heading for the crimson glow that I'm almost certain is Supermac Two.

Slumped against a wall in a corner is an old fellow with a bottle of cider. 'Give us 70p,' he shouts at a gang of small boys who are passing. 'Sorry Joe,' they return cheerfully, 'we're after spending it.'

Horses trot past me in the gathering darkness, quite often accompanied by owners. There's a wonderful sliver of moon, and despite a sinking feeling that I'm not going to get this bus, I'm enjoying myself again. I'm on the road, with nothing but my pack and, now, a thin, hot coffee and soggy burger from Supermac Two. (It *is* Supermac Two, unless the cherry-lipped fourteen-year-old with the scattering of tiny spots on her upper left cheek is lying.)

I sit on the pavement against a lamp-post and wait. Horse-boxes, cars and more horse-boxes rattle past. Perhaps I should try hitching? No. 8.00, 8.11, 8.33. The two lads over the road are not, after all, also waiting for the bus – they're after a taxi – and they think the bus to Tuam goes from Keller's. If not there, it'll *definitely* stop at Hayden's.

At 8.43, my persistence pays off. Here is my bus, taking the bend on the corner of the green very carefully indeed. I dance in front of it, but it's the wrong bus and nearly runs me over as it turns right into Society Street and up into town.

Finally, at 8.50, this must be it, a crowd of faces at the long lighted windows, taking the bend at speed and racing along the edge of the green. I wave eagerly at it, but it speeds past, on up the road to Tuam. Jesus Christ, I think, sitting there disconsolately watching its disappearing tail-lights. How is one supposed to get around in this bloody country. Citylink, indeed! Now I've got to traipse all the way back to Hymany Park and spend another night with Pat and Joe.

Of course not. Why on earth do I fill my head with such untrusting fantasies? The bus purrs to a halt and the automatic doors swing open.

'There is one here,' I hear the driver say over the radio to his controller. I slump down in the third row of this really delightfuly efficient and clean coach, gradually realizing, as I relax in the cosy warmth, that I smell quite, no very, strongly of horseshit. Both me and my knapsack.

The bus sails on, almost too wide for the narrow roads with their drystone walls on either side. There are neat little towns along the way, with cars parked silently in triangular squares. Out in the middle of nowhere is a tall Madonna in a roadside grotto, stage-lit by our headlamps. 'Holy Mother of God', it reads.

17

The Wards of Tuam

There were many reasons why I might have wanted to visit the little market town of Tuam. The last High King of Ireland, Rory O'Connor, had reigned from here (before being superseded by the Anglo-Normans in 1175). There were two huge cathedrals in the place, one for the (thousands of) Catholics, the other for the (twelve or so) Protestants, each with a bishop. The town was a model of self-reliance, having set up a community-owned industrial plant worth half a million pounds to counter the unemployment that had followed the collapse of the local sugar industry. And finally, 'Choom', as its inhabitants pronounced it, in their singing Galway accents, was the home of that celebrated pop group, The Saw Doctors.

But though the locals would, of course, have mentioned something on the above list, in wider Ireland Tuam was known for its large traveller population, the huge fights that erupted among them from time to time, and for 'the Gilmartin Road' which, if I wanted to see travellers, huh, well, I should just see *that*.

I didn't just want to see travellers; I wanted to meet them. Ever since Dublin I had been hearing about them. In that city they had been 'knackers', to be watched out for when you parked your car on a dark side street; in Kilkenny they'd been 'tinkers', to be chased away from your country house; at the Rose of Tralee my friend Leah had fallen out mightily with a man from Waterford Crystal about their rights and status; in Galway, Athenry and Ballinasloe I had got closer.

Now I was looking 'a traveller' in her frank, friendly, just possibly slightly suspicious, green-brown eyes. She was Ellen Mongan, a Tuam pre-school teacher who was the first itinerant in Ireland's history to be elected to a town council. The eyes were set in a wide white face topped by a sharply cropped mane of jet-black hair.

'White' was important; for the terms in which I'd heard travellers discussed reminded me repeatedly of the way bigots in other places talk about people of colour. They were dirty and they were lazy. Give them a house and see what they'd do with it (have the stairs for firewood, for a start). They were violent, treated their women dreadfully and were promiscuous to boot. They were scroungers, most of them were on the dole, and yet look at the cars they drove, brand new Mercedes with '97 plates – now where did they get the money for those?

Fortunately, Ellen was both robust and well informed. She wasn't offended when I said that I wanted to put the myths and criticisms of outsiders to her. It was hardly a surprise, she said, that people were bigoted, for over the years the media had portrayed the traveller community in a very, very negative fashion. 'And because we're a group that doesn't have contacts or links or a power within the media, we were never in a position to challenge them.'

A large part of the problem was that the differing culture and values of travellers were misunderstood by the settled community. For example, she remembered when she was about ten or eleven years old, her mother being incredibly angry at a suggestion by a settler woman that because they'd lived in canvas tents by the side of the road they must be sleeping with anyone and everyone. 'But it was actually quite the opposite.' Moral values among travellers were high; separations and divorces were low.

And these values were formed very early. Even today travellers deemed that when a girl reached thirteen and went into puberty she was a woman. 'Your time of playing with the lads and all the rest is over and done with, you take on a bigger responsibility.' The sexes were separated, and the girls would be married young. In Ireland, of course, they couldn't legally be married until they were eighteen, so often they would be married 'over the water' at sixteen.

This didn't mean, of course, Ellen went on, that all traveller marriages were perfectly happy. It was just that, contrary to that myth, within the traveller culture the idea that marriage was important and for life was very strong. 'If you're not married, you've missed out; if you don't have children, you've missed out.' It was part of a cycle, where travellers viewed people as part of the group, the extended family. The individual was less important than the group. In the whole of Galway, for example, to her knowledge, there was only one old person from a traveller background in a home. She smiled. 'And Galway is a big place.'

The negative side of this, of course, was that people weren't given the opportunity to shine as individuals. For someone like her, setting up in a career on her own would often be viewed, by people within her community, 'in a very, very negative fashion'.

'But I've created an identity of my own. I don't always want to be known as my father's daughter, or some man's wife. I want to be known as me.'

Her digression had brought us neatly to another of the criticisms on my list: that women were secondary citizens and that violence against women was high among travellers.

It was true, Ellen said, disarming me with her lack of defensiveness. Men traditionally had been in charge. They had a very strong sense that they need to be in control. That role had been slow to die. Even now, it was very much part of the heritage, with the man being seen for his strength rather than his brain. The idea of challenging someone to a fight to establish the finest man was very deep-rooted. ('Personally I think, excuse my language, it's a load of shite.')

But again there was a cultural reason for this. Until the mid-1960s the men had been the ones who'd been the bread-winners, with their traditional crafts of tin-smithing and horse-dealing. Then things had changed. The arrival of plastic had made tin-smithing pointless, and increasing mechanization had destroyed other work – farm labouring, for example – that a community that was still 80 per cent illiterate and unskilled could do. The arrival of hand-outs, first from Christian clergy and societies like the St Vincent de Paul, then from the State in the form of the dole, had completed the redundancy.

Ellen remembered her uncles telling her that the first traveller to get the dole had been 'abashed'. 'He should have been out earning it, you know.' But in due course, more and more

travellers had taken the dole; now the majority did. 'Not *all*.
But a certain number are very keen to take the cushy way out,
the easy number.'

We had come to a third settler criticism: not just the dole
but the brand-new Mercedes vans with the '97 plates.

Ellen laughed. She had yet to see a traveller driving a
Mercedes van (though she'd love to own one herself), let
alone one with '97 plates. But of course the point there was
that travellers didn't put what money they had into houses,
they put it into, 'what they're sitting in and driving in, they put
it into their trailers with their beautiful fancy windows, and all
the rest'. They had no other overheads: no rent, no electricity,
no council tax; which might explain why some, but only some,
and mostly those who were in work, might be driving a '97
van. After all, travellers were only entitled to the same dole
as anyone else.

Yes, she said, anticipating my next charge, there was a black
market. People were involved in work outside the dole, but
this didn't just happen in the traveller community; it happened
across Ireland. And as for outright crime, the police superintendent in Galway himself had maintained that the figures
were no different from the settled community. Likewise, the
actual level of vandalism by travellers in local authority housing was very, very low.

But this was the problem, Ellen said. Whenever settled
people addressed the issue of travellers they did so in critical
terms. They never saw things from the travellers' point of
view: that it was illegal to park along the side of the road; that
if you did try and stop you'd be moved on, often roughly, by
the Gardai; that places in halting sites were hard to come by;
that trying to buy a house was often all but impossible. 'I can't
go into an auctioneers and say to them I want a list of houses
and sites for sale, because when I do, when I did in the past,
the "For sale" signs were taken down straightaway.' She'd had
to get a settled friend, who nobody knew was connected to
her at all, to go in and do all of that. And that was typical.

There was very little dialogue between settled people and
travellers. On a *Late Late Show* last year they had got travellers on with a group who were critical of them (ironically called
MEAS, which was the Irish for respect) and wanted them

tagged and monitored from town to town. 'Not once did a member of that group say, "Let's meet after the show, let's *talk* about all this."'

Had they only done so they might have learned something. For Ellen could completely understand why settled people might take against, for example, halting sites. Local authorities didn't need planning permission to put up halting sites, whereas for everyone else, building even a dog kennel required planning permission. So local authorities sneaked in the dead of night to put up these places. It was hardly surprising people's backs were up.

Then there was the matter of 'the small bit of affirmative action' there was around travellers in Ireland. A Department of Environment grant, for example, of £3000, to help to buy a house. But what settled people who criticized this didn't realize was that the set of conditions that surrounded that were incredibly stringent: nine times out of ten a traveller wouldn't qualify. There were other myths bandied about – free school books, for example; but nobody in Ireland got free school books.

When did anyone stop criticizing and ask: what do travellers *aspire* to?

They wanted to have an equal part in Irish society, and they wanted to be recognized for the heritage they had, in law, in educational curricula, in museums, in history books. They wanted 'to be given a fair crack of the whip as regards training and education accessibility'. They wanted, hardest of all, to draw back the values that they'd had before and start living them again: to bring back, for example, a little of the respect that was there for the elderly; to bring back a sense of identity and a sense of pride. They wanted to become, in other words, constructive people who had something to offer. That was her experience of travellers.

And what settled person could have argued with that?

All so much hogwash, I can hear the bar critic say. Naive English *eejit*, let the knackers pull the wool over his eyes. But just down the road, over the rusty railway tracks, was the concrete embodiment of Ellen's go-getting attitude, the Tuam Travellers Education and Development Association – 100 per cent traveller-led, dedicated to getting individual travellers trained and into constructive work.

Caroline Ward, the supervisor, and Martin Ward, the youth worker, showed me round. (They weren't brother and sister; Ward was just the surname of most of the travellers in town. Indeed, said Martin, if you said your name was Ward when you went for a job, they'd say 'Good luck!' and wave you goodbye.)

The big upstairs rooms where the electrician was working away on the exposed beams was going to be a conference/ seminar room. 'Most of this work,' said Martin, 'is being carried out by travellers, which would belie the fact that travellers aren't interested in their own destinies.'

Downstairs was going to be the community hall. There was a need, for example, for senior citizen travellers to have a place to come, as they wouldn't be welcome at the ordinary senior citizen group.

That these things were said matter-of-factly, without a whinge of complaint, made me feel they were true. There was an unofficial apartheid going on here. Over tea, they mentioned that being kept out of pubs in town was a fairly common experience for travellers. Caroline herself had been refused three times. How did they know she was a traveller, I asked, looking at her milky skin, huge brown eyes and auburn curls. She and Martin laughed. 'Oh they know. You've not been back long enough!' It would be the way people dressed or had their hair, and travellers wore a lot of jewellery too.

Wandering, like me, around Tuam that evening, you might have wondered why the travellers *wanted* to go into the pubs. In the echoing back room of the Imperial I was alone but for a man watching *Coronation Street* so loudly that I couldn't relax with my *Irish Times*. I tried the Abbey Tavern, but the two fellows drinking in there were glued to *The Thin Blue Line*. In the Town Hall Tavern the TV was visible from the window. I hurried on to Edward G. Canavan, which looked nicely authentic, and was, with a dark wood interior and a snug at the back, but, oh dear, it still had its goggle-box up by the optics, relaying a programme about the lifecycle of bees that not one of the assembled gaffers was watching, but was enough to send me hurrying off.

Back at the Square Inn, where I was staying, only the television way over on the far side of the big bar was on. Hurrah! But as I sat down the barman looked up. 'Oh, this is interesting, Charlie Bird following Mary Robinson around. I'll put it on for fifteen minutes lads, and if you get browned off I'll switch it off.'

Jaysus! The men up at the bar, in working clothes, clearly couldn't have been less interested in Mary Robinson, as she flashed around the world bringing comfort to, it seemed, every unfortunate under the sun. I'm a fan of Mary Robinson, I really am, but her slightly foaming delivery and nodding dog manner was altogether too much for me this rainy Wednesday night in Tuam. It wasn't her fault anyway, it was what the Irish were doing to their culture with that fecking box. The English had had more success down the airwaves than they'd ever had with their statutes and their swords.

The next morning Martin and Ellen took me out to the famous Gilmartin Road. First, though, Martin wanted to show me a grotto to the Virgin Mary he had built to commemorate a site where travellers used to stop (in the days before they were restricted): 'This statue stands on a traditional traveller camp-site. It is dedicated to peace and all the people of Tuam.'

Martin had originally decided to do it, he said, because when the council had blocked off the original site with boulders, 'it looked awful gaunt'. It had been travellers, Martin stressed, who had helped him fill in the space and build it.

Then Ellen wanted to show me the official town halting site, where travellers *were* allowed to stop. There were two concrete parking bays alongside each square brick facilities building. These consisted of a tiny kitchen (5 feet by 8 feet) in which stood a sink, a brand-new washing machine, and a fridge. Next door was a box bathroom with a toilet and a short bath full of children's toys. *You see! What did I tell you! Give them a bath and they fill it with children's toys!* But there wasn't room for the toys anywhere else, that was the problem. If you wanted a bath, one of the men in the parked-up caravans said wearily, you had to move all the stuff out.

I sat with him and a colleague over a cup of tea at his kitchenette table. They were John Ward and Laurence Ward. The rain drummed on the roof and it was cold. Hardly a situation to get madly envious about.

These days, Laurence said, many travellers actually wanted to settle, but they didn't get a chance, because in a lot of places if a traveller moved into a house there was a big uproar over it. 'They say the prices are going to go down and this and that.'

He'd had an experience trying to rent a house in Mayo with the Rural Resettlement people, whose slogan was 'Without Discrimination and Without Prejudice'. He'd decided to be straight from the beginning, tell the fellow he was renting from that they were travellers. That should be no problem, the man had said. But two or three days afterwards the house had been withdrawn, and later Laurence had discovered it had been offered out again.

He'd been over in Manchester for eleven years and he was going back. Over there, 'you were treated for the way you act yourself. Even the Irish people over there, they treat you the same as the other Irish.'

John was trying to get a house in Portumna. So far he'd had one letter, saying he was considered. 'That was a year ago.'

As for work, Laurence said, a lot of travellers were on the dole because people didn't want to give them work. Yet Ireland was crying out for workers. In Manchester they were *advertising* for workers in Ireland. He was going back to England. It was a lot easier. They didn't care who you were as long as you did your work.

As for the violence, John said, if four travellers had a fight it made the news; if it was four town lads, nobody turned a hair. Laurence didn't drink any more, but he remembered going into pubs and seeing settled lads fighting; they wouldn't even be barred. 'But one traveller is in an argument and the whole lot is barred.' There were thirty-six pubs in Tuam; there'd be one or two they could get into and that would be it.

The other thing was that if travellers got into an argument, they'd go on to the street and have it out there. Settled people would always argue behind closed doors.

Their women, Joan and Julie Ward, echoed their story. Joan

wasn't putting up with it any longer. In Manchester she could ring about a private house and you'd be told to come and have a look. But the minute you mentioned your last name back here it was, 'Oh, I'm sorry, it's gone.'

She'd love to move into a house, she said, but part of settling down was how were you going to be treated by your neighbours. 'When you're with your own people, in a caravan, you know how they're going to react towards you. When you move into a house and there's a lot of settled people, you are classed. It doesn't matter where you come from or what you did, you are just classed.'

Before she'd come here, Julie said, she'd been out on the road for twelve weeks without finding a site. 'Just living in a common, on grass. Because there was nowhere else to go.' And she had three small children.

Travellers remained within their own world, Joan said, because they saw the prejudice as they were growing up. 'So they won't even *try* then. For fear of being turned away. It's like, "Well there's your group, you stay with that and we'll stay with ours".' In other words, Julie said, travellers wouldn't try and push forward. 'For fear of rejection, because they think they're just going to be pushed back anyway. You know what I mean. They've seen it happen to their fathers and mothers or whatever.'

Joan, who was going back to Manchester soon, was bright-eyed and lively. Julie, older, with a place in Portumna only a distant prospect, regarded me throughout with a look that made me feel a fraud, coming in here brightly for an hour or so one morning, to discuss a predicament I didn't have to share.

On the roof two feet above us, the rain continued to fall.

Ellen and Martin were enthusiastic to show me everything. Next stop was St Benin's, where a row of young women in blue overalls giggled shyly when I asked them about discrimination. The three lads with them sat silent.

'You couldn't get on to a bus,' one of them said eventually. 'You had to give a settled person's name to get on.'

'If one traveller did something wrong,' said another, 'all the rest gets blamed.'

They were all on training schemes, learning metalwork, woodwork, crafts, upholstery and cookery, for a weekly allowance that exactly equalled the dole. It increased their chances of getting a job, but there was only one man in town that employed travellers in 'a shop setting': Joe Burke, who ran the supermarket.

Finally, we came to the famous Gilmartin Road. From what I'd heard I'd been expecting a shanty town, with caravans outside beaten-up shacks, dogs roaming, smoke, hens. But it was just a long street of semi-detached, pebbledash, local authority houses. A few had caravans parked to the side, a couple had a bit of junk in their front gardens, but it was hardly the slum of myth.

Martin took me to call on one of the residents. He was Bernie Ward, a heavily built old fellow in a brown baseball cap, stained grey-brown jersey, with black trousers tucked into his gumboots. 'If we'd known you were coming,' said his wife, who wore a baggy green jersey over a purple and white dress, 'we'd have cleaned up.'

We took tea in a room where two huge blackened pots simmered on a stove. Washing hung criss-cross above. Behind me on a sideboard was a neat collection of china; on the otherwise bare walls were framed photographs of family.

Those numerous critics of travellers I'd heard around the country would have loved Bernie; there was no fudging of the issues for him. The problem with the young ones, he said, was simple. 'They can go down to this exchange here and get £65 a week into their hands and none of them working at all.'

When he'd been young he'd worked on the farms every day from quarter to eight in the morning till half-seven in the evening, and a half-day Saturday, for £4.50 a week. You never heard of a fight then; if there was a fight then you'd be talking about it for a week – 'how did that start, and how was it over?'

'Now they can walk down there Thursday, draw their money and feck off any place they want to. Or they can sleep half the week, and still go back the following Thursday and get it. They're getting the money for nothing, so they've no respect for it.

'There's old people with houses now, that wants to be done up, wants to be painted, the gardens want to be cleaned. Why

don't they put them working on them jobs, and pay them their
money every week that they're getting on the dole and a
couple of pound with it, and when they get that money they'll
know they have to work for it the following week or they
won't get it. That'll change their minds when they get out
there and get a couple of cold days.'

Bernie was happy enough talking in this vein, but what
he really wanted to do was show me his daughter's house
over the road. Which was, he insisted, 'as clean as any bank
clerk's'.

Her front room wasn't just clean. On a sideboard there
were rows of gold-rimmed Mason porcelain; in pride of place
was a 'pony set', with gold rims, around pictures of travellers'
caravans in yellow, brown and pink. The low sofa was the
comfiest nest of pink satin and lace you ever saw, scattered
with huge pink satin 'heart cushions'. On another dresser
stood a 'grand gold set' of fruit-decorated porcelain. On the
little table in the centre, above a pink satin tablecloth, sat a
bow-bedecked basket of pink silk roses. The effect was completed with lavish arrangements of dried flowers in vases. It
was a pink and gold Aladdin's cave.

I was aware, of course, that I'd been shown the edited highlights of traveller existence in Tuam. But that didn't detract
from what I'd seen. Ellen and her associates had a hard job
on their hands, trying to turn round a group of people who
had been marginalized by history and then (how could such a
thing happen in this devoutly Christian country?) kicked when
they were down.

Nobody quite knew where the 35,000 travelling people in
Ireland came from. Out of the dispossessed of the Famine,
some said. No, said others, they'd been around long before
that. Henry VIII had outlawed 'tinkers' in 1528, and they'd
been here a while then. Were they perhaps the original pre-
Celtic people of Ireland, descendants of those short dark Fir
Bolg? Was that why, like the Australian Aboriginals, they
were so reviled? Ellen's mother had told her that the old
people she'd listened to had always said they were the original
royal blood of Ireland. ('Are they saying we came from the
gentry,' said Ellen, 'or what?')

Whatever the truth, they were, their whiteness notwith-
standing, a discrete group. Once, when there was more green
space and they'd jaunted around in those horse-drawn, barrel-
topped wagons, they'd been a colourful addition to the scene,
a memory to bring tears to the eyes of the old men of
Killorglin. Now, in the less picturesque trailers of today, they
had gradually become victims of that gentlest of stranglers,
the Welfare State, and it was going to be a hard struggle to
find a significant destiny for their old culture.

After the famous fight of the previous year, which had gone
on for three days and had been much written about, Ellen
Mongan had been told by the heavies within her own community not to make a statement to the press. But she was, she
told me, sitting on the Board of Commissioners. She'd been
elected by the people, two-thirds traveller, one-third settled.
The press were picking up on the most negative vibes going. 'I
couldn't sit there with my mouth shut. That would have been
an insult to the community that elected me.'

When she had spoken out and condemned the violence of
her own people, she'd had travellers coming up to her and
saying, 'I'm glad you did it. I wouldn't have the courage
because I'd be afraid they'd be down on my doorstep.'

She'd been attacked – the wings of her car had been kicked
in, and she'd had it scraped. 'But they know my stand now.
They know I'm not going to be like Mary down the road
who's been beaten up on Friday night, and on Saturday
morning makes a statement, and then withdraws it on a
Sunday. Ellen is not going to do that. If someone hits me and
it's unjustified I'll make sure that the full rigours of the law
will be down on them. You've got to make them see that the
law points at everybody. It's a minority that creates problems
within the traveller community.

'They've got this sense that they're above the law, and that's
got to change, and the only way it's going to change is by
more and more travellers saying, "It's not acceptable what
you're doing, and furthermore you're bringing us down."
We're always being painted with the same brush, but I mean
if you ran outside and looked in you'd say, "Is it any wonder
you've been painted with the wrong brush?"

'There's a wall of silence within the traveller community.

But there's a reason for that, that the settler community doesn't understand. It's down to the fact that we all live near each other and help each other, we're all related, we're all intermarried into each other.'

It took courage – and a certain bloody-mindedness – to tell the truth about your own people like that, but it was only such courage that would find a way forward.

Ellen Mongan got my vote.

18

Is There Wind Up There?

North of Tuam the countryside rolled green and fertile under the randomly strewn sheep. Gazing idly through the window of the packed Bus Eireann I tried to think which English county it reminded me of. None of them – a dream-melange, altogether emptier. A derelict country house was now a potential home for travellers – and why not? Because, of course, a hundred yards down the track was its green-field replacement, a Detached House Ecstasy in bright yellow and blue with matching yellow and blue kiddies' swing in the pristine garden swathe surrounding.

It had been interesting, I mused, finding an Irish problem that had absolutely nothing to do with the Catholic–Protestant divide, or with the British. Indeed, having got face to face with a group of people who were persecuted by the Irish, I felt somehow liberated, as if I could say what I wanted without fear of being thought, help me God, patronizing, or any other of those epithets that might be attached, because of my 'nationality', to any negative comments I made.

With a morning to kill before the one daily bus to the north arrived, I had visited Tuam's two cathedrals, most concrete of symbols yet of this divided island. The Catholic Cathedral of the Assumption had simple, businesslike pews, an uninspiring stained-glass window at the end of the nave and grey stone pillars hung with hand-painted cardboard banners: 'The Lord reaches out to us', 'Believe mightily, hope joyfully, love divinely' and so on. This was clearly where the worship got done.

The Protestant St Mary's Cathedral was locked. It was only by chatting to the friendly (Catholic) gardener, at work in a spooky avenue of yews, that I got in at all. Inside it was wondrous – a Romanesque arch; older and altogether more resonant stained glass; a long row of empty crimson thrones (marked for their absent clerics, *Praepositus Balla*, *Kilmainmore*, etc.); a magnificent east window; cloisters on either side of the nave; and an ornamented high cross. But the Church of Ireland dean resided in Cong, the current bishop (whose diocese reached into the six counties of the North) had been promoted to Cashel and awaited a replacement, and the weekly congregation, I was assured by the gardener, numbered ten or twelve.

At Claremorris I said goodbye to the coachful of beautiful young people speeding north to that foreign city, Derry. The connection to Westport left, incredibly, ten minutes later with a contrasting scatter of coughing and gossiping oldsters. We jolted painfully over wilder and wilder green hills as mountains reared up behind. A little house on a steep slope was entirely painted in the Mayo colours of deep red and green. 'Good luck Mayo', it read. Was it now a permanent memorial to their defeat or did they keep it hopefully dolled up for next year?

The bus chuntered down a long hill and came to its final halt in the circular Westport square, where the market stalls clustered damply round a fountain that was failing miserably to compete with the teeming rain.

I dashed for the shelter of the Grand Central Hotel, where the receptionist was scoffing down a plateful of lunch hidden away behind her counter. Could I get a sandwich, I asked. With mouth stuffed, she nodded sideways in the direction of the bar, then appeared a minute later wiping her lips to serve me. Next to me an old boy in a dripping grey mac sniffed at two-second intervals, like an accelerating steam train.

After half an hour or so Dermot Seymour arrived. He was my friend Leah's boyfriend, a 'Protestant artist from Belfast', now revealed as a stocky character of around forty, with a pouchy face, a shock of thick black hair, and a sudden smile that opened wider to the left, like an American cartoon character. The idea we'd had in Tralee was that I'd come up and stay with the pair of them, but everything had taken longer than I'd intended and Leah had long ago gone back to London. So poor Dermot was landed with this strange itinerant writer, me.

The plan was that he was going to take me round some of the sites of the Great Famine, but today, he flashed the cartoon smile, it was too wet, so he was going to show me a couple of local sights. We might stop at a bar or two and have 'a few scoops'. (Scoops were drinks, but you could also be 'scooped' by the police for driving after too many scoops.)

We drove out along the narrow coast road, around the edge of a huge bay, full of slug-like little islands. There were supposed to be 365, Dermot said, but it was like anything with a large number, there were always 365, weren't there? One of them, Dorinish, had been bought by John Lennon, and a commune had been set up with a high priest called Sid. All the locals had thought they'd never leave, but eventually, they were, in best Irish fashion, burned out, when the oil-filled lantern toppled over in the communal tent where they slept.

As a blow-in, Dermot was full of such local tales and titbits. Westport Protestant church was lined with marble. The minister, the Reverend Hastings, was one of Ireland's best flute players, which was mildly ironic, as traditional music was generally a Catholic Southern thing. This mighty mountain to our left was Croagh Patrick, on the top of which St Patrick had fasted for forty days and nights, and to whose cone-like summit, today half-hidden by a curtain of cloud, Catholic pilgrims climbed every year barefoot. The last bit, Dermot added, to the little chapel at the top, was almost like rock-climbing, with shale that slipped away under you terrifyingly. 'Rick' was the mountain's local name, and this little bar we were stopping at now was the home of Rick's two guardians, Owen and Michael. They had recently been fighting a losing battle to stop an interpretative centre being built alongside them.

Campbell's, it read, in simple white letters on a black background. Inside it was bare-floored, half-shop, half-pub, with chocolate bars and crisps in front of rows of shelves displaying a collection of toby jugs and unusual whisky miniatures. Behind the bar a blond teenager leafed in bored fashion through the *Independent*. At the square red table in the window a high-cheekboned backpacker in a woolly hat sipped a coke and studied Plato's *Republic*.

'Is Owen or Michael in?' Dermot asked, as we waited for the Guinness to settle.

'Owen's inside. Will I call him?'

It was OK, Dermot said with a nod. Sitting at one of the wooden-rimmed white tables to one side, he explained that the guardian of the mountain got depressed at times. 'Today's probably one of the days he's down. With this weather.'

I was finding Dermot's thick Northern accent hard to follow but didn't want to embarrass myself asking him to repeat for a third time the phrase he'd used for this sort of bar, which was, I thought, a 'spurrer-grocer'. It was ironic, he said, that a lot of those things that we thought of as quintessentially Irish, like these spurrer-grocers, had originally been very British. Because Ireland was the most western part of Europe, it was the place you found the last remnants of everything. So if you wanted to find intact Victorian and Georgian architecture, it was still alive and kicking in Ireland. In the North, of course, you'd find the last remnants of all the religious wars they'd had in Europe in the fifteen and sixteen hundreds. And these little spurrer-grocers had been all over these islands until they changed the law to keep people out of them and in the munitions factories during the war. (I had realized at last that the phrase was 'spirit-grocer'.)

Owen appeared at the door, like a ghost. 'How's Owen?' asked Dermot, and he nodded sadly and silently. But as we left, half an hour later, Dermot introduced me as an Englishman who was writing a book, and his interest was suddenly ignited. Before I knew it he'd gone back inside, and returned with a pamphlet on Croagh Patrick and its history which he warmly insisted I take back with me.

From this I learned that the great Irish saint had spent much of his forty-day fast atop the mountain having a heavy bargaining session with God, using an angel as a go-between. Patrick negotiated promises that Ireland would avoid Armageddon, all the Irish would be saved and that at Judgement Day he, personally, would be allowed to be their judge. The Almighty refused this last demand, but gave in when the saint threatened a lifelong sit-in on the summit.

We drove round the mighty haunches of the holy eminence to another little bar opposite the wild, dark sea. T. Staunton turned out to be a tall young woman with long blond hair and film-star good looks, manfully pulling pints behind the bar she'd inherited from her aunt, having abandoned a nursing career in Dublin to return to Mayo and run it.

'You're a foreigner, where ye from?' said the man at the bar to Dermot.

'I'm from Belfast.'

Lips to the creamy white froth of our second pint, we began to touch on all that. He didn't want to influence me in advance, he said. I'd see it for myself when I got there, the madness, the sickness up there. But it was also so provincial, so 'deadly'. And yet, he chuckled, I'd find the people, once you'd got over their initial suspicions – well, the floodgates would open.

Outside dark clouds massed on the horizon against an orange sky. We sped back to Westport and parked up outside M. Molloy, where a scrap of paper against the payphone read 'Trad musician wanted for trip to China to play in Irish pub – Leaving first week November'.

The bar was packed with faces Dermot knew (and we were invited to a wedding the following day), but in the little restaurant next door there was nobody but a chubby American professor with a patterned jersey and an educatedly ironic smile whose surname was Mayo. 'Nobody in Ireland's called Mayo,' said Dermot, laughing. 'Any more than anyone's called Leitrim or Kerry.'

But in the Famine times, the starving emigrants who survived the passage to America would on arrival mutter the places where they were from, and these would have been taken as their names. So this prosperous, clean-cut gentleman who'd driven from Shannon airport in a day and was driving on to Dublin tomorrow to catch a show before flying to Edinburgh (and was there anything special he should see on the way?) was almost certainly the descendant of a half-starved Famine victim.

Much later we were crawling up tiny lanes whose central ridge of grass shone vividly in the headlights. There was a gate to be opened with an impossible latch and a Mayo flag fluttering wildly in the wind against the now clear and brightly starry sky.

*

I woke under a heavy pile of blankets to see three sheep's skulls hanging in a row on the back of the door, one with a red rosette saying First Prize. Dermot's little kitchen, to which I padded barefoot, was also clearly his studio. The table was a scatter of oil paints, a large white canvas was propped length-ways against it, and on the sideboard, food was piled in packets. I found a half-loaf, and, somewhat warily, made a slice of toast and a sickly brown cup of Nescafé.

Outside it was a bright and blowy blue morning. We began our Famine tour with a walk up the lane to see some 'lazy-beds', the long parallel ridges and dips where the potatoes had been planted, still clearly visible beneath the brilliant green grass. The point being that even right up here on this rough and stony ground every spare foot had been under cultivation.

Way out on a headland beyond Louisburgh, where the khaki mountains swept down to a silver-pooled, blue-black sea, the picture was the same, if clearer. Soggy troughs and drier humps scarred the ground from way up on the slopes to the very tip of the granite-strewn point.

Here, by a mound, were the ruins of a village. Great grey clouds had swept in, bringing a sudden squally shower of rain. I crouched behind a hillock under my disposable umbrella (blown inside out) trying to stay dry. 'Imagine *living* here 150 years ago,' Dermot shouted against the wind.

But we weren't going back yet. Dermot strode on across the bog, down through dunes to a mile-long strand of surf. At the far end a man was shovelling sand into a tractor trailer.

'What's he doing?' I asked, catching up.

'Stealing sand,' Dermot replied, with a nod; he seemed in an altogether brusquer mood today.

Round the bend in the sudden sunshine another man had driven a flock of sheep on to the wide bay before us. On the far side, beyond a broad and shallow stream that ran claret-red down to the sea (it was the peat that stained it) was our destination, the Famine mound.

It had been the place where they'd piled the bodies they couldn't bury. And even five years ago, Dermot said, it had been a great heap that you'd had to climb up on to. Now giant tides had made it even flatter than the last time he'd been here, a circle of stones and sand just a foot or so high.

'I came down here two summers ago and found all kinds of things,' he told me. 'A pelvic girdle, leg bones, ribs. Then I came back with Leah this last summer and there was nothing, just a few digits.'

While I took photographs he scoured around, eventually finding a sand-bleached joint, which he thought came from a finger. 'It's really deteriorated,' he muttered, handing it to me. 'I usually get better things than that.'

'Would you take them away?'

'No, I wouldn't be happy with that.' He turned and strode off across the beach.

I stood for a while contemplating the little bleached bone in my palm. It seemed extraordinary that all this could still be here; that only in the last few years Nature had decided it was time to sweep the reminder of that cruel catastrophe away, as if 150 years was long enough to remember.

The dreadful events of 1845–9 had been brought about by the failure, in three seasons out of four, of the potato crop, 'on which,' in the words of a contemporary writer in *The Nation*, 'millions of our countrymen are half-starved every year'. Many of these super-impoverished people lived, effectively, beyond the normal economic world, having no contact with industry, commerce or, indeed, money, and subsisting from year to year on their nutritious staple potato. When the *Phytophthora infestans* fungus arrived via Belgium, from, it is now thought, South America, it was a disaster. The potato-eaters dug open their lazy beds in October to find only stinking black slime. That was the first autumn. 'No language,' wrote a Mayo curate just over a year later, 'can describe the awful condition of the people – they are to be found in thousands, young and old, male and female, crawling in the streets, and on the highways, screaming for a morsel of food.' This was just one of numerous pleas for help from educated people, clergy, charity workers and liberal landlords, living amid the devastation.

Altogether, over a million died from starvation or, more commonly, disease brought about by weakness and vitamin deficiency. Typhus and relapsing fever, xerophthalmia (causing blindness in workhouse children), scurvy and complaints now identified as marasmus and kwashiorkor, all took their toll.

Others emigrated, or attempted to emigrate, often dying in overcrowded ships on the way. In 1847 100,000 left for British North America, of whom 17,000 died on the crossing, 20,000 in Canada, and another 1,000 in New Brunswick – over one in three of those who set out. The Irish population was reduced from 8.2 million in 1841 to 6.5 million ten years later.

Meanwhile, as the children of those sub-peasants were left so wasted and yellow they smelt, in one account, like corpses, exports to the mainland continued unabated. Indeed, as the tired old Liberator Daniel O'Connell pointed out to the House of Commons at the time, more wheat, barley and wheatmeal flour was imported into Britain in 1845 than in any other of the three previous years. Between October 1845 and January 1846 alone, 30,000 oxen, bulls and cows, over 30,000 sheep and lambs, and over 100,000 pigs were transported to English ports. Throughout the rest of the stricken years, not just livestock, but oats, barley, bacon, eggs and butter continued to flow in.

The landlords – British absentee, Anglo-Irish and Irish – continued, by and large, to demand their rents. (They, too, had to survive, and between 1843 and 1849 estates in receivership went from £700,000 to £2m.) So if their tenants failed to pay they would be evicted from their patch, no matter how humble. There were some notable exceptions. The young Marquess of Sligo, for example, sold most of his possessions and gave up hunting and entertaining in his attempts to help his lessees. The Martins of Connemara lost their family estate supporting their tenantry.

Far away in England, the two British administrations, first a Tory one under Sir Robert Peel, then a Whig one under Lord John Russell, did little to help. Some did not take it seriously. The Duke of Cambridge, for example, said flippantly that they 'all knew Irishmen could live upon anything, and there was plenty of grass in the fields, even though the potato crop should fail'. Others subscribed to the powerfully prevailing *laissez-faire* ideology of the time, which held that tampering with market forces would dislocate trade. There was a belief that the collapse of the potato economy would provide an opportunity for agricultural reorganization. The government was also concerned to make Irish landlords meet the cost of a crisis widely blamed on their greed and negligence. Indeed, Sir Charles Edward Trevelyan, who was responsible, as Assistant Secretary to the Treasury, for government relief in Ireland, wrote that 'the Irish landlords alone had it in their power to restore society to a safe and healthy state'. Finally, for many evangelical Victorians, both English and Irish, the Famine was seen as the workings of divine providence, acting to correct the ills in Irish society. 'God's visitation', some called it.

As the crisis continued, repetition blunted the response of the British public to reports of Irish misery, and severe economic recession in Great Britain in 1847 further limited sympathy.

It is hard to believe now, perhaps, but how, you wonder, will historians write about our attitude to parts of the Third World in a hundred years' time? It is far quicker to land a plane load of grain in Sudan than it was to deliver a cartload of Indian meal to Skibbereen.

In modern times the Famine has become perhaps the most potent symbol, for jaundiced Nationalists at least, of the way the British treated, and in some minds, still treat, the Irish. Prominent among those house-end murals near the Upper Falls Road in Belfast is one featuring some gaunt grey peasants desperately hoeing away at the barren lazybeds. 'Britain's genocide by starvation,' it reads, in large white letters. 'Ireland's Holocaust 1845–9.'

Dermot and I drove back down a valley whose sides of orange bog revealed, to the practised eye, yet more swathes of lazybeds, to Campbell's, where Owen, like the mountain he guarded, was in an altogether sunnier state than the day before.

Dermot, too, with a pint in his hand, had relaxed back into story-telling mode. On the beach we'd been on today, Silver Strand, he had once met an old fellow carrying 'a single waterboot'. He'd seen him coming, a little dot way down the beach. When they'd finally drawn level they'd stopped, and the old fellow had asked Dermot where he was from.

'From the North,' he'd replied. 'From Belfast.' The old

fellow had looked at him, 'and there was a long hestitation, and in that hesitation I thought he was going to say, you know, "Oh it must be awful up there with the Troubles," and all that sort of stuff, but he didn't. He just turned round to me and said, "Is there wind up there?"'

'And I said there was, and really he was very disappointed, because living where he lives he knows nothing else but wind, battering away at his house or whatever, for years and years, and somewhere he thought there might be a place that didn't have wind, and that was his dream.'

While Dermot was over with Owen, I explained to the other man up at the bar where we'd spent the day. He immediately began telling me about how Lord Lucan ('Lucan the loony, you know, that led the charge') had got £250,000 revenue from his estates in the Ox Mountains during the Famine, 'from people who never saw money'.

'Now what was happening, of course, was the steward would come and they'd have a pig or something, and they'd sell the pig, there's no mystery about it. They didn't have a cash economy but there's no mystery about how he got his £250,000. The mystery is that it could have been collected.'

Eventually, he went on, the Famine became a scandal. American Indians started sending money to Ireland, for relief, it was such a scandal. 'That was the catalyst. Then the Government started to ship 'em out, subsidize their fare to America, better still Australia – the further away the better.'

You could read reports of how many hundreds of thousands died, he said, but it wouldn't bring it home to you. What had brought it home to him was the accounts of the children coming down from the mountains. 'When the Irish peasants started coming down to take ship, at Killala, Ballisodare, Sligo, the children had never seen trees, bushes, they'd never seen anything taller than their father, they fell into hysterics, they couldn't be calmed, they didn't know what these things were.

'It's all very well quoting a million died. That to me means nothing. They'd be dead now anyway, if you want to be crude about it. Number-crunching does no good. You have to see the result of it, and that struck me.'

Anyway, he said, with a sudden smile, you couldn't talk to

an Irishman about the Famine. 'He either says it didn't happen, or he goes silly about it.'

'And what are you doing?'

He laughed. 'Yuh. I'm going silly about it.'

The thing was, the Famine had been a giant trauma that, 'if you want to talk Freudian talk, was pushed into the unconscious'. He had a psychiatrist friend up in Sligo, who'd asked him 'a very trenchant question, years ago. He said, "What do you know about the Famine? Not what you've *read*, but what did you actually hear, personally, about the Famine?" And what I heard personally was that it didn't happen here. And he was delighted with that, because that's quite common. You get folk in America who say, "My people left from Tory Island in 1848, but of course there was no famine in Tory Island."'

He had another friend, an Irishman, from Skibbereen. 'It has only recently started to dawn on him that the family stories don't make sense. They were from Skibbereen; there was no famine in Skibbereen. But Skibbereen was one of the worst hit places in Ireland, yet his family history says that there wasn't a famine there.

'Now this is survivor guilt. If you were of the peasant class, which most people were, you survived on the backs of your contemporaries. If you were of the landlord class, everybody knows that they were at least careless, at worst evil.'

Had we brought some strange Irish jinx with us back from the Famine mound, I wondered, as the evening progressed. Arriving, a little later, at the wedding, no sooner had we kissed the bride – who stood, businesslike in white satin, on the hotel steps – and got our celebratory pints in our hands, than the lights went out, there were shrieks and giggles, and candles were brought on saucers from a back room.

The bride was from Dublin, and her sophisticated urban friends were making extra-merry, far away from it all, in the wild wild west. Watching them, I hankered for the perfumes and outfits and *savoir faire* of the city. I could feel its tug from here.

And moving on to T. Staunton, we arrived to find the bar on fire. Smoke poured from the two front doors. We rushed in to find T. Staunton herself and a man with an extinguisher emerging, coughing, from the inner room where the spirits were kept. It was OK, out, thank God. She'd put some embers from the fire in a black binbag with a load of rubbish and it must have been quietly smouldering all day. Thank God the smoke alarm had gone off before the spirits had gone up. Suddenly she was in tears, crumpled in Dermot's arms.

In the main bar the rest of the Saturday night crowd seemed none too bothered. Only a few had even moved from their seats to have a look. We left them as we found them – ghostly figures drinking, laughing and talking in the smoke.

A Northern Accent

In the morning Dermot had planned to take me out to Achill Island, to show me the ruined Famine villages there, but the weather was atrocious, lashing rain, so we sped up a big new road to Sligo, to see an exhibition of his paintings at the Model Arts Centre.

It was not the little gallery I'd imagined, but a great echoey place with two floors of bare-boarded little rooms, entirely given over to his work. Leah had not fully explained her boyfriend's stature.

The paintings were big, with (it seemed at first), surreal subject matter and quirky titles. *The Queen's Own Scottish Borderers observe the King of the Jews appearing behind Sean McGuigan's sheep on the fourth Sunday after Epiphany* read one. *Standing back from the Tubercular Air* was another. They featured photo-realistic cows and sheep and badgers and hares and swallows and fish, and occasionally people, set against haunting backgrounds whose green hills and lurid orange and blue-grey skies were often busy with military paraphernalia – uniformed soldiers, watchtowers, helicopters. At first glance they looked about as chock-full of symbolism as you could get.

In the car Dermot had told me that he didn't like talking about his work, it spoiled the mystery. Now it seemed, he'd decided to open up, and I was learning more, about not just his paintings, but his background and upbringing in the North, than in all the bantering conversations we'd had in the previous forty-eight hours.

Take this picture, *The Queen's Own Scottish Borderers* ... , for example, which showed a sheep on a hilltop under Christ on his cross; in the background, two military helicopters hovered around two more hills topped with pillboxes. You might want to read it as symbolic or overtly political, he said. But in Belfast he'd grown up in a world where the helicopter was always there, day and night. 'I've never known it not to have been in the sky.' Children in Northern primary schools always put helicopters in their drawings, the same as they did the sun.

When he had subsequently lived on the border, there was an army base there. 'So you'd be going for a walk on the Southern side of the border, and on lots of these little hilltops in rural Ireland there's a cross on top, so you'd walk past this cross and see sheep grazing. And an awful lot of people round there are called McGuigan, so it's probably Sean McGuigan's sheep that you're looking at. And then you'd look the other way and see the British Army watchtowers on the Northern hills, and they'd probably be looking across at the cross in the same way you were. Everybody would be looking at everybody else kind of a thing.'

So this picture of Christ and a sheep on a hilltop watched by helicopters and pillboxes, was, on one level, just what was there.

'Of course it's political. It's not normal to have helicopters flying around your skies, it obviously means that something's not quite right, but if you ask me am I being political, I would say "no".'

But yes, there were lots of references to disease in his titles: tubercular this and malignancy that. And he supposed it did have to do with that whole Northern thing: the inability of the place to heal itself, 'like a tumour'; and a lot of the Troubles being 'malignant, and just going on and on, and getting worse'.

And this goose here, with a shamrock in its beak? Was that just something that was there? Or was there some symbolism?

'Of course there's symbolism, but then again you could just say it was eating clover. I mean, who makes symbols? Humans make symbols. Clover is clover is clover. The clover doesn't know it's clover, or because it's green it's Nationalist, d'you know what I mean? It doesn't mean anything, but, of course, it means a million things, because everything in the North has to mean something – that's why the flags fly everywhere, that's why the roadsides are painted the various colours, that's why everything is loaded and that's why you grow up in a world where everything has to be either one thing or the other. From birth you just intuitively know that things are Protestant and Catholic. Of course, when you grow older, you throw all that baggage away, but you still have an eye for it.'

So if somebody wanted to see that as just a goose that was fine. 'But then of course nothing is ever what it seems; if you come from the North that's the fascination, you kind of grow up with it.'

And you used that as a way of trying to explore or understand what was around you, rather than fall into 'the easy ways of being either one thing or the other. I mean, to be an activist on one side or the other isn't very radical, because you're just falling into ancient camps, you don't really resolve anything.

'So when you're in the old art lark,' he concluded, with a flash of the cartoon smile, 'you put yourself outside, on a detached limb, observe it all. That's why you explore this sense of the daft. Which seems to be everywhere. Paradoxes and contradictions and nothing is ever what it seems.

'Because I come from the North I've been exposed to all that. And it's like your accent, no matter where you go, the west of Ireland, or Antarctica, or Brazil, you're still going to be looking at things in that Northern Irish way.'

19

The Lake Isle of Innisfree and the Korean Videotape Factory

Some miles north of Sligo, out on the coast by Rosses Point, we bump up a narrow lane to Ellen's. In the outer room of this bar, whose name brought a smile to the lips of the pair of Sligo writers we met in town an hour ago, is the deep orange glow of a fire burning in an old cast-iron stove that fills the chimney cavity. The extravagantly laughing, wild-looking old woman with the pint of cider in front of her is Leland Bardwell, who's a well-known poet. Dermot crashes in her cottage on the days he teaches at the Sligo Art School.

With her is a forty-something blond-haired fellow who looks like he might be a famous actor or something. He's very gentle and courteous, standing up when we come in. Now, when I return from the loo, to find Dermot and Leland gone, 'We're in here, Mark,' he calls in his soft brogue, putting me at ease as the new arrival who hasn't yet got a drink in his hand.

I wonder if he's Leland's son. Who knows, perhaps even her boyfriend? As the evening wears on it turns out that he's fixing a few things in her house, he's some kind of Sligo odd-job man. Then Dermot refers to him as 'the old IRA man over here' and later he talks about himself as 'a Sinn Feiner'. And when the night is over, and the musicians in the next room where everyone's been dancing play the Irish National anthem, 'The Soldier's Song', and everybody in the pub has stood solemnly to attention, Dermot jokes that what we're going to do tomorrow is drive up and meet Billy's friends the *cack* lads, by which he means the CAC lads, the Continuity Army Council people, one branch of which recently disrupted the peace process by exploding that bomb in Markethill, Armagh.

So I wonder about Billy. Is he really an old IRA man? Or perhaps it's just a *façon de parler*; because, after all, with Dermot, nothing is as it seems.

While we've been out, Leland's boiler has exploded and all the bedding is soaked, so I spend an uncomfortable night under a grubby duvet on a naked sofa-bed, wondering in the darkness if that Famine jinx is still following us. The dogs are yapping and yapping outside in the cold wind, banging repeatedly against the slats of the door – should I let them in? Then Leland crashes through to go to the loo, then she's coughing repeatedly, then I can hear her muttering. Or does she talk in her sleep?

In the morning I surface groggily to focus on an elaborate still-life on the white-painted wooden dresser against the wall: two lightbulbs in boxes, an enamel jug, a cellophane-wrapped brown loaf, an assortment of willow-patterned plates, a packet of Lemsips, a rusty pair of kitchen scissors, a tin of stewed steak, a car key, a black bead necklace, a brown-stained packet of *Siúcra* granulated Irish sugar, an antediluvian weighing scale.

On the walls the framed sketches and paintings are originals of quality, and outside, *wow*, it really is 'right on the sea', five yards from the house to the low cliff that crumbles rockily down to a ruined stone pier from where, Dermot tells me, the ships to Inishmurray once left. Ahead of us, that island is a beguiling green hump against the cobalt horizon beyond. It's now deserted, although once there was a community there who lived by making poteen. Across the huge bay are the low and lovely mountains of Donegal, shimmering a bracken brown in the sunlight.

We *are* going to see the CAC boys, or at least the C.A.C. bar, but first, at my request, we're going to call in at Lissadell House, about which Yeats wrote a famous quatrain:

> The light of evening, Lissadell,
> Great windows open to the south,
> Two girls in silk kimonos, both
> Beautiful, one a gazelle.

The girls in question were Constance and Eva Gore-Booth, whose Anglo-Irish family had lived at Lissadell since 1604. (None of them remained there now, Billy said, although Leland thought there was one, off and on – 'Jasper or Juniper, or something.')

When Yeats had visited the big house in 1894, it had been a defining moment for him. 'My uncle,' he wrote in his *Memoirs*, 'had always had faith in my talent, but I think that now for the first time the few others that remained of my mother's family began to think I had not thrown away my life.'

He had spent the summer holidays of his youth near Sligo. His mother's family were the long-established merchants, the Pollexfens. 'In my childhood I had seen on clear days from the hill above my grandmother's house . . . the grey stone walls of Lissadell among its trees . . . we could never be "county", nor indeed had we any desire to be so. We would meet on grand juries those people in the great houses – Lissadell among its woods, Hazelwood by the lake's edge . . . and we would speak no malicious gossip and know ourselves respected in turn, but the long-settled habit of Irish life set up a wall.'

Through his later boyhood, he wrote, the figure of Con Gore-Booth, who had often passed him on horseback, and was an acknowledged beauty of the county, 'had been romantic to me, and more than once as I looked over to the grey wall and roof I had repeated to myself Milton's lines':

> Bosomed deep in tufted trees
> Where perhaps some beauty lies,
> The cynosure of neighbouring eyes.

Now, on closer contact, she resembled for him the fiery and beautiful British army officer's daughter who had repeatedly rejected his proposals of marriage, Maud Gonne.

He was closer in sympathy to Eva, who 'for a couple of happy weeks' was his 'close friend, and I told her of all my unhappiness in love; indeed so close at once that I nearly said to her, as William Blake said to Catherine Boucher, "You pity me, therefore I love you." But no, I thought, this house would never accept so penniless a suitor, and besides, I was still deeply in love with that other.'

Who knows what might have happened had the poet

uttered? As it turned out Yeats didn't marry until he was fifty-two, and Eva and Constance went on to become famous in their own right: Eva as a poet and suffragist who worked for years among the poor of Manchester, and Constance as the Irish revolutionary Countess Markiewicz (the very same who was at Tom Barry's wedding). After a brief marriage to the Polish count who gave her her new exotic name, she worked closely with James Connolly, the Republican whom Pearse called 'the guiding brain of our resistance', set up the Republican youth organization the Fianna Eireann and took part, as a commandant of the Irish Citizen Army, in the Easter Rising of 1916. Sentenced to death she was pardoned and gaoled, and on her release in 1917 stood as a Sinn Fein MP, becoming the first woman ever elected to the House of Commons in 1918 (though as a member of Sinn Fein she didn't take her seat) and, subsequently, a minister in the first Dail.

After that Lissadell visit Yeats had written to a friend: 'These people are much better educated than our people and have a better instinct for excellence. It is very curious how the dying out of party feeling has nationalized the more thoughtful Unionists.'

But although he admired their nationalism then, he didn't like it much when they overstepped the mark of thoughtful gazelledom. In 'Easter 1916' he regretted that Constance should have sacrificed herself in 'ignorant good will' until 'her voice grew shrill'. And that summery quatrain above, which begins 'In Memory of Eva Gore-Booth and Con Markiewicz' continues:

> But a raving autumn shears
> Blossom from the summer's wreath;
> The older is condemned to death,
> Pardoned, drags out lonely years
> Conspiring among the ignorant.

A raving autumn had sheared Lissadell too. The steps where the two young women must once have stood with the turning-thirty Celtic dreamer were now tattered with grass and weeds. The flower beds that ran either side of the lichen-speckled bollards were awash with purple-headed thistles. Despite the telegraph pole in the field, the view out towards Drumcliffe

Bay was still fine, the dramatically swerving outline of Ben
Bulben away to the left. But you could never have lived the
life Yeats had celebrated there now, even if the tall windows
of the square grey mansion weren't shuttered and closed. In
the twenty minutes or so we were wandering round the gravel
path and unkempt lawns, no fewer than three cars drew up to
disgorge their camera-hung sightseers. The poetry had gripped
too many imaginations. Like me, they wanted to compare it
with reality; to dare to hope that something of the flavour
might still linger.

Fat chance.

> The light of morning, Lissadell
> Great windows shuttered to the weeds
> Five sightseers with videos, all
> Hideous, wasting their time.

We piled into the car and drove up the coast where, prominent
on the bare green sweep of a headland, stood the tall keep
and witch's hat faery tower of the neo-Gothic castle that had
once belonged to Mountbatten. The stone gateposts at the end
of the drive still carried his crest, a large M superimposed over
a smaller B (though Billy didn't think they were going to be
there much longer, he knew a fellow who wanted to steal
'em).

Down by the sea was the neat little harbour of Mullagh-
more, with a wide curve of beach adjacent. The locals were
very upset when Mountbatten was blown up, Billy said, it
being, despite its dominating convent, a Protestant sort of
place.

But they weren't going so much for Mountbatten, as for the
braid on his shoulders. What was he, first Lord of the Admir-
alty or something? And this was right by the border here, ten
miles as the crow flies, maybe fifteen by road. He must have
known the risk he was taking, coming out here at that time.

Another few miles up the coast, in the tatty resort of
Bundoran, you could almost smell the North. The Tyrone
Stand, Hotel Holyrood, the Great Northern – it was a different
feel entirely. It was O'Neill's they wanted to show me, the
scariest bar I'd yet been in, with a gang of very heavy-looking
customers going quiet at the far end as we came in, a pile of

the hardline Republican newspaper *Saoirse* for sale on the bar, a 'Brits out' banner above the optics, and walls lined with eye-opening posters. 'Put it back, thief,' said one, which featured a British hand stealing the Six Counties from the remaining mainland of Ireland. '26 + 6 = 1,' said another, over a similar divided-island logo. 'Loose talk costs lives' read the message by a sinister, balaclavaed silhouette.

'Keep your voice down, Mark,' says Billy, and I get a real shiver of what I'm heading on into. But no, says Dermot, it wouldn't be like this in the heart of Belfast. This is an exaggeration that comes from being this side of the border.

'That fellow there,' says Billy, nodding at the barman as we drink up and leave, 'once got up at four in the morning to fill my car with petrol.' But they're not so matey now, now that mainstream Sinn Fein are behind Gerry the Peacemaker and the CAC boys are still holding out for a United Ireland. (Though he doesn't, of course, ever discuss what Sinn Feiners call 'the other side of the house' I get the strong feeling that at some time in his life Billy's been through that green baize door.)

That evening, in front of the roasting cast-iron stove of Ellen's, we get into a political discussion. If the British government would make a deadline to withdraw, even if it was in fifty years' time, that would be acceptable to most Republicans, says Billy.

Surely not, I say.

Billy nods.

Fifty years!

No really, says Billy, then people could start working towards that. If they knew the deadline would stick.

But fifty years, I say, is a hell of a long time.

Well maybe, twenty-five, Billy concedes. Dermot thinks that would be about right. Anything less and you'd end up with a Bosnia situation. 'It's a family feud.'

I like these two, I think, as the Guinness goes down. And Ellen's. With its advert for Tennant's Lager bang next to its Sacred Heart, its brick wallpaper that, Dermot chuckles, covers real bricks, its cast-iron stove, which was made, we discover, after a bit of peering and scratching, in 1750.

'Wolfe Tone was still a teenager,' Dermot says, and Billy laughs.

Sligo is a delightfully tiny place, whose centre you can walk around in two and a half minutes. Time expands, and within a day you've caught up on all your notes, met six new people, nosed round the seven bookshops, discovered that the town has a strong choral tradition, that it is called Little Belfast on account of its large number of Protestant 'settlers' and that 'the shadow of landlordism' is still strong. (Prince Charles, for goodness' sake, owns huge Lough Gill, just outside town, as well as the land around the River Garavogue, which races in a whitewater cascade through the centre of town, right under the windows of my hotel, the Silver Swan.) And still you've got time to meet Billy for a pint at Shoot the Crows, which happening hostelry has a darkly panelled interior and a new window every month, painted by Robbie Cadman, who, like a lot of the other New Agers hanging around the place, is heavily into Irish mythology.

Ronan the barman is Sligo's Sam Malone from *Cheers*, with a long ponytail, a broad white-toothed smile, and a cute French girlfriend who sends a shiver of envy up your spine as she fingers his palm and kisses him lingeringly just below the ear.

'She's lovely,' says Billy, as she slides off, fringed bag dangling.

'You should have seen her at 4.30 this morning.'

'Don't be bragging now.'

'So what should I write about in Sligo?' I ask, to change the subject.

'Me,' says Ronan, with a gurgling laugh. 'Playboy of the Western World.'

Looking round, he certainly has plenty of choice. If I were twenty-one I think I'd stay right here and brush up on my European languages. But this afternoon Billy has kindly offered to drive me out to Lough Gill, whose 'Lake Isle of Innisfree' is another of the dream-poems of my Yeatsian late adolescence.

I will arise and go now, and go to Innisfree,
And a small cabin build there, of clay and wattles made:

Nine bean-rows will I have there, a hive for the honey-bee,
And live alone in the bee-loud glade.

And I shall have some peace there, for peace comes
    dropping slow,
Dropping from the veils of the morning to where the
    cricket sings;
There midnight's all a glimmer, and noon a purple glow,
And evening full of the linnet's wings.

I will arise and go now, for always night and day
I hear lake water lapping with low sounds by the shore;
While I stand on the roadway, or on the pavements grey,
I hear it in the deep heart's core.

The lovely lough is long and narrow, edged with wooded slopes just starting to tinge brown. At the far end, by a Waterbus tourist-trap called Parke's Castle, is a sign saying 'Waterbus rides to see Lake Isle of Innisfree. Live poetry readings'.

The Isle, a quarter of a mile across the choppy water, is a steep, wooded mound, fifty yards long. 'That's all you're going to see,' says Billy, quoting the first stanza of the poem from memory. 'It's just something he dreamed up.'

He's standing studying a nearby notice which reads:

ALGAL BLOOMS ON LOUGH GILL

Sligo County Council today confirmed that algal blooms (or scum) have appeared on stretches of Lough Gill. As a precautionary public health measure, the public is advised to avoid any contact with any blooms/scum and with the water close to it until further notice. Animals, both farm and domestic, should be prevented from drinking water from the lake as serious illness and perhaps death might result.

Billy's shaking his head. In all the years he's been coming up here he's never known anything like this. It's got to be to do with that Korean videotape factory. The place has a system where it takes up water from the lough, God knows exactly what they do with it there, but there sure as hell weren't algal blooms on here five years ago.

On our way back into town we decide to check the place out. So we cut through Doorly Park, where the courting couples go, and up to the tall black metal fence. Inside it's a great grey block of an industrial unit opposite – well, well – the ruins of Hazelwood House. Despite Billy saying he's after an application for a job, we get no further than the security barriers.

Back in Sligo I see the rushing white river with new eyes. But there have always been algal blooms on Lough Gill, says Michael Quirke. The videotape factory's got nothing to do with it. If anything, the water they put back in is *too* clean. No, the problem with the Garavogue is the sewage they pour into the poor misbegotten thing further down. The whole estuary is polluted now, and there's just no need for it. 'As a boy I used to swim down there,' he tells me. 'I wouldn't let my dog paddle there now.'

Quirke is one of the town's 'characters', a butcher turned carver who is celebrated enough to have made it into the *Rough Guide*. As a younger man he used to have his carvings in the window with the meat. Then one day he realized he was making more out of the carving than the cuts and became a full-time artist. Now he chips away furiously with hammer and chisel, talking twenty-nine to the dozen to his endless drop-in callers, who range, in the short while that I'm there, from a pair of Australian backpackers to a furious 'local joskin' with a mobile phone, 'giving out', says Quirke when he's gone, 'about Yeats. Said he was only a story-teller, as if there's anything wrong with that. That he only listened to people, as if there was anything wrong with that. Of course *he* never listens to anyone.'

If you want to know your Irish mythology, Quirke's your man. The wonderfully cavorting and embracing figures in the window are the magical characters from Irish legend, the Fergusses and Cuchulains and Maeves beloved of Yeats and Lady Gregory and all. Indeed, as Quirke chips away, he will quote Yeats at you verbatim, line after line. 'Who will go drive with Fergus now, And pierce the deep wood's woven shade . . .'

Queen Maeve is Sligo's guardian spirit. On top of Knocknarea, the mountain on the other side of town, is an unexcavated burial mound known as Maeve's Lump. Legend has it that that's where she's buried, and it surely is, says Quirke, a magical place.

'Does she actually exist up there?'

'I wouldn't be surprised. I don't know in what form anything like that exists. I very much doubt if there's a Queen Maeve hanging around in spectral form, but that there are images or ideas imprinted or floating or something I've no doubt. There's just too many little things happened.'

The hare is Maeve's animal, so if you're up on Knocknarea with your dog one day, and against all the rules of nature, it's sent scampering with its tail between its legs by a staring hare, that may just be Maeve. But no, Quirke adds, what with all the New Age travellers and others who've visited in the last few years, he wouldn't bother sending me up there now. 'They've leeched away any magic there is there. There are other places around Sligo, around Lough Gill, around Donegal, that have more power.'

That evening I caught up with the ever-available Billy in Hargadon's, another famous Sligo bar, with another dark wood-panelled interior, this one full of snugs and secret corners. In one of these Billy pulled out a thick envelope he wanted me to have. Was it an incendiary device to be taken back to London with me? Of course not. It was a collection of papers that he'd found in a skip when he was doing a bit of repair work on Lissadell House. There were letters to Lady Gore-Booth – 'I have asked Mrs Miller how she makes the soap,' went one of the more controversial ones – and recipes and programmes from long-ago pianoforte concerts. Best of all was a thick 'Nature Notebook', for the year 1930, full of skilfully drawn little watercolour sketches, with entries like: 'May 4th. Watched Ravens eating Carrion on the shore. When we came down they flew up with their harsh cries. I found birds-foot trefoil, also yellow pimpernel.' A whole gentle year is passed like this, the most alarming moment being when our heroine (I feel sure it is a heroine) is 'scolded' by a herring gull. Yeats would have been happy. Whatever 'ignorance' her

spirited ancestors fell into, this little girl is keeping up the
enchanted traditions of the Anglo-Irish.

Billy wanted me to have it. No, I said, it's probably worth
something. No, he insisted, I must have it.

A little later, I asked him, innocently enough, how he first
got interested in Sinn Fein. It all started at school, he told me.
'The history lessons we had were all in the line of stories, and
each time we'd be fighting the British, and although you'd
know the outcome, that they'd never actually beaten the
British, each story kind of heightened up to a point, 1798,
Wolfe Tone, went into Robert Emmet, and so on, right up till
the 1916 Rising, and the teacher told it with such passion that
we were riveted.'

His mother, too, had been a Republican. She'd worked in
the North as a servant in a big house, 'and she hated the
Protestants with a passion. She transferred that on to us as
well. I don't think my mother fully understood Loyalism, so
she blamed all the Protestants for it.'

Then 1966 had come, the fiftieth anniversary of 1916, and
they'd hoisted the flag outside all the schools and gone on
marches. Then it was '69, 'the battles in the streets in Belfast,
we all wanted to be part of it. Imagine, at fourteen, you'd
been sitting in school for the previous five or six years talking
about fighting the British and now it's actually happening on
the street.' *En masse* he and his friends in Drogheda, where
he'd then lived, had joined Fianna Eireann (the nationalist
youth organization established by Countess Markiewicz).
'There'd be more history, more talks, training camps, mock
battles, and all that kind of stuff.'

But then in 1970 'the split' had come, between Official and
Provisional Sinn Fein; between 'those who wanted to play it
politically and stand for the Dail, and those who believed in
the armed struggle.' There was a feud in Drogheda, and one
fine evening the very man who'd recruited Billy into the youth
organization turned up at his house with a gun. Luckily, they
realized they'd got the wrong person and he wasn't knee-
capped or shot dead, but he didn't have much to do with them
after that. 'It was the first time I'd seen a gun and I didn't
want to see another one,' Billy chuckled now.

But years later, in the 1980s, he'd got pulled back into active support for Sinn Fein through the trade union movement, in which, as a local factory worker, he'd been heavily involved. There were trade union protests against the hunger strikes and internment; he'd had the hunger striker Joe McDonnell's mother to stay and got to know Mairead Farrell, who'd been shot by 'the *sass*' in Gibralter.

The last time he'd seen Mairead was in a supermarket in Sligo and she'd told him she was pulling out of active service. 'So what are you going to do with your life now, Mairead?' he'd asked. 'I'm thirty years of age and I want to have a baby,' she'd replied. And a month later she was dead.

I was intrigued by Billy's status around the bars of Sligo. Everyone seemed to know him, from the receptionist of the Silver Swan, who gave him coffee, to the fiddle player at the bar on the edge of town, who'd play 'Carrickfergus' at his request. Whatever his role in Sinn Fein was, he certainly wasn't reviled for it.

She Came up the Mountain with Two Plastic Forks

Billy and I had been talking about the New Age travellers you'd see around Sligo and who mostly lived, he told me, in the empty valleys of Counties Sligo and Leitrim. It turned out that his daughter Katrina was one of them.

He wanted to visit her anyway, so the next morning found us winding through the lovely autumnal woods beyond Lough Gill and down the long valley between the flat-topped Darty Mountains and another mightier range, beyond which was Northern Ireland.

'The bridge up there is blown up,' said Billy, nodding up a narrow winding road that disappeared behind a scree, 'so you can't get in.' They made you go in where they wanted you to go in, in this case through the checkpoint at Belleek.

In a scrapyard at Kinlough we found Katrina's boyfriend Ross, a brown-eyed Glaswegian with cropped black hair and rings through ears and nose. He directed us to 'Josie's' which was a cluster of caravans round a derelict farmhouse. As we stepped out into the mud, four skinny Alsatians raced across from the rusty shed on which hung the banner that read 'Congratulations Pete and Josie'.

And here was Katrina, a soft-eyed beauty in black leggings. She was delighted to see her Da. Josie looked more like the tabloid idea of a New Age traveller, with spiky black hair, nose and earrings, and a strip of pink leg between long black shorts and heavy walking boots. Her brand-new husband Pete was a thoughtfully nodding Scouser with a half-beard.

We're welcomed into their little caravan for a cup of tea. I'd like tea with no sugar. Billy wants coffee with two spoons. Josie ends up giving Billy tea with two sugars, and me black coffee without. She laughs loudly as we swap. She's been doing a lot of mad things like that since she got pregnant. She's five months gone. It's a boy, and he's going to be called Oldham after her husband's dad who's had like 'rakes of cancer' and is dying. 'He's going to have a British name!' she says with a laugh. 'What is that anyway? Old ham. It's like rotting bacon. My son's going to be called that!'

Of all the New Age travellers here and on 'the mountain', she and Katrina are the only two Irish. God knows why, but all the others are from England. Yeah, it'd be 'sound' me going up there to see it, but first we must come and look round the 'derelict' that their friends who live in the other caravan are doing up. There's a lot of careful work in progress in the little ruined cottage. A new roof, piles of new wood in the downstairs rooms – it's going to be just beautiful when it's finished.

Some miles away, up on the mountain, the battered trailers are parked along a narrow back lane. In the wonderful little polythene-roofed round-house where 'T.B.' lives, Billy gazes from the kettle on its hook to the neat makeshift shelves by the mattress. 'I don't mean any offence to you,' he tells his daughter and her friend, 'but d'you know what New Age travellers always remind me of. Kids playing house.'

In the marooned blue bus at the end Maggie is sitting on the purple carpet talking to a boy with curly black hair and the kind of rather studied mockney accent that makes you almost certain he went to a fine English public school. Maggie has wild grey hair and is, Katrina has told me, like everyone's older sister, like their mother. 'She's great,' Josie added, 'she's like the camp's PR because she's got one of the local farmers in love with her – he kind of courts her with like bunches of rhubarb and stuff. It's hilarious.'

Now Maggie's in a panic about the catering for the big wedding they're having this weekend (between one of the travellers and a visiting Australian), but no, yeah, she's up for an interview. We return down to the lane to her caravan. 'Not that way, the dog's got diarrhoea.'

So we tiptoe over the mud and into her tiny trailer, with its neat shelves above its little gas cooker, and suddenly she's terribly nervous. But after a few sips of whisky and a joint she's better. 'Sorry, I'm being very formal, I'll relax in a moment, it's grand.'

Basically, she's been on the mountain for sixteen months 'through a combination of a series of disastrous circumstances plus a deep love of this country, first instigated by a love of Celtic mythology and blah de blah . . .'

She's currently working on a play. 'The reason I haven't got it together properly so far was that I was terrified of failure. How could I deal with failure?' But her big fantasy is, she says, to be interviewed by Melvyn Bragg, about her controversial and brilliant new play on Channel 4, er, Radio 4, one of the great cult institutions in Britain as far as she's concerned.

We laugh. I tell her I've had the same fantasy.

Maggie came, originally, from an Air-Force background. A lot of New Age travellers came from military backgrounds, did I know that? She'd grown up in the 1960s, and as an adult lived the hippy life, albeit in a council house, for sixteen years. Now she realizes she was very unhappy with it. 'I suppose basically, if I'm honest, I was just too damn scared. To do this. What I'm doing now.'

Living the hippy lifestyle, but in a council house, hadn't gone down too well with the neighbours. 'Someone that kept chickens in the garden because they believe in proper eggs, that grew vegetables rather than having shingle and paving slabs and satellite dishes – I was like a pork chop at a Jewish wedding.'

Most of this time she was a single parent family bringing up two boys (one of whom, paradoxically, considering everything, was now in the Paras). She'd been unhappy, basically, so unhappy that she was drunk all the time. In that state she'd made some bad decisions, one of which was to marry a very strange man, a Christian, an only child who didn't have a clue about how she felt about life, who basically didn't want a wife he wanted a mother. 'We're basically talking about a Norman Bates figure here, sexually and physically abused by his mother, didn't leave home until he was thirty-eight and married me.'

The mother had died shortly afterwards. 'Out of temper, I think.' Maggie laughs.

After a while they had split up, although they continued to live in the same house. 'I left him and took court proceedings after one evening he pleaded with me and cried, would I please beat him with horsewhips and sticks to show my authority. An agreement was reached by the County Court, which he told me he was at peace with – separate bedrooms, separate lives type of thing.'

Then, one fine day in May, she'd gone to a friend's to babysit and she'd got this phone call from her estranged husband. 'Saying, "I'm burning all your stuff." Thirty-one years of albums. I'm forty-six, Mark, can you imagine the record collection I had from the sixties?' She went back home to find her possessions a blackened heap and her two dogs – 'who weren't just pets, I'm talking one mind, teamwork stuff, we knew how the other thought, I couldn't be that close with a person because humanity gets in the way' – with their throats cut, feet up at the bottom of the garden.

'I was gone over here the next week. Ireland was, in the strangest way, home. When I first came here seven years ago, I cried all the way back, it was a spiritual thing.'

She had already met someone else. He was fifty-three, the oldest hippy on the road. They hitched and bussed to Galway and were robbed of everything they had, £700 and three big bags of clothes.

In Sligo they heard of this community. 'I walked up this mountain with nothing.' Maggie laughs. 'Two plastic forks. I thought this a big change from running a three-bedroomed council house with two freezers and a downstairs toilet.'

It was only when they were settled that her new companion's raving temper and alcoholism became apparent. 'I thought I'd met my Celtic Viking warrior, and all I really got out of it was lots of black eyes, lots of nosebleeds, a damaged left kidney and a broken cheekbone.'

So he went. Now he lives, when she'd last heard, in a British Home Stores doorway, begging for money for Special Brew.

'I just thought then it was shit or bust time for me. Get a life or it's all been a waste of – personal evolution, really.' So she lived very frugally, got the money together to buy this trailer. Now she has two, this and the one next door. She's as happy as she's ever been. 'This is a community of people that are healing; that truly do know that they need to heal somewhere loving and somewhere quiet. Mostly people are up here trying to get away from heroin and alcohol. OK, so we still drink, but in moderation, really.' Otherwise she lives the simple life.

There's no leader on the mountain. It's pure anarchy. 'Self-rule, for me it's beautiful.' Since she's been here she's had the warmest winter she's ever known. 'I can go out and cut wood, it doesn't cost me anything but my labour.'

Yes, they are all on the dole. 'Because we're not fit to work. We don't believe in the system that's out there. We believe in – if you want a carrot, plant your carrot seed. If you want a rabbit, go and get one.'

And what would she say to people who'd say, 'We're paying for that carrot seed, we're subsidizing your anarchy.'

'I'd say it'd cost you a bloody sight more to keep us in an institution,' she replies, after a pause. 'Because we can't be out there. We don't believe in all those concepts. In jobs. I've done that, earning a fiver from some fat cat who doesn't even know my name. We can't live like that. It's so wrong for us.'

Billy and Katrina and Josie came back, and we all squashed into the little caravan and drank our way guiltily through Maggie's wedding beers.

'Oh go on! Have another!' she cried generously. She was drinking and smoking herself, she said, because she was worried about the twenty guests from England who were turning up at midnight 'expecting some kind of wild Irish wedding'. How were they all going to fit in the other trailer?

They were driving straight from Rosslare and would be – her eyes spun with anxiety – coked up to the eyeballs.

'Well,' she said, letting out a sudden long cackle, 'so long as they bring lots of coke with them!'

They'd been rolling up fat spliffs of green leaf and baccy, and Maggie was well away now, rhapsodizing about the naturalness and spirituality of Leitrim, the slow pace of life, the beautiful, green, unspoilt lack of concrete. 'Like nothing's tolerated in England. It's the sheer numbers thing. It's so densely populated that if you don't fit in with the rat-race mainstream way of doing things you've just got endless hassle.'

In Oxfordshire, where she'd lived, she'd been arrested for *planting flowers* on the verges of the roadside. The police had come and warned her, but they didn't take action. They couldn't, luckily. Planting flowers wasn't yet a crime. 'But d'you want to live in a country like that? I mean, the *Sun* is the biggest-selling newspaper. What does that say? People just sit there with their satellite dishes and their jobs, but we have a human side and an animal side and it's like we've just forgotten our animal side in Britain.'

The others agreed. 'D'you know what I really like about this life?' said Josie. 'We all help each other. Like families in the old days, you had aunts and uncles and grannies. Now Katrina's like my sister and Maggie's like my nanny—'

'Anyway,' her nanny continued, cutting in wildly, 'there's going to be a poleshift in a few years' time. And I tell you what, if I look out of that window and see that tidal wave, coming in across the plain, d'you know what I'm going to do?'

'What?'

'Welcome to my poleshift party!' Maggie screamed with laughter. 'God, if we're wiped out as a race we deserve it.' People didn't understand half – no, less than half – of what was going on. If you'd grown up, as she had, with a father in the air force, you'd know. If you'd listened, as she'd listened as a little girl, to some of the things your father had said when he'd had a few drinks, you'd be frightened. England was basically a nuclear dustbin. She'd grown up, a little girl skipping and dancing in a pile of radioactive waste.

'I am *scared*,' she told us, as we sat huddled in the candlelit caravan. 'My father died of leukaemia from an incident that happened a long, long time ago. He'd been flying back so-called time-expired nuclear weaponry.' Maggie shook her head angrily, and there were tears in her exhausted blue-grey eyes. 'Time-expired nuclear weaponry!' she scoffed. 'Every one of that crew died of leukaemia. We're nuclear prostitutes in Britain. We'll take anyone's waste. And I watched it kill my dad.'

20

Away with the Faeries

In the dining room of the Sandhouse at Rossnowlagh those familiar Irish tunes were no more than piped muzak – 'Carrickfergus', 'The Fields of Athenry', 'Danny Boy', uillean pipes to the fore. The waitress with the floppy dark hair almost giggled as she presented the wine; it was clearly a struggle to be pretentious, especially to a man dining on his own.

As I savoured my Coquille of Donegal Bay Seafood I thought of Maggie and Katrina and Josie and the wedding celebrations that would be taking place *right now*. I, dry and bubble-bathed after my long sunset jog along the magnificent bay, was undoubtedly more comfortable; they, equally undoubtedly, were having more fun than me, alone again, half-listening to the murmured chatter of fag-end-of-season guests.

Even in a super-cosseted retreat like this, though, you could never quite escape humanity. Three tables along a white-haired old lady with dementia was cutting through the politeness with an uninhibited screech of laughter.

'Oh no, no, no, *nooo*,' she gargled.

'Is that nice?' asked her plump, patently kindly, moustachioed son.

'Aye. Ah do, ah *do*, ah, ah, ah *doo* . . .'

Later, in front of the efficiently blazing fire, the Moustache sipped a pint while I and a stick-thin old lady in an embroidered top studied our respective newspapers.

'You got Mother to bed,' said the impeccably suited manager, hovering for a moment.

'Yes.' 'Tache led off into a detailed account of Mum's medical history, the stroke she'd had last year, the excellent recovery she'd made, her garglingly *happy* present state.

'Can I talk to you a moment?' asked the stick-thin lady about four minutes later, throwing down her crossword.

'Of course,' Moustache replied.

She moved over. 'My brother had a stroke . . .'

Despite everything, the details of these mutual medical histories cut across my reading. Eventually I joined them. I had my introduction ready.

'My brother also had a stroke,' I said. 'At forty-one . . .'

'That *is* young . . .'

We discussed strokes and families for a while.

Although Donegal is in the South, much of it is to the north of Northern Ireland. The voice changes, to the harsher, more glottal accent of Ulster. 'Aye,' they say, and 'wee'. Which is as it should be, for Donegal, along with Cavan and Monaghan, is one of the nine counties of historical Ulster. Indeed, after the Flight of the Earls, the six counties planted with British settlers by James I were Donegal, Londonderry, Armagh, Cavan, Tyrone and Fermanagh, not the Six Counties of today. And in 1912, when Partition was first mooted, it was all nine of Ulster's counties that were going to be excluded from Dublin rule. It was only in 1916 that the idea of the six-county statelet was discussed by Edward Carson and Lloyd George – this was to ensure that the Protestant section of the community would be in a majority.

This different Northern accent is reflected in a tangibly different Northern flavour. The children outside the pub at the far end of the beach the next day looked trim and spruce enough to be in a breakfast cereal commercial. 'Aye, aye,' went their Scottish-looking parents, and who knew what their religion was? Perhaps, indeed, they were Protestants, because Rossnowlagh, as the real priest of Ballykissangel had long ago told me, although in the South, had a 12 July march every year.

And what could sound more Scottish than Ardnamona, where I was headed now, alone with an incomprehensible driver in a blue minibus that read 'People to Places' on the outside, this being the transport you get round here when you ask for a taxi.

Out beyond Donegal Town the little road wound through an autumnal feast of colour: browns and golds and maroons and yellows and even, on one dangling leaf, a neon pink.

'Beautiful scenery,' I tried.

'There's been a lot of beautiful bungalows,' he replied slowly, with a nod. 'Built along here. In the last ten years.'

At least, that's what I think he said.

Ardnamona turned out to be a maroon-painted mansion overlooking Lough Eske. There were brown, brackeny mountains away to the left, green hills on the far side of the mirroring water below. The sloping demesne that surrounded the house was thick with stylish vegetation – rhododendron bushes, a giant ornamental Chilean rhubarb and tall evergreens of various exotic species.

At the gate a sign said Accommodation, and when I met Amabel, the English lady of the house, her hair in an Alice band, making lunch for her baby in the cluttered back kitchen, I found out that they were part of Hidden Ireland. So I could, technically, invite myself to stay as a paying guest. Or perhaps I already *was* a paying guest? Or perhaps I would be back in People to Places by teatime, spending the night at a grim B & B in Donegal Town?

I hung on, uncertainly hopeful, as coffee turned to a glass of wine to a light lunch. Another elegant female appeared, also the châtelaine of a Hidden Ireland house. She was with Kieran, the owner of the place, who was not at all as I'd feared but lean, with thick black glasses over a narrow intelligent face, thin but expressive lips and clipped greying hair. At first, from the copy of the *Spectator* under his arm and the interest with which he received my descriptions of the welfare-strangling of Tuam and Limerick, I took him for a New Right type, born to this lakeside idyll, but it turned out that he'd grown up just up the road in Letterkenny. He was a Catholic who had gone to London in 1969 and become a hippy. Long-haired, he had squatted in Hampstead for a few years, making his living as a piano tuner.

This latest role as post-Ascendancy country gent had, it seemed, been hard-earned, and he and Amabel were having to do all those daily things you have to do to satisfy up-market paying guests, to make it work.

Most of this I discovered after I'd been invited to stay. They had a couple of Hidden Ireland people turning up later, but as long as I didn't mind talking to them . . .

I didn't. My uncertain status had been resolved, and I could spend the afternoon sitting on the jetty in the sunshine, gazing out over the restful reflections of the lovely lake. Only one problem troubled me – the misapprehension that both Kieran and Amabel were labouring under that I knew, pretty well, our mutual contact. But Tom H. was, unfortunately, no more than a good friend of a good friend. I'd spoken to him on the phone, but we'd not yet met. He lived north of here, in Ramelton, and I was planning to call on him, but for the moment I barely knew what he looked like. Remarks like, 'So how's Tom getting on?' and 'Has Tom been spending a lot of time in London?' sent me into quiet paroxysms of terror. Would my mumbling 'fine's and 'yeah's be rumbled? Would I end up being cast out at midnight on to the gravel? It seemed altogether too late to explain the situation now that I'd been shown the spacious Pink Room.

But it's not so bad being the non-paying guest in a paying establishment. You get to lurk in the kitchen with the owners and make jokes about the guests. And as you're non-paying, you get asked to do homely things like bring logs in for the fire. There's none of that professional niceness that goes on when they already have your credit card number.

The couple who were now officially in the armchairs by the fire were a plump greybeard from Blackheath and his correspondingly skinny wife. They had a treble-barrelled name, each barrel of which proclaimed the very finest (Anglo)-Irish ancestry – the building of Limerick, the would-be Catholicization of Church of Ireland theology, the planting of Sligo, all were contained therein.

At 7.03, the jovial Mr Treble-Barrel was, like me, gasping for a drink, but Kieran, straightbacked and talkative, didn't seem to notice at all, even when heavy suggestions were made.

'Is there a bar here?' the greybeard tried eventually.

'Oh yes,' Kieran replied, 'there's a good bar at Harvey's Point, you can get a drink there before dinner.'

Only the arrival of Amabel relieved the situation. Having got her son to bed she was *exhausted*. 'I'm going to have a

cigar,' she announced, when the Treble-Barrels had driven off
for dinner.

In the morning Kieran was off to Mass with the family in a
Victorian-looking black corduroy jacket, buttons done up at
the waist. I'd be welcome to stay around for the day, he said.
They had the artist Derek Hill coming to tea, *en route* back
from lunch at – well, well – Lissadell, with the last remaining
Gore-Booth, Jocelyn. (So Leland had been right.) Derek was
a definite Donegal character. He'd taught Prince Charles to
paint, he knew *everybody*, and if I played my cards right I
might get a lift up to Churchill with him, from where there
was an easy bus over to Tom at Ramelton.

'Great.'

'He's a good friend of Tom's, too.'

'Is he?'

I hurried back down to the jetty. The sun was so bright on
the silver-white water it hurt my eyes. At my feet the ripples
made the long reflections of the yellow-brown reeds into
wonderful squirling wriggles, none of which had ever met Tom
either.

'It's like champagne,' said Amabel that afternoon, as we
pushed young Theo up the bumpy drive, to the Famine pot
that he loved to throw stones and conkers in. Guess who'd
been outside Mass that morning in Donegal Town? Dana. 'I
went up and congratulated her for having a go,' Kieran said.

They went back to get tea ready for Derek Hill and I strode
on, out down the lane under the golden-brown trees. At the
Lough Eske viewpoint three late-season backpackers,
wrapped from head to toe in fluorescent plastic, were flat out
on the picnic tables, eyes closed. Beyond was just bracken on
mountains, sienna brown under the cerulean blue. I prayed
that Derek Hill would be uninterested in my relationship with
Tom.

But when I got back he hadn't arrived. Finally, at six, the
phone went. He was back at home in Churchill.

'Stay the night, if you like,' said Kieran.

The Treble-Barrels had been replaced by a family of travel
agents from Willesden. They were partly on business, partly
on holiday, and highly critical of Donegal's facilities for tourists. They had spent the day going around Glenveagh House,

and the girl who'd guided them was 'so beautiful, why didn't they put her in traditional costume?' In the kitchen Kieran's rich Donegal accent modulated to a monotone north London whine, as he spun a fantasy around the idea that he should suddenly pop in to serve them drinks in traditional costume.

When they'd departed we sat up late drinking whisky. He was full, like all the best Irishmen, of theories and paradoxes about Ireland. How emigration, for example, had been wept and wailed over by the Irish, but there were similar circumstances in Scotland, the Clearances had been at the same time as the Famine, yet you rarely heard the Scots grumbling about those.

On our second glass we got on to a conversation about Catholicism. It was a shame, I thought – I said – that if I'd gone to Mass with them that morning I wouldn't have been able to take communion. People were forever saying that the situation in the North had nothing to do with religion, and in a sense that was true, it was tribal and political, but in a deeper way it had everything to do with religion. Imagine an ecumenical future, where everyone could worship their Son of God in the same churches. Places like St Mary's Cathedral, Tuam, could be for everyone, and the twelve Protestants might make a few new Catholic friends.

Kieran, despite – or perhaps because of – his hippy past, was surprisingly orthodox. No, he said. It was right that the Catholic Church disallowed Protestants from communion. Not just because of transubstantiation, and the differences in belief as to how Man was reconciled to God, but his Church had, after all, observed societies of numerous different kinds over its long period of existence. So the rules were important. Once you dropped one, what went next?

Engrossed in my argument, I half-thought I'd seen a white horse's head bobbing past the high kitchen window. Now, suddenly, two mournful eyes appeared round the door from the larder. 'Oh Trestle!' cried Amabel. 'How did you get in there?'

It was my fault. I hadn't shut the gate to the field properly. Trestle and the donkey, Debbie, had seized their opportunity. So now, having given them carrots and cuddled them thoroughly, Amabel led Debbie and Trestle back over the front lawn and down through the dark rhododendrons to the field. It was magical, the big white horse under the moonlight, the lake shining silver below, the blue-black shadows of the evergreens cutting across the path.

Once, Amabel and her kind had lived these enchanted lives, and the only creatures they'd had to expend their daffy upperclass charm on were horses and dogs. Now, here at least, the masters had become the servants, and the animals had been joined by absurdly grateful travel agents from North London, to the undoubted benefit of all.

'Send our love to Tom,' said Kieran, as he dropped me at the bus stop in Donegal Town.

'I will,' I replied, shaking his hand gratefully, and dashing for the bus steps.

Cut off from the rest of Ireland by the North, Donegal is a remote-feeling and empty county. The bus I was on now, Fedar O'Donnell's, was one of two private services that supplemented the barely existing Bus Eireann. 'If you don't have a car in Ireland,' Kieran had said, 'you're a pauper.' I looked round at my fellow travellers with new eyes.

With Scottish 'ayes' in my ears, we jolted on through Scottish scenery. Rocky streams by the roadside; flat rustbrown moors. 'Release all Irish POWs now,' said the signs on those telegraph poles that weren't adorned with the evergrinning Mary McAleese. At a question and answer session at University College, Dublin (the *Irish Times* reported) a student had asked Mrs McAleese this question: as a resident of Northern Ireland, should she be running for the Head of State's job in the Republic. 'I am an Irishwoman,' she had replied, 'nothing more, nothing less, and I am no less an Irishwoman because I was born in Belfast.'

In Letterkenny I stopped in the Quiet Moment for a hoagie. 'How are ye?' asked the people of each other. The two blondes in the corner, hair scraped back harshly off their necks, definitely looked more Glasgow than Dublin.

In his cottage out beyond the tiny hamlet of Churchill, the celebrated artist was waiting with tea. I'd imagined someone thin, twittering and rather fey, but even at eighty, Derek Hill was a solid concave bulk of a man, the front curve of his body divided in the middle between the navy blue jersey and the battered green cords. At first sight his expression was serious enough, worried almost, but after a minute or two a little oblong smile made an appearance.

He had an English voice of the old school. 'Yes, yes, exactly,' or, 'Oh, I'm *sure*,' he'd say, mind wandering, if I rambled off the subject *du jour* for too long.

He had painted everybody, it seemed. 'Too many perhaps . . .' he half-muttered, drifting off again at the end of our chat. Prince Charles 'about three times'; the Queen Mother; '*not* the Queen'; the Duke of Kent; John Hume; Mountbatten; Hailsham; lots of bishops, *endless* bishops; three presidents, the President of India, Erskine Childers and Mary Robinson; and right now, Mary Robinson's cartoonist husband Gerald.

'I admire her *immensely*.' But no, she hadn't been a cosy person. Exactly. 'But he *is*.' He's extremely cosy and jolly and easy, but I felt with her she was slightly nervous of what she said, being the President, which was perhaps natural. But I admire her *immoderately*.'

He was of that estimable generation that wouldn't have a bad word for anyone in public. On the record, the world was as it should be, full of admirable people doing admirable things.

'Being so close to the North has never been a trouble to you?'

'Touch wood, no. All the people have been terribly nice to me, ever since I came here, that's why I left my whole collection of everything to them, except what's in this little house, so they've got everything.'

In return, or perhaps anyway, they had made him Irishman of the Year. 'To my surprise, not having a drop of Irish blood. I was very very deeply honoured and impressed and I was also given the freedom of the city of Letterkenny, so I was *very* impressed indeed.'

'Everything' was the lovely square Glebe House, painted, except for its white windowframes in a bold rust-red, with its 'almost wild gardens' of beech and fern and cow-parsley and Chilean bamboo running down to Loch Garton. Inside was

Hill's wide-ranging personal collection: a Landseer in the dining room; a Victor Pasmore in the drawing room; a Sidney Nolan on the back stairs: prints by Kunisada and Toyokuni in the Japanese Room; a ceramic plate by Picasso in the kitchen; as well as paintings by Irish artists such as Louis de Brocquy and Evie Hone; and, of course, works by Hill himself, although he insisted he wasn't, despite his recent honour, an Irish painter. 'Personally I don't know what I am – the point is I'm a painter.'

He had bought the house for £1,000 in 1953, having first visited Donegal as a guest of the American millionaire Henry MacIlhenny four years earlier. MacIlhenny had owned Glenveagh (the very castle that the Willesden travel agents had grumbled about), which was on the next lough along. Visitors to the castle had been numerous and distinguished, and as the years had progressed, there had been a certain amount of guest-sharing. Greta Garbo, for example, had come over for tea with Derek. 'Which was *silly*, to see this mythical figure sitting in the kitchen pouring out the tea. She didn't have much conversation, though. She said to me, "Oh, Derek, for the first time in my life you make me feel quite tidy." Because I live such a hugger-mugger, cluttered existence.'

Yehudi Menuhin had visited Derek too, 'and we gave a little *ceilidh* for him in the kitchen one evening, and all the local boys came with their fiddles and he had his fiddle and they swapped fiddles and anyway, it was a great success. And the following day, my old housekeeper Gracie was asked what was the name of the famous fiddler who came to *ceilidh* last night and she said, "I'm very bad at names but I *think* he was called Heudi McMeneman."'

We laughed.

'Which is a very nice story, but quite true.'

Hill seemed indeed to have met everyone who was anyone in the twentieth-century artistic world. Cecil Beaton had photographed him; Benjamin Britten had composed a hymn for him; he'd journeyed to Anatolia with Freya Stark. And yet what he really liked was islands, in particular Tory Island, off the north coast of Donegal, where a chance encounter between Hill and one of the local fishermen had led to the Tory Island naive school of painters.

'Yes, I love getting away. And I met in the train a man who was sitting opposite me going from Belfast to Derry, and I said, "The one place I'm longing to go is Tory." And he said, "Well, you're sitting next to the man who can help you." And I said, "Why?" And he said, "Because I'm the lighthouse keeper."'

Ensconced on the island, Hill had been painting away quietly when an old man called Jimmy Dixon had come up behind him. 'And he said, "Oh, I can do better than that." So I said, "Well, why don't you?" And he said, "Oh, I don't have the paper and paints and everything."' So the ever-generous Hill had offered to send him paints and paper from the mainland (Dixon had made his own brushes from the hairs of a donkey's tail) and 'soon there was another man doing it, then three or four of the old boys'. Now Dixon and the others were no more, and a new generation had followed on, led by the King of Tory, Patsy Dan Rodgers.

Derek could arrange for me to meet him, and see the work, and the island and everything, but first there was someone right here in the village I really ought to talk to, Elizabeth Wilde, who was a witch. 'No, she really is, a proper White Witch, and she believes in faeries, and all that sort of thing.'

The Wee People

To my right five crimson tapers blazed on a candelabra that was heavy with great stalactites of dried wax. A dog snored fitfully on the terracotta tiles in the corner. There were baskets and oil-lamps hanging above us, a dresser was chock-full of coloured pottery jugs, one window was crammed with empty blue and green bottles, and a calendar on the wall spelt out *moonths*.

Elizabeth had wildish ginger hair, a plumply filled green jersey. As a young woman she had been a beauty, as a photograph she showed me attested. As she told me about her friends the faeries, her eyes grew moist, she spread her hands flat on the table so you could see the tendons to her fingers, then she gestured furiously, then suddenly flashed me the sweetest smile.

Obviously this was Angus Deayton country. Someone who believed in the faeries was clearly crackers, and all I had to do was nod politely and keep a straight face and I'd end up with some amusingly kooky footage. But for a born sceptic like me, Elizabeth was alarmingly convincing. She really wasn't some country nut to chuckle over in the edit-suite.

Born in Antrim, she'd been educated in England and worked successfully for some years as a journalist. She had gone into the Malaysian jungle for *She* and Cambodia for *Newsweek*, and had ended up being the *Sunday Times* correspondent in Iran. Now in her retirement she was dry and funny and did comic impersonations of Churchill and Donegal characters. One moment she was Derek Hill, the next, the woman who'd ended up getting the Presbyterian house in the village because the pastor was *frightened of her*, and the next, a lady professor from Belfast who wore stockings that only went up to the knee.

And yet, she'd not only talked to 'the little people', she'd even seen them. The first time as a young girl in Antrim. 'They were about two, two and a half foot high, and they had these little brown cowls, they looked like tiny monks.' She and the little boy she'd been with had realized they weren't people. 'And we were afraid.'

So were they spirits, I asked (certainties crumbling) or actual solid little people. No, Elizabeth said, they were flesh and blood people. She'd seen them cry, and she'd also seen them very, very cold. She'd seen them pick things up and move them around, and eat things. She smiled. 'There's special things they like to be taken,' she said. 'Little flat cakes, made with honey and oatmeal. Baby clementines.' They loved sweet things, and colourful things, because they mostly lived underground and in very dark places.

So would she know where they lived round here?

'Yes.' But so many of the faery places had been bulldozed or desecrated now. In fact, she was moving shortly from this house to one at the foot of the Poisoned Glen in Dunlewy, where, as they'd asked her, she was building them a little round tower. 'For when they have to run away.'

I was still, let's face it, sceptical.

That was OK, Elizabeth said, I could think what I liked.

But it wasn't just her that saw the faeries. A lot of Irish people, often the ones you'd least expect, had come across them, one way or another. Elizabeth also told fortunes, and one day this big tough man from Derry had come to get his fortune told, and it turned out that he'd seen faeries in his scout camp in Antrim (about three miles away from Elizabeth's childhood sighting). Then, another evening, here in this very house, she'd been sitting with this hard-boiled lawyer from South Carolina, and there'd come a knock, knock, knock, on the door. As I could see, the door was glass on the top half and wood on the bottom. 'We could see nothing, and knock, knock, knock, it came again. So I got up and opened the door, and there he was, *wheesh*, he was off like that. And this lawyer said, "Miss Wilde, are you gonna tell me, did I see what I thought I saw?" I said, "That's a really great honour for you because they never ever ever come to the house when there's anybody else around."' And other people, Irish people, builders and bulldozer drivers, big tough men, would often do things for her and when it was time to pay would say, 'Never mind, just tell the wee boys it was me that did it.'

We shared a bottle of red wine and a glass of her home-made fruit poteen, and were just starting on an oven-ready pizza when the phone rang. But no, it wasn't the Queen of the Faeries, summoning us to conference at the top of the mountain, it was Derek. Was I *still* there? Anyway, he'd arranged for me to go and see round the Glebe House gallery tomorrow at two. Unfortunately, I couldn't get into the house because of the insurance regulations, but I could peep through the windows . . .

'Oh dear,' I began. 'I've just agreed to go with Elizabeth tomorrow and see her faery tower . . .'

I was no match for the painter's will. 'I'm eighty years old and I can't be expected to keep changing these plans,' he told me curtly.

Now I'd upset Elizabeth. She gave me a thin smile. Honestly, couldn't I stick to my commitments? Oh well, we'd have to see the faery tower the day after.

Oh dear, oh dear, I thought, as I paced back under the

super-bright stars to my room at the pub in Churchill, I've
only been here five hours and I've upset everybody.

It was an eight-mile walk out over the green valleys and rustbrown moorland to Glenveagh. I strode along in the morning
sunshine, smiling cheerfully at the occasional passer-by, thumb
out hopefully. The very first car that passed pulled to a halt,
reversed and offered me a lift. Glenveagh. That was quite a
step, said the white-sideboarded gent at the wheel, but he
could take me up as far as his house, which was some of the
way anyway. That was the one, that bungalow there, by the
clump of trees.

'There's new bungalows everywhere,' I said.

'Sprouting up like mushrooms.'

At the top of the hill I was outraged to be passed at speed
by the next car, but twenty minutes after that a battered white
lorry restored my faith in Donegal, dropping me just yards
from the Glenveagh interpretative centre. From there an
empty shuttle-bus transported me along the edge of the lough,
its timeless bracken-covered islands making a bizarre contrast
to the loud phone-in on the radio about divorce in Northern
Ireland.

The next tour of the grey castellated pile wasn't until 12.15,
so I wandered out through the conservatory to the gardens,
where three Alice-in-Wonderland gardeners toiled over the
late roses. Beyond, among the gravelled walkways, there were
statues everywhere. Up here in this stone-flagged little rest-
awhile spot, a hunky god with fruit and leaves twined in his
hair, and fearfully strong loins, hugged a massive fruit-filled
horn. Opposite, a fig-leaved but beefy androgyne had her
hands round a cross eagle. Or was it a griffin? Jolly peeved
anyway. At the exit these two stone heads weren't getting on
at all. He grinned winningly at the escallonia; *she* pouted
crossly down at the gravel. Clearly he'd been ignoring her for
some time.

Back at the house I was joined on the tour of MacIlhenny's
fabulous interiors by a late-season coach party of pensioners
from Yorkshire. We learned how the original owner, John
George Adair, had cleared his park by evicting 240 tenants in
1861. According to local myth, the evictees had laid a curse

upon Glenveagh: that the castle would never have an heir.
And so it had turned out. Adair had been childless; as had the
second, Bostonian, incumbent. Kingsley Parker, the third master of the house, had mysteriously disappeared on a fishing
trip to Inishboffin. The last private owner, Henry P. Mac-
Ilhenny, hadn't had an heir either. Our tour guide, who was
the wife of his one-time chauffeur and sister-in-law of the
butler who'd gone with him everywhere (to Salzburg and Italy
in August, to Australia in February, home to Philadelphia in
the winter), was magnificently discreet about why. 'He was a
single man, very artistic,' she told us. 'House guests would
come from the theatre world, the art world, the film world,
and the music world . . . It was strictly private.'

Even in the lavish bathroom to the master bedroom, where
above Henry's footbath and below the three chandeliers, three
Greek-style male nudes posed proudly, no comment was
passed. Kieran had already told me that the ice had once
been broken on this tour when, pausing in this very room, the
guide had drawn attention to the nudes, which demonstrated,
she'd said, Henry's great interest in the artistic world. 'I'm
glad you told us that,' an American in the tour group had said,
'because otherwise you might have thought he was a bloody
faggot.'

'You don't realize the havoc you've caused round here,' said
Elizabeth, picking me up from the pub as agreed at six. A
young woman had been murdered in Mayo the previous
Thursday and the suspect was a dark-haired Frenchman. I'd
told the landlady of the pub I'd come from Mayo, apparently,
and now, after somebody else had decided I looked French, I
was 'the Mayo murderer'.

'I could give you some liver,' Elizabeth said. 'You could rub
it over your face and hands and go staggering into the pub
saying, "I need to *talk* to somebody."'

That night, over a shared bottle of whisky, and Elizabeth's
speciality, a venison and nettle pasty, she told me the story of
her life. It had, despite its excitements, been a hard one. She'd
been married twice, the second time to an Iranian who'd run
off the day after the wedding. Her son had 'not turned out
well'.

Was it a kind of despair, I thought, as I sat there beside her in the candlelight, that had made her turn to the faeries? Were the wee people the only ones left to trust? Was that why they were so important to her? Or was I just a foolish sceptic who should open his mind?

'People would find it incredibly hard to believe all this,' I told her.

'Well tough. I'm afraid I find it very difficult to believe some of the garbage that's handed out in church on Sunday.'

As we finished the whisky around midnight she smiled and said, 'I was just thinking I might take you up the mountain to meet the faeries . . .'

I'm ashamed to say that, exhausted and ready for bed, I declined this invitation. It would be a long cold walk in the wet and mud, and of *course* we wouldn't see any faeries. But in the morning I regretted my idleness; maybe there really were little people in Donegal?

We rattled off over the empty moor in Elizabeths's £60 car. 'It's not a moor,' she cried, 'it's a bog.' What, even up there, where the bright orange bracken stretched right to the grey, rock-strewn peaks of mighty Muckish. 'Even up there.' Beyond Muckish, Errigal was a giant, breast-shaped mound of shale, kissed at the top by shifting white tendrils of cloud. The shale was quartz, Elizabeth said, faery stone.

At the top of the third of this row of loughs, on one side of which the Guinness family had their summer retreat, was Elizabeth's faery tower, buried in woods beneath the roofless, fire-blackened Protestant church.

She was building it at one end of a little ruined cottage, with a basement room just four feet high, which already contained a giant crystal the faeries had asked her for. 'They've told me that this is where they want the tower to be. And I thought it very strange that they wanted it to be at the mouth of the Poisoned Glen, but they said, "No, it's the wrong name." This is the way they work. They tell me something and then within a few days something will happen that explains it. I didn't know what they meant, and then a week later a friend of mine said he had met this old Irish scholar who'd told him the Poisoned Glen shouldn't really be called the Poisoned Glen, it should be called the Heavenly Glen. The old Irish for 'poisoned' and 'heaven' was similar, and when the mapmakers had done their survey they'd got the wrong word.'

So Elizabeth's tower was at the mouth of the Heavenly Glen. The faeries had told her that the place was a portal. Something of great import was going to happen at its mouth. 'They haven't yet told me what it is.'

Originally, the old lady who'd owned the cottage to which it was being attached wouldn't sell it. 'It can never go out of the family,' she'd told Elizabeth. But then, suddenly, mysteriously, she'd changed her mind. 'You see,' said Elizabeth. 'Things like that just happen.'

There was no doubt in her mind as to why.

The King and I

The mountainous headlands of northern Donegal stretched away to the north, a long, blue-grey silhouette receding against the inky washes of sky, just a few streaks of ochre down by the horizon. That bluest, most distant one was surely Malin Head, famous from the Radio 4 shipping forecast; the most northerly point in Ireland, yet still, of course, in the South.

All of a sudden we were at Tory pier, which was crowded with old-fashioned faces. Bags and crates were hoisted up from the boat; as was I, pulled up under the armpits by two burly Torymen. As I looked for Patsy Dan, the King of Tory, I heard a short American in a flat cap say, 'Did the important person arrive? The British writer.' (Goodness. Was there another British writer on board?)

But no, it was me, and in a moment I was shaking hands with Patsy Dan, who seemed, despite that just-overheard remark, considerably less interested to make my acquaintance than he'd been on the phone last night. Perhaps he was just flustered. His daughter had arrived and he needed to deal with her. Where was I staying, he asked briskly. Right, that was the tall dark man over there. Eamon. He'd see me later.

We drove off in Eamon's Land Rover. I'd arrived on a historic day. Tory's only road was being tarmacked. The place was crowded with lorries and heavy machinery from the mainland. We waited patiently in the Land Rover. There was no huge hurry.

There was a wedding on Saturday, Eamon told me. That was why the pier had been so crowded. A Tory man was marrying a girl from Scotland and half the island was headed for the mainland. The place'd be deserted tonight.

We got past eventually and down the still-unmetalled track to East Town, where I was shown into a smart new bungalow and offered tea and biscuits by Eamon's pretty young wife at a blue-check-clothed table with a wonderful view over to that long, blue mountainous silhouette of Donegal.

There are no trees on Tory. It's just a bare strip of land, three miles long and half a mile wide, rising from the stony shores of the south to the sheer cliffs of the north. In the middle are East Town and West Town; the latter the bigger of the two, with the pier, the hotel, the chapel and two of the three shops.

I walked back down the connecting road on pristine black tar. On the stony track beyond West Town I caught up with a grey-haired priest (*the* grey-haired priest, of course), striding along with a walking stick.

'D'you know where Derek Hill's hut is?' I asked.

Surely he did. He was going that way himself.

I'd met him, I said, on the mainland.

Had I? Yes, well, he'd been over recently, as a matter of fact, with the French photographer Martine Cartier-Bresson. (I should have expected nothing less.) He himself was from a Jesuit church in Limerick, the city in which he'd grown up. He was here by choice, he stressed, just in case, presumably, I should think he was a real-life Father Ted. (Though if anywhere could have been Craggy Island, this certainly could.)

We passed a gaggle of hens, clucking around by a low, circular stone wall. There were no foxes or rats on Tory, the Jesuit said, so hens running free like this were a common enough sight. People left them near these little stone huts, then came out once a day, fed them and collected the eggs.

We passed a tiny inland lake and came to the lighthouse, where there was, sadly, no longer a resident keeper, but today, nonetheless, three men polishing the glass. Why they didn't just have someone permanent, the Jesuit couldn't understand.

The lighthouse was automatic all right, but these men had to keep coming out to polish the glass. By helicopter, every fortnight at least.

Anyway, that was Derek Hill's hut over there, on the headland.

It was the old lighthouse hut, and Derek had rented it, he had told me, 'until my death'. Close up, it was rather more than a hut – a little one-roomed concrete house with a slate roof, the guttering and exterior bolts picked out in the same bold red as Glebe House, the door bright green.

Leaning against it I was actually in the Corotesque *Tory and the Mainland from My Hut* (25 × 50cm. Oil on board). Although there was no sunshine on the straight today, the undulating mountains were the same, the cone-like breast of Errigal in the middle. It was a wonderful studio for somebody who wanted to try and get to grips with the ever-shifting tones and chromas of landscape.

Outside his bungalow on the edge of West Town, the King of Tory was sawing wood in the door of *his* little studio-hut, which was painted inside in a bright yellow. He had entirely recovered his mood and greeted me with the warmest of handshakes. He was a wiry enough old gent, with a bristly grey moustache and stubble, dapperly turned out in a black peaked cap, which served the double function of keeping his pate warm and taking twenty years off him.

We went into the hut to look at some of his most recent paintings, which mainly featured scenes of the island by night. 'I use my eyes like the cat's eyes,' Patsy Dan told me. 'I like the night. I have great love for the moon, and great love for the stars, and I like the way all the different clouds don't look friendly, the clouds you get with the moon at night.'

He didn't draw at all, he said. By which he meant he didn't sketch first. He just 'started off the ground from my own mind', very rarely using photographs, because, like Dr Derek Hill, the father of the Tory School of Painting, he didn't like them. 'Occasionally I come to the point where you might like to use some, but mostly it would be imagination for me.'

The results would sell in the gallery on the mainland for about £120 for a small one and £200 for a larger one. Northern

308 *Mark McCrum*

Ireland would be their best buyers, although Dubliners were getting quite keen on their work as well, and they had sold paintings to Americans, Germans, French, Austrians ... Indeed he, Patsy Dan, had been to America twice in the last few years to promote the Tory School of Painting. Last January he'd been invited by a holiday company there to visit six states and had 'totally and thoroughly enjoyed it'.

When he was not painting he continued his promotional work as King. His line was to go to the pier as often as he could on summer days 'to welcome friends and visitors off the ferry to my island'. He played music for them and sometimes wore a cloak, and now he was well known all over the world.

It was important work, for tourism was 'the only backbone left'. Under EU rules, salmon fishing was now illegal, which made it 'a cat and mouse game'. In the winter a few families might collect periwinkles, for sale in Germany and France, and sea rods were still saved and burned for kelp ('harsh work'); but that was it, apart, of course, from the social welfare.

In the early 1980s the authorities had tried to close them down entirely, encouraging 120 members of the community left to go to the mainland, 'saying to themselves that this was an island underdeveloped, and it would cost millions to be developed, but we didn't agree'. The islanders had gathered 'our soldiers together and fought all departments of the government that we thought had the responsibility of doing something for the Gaeltacht island and the Gaelic-speaking islanders.

'And gosh, I am happy to say now that we have won and that they were willing at the end of it to throw us a lifeline.' Now the island had a hotel ('hopefully not a second one'), a café ('hopefully not a second one'), a clubhouse ('hopefully not a second one'), a hostel ('and I wouldn't go for the second one'), and life had improved a lot.

There was the new road, the £4.6 million new pier under construction, and this summer, for the first time, they'd had a Guard. Many people hadn't liked that at first, but, 'the head-line would be that from May to September it's good to know the law's there'.

You could see why the islanders had given Patsy Dan the

honour of King. Not only was he a gung-ho enthusiast for the place, he had a politician's way with words. When I suggested that maybe a visitor could get a painting a wee bit cheaper direct from the artist on the island he gave me a level look. 'For you now, Mark, as a friend of ours it would be very unfair to say that,' he said, 'because galleries have to have their business as well.'

And as a friend of theirs I could only agree.

Two hundred yards away, at the other end of West Town, in the gallery for which Derek Hill and an American friend had provided funds, I found the youngest of the Tory Island school. He was Anton Meenan, a jowly thirty-something in a baggy beige jumper. He had just finished a picture of the British gunboat H.M.S. *Wasp*, which in the harsh days before social welfare had been sent to collect taxes from the island. The story went, he told me, that the people of Tory had a cursing stone, which they turned against the ship, and, sure enough, it was wrecked on the rocks behind the lighthouse, all but six of the crew drowned.

Anton could hardly be classed as a primitive painter, having spent a year studying at the technical college in Letterkenny. His style was considerably more polished than the others and raised a sudden question for me about the whole concept of naive art. I mean, you could call some of the artists along the Bayswater Road on a Sunday afternoon naive, yet no one has founded a school around them. Perhaps they should gather up their canvases and move forthwith to a remote Irish island.

Although Anton had refined his practical skills on the mainland, the accompanying study of the lives of famous artists had had the effect of putting him off painting for several years. 'At the back of my mind I always liked the idea to get married and have children, and it did seem to me that none of them had a very happy life, so I thought I would prefer to go back to Tory and be a fisherman and have more chance of a happy life than if I'd gone on with this art.'

Luckily though – for his watercolours were good – the Muse had tugged him back, and now he had the family and the art, plus the bonus of long conversations with the summer visitors to the island. 'You know, you go down the road, you can have a chat with somebody from Italy or Paris. This is a small population, so if you were down the pub tonight I could say to you, "When did you come in and what do you do?" Get a conversation going. When I was over in London' – he'd been laying cats-eyes on the M25 – 'I used to be packed into some of those Undergrounds, and I'd be standing next to somebody and I was often wondering, What kind of a day did you have today?'

If there was an argument between islanders, Patsy Dan had told me, it would be 'cut off within seconds. And you're the best of friends the next day because you can't afford to fall out with anyone. We are 170 people here. To fall out with five or six, I would rather not be here, because you meet that person once or twice a day, there's a possibility that they'll come round the corner and you have to say hello and maybe do them a favour as well.'

As I walked over the little football pitch, and up to the shiveringly sheer orange-brown cliffs of the northern side I understood more deeply what this meant. This would be no walk for two people who had fallen out badly or even for one who was suicidally unhappy. Indeed, I learned later on the mainland, there had been such a casualty the previous year. It had been recorded as accidental death, but everyone knew it was suicide. 'But suicide is still hushed up in this country, the authorities don't like to admit it happens, so accidental death is most often recorded.' It was a woman from Scotland who had always planned to go to Tory with her husband, but he had died a few months before her visit.

I peered over. What unbearable pain or crazed abandon had driven her to jump down to those dizzying blue waters far below? I shuddered back from the edge.

And then there was the case of Sean Rodgers, one of the first group of Tory painters, who'd gone 'very sadly, off the cliffs'.

'He just fell off, did he?' I'd asked Patsy.

'That's right, that's right,' he'd replied, and hurried on without a blink. They, too, clearly didn't like to dwell on private tragedy.

*

I lay on the springy heather in the late afternoon sun. From up here Tory was just a strip of electric green in the foreground, almost too narrow to support life at all. Beyond, the sea was now a shimmering silvery-gold. I saw Derek Hill from a very different perspective now. They had great respect for him on this island, for his contribution, which, if you consider the inept tuition Anton had got in Letterkenny, was significant. Out here, there was none of that particular style of gossip that was part of his life on the mainland. No wonder he loved getting away for a while.

Out at the far eastern end you come to a chunk that's connected to the main island only by the narrowest isthmus of rock. This was where, in legend, Balor of the Evil Eye, Celtic god of darkness, had resided. He had a stony bed of white-grey granite, heaped here and there into rough cairns. The sunset all around was now a glowing extravaganza, but I didn't linger, hurrying back through the shadows for my tea.

Over the blue-checked tablecloth I was face to face with Gunter, a grey-haired but young-looking interior designer from Vienna. He had always wanted to come to Tory, and now he was here he thought it wonderful. Our stop-start conversation became semi-fluent, and by nine-fifteen we were pacing together down the gleaming new tarmac road to West Town.

Tatty red-plush sofas lined the big uncarpeted hall that was the pub. There was a stage, and a huge back-projecting TV screen relaying a two-foot by three-foot image of a hall full of shouting Orangemen. No thank you. Not yet, not *here*.

I grumbled to Gunter about this Irish habit of having the TV on in the bar; but no, he smiled, 'it was like a living room'.

At eleven the King put in a late appearance. Even now he was the professional PR man, extolling the virtues of 'my island' to the visiting writer and his new Austrian friend. I asked him a question that had occurred to me on the cliffs. What was it like being called a naive artist? Didn't they mind?

'We prefer primitive,' Patsy Dan replied. 'But it suits us. Everything on the island is primitive. But we prefer that term to naive.'

Now – goodness – a *woman* had appeared, a bright flash

of colour against the black and blue. She had loose, pre-
Raphaelite ginger curls over her loose brick-red pullover. Pint
in hand, she lay with her feet up on one of the crimson plush
stools, her striped and tasselled skirt dangling down, chatting
eagerly to two white-haired old islanders. The smaller one in
the green pullover had an expression in his eyes that spoke
eloquently of his delight that such a lovely young creature was
deigning to take an interest in him.

She was shagging the barman, it transpired. Mighal, he of
the trendy half-beard. Gunter the gossip-hound had discovered that she'd come for a few days and stayed over a
month. (Now Mighal was worried she'd never leave.) She sat
opposite us and suddenly started analysing me. I had a lot on
my mind, she told me. I looked like she'd looked back in July
when she'd been trying to finish off her art project at school.
That's why she'd had to come here. Because that project, that
school was too much. She wasn't going back; she wasn't even
drawing any more. This was untrue, because she had a little
square journal on her knee full of beautiful drawings. Patsy
Dan had described her as 'a powerful artist', and that particularly Tory adjective was apt. They were as moody and strong
as the turbulent expression in her eyes.

In the suspended time of the inebriated group I found
myself skimming her journal. She'd left the US in late August,
arrived at Shannon at the start of September. There were
references to Robert, whom she couldn't forget, then descriptions of feeling suicidal in a hostel (had she been to Ennis,
too?). Arriving at the island things had improved, there was
hope . . .

Over breakfast Gunter laughed. 'You know, you find
American girls like that everywhere in Europe,' he said. Had
I seen that one big drawing of hers; of the girl with the sword
to her throat?

The pier was crowded with yet more islanders going to the
mainland for the wedding. Even the postmistress had left, and
the priest was trying to find someone to post his letters for
him. Mighal was there, ready to unload booze for the bar.

'You're going to be the only one left on Tory,' I said.

'It'd be nice if we had a busload of nurses arrive,' he

chuckled. But when the ferry pulled in it was nurse-free. Everyone piled on and into the inner room with cans of Budweiser. The King had his accordion out, and the party had already begun.

21

Hallowe'en in Stroke City

The Friday afternoon bus from Letterkenny to Derry was crowded with schoolchildren. I joined the bad boys at the back, effing and blinding adventurously before going back to tea with Mam. The bus took the slow road, up through a housing estate to a row of pristine bungalows with lavish gardens and expensive views of Lough Swilly, then crossing and recrossing the double-track N13 as it wound out into empty farmland, Dermot Seymour cows in the pale afternoon sun, a keep on a headland, Burt Presbyterian Church.

At Bridgend a sign said 'Sterling cash cheques'. Green British roadsigns told us this road was now the A2. FAILTE GO DERRY. The fey, fluting sprite of the BT logo on a phonebox. RELEASE ALL POLITICAL PRISONERS NOW. A red postbox in a wall. PENNYBURK REPUBLICANS SAY NO TO ARMS SURRENDER. We were over the border.

Half past five on a Friday evening is not a great time to arrive anywhere, let alone a dreary pedestrian concourse beyond a drearier bus station just as all the shops are closing. Being back in the UK, I needed English money before I could have a restorative coffee, let alone make phone calls to B & Bs. But my Eurocheque card wouldn't work. Had I reached my limit at the very moment I stepped back into the country? How poetic, ironic, bloody typical. Oh, of *course*, I was no longer abroad.

The few bed and breakfasts there were in Derry seemed to be on the Northland Road. I trudged to the taxi rank. 'Is it worth getting a cab to Northland Road?' I asked. 'Get in,' the scowling driver replied abruptly, then drove me round the corner and up a steep hill in silence. No. 13, recommended by my *Rough Guide*, was closed. Was Clarence House, next door,

a B & B? There were no signs anywhere saying that either
were.

A tall young fellow with a Donegal accent let me in. Did
they have a single? I'll see, he said, departing. He returned
and nodded me in. This here was the key, he said. Which
remained on the hook, here, in the hall. If I went out and
wanted to come back in I should ring the bell. At whatever
time. 'If it's the wee small hours just give me five minutes.'

'Why not just give us a key?' I wondered.

I decided to celebrate my return to the home country by
going out for an Indian. India House, on Carlisle Street, came
highly recommended. On the street a friendly woman directed
me thither. It was 'a wee walk', up to the top of the hill, turn
left through the Diamond, then right out the other side.

Only as I came out through the big gateway of the old city
walls did I realize the subtext of her nervous smile. I was
staying (I was fairly certain) in a Catholic area. This, Carlisle
Street, was a Protestant street. I intuited this from the Scottish-
sounding shop names, from the man in the tartan tie in the
newsagents, and from the Protestant churches, lit up, open
and busy with people on a Friday evening. In the porch of the
big Presbyterian place on the corner a neat lady in a kilt stood
talking to two deeply respectful-looking gents in suits.

And what were the people in the India House? Protestants?
Catholics? Who knew? They all had the same accent. It was
the first Indian restaurant I'd ever been to with white waiters.
The only Indian in the place was behind the bar, making up
bills and taking orders.

As I strolled back up the road, two British Army armoured
vehicles passed by, cruising down the street at 15 mph, each
with two young soldiers on top, blank-faced statues holding
machine guns, which were pointed firmly at the pavement, at
the three young girls who laughed loudly, but not scornfully,
as the uniformed lads sailed past. On closer examination the
second boy had a slight smile on his face. Mockingly superior?
Or just embarrassed at the position he found himself in,
pointing a lethal weapon at civilian children on a pavement of
his own country?

This was, you see, all new stuff to this Britisher. The TV
images of news were, on reflection, closer to film-fiction than

any reality that impinged. Otherwise, why should I be shocked by this commonplace Derry scene.

In the Diamond I jumped at a shout. But it was only an instructor in the Xtress gym club on the corner, marshalling twenty assorted women in leotards. The statue at the little square's centre was a magnificent montage of Republican heroes – Michael Collins, Patrick Pearse, Daniel O'Connell, Wolfe Tone, Dermot MacMurrough. Of course not. It was a maiden with a sword and a wreath: 'To our honoured dead and those who served 1914–1918, 1939–45.' At her feet a soldier far more mature and aggressive-looking than the lads on the armoured car plunged his bayoneted rifle downwards.

At the bottom of Waterloo Street a blue-grey RUC van cruised slowly past (a 'pig' as the locals call it). The gang of youths on the corner (who on Tory Island would have been illegally catching salmon) yelled loud, expletive-rich abuse at its meshed and darkened windows.

In the morning my dour B & B host, Michael, was revealed as a man of irrepressible cheeriness. 'Everybody all right?' he asked the yawning, muttering breakfasters, at frequent intervals. 'Dankershern,' he cried, to a chomping German couple. 'You see! I'm learning!' He hurried round with the coffee jug. 'My German's better than your English. This man's English,' he informed the rest of us, 'is not very good.' The Germans smiled and nodded gratefully, apparently delighted with another fine example of the great British senz-off-humour. 'We're international in here,' Michael continued. 'Germans, Canadians—'

'International house!' the German chipped in cheerfully. 'Dankershern,' quipped Michael.

I gulped down my tea and headed out into the sunshine. Walking down the steep street towards town, I realized there was water at the bottom. Lough Foyle. Beyond the busy road, the terraces and warehouses and church spires and trees and surrounding green hills were reflected smudgily in the gently rippling sheen, pretty enough for any postcard.

At the end of the street was the RUC station, with a cordoned-off road outside it and a heavily fortified, high stone wall around it. High up on the corner a look-out tower bristled with spirals of barbed wire.

Four scruffy kids in woolly hats ran shrieking past. At home – sorry, on the mainland – they would, at this time of year, have been annoyingly asking for 'a penny for the guy'. Here, of course, there was no guy and no celebration of that particular roasted Catholic. The big autumn festival was Hallowe'en, for which the shops in the centre of town were already fully geared up. Devils, witches, saucy maids, faeries, ghouls, Ian Paisleys – the trade in outfits and masks of every variety was proceeding briskly.

By Shipquay Gate I climbed up the steps above the crowds shifting around the market stalls and on to the famous walls, which divided the central sloping oval of the fortified city from the housing estates, greenswards and spanking new shopping centres that now surrounded it. They were, I was to discover, the best preserved city walls in Europe, and they gave the old city both focus and character, as well as a great place for bored teenagers to hang out. From on top they were even more substantial than I'd imagined, the ramparts between the parapets being wide enough to drive one, if not two, cars along.

From up here you could see it all. Looking inwards, steep Shipquay Street running up to the central Diamond. Looking outwards, well, here, beyond the graffiti-plastered black cannons (Roly Majella! Michelle! Ciara! Our day will come!) was the brick-floored square outside the ornate Guildhall. In its centre, the upbeat tourist map saying 'Welcome to Londonderry, an historic city,' had had the 'London' blocked out with green spray paint. The Protestants, you see, prefer the official 'Londonderry', which dates back to the charter granted to the London companies who built the walls and the fortified city from 1600; the Catholics prefer the shorter 'Derry', which comes from the Irish *Doire*, meaning 'place of oaks', which is what the settlement's founder, Colum Cille, called it in the sixth century. Hence, to worn-out local cynics, London/derry is known as 'Stroke City'.

Strolling on, you can see, over the gleaming retail outlets of the huge Foyleside Shopping Centre, the river below. Up here, on 28 July 1689, came two ships. They had smashed through

the Jacobite boom blocking the Foyle estuary and were laden
with food to break the 105-day seige, which had reduced the
pro-Williamite Protestant inhabitants to eating rats, mice, and
dogs fattened on human corpses.

The city had originally cut itself off on 7 December of the
previous year, when, as the advance guard of Lord Antrim's
Jacobite troops approached Ferry Gate, 'thirteen resolute
Apprentice Boys . . . by a strange impulse ran in one body and
shut the gate'.

It was a bold thing for these teenagers to do, because the
city was technically still loyal to James II. But they had heard
of – who knows, maybe even read – an inflammatory letter
that threatened a massacre of Protestants and were taking
matters into their own hands. It wasn't until March of the
following year that a Williamite commission arrived for
Lundy, the garrison commander, and only in April that James
was turned away from the city's gates with gunshots and cries
of 'No Surrender'. At this point Lundy had advocated capitu-
lation to his previous master, but was deposed by supporters
of continued resistance and fled the city.

All this has been simplified in modern times to one Protestant word – 'lundy' still means a traitor – and two Protestant
commemorations – the shutting of the gates on 18 December
by the modern-day Apprentice Boys, when a giant effigy of
Lundy is burnt, and the lifting of the seige on 12 August. (The
difference in dates being accounted for by the gap between
the Gregorian calendar of then and the Julian calendar of
now.) On both occasions the walls are paraded around.

The river curves away to your left as you walk on. Initials
of the modern struggle vie feebly with love-troths: UDF and
CAC are merely sprayed, while 'Terry loves Margaret' is
carved deep into the stone. At the top end, just inside the
walls, is St Columb's Cathedral, in a style all of its own, known
as Planter's Gothic. Just outside is the Fountain area, a tiny
Protestant housing estate huggering up to the walls. It is
protected from the surrounding Catholic streets by a fortified
steel wall, its entrance a single, narrow, steel doorway under
the walls, right by the heavily fortified RUC and British Army
base at Bishops' Gate.

Walking on a few yards to the Double Bastion (where sits

Roaring Meg the cannon), you get a fine view of Catholic
Bogside, streets of terraced housing climbing the gentle hillside opposite, the dirty pink brick ones in the foreground
rising to prettier pastel colours further up.

On the gable ends of the larger houses at the bottom the
famous murals that articulate the grievances of the Bogside
residents and commemorate significant Nationalist events are
laid out for your edification, for it is from here they're
designed to be seen:

NO CONSENT PARADE

YOU ARE NOW ENTERING FREE DERRY

SAOIRSE – FREE ALL POLITICAL PRISONERS

68–96 NOTHING HAS CHANGED

It was riots following the 12 August commemoration marches
of 1969 that sparked the 'Battle of the Bogside', which many
regard as the real start of 'The Troubles'. Exactly 280 years
after the breaking of the Protestant siege it was the Catholics'
turn to feel seriously beleaguered. Rumours of collusion
between the RUC and Orange mobs had filled the Bogside
with the expectation of a Protestant attack. Barricades were
erected in preparation on the 11th August, and supplies for
the manufacture of petrol bombs were hoarded. (One note for
the milkman read, 'No milk but leave 200 bottles'.)

On the 12th the predicted violence broke out. Opinions
differ as to whether the riots were started by Protestants
tossing down pennies on to the Catholics (a traditional gesture
of contempt), or by Catholics stoning the marchers as they
passed the house of Samuel Devenney (a Catholic taxi driver
who had died earlier in the year, three months after being
batoned in his own home by a group of rioter-pursuing RUC
men). Whatever. A mob of Apprentice Boy marchers, accompanied by police, attempted to force their way up into Bogside
and were beaten back by a hail of missiles and petrol bombs.
For the first time in the UK, tear gas was used, choking all but
Bernadette Devlin, who cried, 'It's OK when you get a taste
of it!' and continued to lead the Bogsiders' resistance. Other

key players of later years were thick in the action. The young Martin McGuinness was distinguished by his active stone-throwing; the young John Hume tried to mediate between RUC and mob and got a police gas cartridge in the chest for his trouble.

The rioting spread across the Six Counties, amid Catholic rumours that the Irish Army was on its way to lend them assistance. Prime Minister Harold Wilson was recalled from his holiday on the Scillies, and he and Home Secretary James Callaghan decided to send in the British troops. The initial response of the Catholics was one of relief and delight – the appearance of the British meant the Bogsiders had defeated the hated RUC.

Now, in the Saturday sunshine, the scene was entirely peaceful. On the steep grassy hillside that ran from the walls down to the road by the murals two boys, no more than twelve years old, were practising their golf swings. Now that Martin McGuinness, John Hume, the British government and leaders of those who supported the RUC were all finally meeting to talk in Stormont, could the Troubles finally be over?

That evening I caught up with a Derry resident who was outside the Unionist/Nationalist divide. She was Zena, a young Indian woman who had attended a book-reading I'd done in Covent Garden and expressed an interest in writing something herself. With her 'wee brown face' and John Cole accent, she'd been finding it hard to get taken seriously in London. People, she'd told me, couldn't make head or tail of her. Now she'd returned to a place where the only thing that set her apart from the crowd was her skin-colour. She seemed much happier and more focused. Her brother, Randeep, loved Derry – there was little racism; indeed, the advantage of his colour was that he could go anywhere, mix with anyone.

He laughed when I told him of my uncertainty about Catholic/Protestant areas. Where I was staying was, he explained, almost entirely Catholic. With the exception of the working-class Fountain, most of the Protestants lived over the other side of the river on the Waterside, although you'd find plenty of prosperous Catholics there too.

With Zena's white friend Peter (Protestant, though he didn't believe all that shit) we drank beer in cans, shared a sprawling Chinese take-away and watched *Match of the Day*. Goodness, I thought, as I strode home, what a thoroughly British Satur-day night.

In the morning I walked up through the deserted town centre to church at St Columbs. (Well, after all, the cathedral was Anglican.) But in my blue moleskins, brown GAP jacket, and open-necked shirt, I felt distinctly out of place. The men were all in dark suits and ties, the women dressed up in Sunday best. Not just out of place, but out of time, for the service took me straight back to my childhood in the 1960s. Even then there had been a hapless attempt at trendiness; here the choristers were firmly in their white surplices and red collars, there was no gregarious 'peace', and the liturgy was the old James I text, in which we beseeched our God to defend all Christian Kings, Princes and Governors, 'and especially thy servant Elizabeth our Queen, that under her we may be godly and quietly governed. *And grant unto her whole Council, and especially Ms Mo Mowlam, that they may truly and indiffer-ently administer justice.*

Above us, high in the nave, hung a series of incredibly faded Union Jacks, with regimental coats of arms in their centres; the one right above me was so old the fabric was falling off. I tried not to think they were symbolic.

On the walls, in a prominent position, was a memorial to Colonel Henry Baker, 'A Governor of the City During the Siege of 1689' (he had taken over from Lundy) and 'Michael Browning, Captain of the Ship Mountjoy of this city, chosen to lead the relieving vessels'. The rest of that glorious resist-ance was celebrated in the little museum to one side of the entrance. Here, in glass cases, were the very padlocks, rusty now, with which the rebellious Apprentice Boys had locked the gates. Here were fragments of the French flags captured from the Jacobites on 5 May 1689. The original rods were proudly displayed by the altar; holding replacement flags, but with the original fleurs-de-lis.

And as you come into this place of Christian worship, central in the main porch is the very mortar bomb that had contained the terms for surrender, fired into the city on 10

May 1689. 'With great courage the beseiged refused,' read the notice beside it.

Seeing the English newspapers in the shops I was overcome with a sudden craving for home opinion and gossip. Nolans, with its padded leather seats and little shaded lights at black marble tables, looked just the place to take the spread. Up on the walls were a series of cryptic legends: PEAXE ANΔ ΓOOΔʊILL TO ALL MEN ΣAΨ NOTHINΓ YNTIL ΨOY ΣEE XAYS TEN ΓREEN θA9EΣ ΣTANΔIN ON THE ΩA9Ω ran one.

There had been a murder in Ulster, I discovered, over in Bangor, but it was between rival Protestant factions and was not sectarian. The forthcoming presidential elections in the South merited a piece in the *Sunday Times*, but with a very old stock-photo of Mary McAleese looking like a 1970s academic with long hair and glasses, not the winning made-over creature I had got used to on the roadside placards.

As for the local papers, they were the bizarrest mixture of provincial rag and national newspaper, as you turned from 'Grim warning as UVF–UDA tensions soar' to 'Derry author opens new library'; from 'Trimble's hypocrisy exposed once again' to 'Cattle market to become carpark'. It was *all* local stuff, let's face it – the Trimbles and McClaughlins were no more important than the mayor of Huddersfield; it was just that the local became national by virtue of its viciousness.

As I ate lunch alone, two thirty-something ladies came and sat at the table just along the banquette, talking in lowered tones and laughing loudly. As I got up to go, the darker one, in the white polo-neck and black jacket, said, 'On your own?'

'Yes,' I replied, and before I knew it had been invited to join them. Susan was telling me she just knew I wasn't a Derryman sitting there, and I was replying that I could make neither head nor tail of the city, didn't know which bits were Protestant, which bits were Catholic. Had I been right in thinking Carlisle Street was Protestant?

They laughed. Central Derry was 90 per cent Nationalist these days, they said, but please, let's not talk politics. The two things nobody in Derry talked about were politics and religion. 'Even if a bomb went off right out there in the street we'd still not talk politics,' said Susan.

So we talked about relationships instead. Therese had been married to an Englishman and had lived in Southhampton for sixteen years. She'd had one relationship since, and that was with an Englishman, too. Susan preferred Englishmen as well. *Anything* except a Derryman. Derrymen were too full of themselves. For Derrymen, said Therese, it was football, then booze; women, definitely, came third.

They were spoilt, you see, Derrymen. There were five times as many girls in Derry as men.

'Why's that?'

They looked at me as if I were stupid. 'Because they're having more baby girls.'

But why were they having more baby girls? Was it something in the water?

Now they looked at each other as if I were mad. It was just that more baby girls were born, they didn't know why.

A little later, two well-dressed young men came and sat next to us, at the table I'd been at. I'd taken out my notebook, was jotting down names of interesting things to see around town.

'Put that away now,' said Susan. 'They could see you taking notes and then we could get shot.' She smiled, as if joking; but then, I realized from the look in her eyes, she wasn't joking at all.

It was those eyes that got me, as I wandered up and down the steeply sloping streets of central Derry. The people were terribly friendly, stopping to chat to each other at any and every opportunity, but the look they all had was one of mistrust and exhaustion, it seemed to me. As I was sitting having a cup of tea in Rhubarb and Custard, a Hallowe'en banger went off in the street outside and the four laughing old ladies next to me jumped visibly from their seats. 'Oh,' they went, relapsing back into laughter.

I was right about the eyes, the Bogside Artists told me, chuckling with recognition as I tentatively put forward my observation.

'No, no, that's a fact,' said Willy.

'So what is it?'

'One day you have peace, the next day you don't. One day you have a job, the next day you don't. It's been like that since 1969.'

'I mean,' said Kevin, 'a man born in 1969 would be twenty-eight, so what you're actually observing is people who have known nothing but conflict their entire lives.'

'We holiday in Donegal,' said Tom. 'And once you cross that border, you ask anybody here, you go beyond the British army checkpoint and there's a sign there saying "Welcome to Donegal", it's like a whole weight just lifts off your shoulders.'

The Bogside Artists were the group who had painted most of the murals I'd seen on the gable ends. They were three very different men: Tom a bright-eyed, born-again Christian; Willy a dour and bearded old-style socialist; and Kevin not obviously offering any agenda. But their pictures, articulating the point of view, as they saw it, of the Catholics of the Bogside, spoke with a clear and unified message.

Take the Bloody Sunday mural, for example, which they had painted in 1996, ready for the twenty-fifth anniversary of the massacre in January 1997. If you were an outsider, like me, it might be hard to understand why Bloody Sunday had been so important to them. 'I mean,' said Tom, 'what you see is TV footage and it's over in a flash, and so many other atrocities have happened throughout the world, it's just another string of statistics.'

But from the Bogsiders' point of view, what you'd had was a very small community that had been, for three years, from shortly after the Battle of the Bogside in 1969 until Bloody Sunday in 1972, a no-go area, unpenetrated by the RUC and the British Army. It had had its own police force and its own rule of law. It was run by the people for the people. Now, continuously, because it was a no-go area, it was under threat of invasion from the British Army, and because of that threat, it became a very tight-knit community, everybody knew everybody else. And before the supergrass trials, when the IRA structure had completely changed to a cell system, everybody in Bogside would have known who was involved and who wasn't.

So what 'really made it over the edge' was that everybody

knew the victims. Of the fourteen people shot dead by the Paras, everybody knew at least one or two, 'who lived in the same street, was brought up, played football, played cards and snooker, went to school and all the rest'. And everybody could put their hand on their heart and say: 'These fourteen people were nowhere near involved with the IRA, not a chance. I mean most of them were under the age of seventeen, and most of them were shot in the back, so how can you say they were guilty of this or that?

'So when we painted the mural, we painted it with that type of information, with that sort of feeling. That's the difference, from maybe an artist coming and giving his impression from outside of what happened.'

They didn't need to tell me about the closeness of their community. Just listening to them talk, you could feel it, just as you could feel their shared allegiances and grievances and history.

They were roughly my age. The 1960s they had grown up in had been a time when the Catholic Nationalists of Derry had been thoroughly marginalized. Ever since the Boundary Commission of 1925 had decided to keep this predominantly Catholic city within Northern Ireland, the Unionist council (with the backing of Stormont) had had to go to extreme lengths to maintain control. Here is John Hume's simple statement of the situation:

> Only a third of the population of Derry in the early 1960s was Protestant, but they were able to govern the city through a process of gerrymandering. This was achieved by dividing the city into three wards, and, since they controlled public housing, they were able to put all the Catholics into one ward and then give that ward just eight seats while the other two wards had six seats each. In this way, even though there were more Catholics in the city, the Protestants always won the elections by twelve seats to eight.

In the electoral revision of 1966, for example, there were 20,102 Catholic and 10, 274 Protestant voters in Derry, but the local government elections held the following year returned the usual eight Nationalists and twelve Unionists. To keep the

Catholics in that one ward involved allowing serious over-crowding and even the deliberate construction of high-rise flats.

It was to counter these and other injustices that such bodies as the Northern Ireland Civil Rights Association (NICRA) were formed in 1967, and the sit-ins and civil rights marches of 1968 and 1969 took place. The violent suppression of a NICRA march on 5 October 1968 by a baton-charging RUC, and the attack at Burntollet by Loyalists on a People's Democracy march from Belfast to Derry in 1969 led directly on to the Battle of the Bogside later that year and the Troubles proper. As was remarked at the time, Derry was 'the cockpit of the Troubles'.

But the memories of these three, who had been thirteen, fourteen and twenty-one of Bloody Sunday, were not all of injustice and tragedy.

'You know,' said Tom, 'how, when you're young, one year seems like it'll last for ever. Bogside was a no-go area for three years, so as a teenager that seemed like a very long time, and growing up in the no-go areas to me was the greatest thing. You stepped out of the front of your house and there you had the cars going by with the IRA patrolling the area, and all the main entrances into the Bogside and the Creggan were permanent IRA checkpoints, and then the thing was, from the no-go area you could come up here to the city centre and attack British soldiers all day long.

'So when you're young you'd get used to the tactics of the British Army. What way they were going to operate – the snatch squads – are they going to come down this street or that, which way are they coming? As a young guy you're hooked on what's happening.'

'So were you the guys I'd have seen on the TV, chucking petrol bombs?'

'Oh yeah.' They laughed. 'It was good fun. See, as teenagers, imagine one of the big British Army cars coming down the street, and you're standing there with about twenty other guys and you had rocks and bottles. You say, "Right, as soon as he comes by we hit it with everything." Now, everyone would throw, but when you threw your rock you were watching it, right, so if your rock hit the side of the armoured cars it was like, Yo! You know, you went home happy. But this is the minds of teenagers, you know.'

'And what did your parents think?'

Willy shook his head. 'Sometimes you'd get worse beatings from your parents than you did from the British army.'

Tom remembered a time when the British soldiers were raiding a house and he had three milk bottles in one hand and one ready to throw in the other and someone grabbed him by the back of the neck, 'and swung me right round – it was my father!'

'For us it was great,' said Kevin, 'but for our parents it would have been a nightmare. Looking back now, imagine if you'd had a thirteen-year-old daughter and the word's coming off the street that there's a young girl shot dead, and all the Mas are at the doorstep wondering, who, where, what, what's her name? And then the names start coming back and it's two or three names, nobody's clear. For a parent living in the Bogside it must have been paralysing.'

Just over three months after Bloody Sunday, on the 4th May 1972, a little boy of ten had been taking his usual walk home from school in the Creggan. It was through a field and the playground of St Joseph's secondary school, then up past the army look-out post, which, he remembered, was corrugated iron with sandbags behind, 'and there was like the porthole of the soldiers' look-out in the middle, and barbed wire in front'.

He ran past it, as he always did, and when he was 'about ten feet away, for some inexplicable reason a soldier decided to fire a rubber bullet at me. And it struck me on the bridge of the nose from about eight feet.'

The sandbags were the last thing Richard Moore saw. For when he woke up on the school canteen table he couldn't see. 'I kept saying, "I didn't do anything, I didn't do anything." So I was obviously aware of what had happened to me.'

He was taken to hospital in an ambulance. 'And I can remember the ambulance man saying to my daddy, "There's a woman out here looking to get into the ambulance, will I let her in, who is she?" And I heard my daddy say, "It's his mother, don't let her in."

'I spent two weeks in hospital and during those two weeks I

thought I just couldn't see because of the bandages on my
eyes. And I'm sure it must have been very difficult for my
father and them because, you know, I kept talking about,
when I get the bandages off my eyes, as if I was going to be
able to see, and they knew that that wasn't going to be the case.

'After I got out of hospital my brother Noel took me for a
walk in the back garden. "D'you know what has happened to
ye?" he asked. And I says, "All I know is I was shot and all
that." And he says, "But do you know what damage has been
caused?" And I said, "No." And at that point he told me I
had lost one eye and I wouldn't be able to see with the other
one.'

Now, twenty-five years later, I sat over the desk from those
useless eyes. The right one just a wide open socket of pale
pink skin; the left had a fractional circle of redundant iris
visible in the tiny triangle between the eyelids. They were
shaded from too close a view by tinted glasses.

'I'm not bitter,' Richard told me repeatedly, as he took me
through the stages of his later, blind life. 'Even when my
children were born, I have never felt bitter about what's
happened, I've just felt a sense of loss.

'My daughter Niamh made her first communion last year,
and she was wearing her wee dress and everybody was telling
me how beautiful she looked and she was sitting on my knee
and I was walking with her and all that sort of stuff. I realized
that there is something special about being able to see that
situation, and I haven't got it.

'I suppose I was philosophical in the sense that I would
think about the soldier and think, "Does he realize?" There's
two people, me and him. I've thought about meeting him, I've
thought about how he's feeling. I mean, there was a day in his
life, in the space of one minute – dramatically – I wonder, has
it changed his life, because he's no different from you or me,
and if I'd done something like that twenty-five years ago, and
I was aware I'd blinded a young boy, then I don't think I
could ever run away from that memory.'

Now Richard worked for a charity called Children of Cross-
fire, which helped, as the name suggested, children who were
victims of war worldwide. Not that he'd gone straight into it.
As a young man he'd run a bar for a while, but now he felt

more content helping others. He laughed, self-deprecatingly. 'I don't mean that in a charity kind of way, the selfish thing is I just get more pleasure out of doing that than I did running my own business.'

Micky English was less forgiving. He had lost two of his four sons in the Troubles, and although he seemed to have accepted the loss of the second he hadn't at all accepted the loss of the first. He sat in the front room of his little house in the Bogside, chain-smoking and visibly trembling as we leafed through the papers and photographs that documented *his* fatal day, which was Easter Sunday 1981.

After the annual march to commemorate the 1916 Rising his eldest son Gary had gone off before the orations to play in a football match. The pitch was right beside the Catholic cathedral up on the edge of the Bogside.

And on that day there'd been a bit of sporadic rioting on the junction that had become known, after the Battle of the Bogside, as Aggro Corner. The joint RUC and army forces on the ground had shifted the riot up to a quieter junction by the football pitch, where they would try, Micky explained, and get a pincer action going so they could grab and arrest the rioters in between.

The football match was over and Gary and his friends had been having a kickaround. When the riot had appeared they had, out of curiosity, joined the large crowd that had gathered to watch. Micky had never, incidentally, had any trouble with Gary, in regard of rioting. 'He was a responsible young man, a worker, meticulous about his appearance, never went out without polishing his shoes, no matter where he was going.'

Now while they'd been standing watching, two army Land Rovers had sped down into the crowd, 'on a gradient that's something like 1 in 6, travelling at about 70 miles an hour.'

People were running away from them but one had struck his son, knocking him to the ground. It had then stopped and, in the eyewitness accounts of 90 per cent of the people who were there, reversed back over his son's body, killing him.

This was the point at issue, for the soldier in charge of the Land Rover had denied this second manoeuvre.

The case had gone to court in Belfast, it having been

decided by the powers that be that the soldiers wouldn't get a
fair trial in Derry, and there, their evidence backed by the
trial pathologist, the soldiers had been acquitted of reckless
driving and causing two deaths.

But Micky English was certain of his facts. He still had
Gary's shirt with the W-markings on the fabric (the car's tyres
had been W-tread Goodyears). He had the photograph of his
son's body, with that wheel-thick band clearly marked, a
diagonal right across his back. The soldiers' evidence was that
the first impact of the Land Rover had knocked the son under
the front axle, he had been pushed along with the vehicle. But
if that was the case, asked Micky, why were there no abrasions
on his front? Why were the knees of his trousers unmarked or
in any way torn? Why were there no dragging marks?

Micky English had gone on a speaking tour throughout
mainland Britain. He had fought for and eventually been
granted an inquest, engaging an independent pathologist who
had totally disputed the trial pathologist's findings; an opinion
that was backed up by another British pathologist, who,
according to Micky, couldn't believe that anybody could have
come to the conclusions arrived at during the trial.

Helena Kennedy and Michael Mansfield had agreed to act,
for free, on the English family's behalf, but the Northern
Ireland Bar Association (whose chairman was, coincidentally,
the barrister employed by the Minister of Defence in this case)
ruled that because these two distinguished champions of
human rights had not taken the Northern Irish bar exams,
they could not appear. 'I mean,' said Micky, 'we're supposed
to be British, part of the British legal system, and they were
told they couldn't do that case.'

Nonetheless, and despite facing a jury from North Tyrone,
'with not one Catholic on it', English's family had won two
out of his three points. But Gary was still dead, the soldiers
were still acquitted and Micky was left with a burning sense of
injustice.

A year later Micky learnt that his next oldest son, Charles,
had joined the IRA. He was eighteen years old. 'I sat here
with him, on this very chair I'm sitting on now, till the dawn
was breaking, and we were arguing the pros and cons of why
he shouldn't do this. I was giving him one particular set of

arguments, that that's effectively the end of his life. I said, "There's three ways you can go: you can come in, like your brother, in a box; you can spend the rest of your life being hunted or on the run; or you'll spend the best part of your life in a prison. What happened to all that time you spent training, playing football for the junior clubs, with the prospect of taking your career further?"

'He says, "Look, I went with you down the line. I went to the extent of putting on my brother's clothes at an inquest and standing and showing exactly where he was struck and all the relevant things. I watched you, and I watched me Ma, and the rest of us, slowly being drained away, and at the end of the day who was listening? What do they listen to? They don't listen to people like us. They don't listen to reasonable argument. They protect themselves. They kill us. And that's your answer.

' "I'm going to get into a position to defend myself, and that's the only way I can defend myself because they don't know anything else. The only way they will move, the only way that we'll get concessions is through force. We've come down the line this far."

'He gave me,' Micky continued, 'from his perspective as good arguments for taking up the life that he had embarked upon as I was giving him for not doing it.' He would stand by his son, he said, as would the rest of the family. ' "Because what you're embarking on I can understand to a degree. I don't condone it, and I wish you wouldn't do it, I wish you'd change your mind and see if there's another way to go, but at the end of the day we'll stand by you, you're doing what you're doing because of how you feel, what you've experienced, and where your heart is, you're not being paid for it. And if anything happens I will bury you as a soldier, because to me you're as much of a soldier as anyone who joins the British Army, or the American Army, or the Republican Army of the 26 counties." '

A year later Charles was dead, blown up by his own bomb while on active service. 'He was stepping through the door,' said Micky, shaking his head ruefully as he gazed down at the carpet, 'and he tripped. And we always used to call him – one of his nicknames in the family was Charlie-Muddle. He was lanky and big and he was always tripping over his own two feet.'

Central Stroke City looked very different from Micky English's house. The walls, high up above the grassy slope, were painted with huge white letters reading:

NO MO^{RE}_{LIES} MOWLAM
WE DEMAND OUR RIGHTS

But it was a message you could only see from the Bogside.

Over the Craigavon Bridge and up through the steep streets of Waterside I found, however, a whole different perspective on these dreadful stories of deprivation and injustice.

'This is the thing,' said Glenn Barr, one-time Chairman of the Engineering Union and one of the two men who had organized the Loyalist strike that had brought down the Sunningdale Agreement in 1974, 'that has annoyed me down through the years. When fingers are pointed by Republicans, when they say, "We were discriminated against, we were abused, we were treated as second-class citizens," and all the rest of it.

'I come from these backstreets and my next-door neighbours were Catholics and I could never see that I had anything more than they did. I've always said that the Catholics did not have a monopoly on poverty.

'I was the oldest of ten children brought up in a two-up, two-down, with outside toilets, so nobody can tell me what poverty was. I've come through it. I lived in it. Two children died within a year.

'The one difference between us was that they could object to it. Because they traditionally didn't give a damn whether the State collapsed or not. Indeed they actively tried to bring the State down, so they could afford to attack the Establishment. Whereas we couldn't, because if we brought down the Establishment, the only thing left for us was a united Ireland. So we had to suffer in silence.

'Yes, there was gerrymandering, but it wasn't done for

ordinary Protestants. These guys were gerrymandering for their own power. None of that was handed down to the ordinary Protestant people. I never benefited from it. We lived in these backstreets here, Protestant and Catholic alike, so the guys who were benefiting from that gerrymandering certainly didn't pass it down to me.

'Yes, there was no doubt there was a wee pay-off, you get it in every society, you have it in Westminster, you have it in America, you have it in the South. Southern society is riddled with backhanders and people doing favours to keep themselves in power. And that was exactly what happened here. These guys had it sewn up. The six faceless men as I call them. They were all Unionists, and they had it sewn up, hook, line and sinker. But *I* didn't get any benefit from it.

'I remember a year or two ago I fell on an old Catholic family man, he and I were in the trade union movement together, and we were having a pint one evening and I said, "How's things now, Hughie?" He said, "Glenny, there's no fucking difference is there. All we've done is changed the orange Tories for green ones." I said, "You didn't see any difference when the orange Tories were in power?" He said: "I'm from the Catholic working class, I don't see any difference. It's all jobs for the boys, and where it was a Protestant network before, now it's a network of middle-class and upper-middle-class Protestants and Catholics, and you still can't get on the merry-go-round."'

Central Derry, Glenn confirmed, was now almost entirely Nationalist. Over the period of the Troubles between 15,000 and 20,000 Protestants had been driven out. 'Maybe you weren't shot at directly, but some guy down the street, who happened to be in the UDR, or happened to be in a police reserve, his car was blown to pieces, so you soon got the message that you weren't wanted. There are very few Protestant businesses left over the city side now.'

As I walked back through the little terraced houses where Glenn had grown up, I passed one of the Loyalist murals, on the corner of Bond Street. It was skilfully and powerfully painted, and showed a Protestant warrior vengefully setting fire to the Bogside, a bloody sword in one hand, a tattered Union Jack in the other. The expression on the bare white

skull that was the aggressor's face was more one of insane fury
than control. 'We determine the guilty, we decide the punish-
ment,' ran the rubric above. 'They're hurting *themselves* with
pictures like that,' the Bogside Artists had said.

At seven that evening the Foyle flowed blood-red, lit by the
brilliant squirls of the Hallowe'en fireworks above. Witches'
hats, large and small, bobbed along above the fancy-dressed
crowd, which surged off the Embankment and into packed
Guildhall Square.

At one in the morning the mums and dads and kids had
gone home, but steep Shipquay Street was still a wild street
party between the metal-shuttered bars of the Townsman and
the bright lights of Wheelers fast-food emporium. In among
the crowds of witches and nuns and devils and ghouls and
saucy maids were six Spice Girls in silver, Braveheart, five
people dressed entirely in yellow, Death, a giant bee, an IRA
man ('Up the IRA!' shouts a saucy maid as he passes), a Nazi
stormtrooper, an Arab with a gun, and Father Christmas. The
real RUC man on the corner was echoed and mocked by more
than one false RUC man. The paramilitary quotient, even in
fun, was alarmingly high.

I'd been a bit worried that wandering round taking flash
photos of people with no more costume than a Venetian-style
eye-mask might make me unwelcome. But I seemed to be the
most popular man on the street. 'Take a photograph 'e us,'
they cried, queuing up in inebriated gaggles. Turning from
Superman and his sweet-faced squaw (they'd been 'going
together nine months'), I found I was being approached by a
most unlikely couple: the Pope, swigging from a can of Ten-
nants, with his arm around Ian Paisley.

22

Line Dancing

The waiting room in Derry was packed. For security reasons you weren't allowed to get on the empty train until just before it left; then there was a sudden scramble as everyone surged through. Half the crowd seemed to be students returning to Coleraine University from Hallowe'en. That, for the record, had been another of those Catholic grievances: that in 1965 Derry's Magee College had been passed over as the site for the new Northern Irish University, in favour of the largely Protestant market town of Coleraine.

Enough already! What did these chattering students ('The girls had these *class* costumes') care for the history that had them now gliding past the flat, seaweedy shore of Lough Foyle? Inland, sheep-strewn fields rolled gently away to the horizon.

Somewhere out there was the little village of Greysteel, where on Hallowe'en night four years before two Loyalist gunmen had burst into the crowded bar of the Catholic Rising Sun, shouted 'Trick or Treat!', then riddled the customers with bullets; and Ballykelly, near the garrison town of Limavady, where the INLA had blown up, without warning, the Droppin' Well Inn, a favourite haunt of squaddies, killing eleven soldiers and six civilians.

Hundreds of black and white oyster-catchers swooped and dived over the wide mudflats. There was a wonderfully long sandy beach; a lone man fishing. On the right was a rock-strewn escarpment. The dark flash of tunnels gave way to Castlerock. An old lady in a purple coat embraced her grand-daughter on the platform. A golf course was crowded with men in slacks.

At Coleraine it was all change. The displaced students

hurried off and I was over the passenger bridge and on to an empty local service to Portrush, which was a long curve of elegant bed and breakfasts above a stone-walled harbour and a surf-edged sandy beach. Three teenaged French girls were waiting at the door of the little station to serenade the plump creature who'd been eating an apple opposite me, bite after deeply thoughtful bite. 'Appy Beeyruthday,' they sang, almost in unison. She was blindfolded, crammed into a witch's hat ᵈd led, teetering and giggling, off down the front.

That evening, damp, backlit clouds of drizzle blew across the dark harbour. I felt very alone, pacing the gleaming streets, the cheap plastic handle of my latest throwaway umbrella tugging at my fingers in the wind. Through the open-curtained windows along the front, people were watching the same *Blind Date* in radically different interiors. One street back the Amusements contained just a scatter of leisure-suited desperadoes playing the bandits. But the bingo hall out back was packed, with every grandmother in Portrush and district risking her savings. Beyond, the saloon bars and fish and chip restaurants looked as sad as only such seaside places can on neon-lit, out-of-season evenings.

Down on the beach I took a little energy from the thundering surf, foaming up to my boot tips, looming ghostly white out of the blue-black yonder. The 'What's On in Portrush' board was entirely empty.

The steel chairs and brightly coloured cushions of the Harbour Bar on the breakwater were packed with sociable Saturday-nighters. Damp and exhausted, I couldn't summon up the chutzpah to join them. I slid instead into the Harbour Inn, and took a seat at the end of the front bar, where a loud och aye, aye, aye banter was going on between tattooed barman and loudly laughing customers. Sipping self-consciously through two pints of Guinness, I looked up to find I'd been joined by – goodness gracious, what was *he* doing here? – Tony Blair. Fractionally plumper round the face than in the photos, but undoubtedly the British Prime Minister, wide grin and all. He was down for the night from a village inland. He'd driven his mother and father to a party just outside town, and now he'd booked into the Eglington Hotel and was staying over. This bar was usually really good for women, he confided, although of course – he raised his thick eyebrows – sod's law, it was always better when he came with his girlfriend. Last time they'd been down there had been this one wee girl . . .

Tony was an Orangeman. He surprised me with his contempt for the American Irish. He'd met one in this very bar who had told him how great it was 'to be home'. 'I said, "With an accent like that you must be about 3,000 miles from home." Home! This wasn't their home. Their ancestors *chose* to leave.'

With me tagging along, Tony made a bold attempt to chat up two thirty-something women who had clearly put substantial efforts into their Saturday night make-over. 'So what are ye?' he quizzed. 'Are ye *married*?' When they delicately extracted themselves to go upstairs he explained that the dark one would go. 'She would *go*, big time . . .' He'd *talk* to the other one, he said, but that dark one . . .'

Upstairs Tony posed winningly by the bar, grumbling to the barman about how much 'a policeman' could earn. Could be up to £20 an hour, overtime. During the Troubles, they'd been taking anyone, he told me. 'As long as they were over five foot eight and could write their own names they took 'em.'

The pints were going down and Tony was loosening up. Was he about to tell me he didn't really love Cherie? No. He leaned forward. He was thirty-eight years of age, he confided, and his mother despaired of him ever getting married, but he couldn't envisage ever settling down with one woman. It was always the same. Once they'd been around for a while and they started to get their hooks into ye, then there was no stopping them. His mother was always at him. Now that he was thirty-eight. That's why he hadn't stayed for the party tonight. Because his parents' friends would be *at* him. But his father despaired because none of their three sons wanted to take over the farm. It had been in the family for something like 400 years.

As we left the Harbour Inn and marched out along the front in the drizzle, Tony explained that Portrush was one of the last great Loyalist strongholds. You wouldn't find too many Catholics round here, he said, with a confident laugh.

In the flock-walled splendour of Traks nightclub there was

a band singing cover-songs and a friendly, if not particularly pulchritudinous, crowd. But Tony didn't mind about that. He was going for it 'big time', zooming in on a string of haggard females who might satisfy his increasingly inebriated need.

You had to admire his energy. This one, with a long sulky face and tarmac-thick mascara, was staring frozen-faced in the opposite direction. And still he harangued her, elbow on the bar, smile wide.

He had an ex-girlfriend there, snogging very ostentatiously with Grant from *EastEnders*. But Tony wasn't jealous. He had a *brain*, he told me. So he *knew*. They'd been back and forward, Elizabeth and him, back and forward. On this one. So he wasn't jealous.

He cast one more longing look at her lacy décolletage and dived back into the throng. God had smiled on him at last. A skinny, let's face it, emaciated, blonde in a kind of long string vest and not much else was dancing very enthusiastically with him, now ruffling his hair, now pecking him lovingly on the cheek; and he was returning her intimacies, ruffling her hair, squeezing her close.

But when I looked again she'd gone. And Tony, now covered in a thin film of sweat, was right beside me, bemoaning his misfortune. The wee woman had been ready to *go*. Big time. She'd been kissing him on the neck. Yes, I said, I'd seen. And then she'd just *vanished*. He was sick of this place, he was going to the late bar in the Eglington, did I want to come? It was good *craic*.

Disaster. The bouncer wouldn't let us in. Didn't he know who Tony was? No, Tony couldn't remember which room he was in, but just check the residents' list would ye? Just – check – the – residents' – list – would ye?

So we got in. Tony had friends there. I sat at a central table soaking up the scene. There were three altogether prettier young women in a raised section, two lads with them. 'See those girls,' said Tony, swooping with a drink, 'wee young things of twenty.' He kissed his hand, shook his head nostalgically and all but tripped over a chair. 'I want to ride those thighs,' he cried as he departed. 'Those *thighs* . . .'

Then, as I sat there sipping my rum and coke, the prettiest of the three came to join me, as if in a dream. 'Could you come and protect us from these men?' she said. They'd met them at the disco in Coleraine and they were drunk and *rid*.

The guys seemed a bit hurt that they were now getting the cold shoulder from blond Maire, statuesque, dark Leslie and tiny Christina, who were using me as a foil to escape from them. They were from Derry, three Catholic girls out on the town, or rather, the coast. I knew they were Catholics because Leslie's abuse of the *rid* lads had now got sectarian.

'Protestants,' she mumbled through maroon-glossed lips. '*Rid* Protestants.'

'So what are ye?' Maire asked brightly.

'What d'you mean?

'Which foot d'ye kick with?'

'I'm English. Does it matter?'

'No,' she was laughing. 'But which foot *do* ye kick with?'

I tried to explain that it really didn't matter at home. English people spent their Sundays at garden centres. Here though, even now, particularly now, late, everybody drunk, it was more than a little bit of the story.

Christina, the little dark one, had slumped sideways on to Leslie's lap, kicking her white heels up so they were above the table on the carved balustrade to the next section, her white satin dress awry. Maire was up and slapping her hard on the face.

'Christina! What are ye at?'

Getting no more response than a groan, Maire adjusted her friend's dress so her legs were covered.

'No, Mark,' Leslie admonished me. 'Don't laugh, because if you were to see Christina normally, she's just so dignified.' She shook her head. 'She's going to be so sorry about this tomorrow.'

The *rid* lads had finally given up, driven away by Leslie's spectacularly withering scorn. 'Can't ye do better than *that* . . . That's *original* . . . I'm not *interested* actually,' she told them. Then, loudly, to me, 'They're just so *rid*.'

From one table away I was getting gloweringly aggressive looks from the two rejected Protestants. Tony was nowhere to be seen. Help. I sat tight, wedged between Maire and Leslie until, like bees to honey, another swarm of young men gathered round to hurl themselves at Leslie's flamethrower

invective. There was a chef from Belfast, a satisfactorily beefy
student from Coleraine, and a man with a multicoloured tie
from Donegal.

And when one of the *rid* Protestants careered back, stumbling into the table so that Leslie and Maire and I were
drenched with lager, the man, or should I say the White
Knight, from Donegal saw him proudly, soberly and in a
thoroughly dignified and unsectarian manner, off.

Only when I went to buy another drink did I feel afraid.
'That arsehole,' the rejected Protestants muttered in my direction. 'We were doing all right. There's always an arsehole like
that.' But I had done nothing except what I was asked. I
hurried back to the protection of the White Knight.

On Sunday I slept late, in my airy room with the view through
the stripped wooden shutters to the boats turning slowly in the
little harbour. In the pale sun of the afternoon I walked round
the point, past the Royal British Legion Rest and Convales-
cent Home and the tattered Union Jack fluttering from the
lamp-post on the corner, to the east beach, which stretched
for miles and miles, dunes and the Royal Portrush Golf Club
running all the way to the far end, where a scatter of surfers
caught their waves against the bulbous backdrop of the limestone White Cliffs.

Ahead, and to the north, beyond the dark promontory that
I assumed must be the start of the Giant's Causeway, another
long headland was pinkly visible. Surely Antrim didn't go up
that far? It must be Rathlin Island, chunkier and longer than
I'd imagined. Then it dawned on me. It was Scotland.

Even if they hadn't been brought over in 1603, they'd still
surely have come, these figures I passed on the long strand.
Men in ties and neat grey windjackets and patterned jerseys,
or with clipped moustaches and flat caps. Women correspondingly smart, some still in Sunday best, others looking as if
they'd stepped brightly out of a casual-wear brochure. Which
is not to say that the Southerners weren't well-dressed or neat
on Sundays. It was just a different feel.

It was nonsense, though, that Portrush was a Protestant
stronghold, said Stephanie, my landlady, over a leisurely
breakfast on the Monday morning. Of course, they came down

in the summer and did their marches, rattling their collection boxes along the front, but it was only because the people were here, in groups. You wouldn't collect so much if you just went round the little villages, would you? But otherwise, it was a very mixed, forward-looking town. There were Protestants and Catholics, and plenty of people for whom all that really wasn't an issue any more.

The ordinary people I'd met in Derry, I said, didn't really seem to want to talk about the Troubles. 'That's it!' she said. 'War-weary. That speaks volumes, doesn't it? People just want to get on with their lives.'

In Portrush they were still excited because last year they had got an Independent candidate for the first time. A wee girl who lived a few doors down. And people had said she'd get nowhere and then when the results came she was in with a landslide. Stephanie laughed. She had known she was in by four o'clock, while all the boring old UDPs and SDLPs had been up all night wondering whether they'd still got their seats!

Being the start of November there was no bus out to the Giant's Causeway, Northern Ireland's most celebrated tourist attraction, but Stephanie was happy to drop me there. It was something she often did for guests, she said.

At the swanky Visitors' Centre on the clifftop there was nowhere for me to leave my bag. Security regulations meant that all I could do was ask the man in the sentry box by the carpark whether he'd keep an eye on it. He was happy to. 'Just so long as there's nothing ticking in there,' he joked.

I paced down the tarmac road after the Causeway Coaster and rounded the corner. Was – that – it? William Thackeray had famously remarked, 'I've come all the way to see *that*?' and I shared his feelings. It was just three tongues of rock pushing out, at maximum, fifty yards into the sea. The basalt hexagons that look so huge and impressive in the postcards were barely a foot and a half across. They should rename it the Dwarf's Causeway immediately.

But no, once you were down there, close-up, it was *fine*. The sea was calm, just gentle surges of unbroken waves, foamy fingers puttering in past the bizarre little stacks of hexagons, many of which, this morning, after the rain, had little hexagonal puddles in their slightly concave top surfaces. And when the sun half came out the damp hexagonal ovals haloing these puddles shone silvery-white.

You just had to take your hat off to the Northern Irish Tourist Board (whose work cannot be easy). On this, albeit mild, November morning there were four Indians, two Chinese, four English and five Australian backpackers.

How it gladdens the heart of the uncertain and lonely traveller to pick up the phone and hear an enthusiastic voice. Then, 'D'you want a bed?' Half an hour later I'm being picked up and driven deep into the Antrim countryside, crunch up a gravel drive, to a round oval of grass in front of another fine Irish Ascendancy house.

'This is Glenfergus,' says Alison. 'Goes back for generations.' But it was nothing to do with her. She just married into it. She laughed and ushered me up the steps.

Now I'm standing in a roomy kitchen being offered sherry. On the table lunch is spread: clingfilm-wrapped cheese, chicken legs, rollettes of ham . . .

Donald is the quieter of the two. He stands, nodding, while Alison does the talking. She has an endearing habit of pushing her tongue through her teeth when she's just made a joke.

I'm definitely, if not on the other side, in another camp here. We talk of 'the police', who are not the frightening figures who might smash your windows or baton you in your front room; they're the people you can rely on for a bottle of poteen if you need one.

One of Donald and Alison's sons is in the Army. One night Alison heard him come back late from Belfast. He was retching in the bathroom. She waited for him on the landing. He couldn't believe, he said, the women in the Catholic estates they'd been operating in who would hold their one- and two-year-olds in the line of fire so that their IRA co-habitees could escape. How could they *do* that?

After lunch Alison shoots off to work. She does something with a mobile phone in a car while Donald stays at home and makes coffee for the guest and looks longingly out at the garden. He used to farm the estate, he tells me, but he realized after a while that they could make more by letting Alison do her thing with the mobile phone so it seemed to make sense. He'd got into hens at the wrong time, out of hens at the wrong time. It was virtually impossible to make a living out of pigs these days. Anyway, if I didn't mind, he'd leave me with the fire and the *Telegraph*. There was a man leaning on a spade in the garden who needed some guidance.

At teatime he returned. I complimented him on his trees, which I'd been half-gazing at all afternoon, magnificent in their dying fling of gold. 'Yet it'll all be gone in a couple of days,' he mused, looking out. 'Strange to relate . . .'

That evening, with Alison still elsewhere, we shared a couple of pork chops and a bottle of wine by the fire. Before they'd returned to the North, Donald told me, they'd been in New Zealand for years, which had been a good life, a very good life. To some extent he regretted returning, but if he hadn't, the house would have gone, and it had been in the family so many years.

When they'd returned, within a couple of days he'd had the Orangemen knocking on his door inviting him to join the order. But he'd said, 'No, I'm not going to join the Orange Order thank you very much.' He had pointed out that both his father and grandfather had been in the British Army. 'That saved me, I reckon.'

Another time he'd had a friend staying from New Zealand who was a Catholic priest. Within half an hour of this priest appearing, there had been a knock at the front door. It was the fellow who lived in the gate lodge. 'He's a friend from New Zealand,' Donald had pointed out.

'Ah, from New Zealand, well that's all right then . . .' And the man had gone off happy. But otherwise he'd have moved out of the lodge.

'The truth is,' said Donald with a shrug, 'there is nothing, *nothing* you can do.'

Sometime after ten Alison returned with her mobile phone, triumphant. She'd just closed a deal and made herself a stack of money. She was visibly buzzing as she drank the whisky Donald had toddled off to bring her.

We sat up late in front of the fire. She had three grown-up

sons. The oldest, conservative one, wanted to stay part of the UK, with British justice, as he saw it, and liberty; he didn't like the Southern Irish politicians, whom he saw as corrupt, like the judicial system. The second son had moved to Scotland. The third would be quite happy with a united Ireland.

But her own point of view had been radically changed by going to college in Coleraine as a mature student. Of those bright young people she'd befriended (many from Catholic backgrounds), all but two had left the country. Which was a pity, because the best, most forward-looking brains were leaving the place. They'd just had enough and didn't want to be ground down by the divisions. They wanted to make a fresh start elsewhere. You could understand it, but it was sad.

The Talks were all very well, but the fact was, as long as they went on segregating the schooling they'd get nowhere. 'If they're brought up together, rough and tumble, that's when the barriers will really be broken down.'

What a thoroughly upbeat and generous person Alison was. The next afternoon, *en route* somewhere with her mobile phone, she offered to drive me all the way back down to the coast, and then along past the sandy sweep of White Park Bay to Ballycastle.

I found a B & B above the beach and paced alone up the long uphill road that led into town. To my left, beyond the naked sports field, the Glens of Antrim rose steep and green. I could so easily have been in the Scottish Lowlands.

In the Antrim Arms there was a fire blazing and nobody in but me. I perused the *Irish Times* and caught up on the poppy controversy. Over in Stroke City a dozen Protestant workers at the Coats Viyella factory had been suspended for wearing 'offensive emblems', i.e. poppies. The poor poppy, being a memorial to the bravely dead British and the bravely dead Unionists, had become sectarian; although, as Glenn Barr had pointed out to me, this was absurd, because plenty of Catholics, from North and South, had fought and died with the British Army in both the First and Second World Wars.

There was, however, as always in Ireland, a significant historical twist to all this. The whole acceptance of Partition by the British government had been heavily influenced by the heavy sacrifice of the Ulster Unionists in the First War, particularly at the Somme. Close to 30,000 members of the original Ulster Volunteer Force (UVF) having joined up to do battle for King and Country in the celebrated 36th Division, it was hard, later, for Lloyd George not to pay special attention to Unionist demands.

After a while, bald Ernie came in; then hirsute Peter. I joined them. We didn't even mention the Troubles. We talked about the beauty of the coast and the decline in tourism this year. It wasn't until they'd drunk up and gone that the young barman volunteered the first remarks about Catholics and Protestants. In Northern Ireland, he said (we were still talking about tourism), where you drank depended on your religion, to some extent, certainly with the older people. Of course, they had both Protestants and Catholics in this bar, it wasn't an issue, it would just be a joke, in *this* bar; but there were some bars Protestants wouldn't go to, and some Catholics wouldn't go to. You could tell which the Catholic bars were on 12 July. They were closed.

As for himself – he flicked a long strand of dark hair out of his eyes – he was a lapsed Catholic. He really didn't care about religion or politics. Last time there was an election he hadn't voted. OK, so the vote's secret but what does it mean? Say you vote for Sinn Fein. Is that a vote for peace or are you supposed to be approving of the violence? He reckoned that if somebody put themselves up as a Peace candidate, just that, he'd vote for them.

So where should I go to see an exclusively Protestant bar, I asked.

'In Ballycastle?' McGinn's was the closest. Up the hill. So, after an over-battered 'fresh' cod in the Golden Chip I headed thither, hoping to meet some Loyalists; I'd settle into a bar-stool, and after a while they'd tell me their side of things. But the front bar of McGinn's was entirely empty. In the parquet ballroom that was the back bar, thirty people, in six neat lines, were a-movin' and a-groovin' to an American country number.

'And *turn*, and take a step *back*, and *turn*,' called the slim moustachioed gentleman in black.

'Hall-*oo*,' called three women from a padded corner.

'What are they doing?'

'Line dancing.'

So here were some Prods who liked Americans? Or things American? Or perhaps they were Catholics?

I would never even *begin* to understand.

There was only one bus east along the coast – at 2.15. Well, that was that then. I'd hitch. I trudged off past the empty beach and up the seemingly endless steep road beyond, towards the mighty dark green promontory of Fair Head. Just as I was giving up hope entirely, a gleaming silver saloon pulled to a halt just ahead of me. At the wheel was a man in a pale grey suit and bright crimson tie, who looked at me somewhat nervously out of the corner of his eye. So I chatted away resolutely about the beauty of the scenery, how it reminded me of Scotland, and all of a sudden he'd turned left and was driving me out along the tiny coast road to Torr Head, where on a clear day you got a view, he told me, not just of the Mull of Kintyre, twelve miles away across the strait, but right up the Scottish coast beyond. It was surely one of the finest views in the world. Today, typically, was not a clear day: the thin misty rain obscuring all but the immediate sea.

Having shown me the viewpoint and the steeply lovely meadow-sweep of Murlough Bay, he started in on politics. He was a Nationalist himself, he said, and explained to this noddingly naive English hitchhiker exactly what a Nationalist was. People thought they were mixed up with Sinn Fein, or supported Sinn Fein, but that wasn't the case at all.

'Right,' I said, and added that I knew a little of the history.

He seemed delighted. Well, the Glens of Antrim, he went on, which we were driving through now, would be very strongly Nationalist. The plantation had never affected the Glens because they'd already been colonized, by the Mac-Donnells of the Isles, who came over in 1399, when Scots were still Catholics. Along with the MacBrides and the MacKinleys, they had become Irish Gaelic chieftains themselves. Indeed, in the middle of the sixteenth century, forty years before James I, the famous Sorley Boy MacDonnell and Shane O'Neill had had a terrible row. There'd been a massacre at Cushendun, which we were just winding down to now .. Sorley's son

Randal had, unlike the O'Neills, submitted to the English Crown after the battle of Kinsale. Was I with him?

I was, I said, very much so.

He nodded approvingly. Randal, he said, had then helped the English in the suppression of a rebellion by his own Scottish MacDonald cousins. So he'd been rewarded with 300,000 acres of prime Ulster ground, and in 1620 had become the first Earl of Antrim. It had been his son, the 2nd Earl, whose Jacobite troops had been turned away by the Apprentice Boys of Derry. I knew all about that?

I did, I said.

So, he gave me a broad smile, hundreds of years later, the earls of Antrim were still Catholics and the Irish tricolour fluttered boldly from the lamp-posts of Cushendun. This was actually a recent thing, he said, a reaction to the Protestant flags. You even had the kerbstones painted green, white and orange, which there had never been before; that, too, was a reaction . . .

He reminded me a little of those white South Africans I'd met at the end of apartheid. Resolutely not talking about politics and history; and then, once they'd started, incapable of stopping.

He dropped me in Cushendall, one glen along. Though they all knew the history, he remarked, they could do nothing about it.

On this gloomy November day, the beach was a depressing curve of pebbles littered with rusting lager cans against the spectacular headland of Garron Point to the south. In the hotel there was nobody but a man working his way slowly through a pint of Kaliber; he'd once poured a pint for your man in the James Bond films, what was his name, Timothy Dalton. I repaired to the bright lights of the Baker's Oven, where the woman behind the till was trying to persuade her waitress daughter to go out for a night of traditional Irish music at Skerries pub.

'I don't want to go out and you're *forcing* me, Mam . . .'

'You're like something out of *Absolutely Fabulous*,' I said, after a while.

'Well, Edie's going *out* tonight,' Mam returned, without a blink.

Her two daughters were dating identical twins, it turned out. One was outgoing, the other was really – she made a face – *intense*. The other daughter was keen on the intense one, who wasn't that bothered with her. This one, 'the stupid wee bitch', was pretty casual about the outgoing one, who *doted* on her . . .

Shakespearian comedy in Cushendall! I almost didn't catch the bus.

Which was empty, except for a stocky white-haired gentleman with a huge, dark-blooded sore on his lower lip. He was going up to Ballymena to fetch his car from the MOT. He did the bus trip once a year, he told me, and that was enough; the buses, he chuckled, ran entirely to their own time.

We wound along the narrow road up Glenariffe. Even on this gloomy afternoon the giant valley was magnificent, a collage of damp greens and browns and golds and oranges rising high on either side.

Was I touring? asked my companion.

I was, I replied. I thought I'd come over now the ceasefire was in place.

He nodded.

'Not,' I continued, 'that I'd imagine you'd have had a lot of trouble round here . . .'

He shrugged. Oh, they'd had some trouble. The police barracks had taken a bomb, back in the 1970s, and one of the hotels, too. And the head of the RUC had been shot. But – he laughed – it turned out that that was one of his junior officers. They'd caught up with him in the end; he'd been involved in some fiddling and this senior officer had found him out. But he'd been very popular in the locality, this senior officer . . .

'And he was a Protestant fellow?'

Aye, but he'd been very popular. If you got into trouble out of the Glen, he'd be the sort to phone through and make sure it was quashed. He gave me the broadest smile, revealing a black triangle up on a jagged tooth to the left.

But the people of the Glens had been there for years and years and years, he said. They'd come over originally with MacDonnell of the Isles.

Was that so?

Aye, and since then it was always us here and the rest of Ireland away over there.

This had, indeed, been one of the old Irish-speaking areas. You see, the Gaelic would have been much the same as spoken in the Western Isles. 'That's why you'd see the old Gaelic names still round here; because a lot of them would have understood the Irish from the Scottish.' That was his theory anyway – he smiled – and he was sticking to it.

So we came over the top of the Glen and back into the rest of Ireland, which was now, after a birch wood or two, the roundabouts and garages and shopping centres of the outskirts of Ballymena. One interesting thing, my companion said, was that here in Ballymena, a largely Protestant town, there was a huge interest in traditional Irish dancing. They came out into the countryside to compete. He laughed.

'Things'll work themselves out in the end,' he said.

23

All About Helplessness

In the rainy darkness we drove out of town and parked up at
the end of a puddled back lane. Dermot was keeping an eye
out for the RUC, his hand rubbing at the steamed-up windows
with a nervous circular motion. He'd only got out of gaol back
in September (having served an eight-year stretch for conspiracy to murder) and certainly didn't want to be re-arrested.

At first glance you'd have hardly taken them for terrorists.
Michael was a plump family man with an affable manner and
a gurgling laugh. Dermot, leaner, darker and younger, had the
intensity of a singleminded student; but 'murderer' was hardly
written in his eyes. (Or rather, his eye, because only half his
narrow face was lit by the single orange streetlight outside.
Michael was just a chubby silhouette.)

How, why, had they got into the UFF, I asked them.

Well, Dermot replied, he hadn't gone directly into the
paramilitaries. When he'd left school he'd joined the UDR,
'with the sole aim of what I thought was a chance to take on
the Provies, actually pick up a gun, wear a uniform and defend
your country. It was my chance to actually do something –
maybe even kill Provies.' But when he'd gone through the
training he'd realized the UDR had never been formed to
defend Ulster. His final disillusionment had come one night
when an officer of the British Army had come swaggering into
the mess, 'with his belt on, and his Browning strap to one side,
and one of those "Kill 'em all let God decide" type T-shirts
on, real macho gung-ho crap. And he came over and asked
what we belonged to, and we said G company and all the rest
of it. And he said, "You know why we have a UDR?" He
pointed at the ten of us. "To keep you people out of the

paramilitaries." And from then on I thought, This isn't for me.'

So Dermot had 'drifted towards' the UDA and ended up joining them.

Michael was older. He could remember when the Troubles had started. 'I'm going back to '68, or '69. I was a nipper then, eight, nine years of age, and we were brought up in the Protestant tradition, the Orange Order, the Apprentice Boys, organizations like that. And I can remember my brothers coming home from the parades where they'd been stoned by the Catholics, beaten with batons by the British Army. So that left an impression on me. You know, there is something wrong with my country.

'Coming through my teens, I was always involved in some way with the Loyalist cause, bands or whatever, but I never felt led to the paramilitaries. I suppose that was because of my upbringing. My mother and father would have taken the traditional Protestant stance that, you know, you respect the law, you respect the State, the security forces are here to do their job, you let them get on with it.'

'So what changed?'

'Well, I could see for years that the British government's policy was one of containment. I mean, everybody here knows that if the security forces were allowed to do their job, it would be over in two weeks.'

'How?'

'Isolate the Republican leadership and execute them. I mean, they travelled thousands of miles to the Falklands and took them back. But in my country the government's attitude was, OK, let them shoot the odd UDR man, let them murder the odd policeman, as long as it doesn't affect those on the mainland, and it's not too big an atrocity, we'll let them get on with the business. And eventually, I came to a position where I thought, well, I believe in the right of self-defence. If the government has abdicated its responsibility to protect the people, well then, we have the right, not only the right, the duty, to do it ourselves. Joining the UDA was the best way to go about that.'

Dermot and Michael had met within the UDA and eventually

moved, within that, to the illegal UFF. But although a paramilitary, Michael wouldn't class himself as sectarian.

'I've got nothing against the ordinary Roman Catholic. I've got plenty of Catholic mates, who know I'm in the UDA, but I'll still meet with them for a pint on Friday or Saturday night. It was 'the Provies' who were the enemies.

But it wasn't, surely, just a tit for tat thing?

'Definitely not,' said Dermot. 'When these Troubles erupted in '69, '70, it was solely a Unionist, pro-British fight. It was the Protestant people who wanted to stay British.' But since 1985, the Anglo-Irish Agreement, when the joint secretariat of British and Irish civil servants had been established at Maryfield, there had been a clear, Irish-British dimension to politics in Northern Ireland. 'Paisley, Trimble, McCartney, they won't admit that, or openly say that, but they know in their heart of hearts we've already got joint authority here.

'So the fight now, and for the next ten years, is to see how much of this territory we can hold on to. Either as part of an independent Ulster state or as some part of a federal Europe. It's not about staying British, remaining within the UK, it's about how much land we can hold on to here.'

They talked so enthusiastically about an independent Ulster; so critically about 'the Irish dimension'. But what, I asked, *was* so frightening about a united Ireland?

'Well, to begin with,' said Dermot, 'anybody who has ever been involved in the security forces or Loyalist paramilitarism would never find peace in a united Ireland. Anybody who has been deemed a threat in the past would be deemed a threat in the future. Every time there's a settlement in Ireland, the firing squads come out, the mass expulsions come out. We saw it in 1922, after Partition. The Protestant community is down from what, 10 per cent, to less than 2 in the South—'

'We are *castigated*,' Michael cut in. 'The Unionist people are supposed to have been so bad to the Catholics in Ulster, yet the Catholic population in Ulster has practically doubled since Partition, whereas the Unionist, pro-British population in the South has all but vanished.'

Then you had the instances where, after Partition, the IRA went to a Protestant farmer who had been there all his life and said, '"Right, you're selling your farm." You know, and if he didn't do it, well they shot his son a couple of weeks later. So they had to sell it. No other Protestant was allowed to bid for it. So a Catholic got it at a rock-bottom price. I mean, you had ethnic cleansing. It's a new term, but basically it was happening seventy or eighty years ago in this country. So if there was unification tomorrow, the same thing is just going to happen all over again.

'I mean, they say we are to be allowed our privileges in an Irish state. They can't even have a British Legion parade next Sunday in Bellaghy. And that's while this country is still supposedly British.'

The problem was, I said, that from the people I'd talked to, particularly in the South, I couldn't see there ever being complete peace without a united Ireland.

'Well I believe in a United Ulster,' said Dermot. 'I'm an Ulster Nationalist.' The problem, he continued, was simple: 99 per cent of Protestants wished to be if not British, then of Ulster. Whereas the majority of Roman Catholics felt an allegiance to Ireland, to Dublin. 'They talk about compromise, but they cannot compromise. These are two, you know, opposites. The only compromise is for both communities to give something up. But if there's a united Ireland tomorrow, we've given everything and they've given nothing.'

'I would die before I accepted a united Ireland,' said Michael. He laughed. 'Because I'm gonna die anyway . . .'

'What, one day, or . . .?'

'No, in a united Ireland. We wouldn't last two weeks.'

'You reckon?'

'I know.'

'Who would murder you?'

'You'd probably find another version of the Irish Continuity Army or the Provies. Even if the thing got into place without trouble, once the spotlight shifted, the death squads could get into action. It wouldn't be making headlines any more, so they'd be quite happy and everybody else would be quite happy. Because basically,' he added, 'we're an embarrassment to the British, you know.'

'What d'you mean?'

'I mean, the average English politician. I know he doesn't want me.'

'You do.'

'It's plain to be seen. Northern Ireland's just a problem. If they could get rid of it, well and good ... Look, I feel an affinity with the English people, the Scottish people, the Welsh people. But the mainstream British politicians have betrayed us consistently.'

'And you think the mainstream English people are on your side?'

'Well, we have groups on the mainland, there is support there—'

'But there's just such total ignorance,' cut in Dermot impatiently. 'On the mainland, about what is actually happening here.'

Michael agreed. 'I mean I've been on the mainland and you're just classed as a Paddy, you know. I could say, "My family fought in two world wars, wore the British uniform," but it doesn't count for anything.'

'So what is it?' I asked, 'that you guys are defending?'

There was a pause.

Then, 'Family and friends,' said Dermot. 'First and foremost, family and friends. Then your own community after that. Because there's nobody else in the whole wide world supporting us. There's one million Protestants here and that's that. There's a handful of friends in the rest of the world. Beyond that there's nobody here but ourselves.

'You hear the saying "siege mentality". It is a siege mentality. We're sitting here and there are five billion people in the world or whatever it is and there's one million of us and everybody's against us. There's not one single government, one single institution that would give us any sort of support at all. None at all.'

'And the Americans are not on your side?'

'The Americans,' Dermot replied with enthusiasm, 'are the most detestable people I've ever had the misfortune to meet. That's putting it mildly.' He developed this theme for a minute or two, then concluded, 'Their consumer society is self-centred, they have no interest in anything but themselves, in their own political games.'

'So you feel totally isolated?'

'Definitely. There's no one else there definitely.'

I brought up the peace process. If these Talks succeeded and managed to maintain the integrity of the existing Northern Ireland State, as Blair had promised, mightn't that be an answer? But no, they thought it would be 'another Sunningdale'. As far as they were concerned, as long as the agreement had an Irish dimension, they would continue fighting.

'So what would you say,' I asked, 'to people who say that you, the paramilitaries, are one tiny per cent at the end of the spectrum and that your point of view, enforced by violence, is not important.'

'Well,' said Michael. 'How do we survive, you know? The reason the UDA has existed for the last twenty-odd years is because we have the support of the Protestant community.'

It came back to 'the thing of the territory'. They were doing no more than protecting their own. Take the village of Dunloy, for example, 'a classic example'. 'It used to have a Protestant community, but doesn't now, because that community, over the years, was worn down, intimidated out. Children going to school were spat on. Simple things – cars vandalized, windows broken, houses attacked. Over a period of years that wears people down.'

'And the intimidation is coming from . . .?'

'Republicans in general. Just simply to get us out. It's low-intensity psychological warfare.'

It would be different in Belfast, said Dermot, because there people lived in their own ghettos, you'd never see a Roman Catholic. Out here, though, in the countryside, 'I think it was Rudyard Kipling who said, "Two men fighting in a pigsty with knives." We're cheek and jowl. We're that close to each other. I know who the local Provy is, he'll know who I am.

'Now people out here,' he went on, 'are hard-working. They haven't got much, but what they have, they intend to hold. I think maybe it's got to do with a closeness to Scotland. Do you understand the term *thran*? We're stubborn. In the countryside you'll find – parades are a brilliant example – you say to twenty, thirty Orangemen, average fifty years of age, "You can't walk down that road." That's where a man's lived all his life, he's walked down the road maybe three or four times a day and he will say, "I'm going to, and nobody's going to stop me." And they won't stop him.'

So they weren't going to put up with the intimidation, the stuff that went on throughout the North, when this or that small community was picked on because it was seen as the enemy. 'Over the years maybe a father was shot dead, another had his leg blown off because he was a UDA officer, so there's two more families out of the area, and it narrows down and narrows down.'

Meantime other families would be subject to that quieter war of nerves. Dermot had had relations who'd had to put up with a 'nightly abuse of eggs thrown through the window, stones, excreta, paint bombs, all very low key. No bullets, no bombs, nothing to interest the RUC.' When the RUC had eventually come, their advice had been, 'Why don't you move?'

'So here you have only three or four families left and you have to decide – do I bring my children up in this, where they're getting abused and they can't play in the front garden, or do I go? Next thing you know, it's a total Roman Catholic area.'

'The thing is,' said Michael, 'the people who are doing this at night, nine times out of ten you'll meet them in the street the next day and they'll say, "How are ye?"'

You couldn't prove anything. His brother-in-law, for example, had been murdered by the IRA. 'We've our own contacts within the security forces, and they know who've done it and they know the neighbours set them up for assassination. But, like, the rest of his family's still living there, and those people are still meeting them and waving at them from the car and so on. But they *know* they were the ones that set him up for execution.'

The police force, the RUC, wasn't there to protect them, said Dermot, any more than the British Army. 'Their attitude is, I'm here to protect my family and the local RUC station and sod the rest of the community. So there's no one except yourself. I'm only thirty now, but I remember when I was a young lad, lying in my bed at night and seeing the flashes in the distance. It was the Provies out training. The army knew they were there, the RUC knew they were there, everybody knew they were there. But nobody did anything about it. And you had entire communities terrified. The Provies would be driving up and down in their cars, showing off guns at the windows and all the rest of it.

'The RUC would come in the morning. "Did you see anything?" You'd say, "I saw such and such." And they'd go "Right" and walk away, and the next night the Provies would be back again.

'And this is supposedly a Protestant police force, supposedly biased against Roman Catholics, part of the Protestant Ascendancy, and all the rest of it. So what do you do? If you've a gun you keep it for your own family. Who do you rely on? Nobody but yourself. And then they ask: why do we exist?'

The only difference now, Michael added, was that they were more organized.

For years, continued Dermot, they had just been reactive. 'It used to be we'd have waited till somebody got shot dead, and that's the fun of it, if a local peeler got shot dead, we'd go out and revenge him.'

Nowadays they said 'tough'. Nowadays they were proactive. 'In the sense we'll say, "Right, who's who? He's a Provy, right, we'll go get him." So now we don't wait for them to come for us any more, we go for them.'

Which is why, Michael argued, they had peace now. Because for the first time in the history of the Troubles they'd been giving the IRA some of their own medicine. 'And they didn't like it.'

That was the reason the IRA had pushed for a ceasefire. It was like 1921, when Collins called a ceasefire. The British offered them a ceasefire then when they were being beaten. Every time it was the same.

And did their families know about their involvement?

Of course. 'My mother summed it up,' said Dermot, 'when she said, "If I'd been a young man I'd have joined too." And that's the general attitude. You don't have a choice really. If you're sitting in your house and someone comes to your door and you can't defend yourself, then you're dead.'

'The way I felt about it was,' said Michael, 'when the Provies were active, and an atrocity came on the news while you were sitting eating your supper, at least I'm trying to do something about that. I could have just been the typical Loyalist, gone on my band parades, drunk my beer and then forget about it all till the next 12th.

'Every time the Provies have done something your blood boils, but at least you can say to yourself, "Well I may not have achieved much, but at least I've tried to do something about them guys."'

'It's all about helplessness,' said Dermot. 'If you can do something, it means you're not actually helpless.'

'I can go to bed with a clearer conscience,' said Michael.

'If I die tomorrow,' said Dermot, his voice going quieter and quieter with his emotion, 'I can say, "Well, I've had a few good years. I've done my best. I've tried. I've tried."'

'You've done your best for your people?'

'I've tried. That's all I can do. I canna' do more.'

In the Grouse, in town, I sat with a pint of English bitter over a thoroughly English trio of lamb, duck and chicken in a lamb *jus*. The suits bustling in, introducing colleague to client with the usual gurgles of business *bonhomie* could have been from Preston, Swindon or Tunbridge Wells. The skinny waitress spoke with a birdlike East End accent. On wooden café poles there were the *Daily Express* and the *Daily Telegraph*. On the surface, it was so like home.

Mary McAleese had made the English *News At Ten*. The Irish President-elect (as she now was) wasn't going to wear a poppy on Sunday. In the morning, she was on the front page of the *Irish Times*. 'President-elect decides she will not wear a poppy at her inauguration ceremony.' She had given the matter her deepest consideration and decided that apart from the shamrock, the President should not wear emblems or symbols of any kind. Instead, she was honoured to attend the Remembrance Day ceremony in St Patrick's Cathedral. Clearly Presidential material there (especially as, as a child, she had been burned out of her home in Belfast).

In the bustling streets of central Ballymena they were almost all wearing poppies. A splendid old gentleman in the navy blue uniform of the British Legion (encrusted with medals) was selling them in the doorway of Marks & Spencer. For the first time in my life I paused in my poppy purchase. Despite my neutral accent I had become politicized.

It seemed appropriate that Ballymena's only tourist attraction, Morrow's Shop (an old draper's with the cabinets still intact), had an attached museum room stuffed with military mementoes. The only difference from those similar exhibits in Ennis or Enniscorthy was that these glass cases didn't contain Michael Collins's jockstrap or Patrick Pearse's last laundry list, but equally sentimental and ghoulish tat from the two world wars. There was a Wartime Utility Pencil, a Ration Book, a Celebration of Victory Day programme and a Death Penny ('The Colloquial Name Given to the Memorial Plaque Presented to the Next of Kin of All Soldiers Killed in Battle in the 1914–18 War, or Who Died of War Wounds').

As I gazed in wonder at these reliquiae, I was joined by a diminutive gentleman with a bizarre combination of moustache, stutter and tattooed right arm. He was interested that I was interested (clearly the last tourist he'd seen had been some decades before), and when I explained that I was doing a little historical research, he informed me that in 1798 the United Irishmen had burned down the original Town Hall next door. They'd rolled a flaming barrel of tar up to the front door. In fact, he had this print here, of the scene; also this bayonet from 1798.

It was interesting to me, I said, fingering the rusty instrument of death, that in those days it had been the Protestants leading the fight against the British. Yes, he replied. But look what had happened to them after 1798? Look what the Catholics had done to their comrades at Scullabogue – they had just packed them into a barn and set fire to it. It was important, he told me, to remember what actually did happen in the Irish rebellion, when the Presbyterians and the Catholics were united, because the Catholics, directed by their priests, had turned on their comrades and butchered them. 'So the one crack they had at that, well, we see how it turned out for us in the end.'

These days, though, Ballymena Town Hall, with its surprising Graeco-Egyptian interior, looked out over a peaceful and prosperous little town, which had its fair share of millionaires, Billy at the George Buttery told me. Indeed, people actually drove out of Belfast to do their shopping here, because they could get the range and quality of the city without the hassle. Even McDonald's was here now. 'The golden arches have arrived in Ballymena.'

'You'd be doing us a favour by letting the world know we're not fighting each other,' said Jack Adams, Ballymena's 'local Lord Lichfield', who was retiring next year after 3,500 weddings and thirty-five years of being the town photographer.

Why did the media always dwell on the bad side of things when there was so much good news? Take Radio Cracker, for example, of which he was the chairman and coordinator. It was a local radio station that had a licence to run once a year, in December. It was music and chat, and they charged for dedications and advertising and last year it had raised £50,000 for the Third World, despite Ballymena's – he laughed – reputation for being tight-fisted – 'the Aberdeeen of Ireland', as some called it. And it was cross-community, Catholics and Protestants were all involved. And yet, when they'd broken their record last year and he'd written a press release and sent it to the BBC and ITV and most of the English dailies, it was totally ignored.

Jack was right. The only news to come out of Ballymena was focused on a Catholic chapel in the Protestant suburb of Harryville, where a group of Loyalist demonstrators met regularly to jeer at the Catholic worshippers as they went into Saturday evening Mass. The protest had apparently begun because the Catholics in Dunloy (the very village that Dermot had used as an example of intimidation) had prevented a Loyalist march from going through. Now the ugly sectarian scenes were regularly on TV.

But it was really nothing, said another Ballymena resident, who wished to remain nameless, 'just a handful of yahoos'. The TV news blew it up into this huge fight. You could guess how bad it was because his son had gone down there on the night they'd burned the bus, and taken *his* son, who was six, to have a look. The burned bus had been world news, had looked terrifying on the small screen, but locally it hadn't made a stir. 'He'd hardly have taken the wee lad down if it was going to be dangerous.'

There was nobody at all outside the little chapel when I

walked down there, but the housing estates round about made no secret of their loyalties, with red, white and blue kerbstones, and Union Jacks flying alongside Red Hands of Ulster from numerous lamp-posts and windows.

The cherries in the Ballymena Memorial Park (Outstanding Well-Kept Memorial Park – Progressive Ulster in Bloom 1991) were as gloriously crimson as the Red Hands of Ulster mounted on every twentieth railing beneath them. The trees had been planted by the British Army to Commemorate the Ending of the Second World War, and the poor gardener was having a dreadful struggle keeping their leaves off the manicured lawns beneath. He'd mown them only this morning, he said. And *now* look at them.

24

Concerned Residents

The nasty little protest at Harryville had had its repercussions, and now there was a huge fuss in Bellaghy, a small country town twenty miles or so down the track. Tomorrow, being Remembrance Sunday, a British Legion march was due to parade down the main street, but a group of Catholic residents had objected, apparently because the band that was going to lead the parade had once played at one of the Harryville protests.

Petty and local it might seem, but it had made the *Irish Times* and the English broadsheets. Was Bellaghy, everyone was wondering, going to be the first big disturbance to disrupt the ceasefire, and the ongoing Talks?

But it was all the most utter *nonsense*, said a Bellaghy resident of the Protestant persuasion who wished to remain nameless. The whole controversy had been whipped up by this one hardline Republican, who didn't even come from the village – he had only moved here five years ago. He was on the dole and hadn't done a day's work in his life. This fellow and his supporters called themselves, as did similar Republican groups across Northern Ireland, Concerned Residents, but they just weren't representative of most of the community at all. 'He says the village is 95 per cent Catholic, but it's not, it's at most 75 per cent Catholic. He says he represents National-ists in the village, he doesn't. A lot of them have said to me personally they're sick and tired of this bloody man. But they're too scared to speak out because he has the backing of Sinn Fein.'

First of all, this fellow had said the band had been protesting at the Catholic church in Harryville, and that had turned out to be untrue. Then that it had been at the Garvaghy Road in

Portadown, but that was also untrue. 'Now he's flummoxed. He really thought he had good propaganda to stir up the Nationalist people in the village, but as it turns out he's made a big mistake, this is just a local band.

'Now his latest thing is the band is sectarian and so some other band from outside should lead the parade. But that defeats his whole object because he's always arguing about outside bands coming into the village.'

Nobody knew what was going to happen, but the word was that Tony Blair had specifically said that that march had to go through. 'It's gone right to the top. Presumably the Concerned Residents will have a protest at some stage. I'd say they'll more likely shout and jeer behind police lines, but I don't know, they're keeping their cards close to their chest.'

Robert Overend, MBE, who was organizing the band, didn't mind his name being associated with his views. 'The IRA have been trying to kill me for years,' he told me. He'd had his old house in the village attacked with petrol bombs, then blown up by a proper bomb; then, when he'd moved out here to this bungalow with bulletproof windows he'd been shot at on his way into a church meeting. His son Robert had survived four murder attempts and his pedigree pig-breeding business had been attacked on a number of occasions.

Why were they so keen to do away with him, I asked. (In his slippers and open shirt, a cup of tea in front of him, he seemed an unlikely target.)

'I don't know. I was a Justice of the Peace. That may have been the situation. Then everybody knew I was quite happy to talk to both police and army intelligence.' He was also a Deputy Grand Master of the Grand Orange Lodge of Ireland, 'which would make me one of the most senior Orangemen in this particular area'.

The village had always had a strong Republican element. It had produced a number of leading terrorist figures – among them Dominic McGlinchey (who, as leader of the INLA, had been involved in the Droppin' Well bombing) and 'a fellow who made himself very well known across the world because he was the second person to die on hunger strike – Francis Hughes.'

This little problem tomorrow had arisen only in the last two or three years, since the ceasefire, in fact. 'There's been this group of people, not only in Bellaghy, but in several areas and they've set themselves up as so-called Concerned Residents groups. And these Concerned Residents protest at anything to do with the Protestant people.

'We've lost a lot of Protestant families out of the village here through intimidation. You know, you're sitting in your house at night and somebody puts a window in round you. Well, if you've been working hard all day and maybe your wife's been working too, and you've got young children, you're not going to stay are you? So you just up and go somewhere quieter.'

This Concerned Residents thing, he went on, was just intimidation by another means. It was a way of keeping the IRA 'actives' happy while there was a ceasefire. It certainly wouldn't have the backing of the wider Roman Catholic community at all.

'Since this programme has blown up, I've had a large number of Roman Catholic people that I've known all my life contact me, and they're furious that this thing has given their village such a bad name. But they don't want to say anything, because if their name gets out the small number of thugs who run the Concerned Residents organization will tell some of the young boys to put in their windows, or maybe, far worse, burn them out.'

As far as the band was concerned, Overend had taken up the allegation that it had played outside Harryville with the individual members and it just wasn't true. 'I chased round the band now, and not one of them has ever been there as an observer, let alone taken part in any protest.'

Meantime, the Concerned Residents would be ringing the press, and putting out press releases and making 'all sorts of threats and allegations' – that there were going to be thousands of protesters there, and they're going to burn the village – then the Press made a story out of it. 'We had one parade here in the summertime and there were about six camera crews here, and another twelve journalists from different papers. We even had a group from France, and groups from Denmark and Norway . . .'

*

John and Hazel Gilmour lived right on the main street past which the parades went, in a little house with unbarred, unprotected windows. Nobody had yet 'put them in', but, Hazel said, during the marches in the summer, when protesters would be bussed in from Catholic communities around about, the tension on the street was so bad you could 'cut it with a knife'.

Two years ago, the year of Drumcree, they'd barricaded the window before going to bed, 'for the fear of the house being burned. There was a mob of maybe a hundred people circling round your house – it's only the Protestant houses they circle round. We sat up till about four o'clock in the morning and then I said to John, "I can't stand this any longer." So he went out to the garage and got these boards and poles and put them up against the window and I thought, Well at least if a petrol bomb comes through that'll stop it.'

They'd taken a tip from her brother-in-law, too, who'd told them to fill their bath with cold water. 'Then if someone puts something through your letterbox you'll not be waiting on the water filling.' So they'd taken a bucket up the stairs full of water and kept the bath full. 'It sounds hideous, doesn't it,' said Hazel, 'but that's how we live in the tension times.'

Last year they'd gone on holiday. And now, like other Protestant families before them, they were moving out, to a house they were building in the country. Hazel couldn't wait. She was neat and attractive in her tailored jacket, her blond hair freshly done. John, next to her on the sofa, was more casually attired, in a grey T-shirt and jeans.

They, too, made the point that the residents groups had only got going since the ceasefire. It was something 'Sinn Fein/ IRA' did to keep their people interested, rather than losing support. Most of the Nationalist community didn't really mind. (Either this is the truth or a fine example of how consensus builds up, I thought, hearing it for the third time.)

But all they really needed, John said, was about thirty people, including mothers with small children, and they'd get a protest. 'And then the police are in a no-win situation. They could hardly baton them off the street. But some of the protesters were so young they couldn't even *spell* sectarianism, let alone know what it's about.'

Last year, said Hazel, the wee boy from next door, who was a Catholic, had been standing up on their front wall shouting 'No Surrender'. 'It was just funny.'

The protestors were now, John said, trying to say the Orange Order were hijacking the Remembrance Sunday parade. But it wasn't any different from what it had been these last thirty years. The way IRA/Sinn Fein seemed to be approaching things now was like the Nazis in the build-up to the Second World War. It was either their way or no way. 'And if you happened to disagree with their attitudes they just wiped you out.'

I gave them my perception of the Sinn Fein point of view: the bottom line was a united Ireland, and the trouble was that just seemed to be anathema to most Protestants . . .

'I don't mind a united Ireland,' said Hazel, leaving me silenced in astonishment (for she was the first Northern Protestant I'd heard who'd said this).

'No,' agreed John. 'Personally I would have no worry about that.'

Sensing at last a glimmer of hope, I delved deeper. Well, Hazel said, she would call herself a Unionist, but the way she saw things now, Britain didn't want them any more, so what was the point? John agreed. 'The British government comes over here and dictates what we can and cannot do. And then you watch TV at night. And who's in Westminster when there are Northern Irish questions? Nobody. The rest of them don't care.'

Things were changing down South, too, said Hazel. The Catholic Church didn't have the same control. The government was more forward looking than Britain, wanting to go into European Monetary Union, for example. No, so long as she was able to go out to work in the morning and come home quietly at night and live in peace and harmony she wouldn't mind . . .

I was sitting there quietly amazed. Get these two round a table with Denis and Stephen from Cork, and Billy from Sligo, and the Bogside Artists, and who knew what might come of it . . .?

'D'you think you're representative of a lot of Unionists?' I asked eventually.

'No,' said Hazel, and John chuckled.

'The educated Unionists,' she went on, 'would maybe agree. But the small, polarized person who has never been out of their wee village, who has tunnel vision, would disagree.'

What was the problem?

'I think there is a genuine fear of being downtrodden. You'd hear the older Unionists, for example, saying, "We'll see a day when we'll not be able to get to our churches."'

'We feel,' she went on, 'at the moment that our civil and religious liberties are being attacked. People say once we go to a united Ireland we're going to lose everything.'

If only these people would talk to each other, you think, sitting there. For now John is telling me that there are too many parades in the village. 'Some of them could be done without, really. Most Protestants admit that privately. Yet if you go to a full meeting and say that you're nearly thrown out ... they see it as a divine right that you can parade anywhere you want.'

And Hazel is saying she wished the parades could be interdenominational. And John is saying he doesn't understand why they always have to have their Remembrance services in Protestant churches. 'Why has the Roman Catholic church never invited them to hold their service there, I never enquired into it.' And Hazel is saying it's just a pity we couldn't all get together and share it.

But it has all gone too far, so they don't talk to each other, and don't discover that one of the reasons many Catholics can't support poppy parades is because they include UDR men and RUC men who have, in their eyes, committed the most atrocious crimes on Catholics.

Even though their son Stuart is playing at this moment with his wee friend Michael in the Catholic house next door they would never discuss politics or religion with Michael's dad, whom they know to be a fervent Republican. And when it comes up to the 12th, 'he gets quite bitter and can't really hide it. So he'll stay out of your way and avoid eye-contact till it's all over.'

And such is this bad feeling between (sections of) their two interlocking but divided communities that there may well be, as there have been on other marches, coal and bricks and bottles thrown, and to be honest Hazel is a bit worried about letting Stuart go tomorrow, but then how can she turn round and stop him, 'because all his wee colleagues in the Boys' Brigade are going.' (And this is no idle fear, for only two years ago they lost their other son in a fire; an accident, not that it makes any difference to the loss. 'Nobody,' says Hazel, with tears in her eyes, 'can know the pain of losing a child.')

One wee colleague who won't be going is Michael. And when I put that point to her she shakes her head. 'It's sad,' she says, 'that we have to be divided the way we are.'

Now Hazel nips over the road to a moderate Catholic friend of hers and yes, that'll be fine, her friend's not there, but her husband'll talk to me. And I walk no more than thirty yards along the street and meet a man – I'll call him Sean – who tells me that, yes indeed, most of the Catholic residents aren't bothered, they just want to get along with their neighbours. But then, having said that, if the band were playing with those drunken bigots at Harryville, protesting against people who were only going to chapel, then to show support for them wouldn't be the right thing to do either.

The parade tomorrow, which will be over in fifteen minutes, is no big deal really. But then in the summer, with the big marches, you basically have to stop in your house from six till eleven at night. You can't go out on the street. If you're out of town, you have to phone the police to come back in. So, yes, he thinks the Concerned Residents group has got a point of view.

'And you have to think, without them, people would be walked over, there would be parade after parade after parade . . .'

Sean isn't a protester himself, he doesn't get involved, because it's too complicated an issue and he doesn't think anybody has any answers to it. 'I mean, you can't say, "Don't march," because then you're alienating another tradition.'

But then, if you let them march, some of them were fine, but some were really antagonistic. Scary. 'You see these fellows, three in a row, really military like, with dark glasses, which means they represent paramilitary organizations, and nobody wants to see that. They put the fear of God in ye.

'And then some bands are fine to watch, but when you get these blood and thunder bands, you don't want to see that. I'd say ordinary Protestant people don't like to see that either.

'When I was a lot younger I remember the town was taken over, not just with the parades, there were hangers-on, and there's a play park across from the pub, and these hangers-on used to come into the park and throw stones, and riot around the town, and there was never anything done about that. One time there were forty Loyalists rioting and only four were lifted, then let off down the town, so it was seen as a police force for one side.'

In the morning there was frost on the fields and mist lurking in the hollows. Walking down the lane from my lodgings I was stopped and quizzed at an army checkpoint. My English accent revealed that I wasn't a hired heavy going to join the mob and I was let through.

When I arrived in Bellaghy's little main street, I had never seen so many policemen in my life. There was one every two yards, on both sides of the road, from the Manse at one end of the little town to the Protestant church at the other, a distance of what, a good half mile. In the side streets were the spooky-looking blue-grey Saracens, two parked up in the little close where the main organizer of the Concerned Residents lived.

Just down from the Manse, where the marchers and band were now assembling, the media were already in place, rubbing their hands and cracking jokes in the chill November air. The centre of the group was the well-known BBC presenter Dennis Murray, plumply resplendent in a padded crimson windjacket and sending himself up, as media folk do. 'Is Lord Murray of Gobshite going to be present? Well then it must be important.'

'We just want it all to go quietly,' said one of the pack, with a wink.

Now, from the side road opposite ('a Nationalist estate') two or three scowling teenaged lads appeared, loping along with an odd mixture of defiance and uncertainty. They were followed by three little boys of ten or so, one in a united Ireland sweatshirt; they weren't smiling either. And here, down the middle of the road, were the Gilmours, smartly turned out in dark blue coats and poppies, with wee Stuart in his Boys' Brigade uniform between them. 'You wouldn't know us now,' said John out of the corner of his mouth (a remark I wasn't quite sure how to take).

I followed them up to the front drive of the Manse, where the rest of the marchers were gathering, piling out of cars in their spic-and-span navy uniforms. I chatted to a bald gent with a fine row of medals. The protests, he told me, represented a gradual chipping away. 'You almost have to ask permission to walk up the street to the shop now.'

The band had arrived! In several cars, having finished playing at the memorial march in nearby Castledawson. They were in white shirts and blue and white caps, the women in bright blue skirts. And here was Robert Overend, organizing everybody into line, in good-humoured fashion. 'Just give me a wee bit of room. Get the band out!'

But when they were all in line, and had moved off down the hill to the main part of town, past Dennis Murray and the big shaggy microphones of no less than three TV news programmes, their jolly smiles were replaced by blank and frozen stares.

Past the little Nationalist estates they marched, in absolute silence. The Concerned Residents, (under strict orders from above, it was rumoured) had issued a statement earlier saying that in the interests of cross-community harmony they were dropping their protest. So, commented my anonymous Unionist, in the eyes of the world's media, Sinn Fein were seen as thoroughly reasonable, and once again the Unionists would come across as cold and intransigent. 'They really are absolutely hopeless,' he went on. 'The world generally looks at the Unionists and thinks, you know, they say "No, no, no," to everything. They come across desperately badly, they really do. It's pathetic. While the Nationalists are so much cleverer, they'll tell the media exactly what they want to hear, meaning always, of course, the exact opposite.'

The rumour of powerful forces in the background was certainly easy to credit. For the discipline was excellent. Not a word did those angry Nationalist faces utter. Not a word did those proud Unionists say, as they strode on by. Until the band struck up you could have heard a regimental pin drop.

It was one of the most tragically ridiculous things I'd ever seen in my life. Two communities, sharing the same tiny townland, behaving *en masse* like a couple who've just had a huge row and won't speak to each other. Unable to meet each others' eyes, yet determined they make their furious point.

And what were the paid representatives of the wider world doing about it? Rushing forward to say 'For God's sake snap out of it!' No. Waiting in hope that a spat would break out, that the righteous anger of both sides would flare up into something entertaining enough to make the headlines.

Bang! Everybody jumped. But only a little, for it was just the kid in the united Ireland T-shirt chucking a banger in the direction of a knot of RUC men. Well-disciplined too, they barely moved a muscle.

Once beyond the Nationalist gauntlet (all twenty-five of them) the marchers relaxed again. Piling down the steps into the little church at the far end of the village they were all smiles and greetings. Up above, on the pavement, the media rubbed their hands. It was a waste of time hanging around for the service, they said. The Lord Murray suggested heading off for something warming, 'preferably with cloves in it – and the wimps can have coffee.'

I walked back down the street past the ranks of RUC men. One or two nodded and smiled, most looked fixedly at a point in the middle-distance. By the parked-up Saracens I knocked on the door of the leader of the Concerned Residents.

In the spartan front room of their council house, the leader's family and attendant hangers-on were seething with visible outrage. The man himself, a lanky figure with a thick head of grey hair, was sprawled in an armchair in the corner. Was this his wife who was now addressing me?

'My grandfather *dayed* at the Dardanelles War,' she all but shouted. 'And *aye* feel that knowing my grandfather the best way I can honour him is just say a prayer at my parents' grave. *Aye* don't need to parade through any town, or any road to show that I honour him . . .'

It was not, she continued, the dead those people were

honouring, but themselves. 'I was listening to it on the news,' she told me. 'This man, he said, "We *will* walk." Well to me that was: we will walk whether it's for the dead or for ourselves.' In fact, she thought, they were *degrading* the dead.

And what about her? What about her rights? She'd been living in the centre of the town and putting up with this for *years*. It hadn't been easy, rearing your children, trying to bring them up in a way that they wouldn't show hatred, 'towards these people, that God made just the same as he made us'.

This was, said the leader, leaning forward, the seventh parade they'd had with a curfew this year. 'That's seven times people's movements have been restricted. There was people stopping you going to the shop, there was people stopping you coming into the village. People wanting to leave the village for one reason or another were told, "No, you can't go, the road's closed."' Last year they'd had thirteen parades. In a 95 per cent Nationalist village . . .

Was it 95 per cent, I asked. I'd heard otherwise. No, he replied, it was 95 per cent, most certainly.

I pressed him. It depended, his wife cut in, on where you drew the line. But within the thirty-miles-an-hour signs it would definitely be 95 per cent.

People had said, I told him, that the Concerned Residents was a political thing and that he and his group didn't represent the wider residents.

'We disagree with that. We have the petitions to prove it. We went from door to door and got them signed. And an overwhelming majority of the people said they were sick to the teeth of this happening.'

'How would they feel,' his wife cut in, 'if it was Nationalists parading through a Loyalist area. Would they enjoy it? What do they expect? Of the Nationalist people? That they're singing joyfully?'

'Here's a point,' the leader continued, 'that I tend to put over when I get a chance, because it symbolizes what's going on in Bellaghy. Bellaghy's very much steeped in Republicanism, there's a strong local tradition. Now up in the local churchyard there, there's a number of Republicans buried. I'm not going behind any bush to say it, we see them people as heroes. They are our soldiers, and we honour them every year. But that commemoration is done up in the graveyard, where it's not offensive to anyone. It's done in a nice, peaceful, dignified manner. The people come out of that graveyard, they step into their cars and they go home.'

And their Hibernian accordion band, which marched through Castledawson every year, was allowed only as far as Castledawson bridge. 'Because there's a number of people there saying they find it offensive to see that band marching through Castledawson. Yet they can turn round today and force this parade through Bellaghy.'

Church over, the Protestants marched back. Back through the silently watching village again, the boys' line rather raggedy now. At the far end they stood stiffly and in silence as the National Anthem was played. I hadn't really listened to the reassuring old tune in years, and I felt almost embarrassed to be taking a photo of them, my click surely heard from one end of the street to the other.

Then, 'Parade dismissed!' and everyone was at ease. The numerous flags were rolled up and people were smiling and chattering again. There was a definite, if not triumphalism, or even smugness, at least a sense of quiet pride in the air. 'We've done it,' the faces seemed to say. 'We've marched our march.'

The curly-haired photographer from the *Irish News* was disappointed.

'Back to Belfast then?' I said.

'With nothin'.' He made a face.

I walked back down the street with an affable RUC man who was relieved there'd been no trouble. Made their job easier, he said.

At the crossroads I pushed through the door into the Central Bar, remembering only as my eyes adjusted to see everyone silently staring at me, that this was a staunch Republican bar. Just a glass of Guinness then, but the well-oiled old fellow with the flat cap and the very thick accent at the next stool along was the nearest thing I'd met to a Southerner since I'd been this side of the border.

I couldn't make out everything Flat Cap was saying, but the gist of it seemed to be that Bellaghy people were very friendly. As I became accustomed to the gloom, so I became accustomed to his accent. Had he just said that he'd been an IRA man these last fifty years? I rather thought he had.

But the fellow who organized the Concerned Residents, he told me, had been set up, he reckoned. There was nothing wrong with him. He was a bit simple perhaps, but he was being used. And he'd got himself into a very difficult situation, organizing these protests. He'd make himself a target, if he wasn't careful.

A 'target' being hardly pleasant when you consider what had happened to poor Sean, the chairman of the local Wolfe Tone GAA Club, who'd been abducted by the LVF as he was locking up the gates of the sports field one evening last summer. The paramilitaries had driven him out of town, tortured, then murdered him. For no other crime than being a prominent local Catholic.

When we repaired back to Flat Cap's house (at his absolute insistence) for tea, his delightfully hospitable wife told me that she wished she'd not been up to the wake to view poor Sean's body. Half his face had been eaten away by acid.

It wasn't just tea this good lady was offering. Hadn't I had lunch? Well now, it wouldn't take her a moment to make me a sandwich, or, rather, a huge pile of warm chicken sandwiches. And not to make strange with these pink iced cakes here.

Walking back down the lane to my lodgings I stopped at the Bawn, which had once been the fortified house for the defence of the Protestant planters who had laid out Bellaghy (they called it Vintnerstown, after their London guild) against the native Irish around. It was now a museum with a special floor devoted to the Nobel Prize-winning poet Seamus Heaney, who was a son of the area. I read his line about 'man-killing parishes' with considerably more understanding now.

25

Cross Community

Swirling slow movement (Dvořák's *New World*), tall cream pillars with functional fans and tiny spotlights at the top, square mustard formica tables, moulded plywood chairs with chrome legs, *Caffe Latte, Caffe Mocha, Espresso, Doppio, Lungo, Espresso Affumicato*, 'Dek' (decaffeinated coffee), *Te Altos*, Herbal Tea, *Tè Freddo* (iced tea), pot of tea for two, Muffin (chocolate or blueberry), Moroccan Lentil Salad with Merguez, Grilled Turkey Escalope on a Baguette with West Indian Spices and Sause *Chien*, Ramekin of Mixed Olives, Polenta (god!) alla Griglia with Wild Mushrooms, Grilled Chump Steaks with Gorgonzola Sauce, a blonde in black flicking her eyes away to the right, six inebriated professional women gurgling at a bad joke, two bespectacled thirty-somethings waiting for their mobiles to ring first, a ponytailed barman, wine of the week from the Hunter Valley – oh nineties city life how I've missed you!

I am, as they say up here, 'scunnered', but I don't care. So what if my horrid bedroom on the Golden Mile smells as if 400 men have checked in, masturbated extravagantly and left – I've made it! To this city with the green hills all around that the tourist brochures call a Hibernian Rio.

Everyone has heard of Belfast's famous Crown, but it really is rather spectacular, the Dublin bar I never found in Dublin. Outside, its ornate gold-on-green lettering lights up the dirty brick and concrete of drab Great Victoria Street. Inside, there's a dark green ceiling, a wonderful row of panelled snugs, pillars with giant crocodile-skin-style flamelets running down towards a black and white diamond floor. Up at the bar with its brass-topped barrels a scruffy gent with long grey hair

is madly scribbling, what, poetry, all over his *Irish Times*. I
look sideways as I order and see:

> Guinness
> It makes you drunk

Hm. In a stronger mood I'd talk to him, but he really does
look cracked, his manic scrawling covering most of the page.

At home in London and round Ireland, I've met plenty of
people who've moved away from Belfast to 'escape the madness', in the words of Dermot Seymour, but never, yet, one
who's settled here from somewhere else. But Sarah Morrison
loves the place. Having spent the ten years since Art School
here she could never imagine going back to Kent now. She's
even picked up a wee accent: 'Aye,' she says, and even, at
times, 'Och aye!'

The card she gives me at the end of the night says Sarah
Fay Morrison over a pale rubric which reads:

> Woman. Artist. Sculptor. Human. Lover. Piss-
> artist. Aries. Stubborn. Brown-eyed. Strong. Alive.
> Creature. Guinness-lover. Traveller. Hot whiskey
> enforcer. Independent Sister Daughter Worldly
> Wise Flower-lover. Voyeur. Cyber-punk. Humorist.
> Woman. Artist.

But she's changed since she made that, she says.

'You're no longer a flower-lover eh?'

Now, at lunchtime, we meet outside the post office on Royal
Avenue. Sarah's wearing a battered leather jacket over a big
woolly new polo-neck, which she bought this morning, but
thinks is a mistake because it's too hot. For some reason she
didn't put Blonde on her card, but blond she is, over skin that
is Irish white.

'What d'you want to see?' she asks.

Whatever, I say. You decide.

She suggests that we go up to visit the graves of the hunger
strikers on the Upper Falls Road, but first we call in at her
studio, a curtained space in one of those half-derelict city
centre buildings, where you tramp up stone stairs and clang
through metal doors. There's a map of Berlin on the wall, a

rough wooden floor painted dark red, Chinese-type scrolls featuring Chinese-type angels hanging from a yellow washing line on red, blue, yellow pegs. Sarah's getting together some work for a show in Berlin, remoulding the backs of some plastic toy soldiers into tiny golden wings.

She loves her view, over the mass of brick-red chimney stacks that is the Falls and Shankill, to the green mountains beyond.

On the floor downstairs is a cross-community group called Belfast Exposed. 'Welcome to Belfast Exposed' says a sign on the door. 'This is a neutral venue. Please leave your politics at the front door.' They aim to bring Catholics and Protestants together through photography, and have currently got an exhibition of black and white ten-by-eights taken by children from both sides of the Peace Wall: 'Washing Day', 'Mum and Me', 'It's a Hectic Social Life We Lead' they're called; this last shows a gang of flirty teenagers partying by an alleyway.

They've mixed them all up, so apart from one with a poster of Gerry Adams in it, you wouldn't have a clue which side they came from; they're indistinguishably larky images of urban poverty.

In the room off the gallery I meet the team, three receding-haired guys in jeans and T-shirts, who find it highly amusing that I'm kneeling on the floor to interview their leader, and before I know it are kneeling beside me, hands in prayerful attitude, asking the Holy Mother for absolution. But when I don't take offence at this 'slaggin' I get offered a coffee, which is tongue-burningly instant and comes in a chipped cup, which has almost certainly been washed up in the sink of the loo outside.

'I'll have a decaffeinated cappuccino,' says Sean. 'With goat's milk. There's a goat in the darkroom.'

The kids take photos of their own communities but visit each other's areas for cross-community 'activities' (Sean makes inverted comma signs in the air) like drinking, smoking, groping . . .

'Gobsucking,' adds Sarah.

They've recently got a lot of money from the lottery. There's loads of European cash available for these cross-community projects. Soon they're going to be getting three Digital computers.

Just round the corner on King Street is the rank where the black London-style cabs queue to take the Catholic residents home up the Falls Road. (It is matched by one three blocks up, for the Protestant Shankill Road.)

The cabs are shared and stop anywhere to pick up or drop off. The only other place I've seen this eminently sensible system of transport is in South Africa, where identical rules operate for the minibuses that ply back and forth to the townships. (Did one copy the other; or is it just a function of a sharing spirit of hardship?)

'It's a great way to meet people,' Sarah has told me, but the three men with us say nothing as we rattle across the Westlink (which the RUC can use to seal off both Falls and Shankill in riot times) and up past the huge Madonna and child mural opposite the tall block of flats whose entire top storey is a British Army observation post (supplies and personnel are ferried in and out by helicopter).

On we rattle, stopping to let out the ginger-haired man next to me, stopping again to pick up a large lady with shopping bags, then on past the mural-covered Sinn Fein headquarters (Vote for peace, Vote Sinn Fein); the Irish cottages where people speak only Irish; Culturlann, the Irish culture centre; and up the hill to the gates of the huge Milltown Cemetery. Above us hover two Dermot Seymour-style Army choppers. 'See those things sticking out either side,' says Sarah. 'They're cameras. They can home in incredibly close.'

So, watched by Big Soldier, we stroll down the gentle hill through the packed mass of stone crosses to the plot where the hunger strikers are:

VOLUNTEERS
TERENCE O'NEILL
BOBBY SANDS
JOE McDONNELL

all on one simple black marble slab, surrounded by a profusion of flowers: real chrysanthemums, silk roses and a wreath of carnations in white, green and orange, the colours, of course, of the tricolour.

Sarah has forgotten what a strong place this is. 'My heart's in a knot here,' she says quietly.

'In proud and loving memory of all those who gave their lives in the cause of Irish freedom,' says another stone. Here, at the end, are 'Thomas McErlean, John Murray and Volunteer Kevin Bray, killed in defence of their people, 16 March 1988, at the burial of the three volunteers murdered by the British in Gibralter 6 March 1988.'

That was Billy from Sligo's friend Mairead Farrell, and Danny McCann, and Sean Savage, 'shot by the *sass*,' at whose funeral in this very spot the wild-eyed Loyalist Michael Stone opened fire and threw grenades, killing the three above and injuring over sixty others.

'It's a very strong place,' Sarah repeats. 'A place of defiance.'

She lives, as it happens, just down the road, and is not ashamed to admit that her loyalties are all to the Catholic side. It wasn't a conscious decision; she just finds the Nationalist community more sympathetic.

Up here, with uniformed schoolkids running along the pavement past the bus-stop and the leafy park opposite, it seems more like a suburban London street than the legendary Falls Road. Only when we turn left into the older, unmodernized estates do you get the battered urban landscapes of myth and TV footage. Grey, grey houses in grey, grey cul-de-sacs. 'I.R.A.' sprayed everywhere and murals listing the POWs.

But Sarah wouldn't live anywhere else. 'This is one of my favourite places,' she tells me, as we pass up a narrow alleyway between a row of terraced houses and the back of an RUC station. The police have expanded their base to within four feet of the front of the houses, casting them into perpetual gloom. Yet still there are people living there. Through the curtains I can see a china shepherdess on a television. J. Heenan, Upholsterer, reads a boarded-up front next door. The shepherdess's view is a twenty-foot high rusty grey steel sheet. Above, thick wire mesh holds a broken milk bottle with a scorched brown neck.

We emerge to a new network of little red brick terraced houses. At the end of each street is the Peace Line, the tall fortified steel wall that divides the Falls from the Shankill. You can read about sectarianism till you go orange and green in the face, but it's not until you see these little streets literally sliced through the middle that the reality comes home to you.

Now we're into Sarah's local, the Fort, a backstreets version of the Crown, with heavy wire mesh all over its marbled brown exterior and scaled-down snugs inside, all packed at teatime on a Tuesday afternoon. We join a pair of old gents in the last of the row. One is white-haired, tall, handsome-featured; the other, younger, rounder of face, with a drooping lower lip.

As Sarah says later, the younger man was clearly dying to talk to us. 'Are ye on holiday?' he asks eventually. No, she explains cheerfully, she's a resident, she's lived here ten years. She names her street. The white-haired fellow corrects her pronunciation; but they seem surprised, impressed almost.

The white-haired fellow has never been to England. Wouldn't go there. No disrespect to us, but the English . . . He shakes his head. It's not just what they've done here, but all over the world. Do I know about the Famine?

Of course, I say. I've seen the lazybeds in Mayo. He nods slowly and raises his eyebrows. There never was a Famine, he tells me. The landlords were shipping the grain out as the peasants starved. They could have fed the people.

He leans forward. I should be careful, he tells me. Round here. 'Ten years ago, five years ago, if you'd walked in here with that accent they'd have had you out the back.' In the toilet, with a gun to my head, finding out who I was. Maybe I *am* writing a book, but then, there were plenty of undercover British soldiers who'd come up with stories like that over the years. I should be careful, he reiterates; I should go up to Sinn Fein headquarters tomorrow morning and let them know what I'm doing.

'OK,' I say, chastened. (I've taken Sarah's word for it that it would be entirely safe to come in here.)

Yes, there is a ceasefire, he says. But things are still going on. There were three killed over the weekend.

Well, I say, I really wasn't trying to upset anyone. I was

entirely open. If I could get to interview Gerry Adams I would.

The round-faced man laughs, loudly. 'Well, you've got the right man here. This is Gerry Adams's brother-in-law.'

The white-haired man nods, quietly, slightly embarrassed, but with obvious pride. 'We married the two sisters,' he says. He'd been trying to persuade Gerry to claim his £50,000 salary from Westminster. It wasn't just the salary, it was the secretarial allowance, too. He laughs. Couldn't he just scribble a few lines on a bit of paper and claim the allowance? For him? But Gerry wouldn't do it. And to think how he'd helped him in the old days, when the police, the press had all been after him.

As he puts on his big blue windjacket and stands to leave, he shakes my hand and bends to give Sarah a kiss. 'The *craic* was good,' he tells us. He's taken my name on a piece of paper and I wonder if our *craic*-capacity will make any difference to my safety in the Falls Road.

Back in the centre of town we called in to another Republican bar. Madden's. It was just up from the Falls Road taxi rank, a pretty obvious first stop for people coming into town.

The Belfast Exposed team were in there with a Guatemalan photographer called Alberto and a petite, pretty woman called Dervla, who was another artist. They laughed when I took the empty side of the table, with my back to the door. You'd never find any of them in that position – force of habit.

In the office there'd been that sign about neutral politics, but here it was clear that sympathies lay firmly on the Nationalist side. What was my impression of the North, Sean asked. And when I started to tell him, he overruled my mild voicing of sympathy for the intimidated Protestants I'd met in Derry and Antrim with a long harangue about how the Catholics had suffered so much over the years. Excuse *me*, he kept interrrupting. Excuse *me*. His own *mother* had been *pulled down the stairs* by British Army soldiers, it was like she'd been *reeped*. There are tears in his eyes as he shouts into my ear. His whole torso quivers with rage. She was *reeped*. And the Irish had lost everything.

'Everything?' I say, confused.

'What language are we speaking now?'

'English.'

'You see. Nobody has any *idea* what other cultural stuff we've lost, in addition to the language.'

Dervla, dark-curled, with intensely affectionate pale blue eyes, doesn't think the Talks will go anywhere. She thinks it's all going to get worse before it gets better. She doesn't want to think that, but she feels it in *here*. But the British must go, whatever happens. They created the situation, now they're perpetuating it. Even if there had to be bloodshed, they should get out. 'We're used to bloodshed,' she tells me, with a quiet nod.

Now, late, a big square-headed man in a broad-shouldered suit has picked up a guitar and is singing, loudly and with such power, such power, 'Something in-side so *strong* . . .' The whole bar is with him, some singing, some muttering, some just watching and shaking their heads. (His name is Cruncher, Sarah will tell me later, 'because of bones crunching', and I am left wondering how much of a joke that is, if it's a joke at all.)

When it's over, Dervla leans over to me, 'That's about us, about Belfast people.' And I get such a powerful sense of this city, or at least of this Nationalist side of it, for they're all Nationalists in here, although as Sean says, there'd be some Loyalists might drink in here too, but they couldn't let that be known back home.

Something in-side so strong . . .

The next day I travelled on a parallel line to take a look at the Protestant side of things. Three hundred yards north of the Falls, back over the Westlink and up the Shankill Road towards those same green hills.

There were two obvious differences. The Shankill was sprucer and altogether less run-down than the battered Falls; and the murals, on the gables of corner houses, did not depict Mary, or say 'Time For Peace', or illustrate the Famine; they said 'Lest We Forget' and 'Ulster Volunteer Force', and they showed hooded paramilitaries posed with weapons by the Red Hand of Ulster and the Union Jack.

Right at the far end, I found Glencairn, a bleak concrete

estate on the side of the mountain. In a tiny office in the Community Centre was Jimmy Creighton, the community development worker, a short, bald, terrier of a man, wearing a bright green shirt that in no way reflected his politics. In the adjacent IT suite fifteen women laughed and gossiped as they learned secretarial skills. In Jimmy's smoky den there was a powerful whiff of No Surrender.

It was the Belfast version of the story I'd heard from Glenn Barr. Deprivation was no one-sided thing. 'Some Protestant areas,' Jimmy stressed, 'are worse off than any Catholic area ever was, or ever will be.' Did I see this photo on the wall. 'The date on that newsletter is 9 January this year, and there's a lady stuck with an outside toilet. Just so happens to be a Protestant.'

Of *course* there had been gerrymandering. Nobody would dispute that, particuarly in Londonderry. 'But let's get right down to the nitty-gritty. The Civil Righters came out and they said, One man, one vote. Very emotive. Very eye-catching for an international audience, and a degree of truth, but not the total truth.' The total truth was that Jimmy hadn't had a vote either. And his three sisters hadn't had a vote, because they had lived with their mother and father. 'I didn't cry any tears because I didn't have a vote,' Jimmy told me. And how had John Hume got into Stormont if none of the Catholics had votes. 'It wasn't the Protestants put him in.'

There were no jobs for Catholics, they said. Well, it was certainly true that there'd been more Protestants working in the shipyards, and the Catholics who had got jobs there had had 'a pretty rotten time, there's no point glossing over that, it did happen'. But the Catholics had come from an educational system that didn't gear them up towards heavy industry; they were more geared towards bar work, restaurants, academics, arts and so on. To put it bluntly, 'you can't ask somebody who fries fish to build ships'.

But *no* jobs. Jimmy shook his head. 'Mark, I worked as a window-cleaner in the early 1960s. There was two Protestants and all the rest were Catholics. It wasn't as black as it was painted.'

And as for violence and intimidation, he could name me twelve Protestant areas in Belfast that had turned Catholic.

'You can't name me one Catholic area that has turned Protestant. So, if we were doing all the attacking, how come we lost all the ground?'

He himself had come from the Ardoyne, where 120 people had moved in one night, back in 1971. 'It had been going on for months beforehand, when Catholics had been coming into the area, shooting, throwing bombs over the roofs of the houses, coming up and picking fights and arguments, shouting in Gaelic so nobody knew what they were talking about.'

And when they left, three streets of houses were in flames. 'Some say it was Catholics, some say it was Protestants – I'm saying nothing – but people had been coming up them streets for months beforehand saying, "I'll have that house, I'll have that house," while the Protestants were still living there. So I'm saying nothing.' His implication was hardly obscure, and I had it confirmed elsewhere. The Protestants had operated a scorched earth policy before they'd fled.

Now, when people objected to the parades, well, of course, he could see their point. 'I still say people shouldn't walk where they're not wanted. But can you understand the logic, Mark, of people who've been intimidated out. The Ormeau Road was Protestant once. So people say, "Well, we originally came from here. We lived in these streets and we walked down this road for years. And now, because the Catholic Republican movement has pushed us out, we're not even allowed to walk down the main road."'

As he sat there chain-smoking Jimmy made a very convincing case for the hard times the working-class Protestants had had. And I believed him, just as I believed the horror stories I'd been hearing from the Catholic side of the wall. The astonishing thing was they thought that by looking on it as a competition anything would improve. From outside toilets to bombing atrocities, neither side was ever going to get the other to say what they wanted to hear – and who else was interested?

And on both sides the arguments were – almost unwittingly, it seemed – so selective. 'We originally came from here,' said Jimmy about the Ormeau Road. But that, on a longer time-scale, was the cry of the Nationalists, and one that the Protestants had plenty of their own good arguments to. Just five minutes later Jimmy was saying, 'Let's forget about the past. Let's worry about *now*, and the future generations.' How often, in both camps, had I heard that switcharound; from angry, violence-justifying reference to past injustice, to platitudinous hope for the imaginary future.

I need hardly tell you that Jimmy was vociferously opposed to a united Ireland. 'If the British government ever said, "We're putting youse out of Britain," not only is it undemocratic, but they will create a situation that is going to take *years* – they ain't seen fuck all yet – if we need to fight we'll fight – people will lift arms to defend this country – they will, Mark, they will.'

Just up from the Community Centre was Fernhill House, 'the people's museum', telling in elaborate detail the Protestant side of the Ulster story, with a whole room devoted to the extraordinary bravery of the 36th (Ulster) Division at the Somme and a full-sized model of Sir Edward Carson signing the Solemn League and Covenant against Home Rule, in Belfast Town Hall, on 28 September 1912 (forever after declared Ulster Day).

The Protestant Ulstermen of 1912 had been as against a united Ireland then as Jimmy Creighton, Glenn Barr, Michael and Dermot of North Antrim, Robert Overend and all were now. In Belfast that day all shipyards and factories had closed, and a procession carrying the faded silk banner that was supposedly William's at the Battle of the Boyne, and escorted by a guard of honour of 2,500 in bowler hats, had marched to the Town Hall to add their signatures to Carson's. Many signed in their own blood. Within a week, the Covenant was 218,206 souls long. (A parallel declaration was signed by 228,991 women.)

I was, of course, interested in the Lambeg drums, and the arrays of uniforms and medals, and the German weapons supplied to the UVF after the First World War, and the exhibition of 'poverty in the Shankill Road', not to mention the blackthorn stick that was used by the RUC to beat the Catholics in 'a Civil Rights march'; but to me, most telling of all was a postcard from Carson's time, depicting Ulster as a beautiful, wronged-looking maiden holding the Union Jack.

Thou Mayest Find
Another Daughter
With a Fairer Face
Than Mine
With a gayer voice
and sweeter
And a softer eye
than mine;
But thou canst not
find another
That will love thee
Half so well—

Next to it, another slightly older woman was now carrying a gun. It read:

Ulster 1914
Deserted! Well – I can Stand Alone.

Not far down the road, at FARSAT, an outfit for retraining Protestant paramilitaries when they got out of gaol, I found Jackie Hewitt, a member (among other hats he wore) of the Shankill Community Council. Two of his colleagues were hard at work trying to sort out the conflict in Moldavia (the Moldavians were arriving at the weekend), so we left his office and shared a pot of tea in the boardroom.

We talked for an hour and a half: about marches not being the issue ('the issue is the whole constitutional position of Northern Ireland'); about the fear of a united Ireland ('I can tell you what the fear is, the Ormeau Road which was once all Protestant is now all Catholic'); about the beleaguered Protestant population of the South ('it hasn't flourished, it's diminished dramatically'); about the relationship in the Republic between Church and State ('apply those rules in England, I mean you'd have a bloody revolution'); about the all-Ireland aspirations of John Hume ('how dare he lecture me about borders don't matter and preserve his fucking Nationalism'); about how he, Jackie, respected other people's religion ('as opposed to sectarianism'), and thought the cultural diversity of the North was rich ('something we can capitalize on'), but nonetheless if the British government tried to force him into a united Ireland he would take up the gun ('and so would most people I know'); if Tony and Mo ever *tried* it, you haven't seen *nothing* ('I would blow the hell out of everything I could blow the hell out of'). But at the end, when I switched off the tape recorder and shook his hand (for he was, like all these people, a thoroughly genial Irishman), he looked at me, and apparently exhausted by the force of his own arguments, let out a deep and weary sigh, and said, 'It's sad.'

To me, that said more than the hour and a half of tape that had gone before.

Kindly driving me back into town, Jimmy stopped to show me the Shankill side of the Peace Line, which was much barer, with a wasteland running up to the tall steel wall.

'This is something that's started happening recently,' he said, slowing the car. The white surface of the wall was covered with slogans from international well-wishers and advisers: 'Just chill out – Luke, Sarah, James, Engadine, Aus.' 'Peace Can Happen – Louise, Brisbane, Australia', 'A society that claims an eye for an eye will soon go blind. What's more important – Land or people?'

'Jeez!' said Jackie. 'That's a question.'

As I walked back over the Westlink, I was smiling to myself. Absurd though it was, 'Just chill out' was probably more of an answer than a detailed understanding of why and how the Sunningdale Agreement was brought down in 1974 could ever be.

Back in Belfast city centre I gazed at the crowds and wondered who was from where. There was no difference in skin pigmentation, language, accent or even surnames. As Jimmy Creighton had pointed out, both Hume and Adams were Scottish names.

In central Donegall Square (how far away the Marquis seemed now) Christmas was already kicking off – on 13 November. With tinny speakers blaring, 'Sim-plee hav-ing a won-der-ful Christmas time' in front of the chunkily ornate City Hall, whose domes and pillars and turrets and pinnacle pots, in off-white Portland stone, spoke as eloquently of the Union's former glory as did the central statue of Queen

Victoria as Empress. (Now, for the first year in its history, Belfast had a Catholic mayor.)

The festive din drove me quietly crazy as I sat reading at one of the jumble of desks and tables in the tall town house that was the Linenhall Library, for which, despite the smartly dressed security man at the front door, there appeared to be no entrance qualification, bar a bookish manner and a baggy pair of trousers stuffed with pens. All the current British and Irish publications were arranged on a big square table on the first floor, and if you wanted to really start understanding the Troubles there was a second floor containing 80,000 publications on Northern Ireland politics from 1966 – election posters, pamphlets, doctoral theses, prison letters – where did you begin?

So why not just leave the noisy couples trying to track down their genealogy ('Oh I *see*, he was born *before* the turn of the century, that's *interesting*') and wander round the corner to the Fountain area, which was not at all like its bleak Derry namesake, but a gleaming pedestrian precinct, full of cafés with pink and grey polished granite tables.

As if I hadn't had my fill of Irish festivals there's one opening right here tonight, in Donegall Square. There's more culture than *craic* and you can take your pick of Irish, UK and European people and shows. Juliet Stevenson is doing Beckett, and Pete Postlethwaite is doing the Scottish play, and Nick Hornby is 'In Conversation' with Roddy Doyle. There's a John Rutter Requiem, a Cavalcade of Song, the ubiquitous Tap Dogs, and the Czech National Orchestra performing Dvořák's Symphony no. 9.

There's not a bed and breakfast to be had in the centre of town, and when I gratefully say goodbye to my malodorous den (you are welcome to it, Czech cellist) I have to spend half a morning and travel right to the far end of the Ormeau Road to find an alternative.

Peter and Michaela have just opened their place, and they have a wonderfully airy room that smells of nothing more noxious than fresh carpets. When Peter appears with a freshly plunged cafetière of real coffee I almost expire on the spot.

'Where were you?'

I tell him.

He laughs loudly. The place is famous. The owner, apparently, rents out the rooms – of guests who go to work for the day – by the hour. Well that would explain the smell, anyway.

Out here in south Belfast, and wandering in through the leafy streets around the university, you could be in any provincial British city. There are some peaceful Botanic Gardens with a huge curvilinear glass Palm House that seems a million miles away from the Peace Line and its dependencies. Needless to say, I'm the only person in there, my nose embedded deeply in a phalanx of purple chrysanthemums.

Just over the park the Ulster Museum is hosting the Ulster Academy's Autumn Exhibition, an open-entry show that contains, as far as I can see, not one painting that addresses, or even refers in passing to, the statelet's war zones. There are birds and ducks and dogs and pigs and deft portraits and landscapes: *Deserted Farmhouse in Co. Down*, *Kingfisher in Flight*, *Burning the Whins*, *Pensive Nude*, *The Mantel Piece*. Even the installations are too busy being postmodern to consider the man-killing parishes. And why should they, I think, as I stroll down the road to find Andrew Motion and Tom Paulin under the white arches of the Elmwood Hall, discussing the issues raised by their new biographies of Keats and Hazlitt. Life must go on.

'I had hoped,' says a woman at question time, 'you had come to Belfast to raise some flag of insurrection . . .'

The sense of normality continues in town where I have been invited to the launch of a book by a thickly-bearded gentleman from the Ards Peninsula.

'You've researched the Titanic, the Union, and the Passenger pigeon,' says the director of the Linenhall Library in his speech, 'd'you see a connection?'

We all chuckle urbanely. I meet the director of the Ulster Museum, no less, and a professor from Queens who tells me that yes, he'd go up the Shankill or Falls Roads. He has done it, um, not on foot, no, but in his car. 'I don't *like* doing it, but I do *do* it, yes . . .'

Then a schoolteacher who has a funny story about a little boy from the Shankill being taken up to visit the leafy Malone

Road. 'These are big houses,' he said, gazing around. 'I bet they don't have troubles up here.'

As the crowd thins out I find myself perched on the central table next to a unicorn. Good God, that I should finally meet such a fabled animal. The single horn that protrudes from the centre of her forehead is of burnished gold and she has a nice habit of touching your arm with her hand when she's making a point. No, she's not really a unicorn, but that equally mythical creature, a Catholic Unionist.

In my comfortable new B & B I gaze out of the window at the geraniums in the conservatory next door and leaf through my list of possible interviews. There are any number of cross-community projects, although, to be honest, most of them seem to be on 'the green side of the game'. 'I don't believe in cross-community,' Jimmy Creighton told me, 'because it's only a way of certain people getting money to do what they want. If I brought a Catholic on to this group then I'm cross-community. There's nothing productive in that. A lot of these groups that are set up as cross-community, you'll find that they are people who are connected to the Republican movement or to the Loyalist paramilitary movement, and it's a way of getting funding to carry on what they're doing. When you try and find these people to do community work, they're not about the place, they're always away doing this and doing that, money is being wasted, hand over fist.'

Who to believe in this landscape of contradictions?

Did Douglas Hurd really ban the funding to Conway Mill, and if he did, was it because he represented the uncaring British Establishment or did he have other intelligence? Is there a reason why the Northern Irish Tourist Board 'don't even mention' the West Belfast Festival, and is it really 'the biggest festival in Ireland'? Did the parents' group that wanted to educate their children in Irish actually get obstructed by the Department of Education? Were they threatened with prosecution? And if so, why?

Who can answer these questions with total objectivity, especially if the answerphone is always on?

But oh dear, if some of the money is keeping paramilitaries off the breadline – Do I believe that? No; yes; no; yes – then some of it is undoubtedly helping comfort their victims. Here, in this reclaimed Presbyterian Church on the Cliftonville Road is Survivors of Trauma, whose curly-haired (Catholic) organizer, Brendan Bradley, has lost four of his immediate family in the Troubles: a brother, a sister and two nephews: blown up by Loyalists, killed by a ricocheting bullet, shot by Loyalists, shot through the head by the IRA.

The pamphlet that details the 630 people who have been killed in the small bullet-shaped postal district of BT14 is undeniably non-sectarian, baldly listing dates, names, ages and murderers, or should we say soldiers, in this war that isn't a war. I plunge a finger into their leaflet at random:

20 Jun 1978	James Mulvenna	28	British Army
20 Jun 1978	William Hanna	28	British Army
25 Oct 1978	William Smyth	54	Loyalists
5 Jan 1979	Francis Donnelly	24	Republicans
5 Jan 1979	Lawrence Montgomery	24	Republicans
4 Feb 1979	Patrick Mackin	60	Republicans

And so it goes on, though the Loyalists seem to have been busier than Republicans and British Army in recent years.

I sit in Brendan's office and listen to the story behind one of these 630 local statistics.

| 13 July 1972 | Terry T— | 36 | British Army |

He was just in the wrong place at the wrong time, says Doreen, his widow, who trembles visibly as she chain-smokes her way to rehearsing the unspectacular details of a death she never saw. 'A knock came to my door, and it was the British Army to say that my husband had been shot. And I just asked them where and how and that, and I got no answer from them. His remains would be at the Manor Hospital. The house just seemed to crowd in all round me, I just couldn't imagine myself being left with six children on my own.'

Nothing glamorous or dramatic about that. Or the twenty-six years of missing a man she'd married at twenty, with whom she'd been perfectly happy, who'd worked all the days of his life, 'And he only lived for me, and for the children, and his rose garden . . .

'It's such a cruel bloody war. The bad's always left behind, they'll never take a bad person, they'll always leave them . . .'

After the immediate aftermath – the repeated Army raids, where floorboards were ripped up and the house was 'literally ruined, because they said my husband was an IRA gunman, and he wasn't, and I kept telling 'em'; the phone calls from strangers telling her he was an 'IRA scumbag'; and so on – she'd gone on to the Valium. She'd become a drug addict. From 1972 to 1988 she was taking the tablets, 'like sweets, because I couldn't live without him, to this day I sit and talk to him, imagining he's there, and I've a son who's his double. There's a picture of him in the front room, and I tell him things, and imagine his lips moving. Twenty-five years down the line and I still feel the same way as I did the night he was shot.'

Two nervous breakdowns later she managed to leave the drugs behind. 'I wrecked the house, put windows out and what have you. I went buck mad.'

She's got to the position now where she fears nothing or nobody. 'If there's a bullet for me I'll get it, because I do my own thing.' She does. On the record she calls Gerry Adams 'buckmouth bastard'. She feels sorry for the boys who get involved on either side. When her grandchildren were growing up she would tell them that if she ever saw any of them pick up a stone against anybody she'd cut their legs off at the knees. 'Those lads join the IRA because they think they're wee hard men and you just look at them and think, I could squeeze you with my thumb.' And the soldiers in the army are just boys too. And they have a dirty job to do along this murder mile of the Croftdown Road.

It isn't just the murders; it's the tortures. 'My sister's father-in-law was murdered and put in the back of a car, tied up with barbed wire, two ears cut off, his tongue, his nose completely off.

'They have to be on drugs, the people who do these things. How else could one human being do that to another human being?

'There's one story sticks heartily and solely in my mind. Frankie Crawson. Who lived in the Ardoyne. His father lived facing me in Ladbroke Drive, and he was a very elderly man

and he came through two World Wars.' Fighting, of course,
for the British Army, as so many round here had done.
Doreen's father was in the British Army; and her brother-in-
law; and her father-in-law. 'There's not a person in this
country could say a relation of theirs hasn't been in the British
Army, because they would be liars.'

Frankie was abducted and his body found the next morning
in T—— Street. 'And they went right up his back, his whole
spine with an electric saw, while he was alive.

'When they brought the remains home to his father's house,
the priest and the undertaker says on no consideration was the
lid to come off that coffin. And Mr Crawson looked at me –
there was me and my two friends and another elderly friend
of Mr Crawson. And I'll never forget that moment till the day
I die.

'That man turned round and he said, "I'll tell you something. I've come through two World Wars. I've lain in ditches
with men, the maggots was coming out of them, and if I can
look at them, I can see my own son." So we were put into
another room. And they took the lid of his coffin off, and that
man let out such a yell I swear to God I thought fucken Hell
had opened. I thought the gates of Hell had opened up, when
I heard that man scream.

'That man never spoke again. At the wake, two nights of
the wake, and that man couldn't speak, throughout everything;
and he died four months afterwards himself.'

He had written down, on a piece of paper, to Nelly C——,
who was Doreen's neighbour: 'Nelly. This is a cruel bad world
and the sooner I get out of it the better. Can't take no more.'

Down at the Irish (Bawn) School on the Falls Road there's a
Christmas exhibition. A music session is going on in one room,
in the other there's wine in plastic cups and Yule faeries, and
Celtic Jewellery, a Celtic Buddha, a Celtic Santa. It's Irish
culture all right, but what squashed, angry, self-righteous,
warped, bizarre Irish culture it is, so far from the irreverent
modernities of Dublin and Galway. The milk from sacred
cows is all they get to drink up here, and what thin and bitter
milk it is.

I end up buying one of Dervla's prints, which has nothing

to do with Irish culture at all. It just comes out of her head, she says. It's a frame full of heads and arms and hands and legs, all swirling around in a maelstrom.

'Belfast,' I say.

She hadn't thought of that, she says, with a smile. 'But maybe.'

26

Great-grandfather's Furniture

A mile or two beyond Armagh the taxi turned left off the main road south. A hundred yards up, the village of my ancestors began. A broad main street of identical little houses in orange-red brick, two similar side streets to left and right. And these half-derelict buildings round this tall rod of a chimney at the far end had to be the old linen factory. Beyond it, on the right, a gate lodge, and then, emerging round the bend ... surely this was the big house? Behind locked gates and up a short gravel drive is a gloomy-looking edifice in grey stone, surrounded by a mini-demesne of oaks and evergreens, a spreading cedar by the oval of grass out front. It is altogether bigger than I'd imagined, with an elaborate wrought-iron porch construction and a tower topped by a green-oxidized copper dome.

Back round the corner I knocked on the door of the gate lodge. It swung open to reveal a short, plump gentleman in a patterned jersey and beige trousers. He regarded me quizzically.

'Are you a McCrum?' he said.

I smiled. I couldn't have scripted it better myself.

'Yes. Mark.'

'Mark.' He shook his head and his eye-lines trebled with his smile. 'I knew you were a McCrum.'

He was the old retainer, the old game-keeper who'd worked for my great-grandfather and still miraculously hung on, keeping the weeds down and the memories of better times at bay. 'I'd 'a known that smile anywhere,' he told me.

Sadly not. He had bought the gate lodge five years ago, and he recognized me from my older brother Robert, who had been here ten years before to make a *Bookmark* programme for the BBC, *In the Blood*. He, too, had been doing that returning to your roots thing.

Now, Pat said, I wasn't going to go straight back into Armagh, was I? I must at least come in for a cup of tea. Then we could walk over and have a proper look at the outside of the old house. Who knows, maybe we could actually get inside?

I slumped back gratefully on Pat's little sofa. His gate lodge was a sweet little Mrs Tiggywinkle house, with steep slate roofs and a single tall brick chimney. Inside, it was chock-a-block with trinkets. On the fireplace was a clock fashioned like a Greek temple, with little shiny brass pillars and entablature; on a side table was a set of saki cups; there was china and framed pictures everywhere. But it turned out that this was Pat's business-cum-occupation, for having retired from nursing a year or so ago he was now a part-time antiques dealer.

Outside, there were other fine *objets*, statuettes, a gnome or two and a full-sized summer house that originated from Birmingham. It squatted right up next to the old stone gateposts, each still topped by the original electric lanterns, splendid in their elaborately curved gilt. My great-great-grandfather Robert (R. G.) McCrum had been one of the first to have electricity in his house in the whole island. 'It appears,' said Pat, 'that he was a man ahead of his time.'

'Can you imagine . . .?' he went on, holding out a theatrical arm. These gateposts and this driveway. It was just a dip in the field now, but in R.G.'s time it would have all been lit up with electric light, a lantern every thirty yards. 'People used to come cycling out from Belfast to see it. People would come from all over Northern Ireland to see it,' Pat enthused.

We climbed over the gate and paced together through the dew-soaked long grass. At the far side of the field, beyond another gate, was the drive proper, leading up to the ornate, wrought-iron portico out front. Pat's delight was undiminished.

'Can you *imagine*,' he continued, 'the coach pulling in to the front door?' He shook his head and chuckled. When my brother Robert had come he'd stood inside that room up there, looked out of the window and said, 'I might have lived here.'

'"I might have lived here,"' Pat repeated now, shaking his head and chuckling. 'He might, too.'

Of course, when Robert had come it had been a home for Special Care children, but now, with the government cutbacks, they'd closed it down, and taken the patients back to a centralized facility. It had been empty for two years, and Armagh City Council were trying to sell it for a country house hotel. In the meantime it was being stripped. Some thieves had pinched half the lead off the roof. Another night the old fountain had gone. It was a beautiful ornate thing, with three or four tiers. 'They blame the travelling people for it, but they wouldn't have the equipment to take something as big as that.' But there were still marble fireplaces inside that would be worth a small fortune.

An engineer Pat knew had told him that it would cost a million pounds to put the old place right. The ceilings would have to be ripped out because, to put it bluntly, the Special Care children had not had quite the control of their bladders they might have wished.

Round the back, the original house had been added to. There was an ugly extension with mean, institutional windows. When my great-grandfather William had had to let it go it had become the Manor Girls School. 'Though it never was the Manor,' Pat said. 'The McCrums always used to call it the Cottage.'

The older people in the village would remember the old gentleman, R.G., as a great one for the working man, particularly because he'd never got mixed up in politics. The McCrum Institute, the village's hall and social centre, had been strictly non-denominational. Nor would R.G. allow any churches in Milford. People would go into Armagh and worship at the church of their own denomination.

We had come, by way of a huge derelict walled kitchen garden, to the green tin-roofed boathouse, with its view over a dell of weeds. This would have been, Pat said, a lake, fed by the diverted river that ran down to the millwheel by the factory.

'Can you imagine ...?' Pat held out his chubby hand. The boatman would have had the boat waiting for them. They'd have gone under the little bridge there and down to the factory. He chuckled. R.G. had had the whole enterprise sewn up. He owned the shop in the village and gave his workers vouchers with which to buy their food. 'Giving with one hand, taking with the other . . .'

And what about William, I asked. The vague myth I had grown up with was that William had been a ne'er-do-well who'd frittered away the family fortune on wine, women and song. Not quite, it transpired.

'How would you put it,' Pat said, as we strolled back together down the ex-drive. 'He was a man who was very interested in sport, in the welfare of the young of the village . . .' He tailed off. William had devoted his energies, he went on, to organizing the cricket in the summer, the soccer in the winter. He'd been an exceptional sportsman himself. Indeed, Pat said, William had been responsible for the introduction of the penalty kick into soccer football. Surely not? No, it was an undoubted, documented fact.

Stranger and stranger. My brother Robert had told me none of this. Despite the fact that I knew hardly anything about football, had never supported a team, had played it only reluctantly, and badly, as a small boy who was trying to keep up with his peers, my great-grandfather had invented the penalty kick. I felt a surge of Nick Hornbyesque pride. This would be one to tell the lads in the changing room, if and when I ever had to be in a changing room again.

But things had not gone well for William. His wife, having produced my grandfather Cecil, had cleared off with a major to the south of France. William, Pat told me, 'took to the old spiritual side of life when things began to go wrong'. We were clearly talking bottle, not religion. More of the family wealth had been gambled away in Monte Carlo. The factory had failed and had been taken over by the bank. William had moved, first to a house in the village, on to England, then back to Armagh, where he had died alone in a single room. Someone had said that at his funeral there weren't enough people to carry the coffin.

We paused at the gate. All these things my father and uncles had never told me. But then Cecil had left them, and my grandmother, when they were children, and I had never even met him. As a child, you just accept these things. There's the silver plate, and the myth, and your mother's stories about how the McCrums had been bootblacks to the McClouds of Skye and had backed the wrong king, Bonnie Prince Charlie, and had moved to Arran, and then to the North of Ireland . . .

Back in the Mrs Tiggywinkle house, we had another cup of tea. So would it be possible, I asked, to go and talk to some of the old people in the village, to see what memories they had of my great-grandfather.

Of course, said Pat. But he would have to tell me now that that film of Robert's, *In the Blood*, had upset a lot of people in Milford. One of those who had done an interview had had a heart attack shortly after it was screened, and some of the villagers would say that that's what had killed him. They didn't like the line Robert had taken on Unionism, you see. Someone had said, 'If that man ever comes here again . . .'

Oh dear, oh dear. The trouble you get into for telling it how you find it. This was not going to be as easy as I'd thought. With my authentic Protestant ancestors I had hoped that here at least (at last) I might hear the deep-down cry of the Loyalist soul.

As I sat drinking Pat's tea, I'd been thinking: 'It's always the same, you get people on their home ground and they're always the most decent, hospitable folks in the world. But now Pat was talking about 'those of the Protestant persuasion', and I realized he was a Catholic.

Now he wanted to show me the factory. 'Can you imagine . . .?' he continued, as we peered through cracked and grubby windows at the derelict halls below the towering brick chimney. In 1980 it had still had a full order book; now it was half-used by a man who grew mushrooms. And here, on the walls round the back, were the inevitable graffiti – UVF, UVF. But out there on the low green hillside was where they'd have dried the linen in the old days. There'd have been a little station; and a railway to take the finished goods right the way through to Dundalk and then on to Dublin.

Over the road the McCrum Institute was being refurbished. The old letters R – M – C – U still hung tattered on the outside, but inside there was a hammering and a sawing and the smell of freshly cut planks. And here was the very lady who'd bought the place, looking like the boss from the Kenco commercial, with a man from the National Trust in tow. Her company sold water filters, and the McCrum Institute was going to become a training centre for her sales people. *O tempora, o aqua . . .*

Pat was taking me in hand. He'd organized me somewhere to stay, 'over in the Moy', a village on the other side of Armagh, in a guest house – his eyes twinkled – which was full of all the old furniture from 'the Cottage'. It had been the doctor's house, and as William had got broker, and iller, he had started paying in kind.

And this evening a journalist, Joe McManus, on the *Armagh Observer* wanted to meet me. Robert had spoken to him.

No, all this kindness was no trouble, no trouble at all. So we drove together into Armagh to pick up his daughter from school; then back a little later to get 'a fish supper'. As we left, a bus burst into flames on the roadbridge right above us. Pat hardly flinched as he put his foot down. There'd been trouble brewing for a couple of days. A man called Duffy, from Lisburn, who was suspected of the murder of two police constables, had been taken back into custody. These would have been some of the youths from the Nationalist estates in Armagh, protesting.

Pat smiled. 'It takes very little, you see.' It wasn't reported, but they lived with this sort of thing all the time.

In Joe's cosy front room on Main Street his ten-year-old daughter was wide-eyed and worried. Did the bus-burning mean they wouldn't be able to go to the Argory tomorrow? Because they were going to make corn dollies and dress up as Victorians. Joe reassured her. If they couldn't go tomorrow it would be another day. No, but they were going to dress up as Victorians *tomorrow*. Joe gave me a broad smile. He was a big man, with a full head of grey hair. A Catholic, though the one thing it was important to stress about Milford, he said, was how there really was a harmony that didn't exist in other places. R.G. had been largely responsible for that. When he had built his McCrum Institute, he had made it clear that this was for *all* his workers.

The story went that the Orange Order had approached R.G.

for some land to build an Orange hall on, but he'd refused. 'The Orange Order was a power and he was a power.' And when the McCrums went out, the Orange Order took over the factory floor. 'To the extent that the Catholics only got the jobs no one else wanted.'

And William had continued the principle. He'd been not just a fine sportsman, but a very generous man. 'Maybe too generous,' said Joe, as Pat nodded seriously beside him. He mixed, he was one of the villagers. The big house would have been open door. He had been very much loved in the village.

But in his old age, when he'd lost the money and moved down to the boarding house, he had been hard to handle. Eventually one of the old men had taken him in. His host had once been a clerk in William's factory.

His sister Harriet had married the local minister. And when the Ulster Bank had taken over the factory in 1931 Harriet had pleaded and pleaded with them that the work force be at least given the opportunity of buying their own houses. 'That's why there are so many people today living in the houses they were born in.'

'But this place,' Joe enthused, 'is a place that could be shown to the world.' Milford had always been successfully mixed. He'd had a fellow up here from Crossmaglen on 12 July, when half the houses in the village had the Union Jacks flying. 'How d'you live with this?' he'd said.

'I wouldn't even notice them,' Joe had replied. He'd grown up with them.

As a Catholic, he went on, he would find more identification with his fellow Northerner than with someone from the South, and the Protestants would have more identification with Northern Catholics than with the English. 'In the back of our minds we know that nobody wants us. The English don't want us, the South don't want us . . .'

'They don't even know us,' interjected Pat.

'Under this European flag,' said Joe, 'there must be an answer . . .'

When we'd finished our tea, Joe's family joined us, and a more bright-eyed and cheerful-looking crew you'd have been hard put to find. It seemed, rather embarrassingly, that we McCrums were all but figures from myth to Joe's son Paul,

who had done a school project on us, which had received the
very highest commendation for its elaborate detail. It was just
something he'd always been interested in, his mother told me,
the big house at the end of the village and the vanished
McCrums. Staring at me as if I was Finn McCool, he whispered in his father's ear. Would I mind sitting for a photo with
him, Joe asked. No problem, Finn replied.

The next day Pat appeared at my guest house in the Moy
shortly after breakfast. The burning bus, and the grain lorry
that had followed it, had already been towed away, and there
was nothing by the road but scorch marks and a pyramid of
wasted corn. We were able to drive into the centre of Armagh
and up to the City Hall, to seek the key that would let me
inside the ancestral 'cottage'.

Pat was in confident mood. 'It's just a question of knowing
which button to press,' he told me, as the smartly dressed
young woman on reception told him to wait, please, in the
corner. If we'd been in South Africa in the apartheid days and
Pat had been black, her tone couldn't have been more
superior, but he hardly seemed to notice. The current chairman of the council was a Catholic, he told me; the first time
there'd been such a thing in seventy-five years. 'It's great to
see it,' he said. 'There is *movement*, if you like.' It wouldn't
have been heard tell of, five to ten years ago.

When he'd first tried to buy the McCrum gate lodge – he
laughed – he'd had a few problems. It kept being withdrawn
from the market. In the end he'd had to ring up the estate
agents and say, 'Look, is this house for a Catholic or not?'
(How much more than statistics do these little anecdotes tell
you, I thought.)

But we were in luck. Pat had been proudly introducing me
as, 'a McCrum, he's writing a book, and he might be interested
in buying back the property'. (Stick to one story, Pat!) And it
seemed to have worked. Suddenly we were under the ornate
porch and the man from the council was letting us in.

It was a heartbreaking sight. Where the lead had been
pinched from the roof the water was dripping through, and it
could only be a matter of time before those deep red ceilings
in the reception rooms collapsed. Downstairs, the marble

fireplaces Pat had told me about had already gone; the faeries had broken in at dead of night and prised away the plywood boxes that had protected them. In one boarded-up room I thought for a moment I was looking at the elaborate pattern of a Victorian carpet. Then I realized it was fungus. The cheery felt-tip drawings of the Special Care kids were curled with condensation, half-falling off the wall. And yes, the overwhelming smell was one of stale urine.

'It's sad, isn't it?' said Pat.

I headed off down Main Street with a shortlist of villagers who would remember William. Old Pastor Armstrong, in maroon sweater and bright red tie, asked me to move closer, he could hardly hear my questions.

'If you are a relative or a descendant of the McCrum family,' he then announced, in stentorian tones, 'I am very glad to meet you. I have very happy recollections of my dealings as a young boy under the guidance and the help of Mr William McCrum. He lived in the Manor House and he was very interested in Boy Scouts. And wolf cubs. And as a young fellow after school hours, it was customary for the boys of my generation, those who belonged to the Scout movement, to go to the Manor House. I still can see him, in my mind's eye, sitting at his desk in the parlour, or the library, writing. He wasn't a very handsome man. He was corpulent, he had very large eyes, but had a great love for youth, and for sport.

'It was customary to be shown into the library and to give the scout salute. And in those days he had a nickname, for nearly all the boys. There was Toot Faherly, and there was Pearly Livingstone, and there was Beattie Hyde, and quite a number of others. They were known, and indeed, to this very day, they are referred to, in the village, by those nicknames. That's one of my recollections of Mr William McCrum.'

But I wouldn't leave, surely, said his wife, some while later, before I'd had a sandwich. Which 'sandwich' turned out to be a tray of huge ham and cheese baps, a mound of sweet cakes and tea in a cosied pot.

Just round the corner, Ivy Dickson had worked for years as a cashier in the factory. She threw back her white curls and laughed. She could remember Mr McCrum coming down and telling them that the Institute was for the villagers, to be used and not *abused* – she'd always remember that.

He'd been a great Scoutmaster, Mr McCrum; in fact, at one time, Head of all the Scouts in Northern Ireland. As for the factory, you left school and in you went. She'd stayed till 1968 when it had been taken over by a new owner.

Milford wasn't what it had been, though, when the factory was going. There'd been many more young people around then, everybody knew each other, the shop was open and the Institute. In the summer there was the cricket, the tennis, the badminton; in the winter, of course, the football. The houses were well kept and all the people mixed. It had always worked well as a mixed village. The wages weren't high, but everybody was happy. In the afternoons they'd all be up at the sports fields.

Her face changed. It was so different now. 'That's the way things go, I suppose. Nobody takes care now.' They no longer played soccer or cricket. 'Sure, the very bridge that you went over is ready to fall in.' She didn't think they did much at the mushroom farm. 'It's going to the bad.'

The village was filling up with people from Armagh. 'Some of the children can be very rough. They seem to have nothing to do, only wreck and destroy.'

Now would I have a cup of tea and a sandwich before I left? Well, if not a sandwich at least a slice of fruit cake?

Harry Carson remembered my great-grandfather as a cricketer. 'You'd think you'd played a faultless innings, and he'd take you aside and say, "I want to see you up at the Big House." Then he'd show you six ways you'd gone wrong.'

As well as the football and cricket and Scouts and badminton McCrum had had a snooker team going too. 'Now there's nowhere for youth coming on. Then you're tortured with vandalism.'

Now surely I'd have a cup of tea before I left?

. . . or Civil War

Back at the gate lodge Pat was waiting with a nice refreshing pot of tea. 'And I've got a little bit of fruit cake here . . .'

Had any one of the old people brought up my brother? No? Well, what had he told me. That was how they were. A different generation. Even when I'd given them a lead, 'My brother came a few years back and made a film . . .' 'Ah. Yes. Is that so?' they'd replied.

Now Pat had a new gleam in his eye. There was somewhere else he wanted to take me before he dropped me back at the Moy. Dan Winter's cottage, the birthplace of the Orange Order. Joe McManus was coming along for the ride.

It was dark and wet and cold in the farmyard where the Orange Order had started, in 1795, following the victory of the Protestant Orange Boys over the Catholic Defenders at the Battle of the Diamond, just up the road. I got the feeling that the two lads in gumboots who were putting the cows away in the shed thought that Pat and Joe were loyal Orangemen. There was certainly a slightly conspiratorial air as they showed us round the low-ceilinged, thatched cottage with all Dan Winter's stuff still intact. Joe bought some Orange leaflets and Pat a book about Orangeism. I, meanwhile, arranged to talk to Hilda Winter, a defender of the faith, the following afternoon.

Pat was visibly humming with delight as he dropped me back at the Moy at the tall white house on the pretty central square where my great-great-grandfather, R.G., was waiting for me when I opened the front door, a white-bearded gentleman of stern expression, who took an extremely dim view of my observations so far.

Just down the square was the Ardross Arms, owned by Pascal and Brona, landlord and lady of my guest house. Now surely we'd stop for a cup of tea? And goodness, what had Brona found but a tray of sweet cakes. Now if I'd seen the birthplace of the Orange Order, Pascal said, I had to see Crossmaglen. Pat agreed. In fact he'd already organized it. Pascal would take me.

*

It's a gloriously sunny November morning as we speed by the orchards of Armagh, and down past Markethill, where the CAC bombing took place in the summer, to Slieve Gullion, which Yeats – says Pascal's brother Liam, who has come for the ride – once called the most mystical mountain in Ireland. If you swim in the sacred lake on the summit you'll find eternal youth.

These round, rolling hills are South Armagh, which Malachi from Athenry had described as the most fortified zone in western Europe. I have not made an inspection of all western Europe's fortified zones, but I take his point. Ceasefire or no, there are army look-out posts everywhere, bristling, as I can see, with masts and cameras and military look-out equipment. Overhead the choppers circle. The Army go everywhere in the air down here; they took to it in the mid-1970s because the roads were so heavy with landmines.

Pascal and his brother were smugglers then. Taking whatever over the border. Even apples at one point. 'This was a smuggler's paradise between these two states,' says Liam.

They used to have a scout car that went ahead empty, to check out the road. The van of goods would follow. One day the scout car was stopped by a trio of suspicious customs men. 'There's a major gun battle up the road,' Pascal had told them. The customs men turned tail and fled to Dundalk.

At Forkhill there's a huge monstrosity of a barracks behind McLarkin's pub. The contrast between the picture-book Irish country village and the dark green steel fortress is instructive. We wind up to a viewpoint high on Slieve Gullion. From here you can see right down the coast to Dublin. On a clear day, twenty-eight counties. Twenty-eight of the thirty-two.

As we approach Crossmaglen the political signs by the roadside increase. 'Sinn Fein all-party peace talks now' and 'Disband the RUC'. The letters I.R.A. are on three pieces of board on a telegraph pole.

Just outside the little town, high up above the sign that points one way to Dundalk in the South, and the other to Armagh in the North, is an adapted roadworks warning. Inside the crimson triangle, the little silhouetted man holds not a spade but a gun. SNIPER AT WORK it says below.

Anybody who has ever dismissed the British 'armed presence' as 'Provo-speak' should take a trip to this nondescript little Irish town of Crossmaglen. Nondescript, that is, if it were not for the border a mile and a half to the south, which keeps it just a few fields inside the seventy-six-year-old statelet. The Treaty that created the line had included a clause about a commission, which was to sit to 'determine in accordance with the wishes of the inhabitants, so far as may be compatible with economic and geographical considerations, the boundaries between Northern Ireland and the rest of Ireland'. Just before it was signed Michael Collins had had an interview with Lloyd George that had convinced him that the wishes of large Nationalist areas of the North, certainly those near the border, would be respected. But it was not to be. When the commission finally sat in 1924, the chairman, a South African called Richard Feetham, argued that he couldn't reconstitute the existing Northern Ireland. The other jurors resigned, the commission was abandoned, and the existing border was confirmed in return for the writing-off of Free State debts to the British.

So it is that Crossmaglen's pretty little central square has been invaded on its northern side by a giant armoured green dalek-head. It's the observation post for the mighty reinforced RUC/Army barracks behind. The village police station, in a parallel history.

We are due in Paddy Short's pub at eleven. At Pascal's request Paddy has opened the place early for us. He is white-haired and genial, giving the warmest of Irish welcomes to Pascal and his brother. A little more suspicious with me, though. What do I want to know?

I'm just canvassing all points of view, I tell him. He nods. Doubtless he's heard it all before. From polite Englishmen who want the story. The best way to get a point of view in Crossmaglen, he tells me, is just to see it. This young man here will show me round.

Sean is in his mid-thirties, I should guess. He's tall and strongly built and you wouldn't need to be Sherlock Holmes to guess that he has been once, or is now, a Volunteer. As we walk around together he's greeted by a lot of the younger people. One or two of the older ones eye us suspiciously, but it's 'Hi, Sean,' from the kids on the bicycles.

We start with the Gaelic football pitch, which the RUC

barracks has expanded right up to (on ground owned by the club). They still use the place to land helicopters. 'One time last year they came down right in the middle of a game.' They're still, apparently, threatening to take the field off them entirely.

Round here, past Joe's Bakery, and the dalek's head, and across the square by Chums bistro, this little circular pockmark in the wall was where a soldier was hit by a sniper. 'From that tree over there,' says Sean, 'just after the last ceasefire broke.'

Just there, there used to be an old picture house, from where the tricolour always flew. The Army would climb up and take it down. So the IRA put explosives behind the flag. 'At that time,' Sean tells me, 'in the '70s and '80s, the soldiers were so gullible.' They used to call the barracks the Conveyor Belt, round about '76.

But the Army drives the locals mad. Even now, in the so-called ceasefire, they're out on their patrols in the fields, cutting the barbed wire so the cattle get out and TB is spread. They fly their helicopters constantly, even at a funeral recently, right over the graveyard, so the words of the priest were drowned out. Young girls coming through the check-points get nothing but verbal abuse.

Back outside Paddy Short's, standing next to another little cavity that marks the last moments of a British soldier, Sean reminds me of those now familiar Nationalist arguments. 'They talk about democracy.' But in 1918 93 per cent voted to keep Ireland united; the British *forced* Partition on them. (This is something of an exaggeration, as Sinn Fein's share of the vote at that famous election was 48 per cent. But I take his point, for they did win 73 out of the 105 seats.)

The British, Sean tells me, look at it this way. If the IRA can force them out of the Six Counties, then how can they stay anywhere else?

It's not that simple, I say. Doesn't he understand how frightened the Unionists are. How terrible their fear of reprisals in a united Ireland. Sean looks surprised. Why should they fear reprisals? 'You ask them *why*,' he tells me. 'We've had all this done to us. Why should we want to do it back to somebody else. It's so degrading.'

I shake my head, for he doesn't sound like a man who's insincere. 'They wouldn't believe you, I'm afraid.' I've heard both sides, I tell him, till I could repeat the arguments in my sleep. But the positions are so far apart. I can't see how the two can ever meet. And if the British army was to leave, wouldn't there be civil war?

Sean stands there, just in a shirt, on this freezing November morning. It's starting to rain, tiny specks smudging my notebook. 'I would rather see a civil war,' he tells me. 'And have it over and done with, than have my children come up and face the same bitterness.'

He doesn't join us in the pub. He doesn't drink, he explains, as he says goodbye. 'There are more decisions taken here than at Westminster,' says Liam as Paddy Short appears with the Visitors' Book.

I sign my name. I pause over the address section, then, on consideration, write 'London'. The brother looks over. 'London's an awful big place,' he says, with a laugh.

It was barely an hour back to the other end of the spectrum. In Dan Winter's cottage Hilda Winter had a huge fire crackling and a thoroughly benevolent view of the Orange Order to put across.

They were just upholding the pure simple faith of our Lord, she told me, that had been brought to Ireland by St Patrick; for it was his church that was the original church of Ireland, not the Romans with all their ideas of paying for your sins to be forgiven, paying to get through Purgatory. And how many people these days in our society were still going to church, to hear the pure simple word of God? The Orange Order had Bible readings, 'you can't get into it unless you're a regular churchgoer'.

What other organization in the world would take in from the highest doctors and surgeons to the dustman? 'And when they sit in that one room they're all equal.' Their Master could be anyone, even the dustman. 'If you go back to the Last Supper our Lord made everybody equal, and this is what the whole thing is based on.'

And what could anybody possibly object to about a parade? It was nice to bring your children out and see their daddy marching in a decent respectable manner, all nicely dressed with the bands. In 1995, at the 200th Anniversary of the Order, they'd had 70,000 Orangemen gathered right here at the Diamond. There'd been a few policemen at the corner directing the traffic, but those Orangemen had walked for three miles in their dark suits and white shirts and ties, five deep, and the only two incidents in the entire day were a child got lost and a tree fell. 'So why should all this be brought up about Orangemen?'

If those people living in Garvaghy Road and Churchill Park would stay in their houses for ten minutes, they'd not be offended. The gables were all facing the road. 'So you've got to come and walk three hundred yards or more to *be* offended.'

It was not so much that she hated a united Ireland, it was simply that if there was 'an all-Ireland' tomorrow, 'we would be burned out of our homes. No, you wouldn't be allowed to live. They just wouldn't stop at the united Ireland. They would riot. Look back to 1969; it's the same story. They get one thing, then they want another. 'No, Mark, they would have every Protestant either killed or out. We hold nothing against our Roman Catholic neighbour, we do *not*, but if there's anyone pushing you and pushing you, you dig your heels in, don't you? You'll not go. Until they stop the pushing we're never going to get anywhere.'

But in any case, to ask her to stand up and sing 'The Soldier's Song' would be like asking her to put her hand into that fire. They'd have to have another national anthem and another flag.

Hilda wouldn't let me go without a cup of tea, which turned out, of course, to be three slices of cheese on toast and a huge pink iced cake. In front of the noisily crackling fire she would put her hand into rather than accept a united Ireland.

Returning the keys

Back at the Moy, Pascal's long-haired son Daniel is minding the bar. He's a thoroughly nice dude, who's been sitting round the Moy, he reckons, for too long holding his head. I encourage him to go backpacking, see the world beyond. With that haircut he couldn't fail to have fun.

He reminds me of the twenty-somethings I met in South Africa, exhausted by politics, somehow beyond the endless arguments and counter-arguments of their parents' generation. Guinness, he reckons with a chuckle, would solve the problem better than the politicians. Offer both sides free beer for a year and then see what happens.

'But what would happen when it stopped?'

Ah well, he says, by then they'd all be friends.

'But Presbyterians don't drink . . .'

'Put Es in the water supply . . .'

Back in the front room of the guest house I am alone, surrounded by this bizarre collection of my great-grandfather's furniture. Were these heavily floral Victorian armchairs his? And that octagonal mahogany coffee table? And what about that absurd pink-tulled flamenco dancer, strumming at a guitar in the window? Did she comfort him as his debts mounted?

There are Irish songs open on the old piano, and I'm still (just) in the North, but tomorrow I'm out of here, on a mobile radio that calls itself a bus, down the A3 that becomes the long straight N2 through Monaghan and Castleblayney and Carrickmacross and Ardee and Slane; sighing with relief as I see the yellow Telecom Eireann boxes, even though it's my own country I'm leaving; wondering how the Protestant congregation of St Finbar's Church of Ireland get on in Carrickmacross – why haven't they been burned out yet?

I see the Gaelic football pitches with new eyes now. Likewise the tricolours, fluttering proudly outside the Shelbourne. In a new basement cocktail bar in Merrion Square I run into – well, well – Noelle Campbell-Sharp, who embraces me warmly and invites me to a Christmas party. And when Therese, my friend from Lisdooonvarna, finally turns up, she tells me she's only been to Belfast once. Was Shanklin the Catholic area or was it the Falls? She couldn't remember. I laugh. And is there even wind up there? And when I get in a cab the next morning and speed to the airport, my cheerful Dublin taxi-driver transforms before my eyes from someone who loves horses and a ride out in Kildare to a furious Sinn Feiner who slams his hand on the dashboard and tells me that the British have created this monster and now it's turned round and bit them on the arse. As his passion rises, his soft Dublin feckings become hard Northern fuckings, and the people that really enrage him if I want to know are the Southerners who are doing so well out of the economy, the Celtic Tiger and all that shite, but have forgotten about the North. And the reason these scumbags have forgotten about the North is because they haven't had their doors kicked in, they haven't been interned, and tortured, and locked up. He has three friends who were sentenced six months ago to *thirty-five years . . .*

'Oh shit,' I said, when I got out of the car at Departures. 'I've taken the keys to my room.'

That wasn't a problem, he replied (and his Irish eyes were smiling), he'd drop them back for me.

Acknowledgements

I am deeply grateful to the composer Pete St John and Dolphin Records for allowing me to quote the first stanza of 'The Fields of Athenry'. (There are a number of different recordings available of this song from Dolphin.) On the road to and from those fabled meadows, my journey was made much easier and more enjoyable thanks to encouragement and assistance from many organizations and individuals who went out of their way to help.

Bord Failte, the Irish Tourist Board, offered useful advice and three nights' accommodation at the charming Lansdowne Manor in Dublin while I found my feet. Les Neal of Travellers' Connections (0181 286 3065) provided me with a mobile answering service that made my dealings with home so much easier. British Midland kindly flew me to Dublin at a cut-price rate. Mr James White, of the White Hotel Group, gave me two nights' accommodation at the splendid Burren Castle, Lisdoonvarna. Oona Murray of Manor Hotels did the same at the Sand House, Rossnowlagh. Thank you all; may your businesses thrive.

Before I left, friends, acquaintances (even kind people I never actually got round to meeting) proffered advice and contacts. In particular, Robert Bathurst, Charlie Bigham and Claire Worthington, Mark Chichester-Clark, Lana Citron, Nick Cochrane, Leonie Edwards-Jones, Benedict Flynn, Sally Garland, Simon Greenwood, Kenneth Griffith, Aubyn Hall, Tom Halifax, Ali Joy, Clare Kavanagh, Peter Kavanagh, Mary Kenny, David Kennaway, Noel Lamb, Caroline Logsdail, Tom Lowther, Angela Martin, Finbarr McCabe, Pauline McCrinn, Robert McCrum, Rosemary Koelliker, Gina Orr, Jenny

Romyn, Sue Stuart-Smith, Alex Spicer, James and Gabrielle Tregear, John Walsh, Tara Williams.

Once over the Irish Sea I met with much kindness and hospitality. What follows is just a shortlist of those who looked after me, lifted my spirits, or otherwise smoothed the way. (I have had to leave out some in the North, who needed to remain anonymous; you know who you are – thank you.)

Leland Bardwell, Glenn Barr, Norah Bennice, Joe Burke, Frank Brody, Edward Byrne, Conor and Maire Cruise O'Brien, Noelle Campbell-Sharp, Parkash and Meena Chada, Kieran and Amabel Clarke, John Colclough, Elisabeth and Geoffrey Cope, Jane Crane, Grainne Cunningham, Anne O'Dee, Tatty and Boihy Dromahair, Pam, Ted, Sonya and friends, Pat Dunlop, Amanda Dunsmore, Anne Enwright, Irene Feighan, Nesta FitzGerald, Andrew and Tina Mc-Morrough Kavanagh, Jennifer Grimes, Vivienne Guinness, James Harrold, David Hammond, Derek Hill, Emma Hill, Christopher Horseman and Judy Butler, Adrian Horseman, Christine Kelly, Mary-Louise Kenny, Danny and Anna Kina-han, Tarka King and Samantha Leslie, Colman McCabe, Molly McCloskey, John McKenna, Joe McManus, Laurence and Margaret McNeice, Maire Moriarty, Richard and Rosal-ind Mulholland, Dervla Murphy, Timmy and Carina Newell, Liz O'Driscoll, Jackie Rudd, Dermot Seymour, Frank Slattery, David Skinner, Richard and Pam Traill, Madelaine Walsh, Vebeka Venema.

Special thanks to: my uncle Tony McCrum and brother Robert who provided helpful background to the family history. My brother Stephen, and Benedict Flynn, who read the first draft and offered useful advice. My parents, for their continual support and for acting as a mailbox. James Kanter, who helped me out of deadline panic with noble transcription work. The staff of the British Library, for their efficient and friendly service. Humphrey Price, my editor, who commissioned and encouraged me from the word go; Lydia Darbyshire, copy-editor, and all the rest of the team at Gollancz. Mark Lucas, my agent, who never lets the sun go down on his return phone call; and Leonie Edwards-Jones, who was her usual enor-mously supportive self.

I am grateful to A. P. Watt Ltd, on behalf of Michael B.

Yeats, for allowing me to reproduce lines from Yeats's *In Memory of Constance and Eva Gore-Booth* and *The Lake Isle of Innisfree* and to Joseph Boland for allowing the use of 'Sonnet to a Cow Dung'.

Throughout the journey I used the excellent *Rough Guide to Ireland* (Rough Guides, London, 1996) for topographical information and the *Oxford Companion to Irish History* (ed. S. J. Connolly, OUP, 1998) as my central historical reference. Other books consulted, in addition to those mentioned in the text, include Robert Kee's *The Green Flag* (Weidenfeld and Nicolson, London, 1972); Edmund Curtis, *A History of Ireland* (Methuen, London, 1964); Gemma Hussey, *Ireland Today* (Penguin, London, 1995); Conor Cruise O'Brien, *States of Ireland* (Pantheon, New York, 1972); Liz Curtis, *Ireland: The Propaganda War* (Pluto, London, 1984); Colm Tóibín, *Bad Blood* (Vintage, London, 1994); Roy Kerridge, *Jaunting Through Ireland* (Michael Joseph, London, 1991); Rev A. E. Stokes, *The Parish of Powerscourt: A Centenary Lecture* (Dublin University Press, 1963); Fergus Finlay, *Mary Robinson, A President with a Purpose* (O'Brien, Dublin, 1990); Richard Roche, *The Norman Invasion of Ireland* (Anvil Books, Tralee, 1970); Mark Bence-Jones, *The Twilight of the Ascendancy* (Constable, London, 1987); Ann Morrow, *Picnic in a Foreign Land* (London, Grafton, 1990); Charles Chenevix-Trench, *The Great Dan* (Jonathan Cape, London, 1984); R. A. S. Mac-Alister, *Ireland in Pre-Celtic Times* (Maunseland Roberts, Dublin, 1921); Mary E. Daly, *The Famine In Ireland* (Dublin Historical Association, 1986), *The Famine Decade, Contemporary Accounts 1841–51* (ed. John Killen, The Blackstaff Press, Belfast, 1995); Cecil Woodham-Smith, *The Great Hunger* (London, 1962); Gifford Lewis, *Eva Gore-Booth and Esther Roper, A Biography* (Pandora, London, 1988); Alisdair D. F. MaCrae, *W. B. Yeats, A Literary Life* (Macmillan, London, 1995); W. B. Yeats, *Memoirs* (ed. D. Donoghue, Macmillan, London, 1995); Tim Pat Coogan, *The Troubles*, (Arrow Books, London, 1996); Brian Lacy, *Siege City, The Story of Derry and Londonderry* (Blackstaff Press, Belfast, 1990); Paul Kingsley, *Londonderry Revisited* (Belfast Press, Belfast, 1989).

The following are sources of quotes used directly: I am

grateful, where relevant, for permission to use them. The statistics in Chapter 2 come from the *Irish Times* 8.7.97; the description of 'Omurthie' from John O'Toole's *The O'Tooles of Powerscourt* (A. M Sullivan, Dublin, undated.) The Wolfe Tone journal extract is from his fascinating autobiographical *Life* (Hunt and Clarke, London, 1828). The description of Vinegar Hill draws heavily on Robert Kee, *The Green Flag* (above). The local history of Bannow quoted in Chapter 3 is Thomas C. Butler's, *A Parish and Its People* (Grantstown Priory, Wellingtonbridge, 1985). The description of the miraculous happenings at Cappoquin is extracted from a leaflet published by the Melleray Grotto Committee, Cappoquin, Co. Waterford. The translated extract from the Statute of Kilkenny may be found in Curtis, *ibid*, p. 112. The ballad 'Flight of the Earls' comes from A. P. Gravet, *Songs of Ireland* (Alexander Ireland and Co., Manchester, 1880). Descriptions of Tom Barry's exploits are from *Curious Journey* by Kenneth Griffith and Timothy E. O'Grady (Hutchinson, London, 1982) and also Barry's own account *Guerilla Days in Ireland* (Anvil Books, Tralee, 1968). In Chapter 13 the report of O'Connell's speech in *The Nation* is quoted in Kee *ibid.* vol II, p 204. In Chapter 14 the quote from Eoin MacNeill can be found in Terence Brown's *Ireland: A Social and Cultural History (1922–79)* (Fontana, London, 1981) p. 51; and that from Tim Robinson in *Stones of Aran: Labyrinth* (Lilliput Press, Dublin, 1995) p. 64. Pat Mullen's *Man of Aran* was published by Faber and Faber, London, 1934; and C. C. Vyvyan's *On Timeless Shores* by Peter Owen, London, 1957. In Chapter 21, John Hume's perspective on gerrymandering comes from *Personal Views* (Town House, Dublin, 1996). My account of the Battle of the Bogside relies heavily on Tim Pat Coogan's *The Troubles* (above).